THE RISEN

DIALOGUES OF LOVE, GRIEF, & SURVIVAL
~ BEYOND DEATH ~

AUGUST GOFORTH

AND

TIMOTHY GRAY

21st Century Reports from the Afterlife
Through Contemplative, Intuitive, & Physical Mediumship

Grateful acknowledgment is made to reprint excerpts from *Alive in God's World: Human Life on Earth and in Heaven,* by Joa Bolendas, ©2001 Lindisfarn Books, Barrington, Massachusetts; with kind permission of Lantern Books.

Grazie tante a John Crowley for unceremonious sanction to quote a tad from *Little, Big,* ©1982 Victor Gollancz Ltd, London.

Nous sommes profondément reconnaissants à Justin for his eagle eyes, technical talents, unwavering commitment, and friendship.

The Risen Dialogues of Love, Grief, & Survival Beyond Death – 21st Century Reports from the Afterlife Through Contemplative, Intuitive, & Physical Mediumship. Copyright ©2009 by August Goforth and Tempestina Teapot Books, LLC. The authors have made every effort to locate sources and obtain permission to quote certain materials herein. Any omissions that are identified by the sources will be subsequently corrected in future revised editions.

Tempestina Teapot Books and the Tempestina logo are trademarks of Tempestina Teapot Books, LLC.

Also by the author: *Dreams, Symbols, and Psychic Power,* by Alex Tanous and Timothy Gray (New York: Bantam Books, 1990).

Book Design ©August Goforth

2nd Edition ISBN: 978-1-365-48699-9

First Printing September 2009

SECOND EDITION
© 2017

TM

TEMPESTINA TEAPOT BOOKS

~ NEW YORK ~

THIS ORCHESTRATION IS DEDICATED TO

Andrew, Annette, Barney, Billie, Bonnie, Carolyn, Deborah,
Dee, Eddie, Eileen, Felicia, Gerit, Jack, Jimmy, Jo, Justin,
Kay, Lynda Lee, Mamie, Marc, Melvin, Noveh, Patricia,
Paul, Phyllis, Rick, Rip, Sally, Serenella,
Sky, Suzanne, Tana, Terri, & Tricia
~ *Who Gifted Us with Their Listening* ~

To Zoë
~ *Who Witnessed* THE RED HAT ~

To Each Other
~ *Dimidium Animae Meae* ~

And with Fond, Fond Memories of
Beakstein
~ *Chanteuse & Mediumistic Assistant Extraordinaire* ~

"Death remember'd, should be like a mirror,
Who tells us, life's but a breath; to trust it, error."
~ Shakespeare ~ *Pericles, Prince of Tyre*

~ DISCLAIMER ~

The authors of *The Risen: Dialogues of Love, Grief, and Survival Beyond Death* endorse neither suicide nor euthanasia in this book. We advocate "a good death"—comprehensive pain control and palliative care for the dying person, and legal guidance for end-of-life choices. There are many resources for these matters, including assistance with grief and bereavement, at the American College of Physicians: see "Papers by the ACP-ASIM End-of-Life Care Consensus Panel"; http://www.acponline.org/ethics/papers.htm.

The material in *The Risen* should not be used as a substitute for medical opinion and guidance, or as a replacement for the services of trained medical or mental health professionals. For appropriate medical and mental health support, services, and treatment, a primary care physician and/or a qualified mental health care professional should be consulted.

CONTENTS

NEW FOREWORD by Wendy & Victor Zammit

The Journey Begins ~ *1*

Signs of Risen Contact ~ *8*

1. ~ Worlds Within Worlds ~ *11*

2. ~ Tim Speaks ~ *15*

3. ~ The Risen ~ *21*

4. ~ Spirit & Science ~ *30*

5. ~ Transition, Formerly Known as Death ~ *37*

6. ~ The Fabric of Beingness ~ *40*

7. ~ Contact ~ *43*

8. ~ Small Medium at Large ~ *53*

9. ~ Grief Transformed ~ *63*

10. ~ Ego-Mind & The Simulate Selves ~ *70*

11. ~ Grief Evolved & Self-Exiting ~ *96*

12. ~ Authentic Self ~ *112*

13. ~ Mundus Imaginalis ~ *118*

14. ~ Breakthrough ~ *129*

15. ~ Psychospiritual Amnesia ~ *136*

16. ~ Kundalini Bells & Astral Kisses ~ *143*

17. ~ Tim Rises ~ *155*

18. ~ Aspects of Transition ~ *185*

19. ~ Liberation Dramas ~ *195*

20. ~ Dwelling Places ~ *211*

21. ~ Krishnamurti Speaks ~ *219*

22. ~ Borrowed From Angels ~ *228*

23. ~ Vibration, Resonance, & Harmony ~ *253*

24. ~ Water to the Ocean ~ *267*

25. ~ The Pastime of Reincarnation ~ *275*

26. ~ Moon Shadows ~ *301*

Oolong Rises ~ *307*

Appendix — The Edge & Waiting ~ *308*

References ~ *312*

The Authorship ~ *315*

FOREWORD

BY WENDY & VICTOR ZAMMIT

Authors of A Lawyer Presents the Evidence for the Afterlife

"I am absolutely convinced of the fact that those who once lived on earth can and do communicate with us. It is hardly possible to convey to the inexperienced an adequate idea of the strength and cumulative force of the evidence."
~ Sir William Barrett, English Physicist and Afterlife Investigator

"Neither was it intended that the two worlds, ours [the afterlife] and yours [the earth plane], should be as they are now—so far apart in thought and contact. The day will assuredly come when our two worlds will be closely interrelated, when communication between the two will be a commonplace of life, and then the great wealth of resources of the spirit world will be open to the earth world, to draw upon for the benefit of the whole human race."
~ Monsignor Robert Hugh Benson, through medium Anthony Borgia, in *Life in the World Unseen.*

While many of the people who purchase this book will be familiar with the claim that genuine two-way communication with those who have "died" is not only possible but frequent and well-documented, some may not have had the opportunity to review the recent evidence.

Since communication between the living and "the Risen" is the central premise of this book, August Goforth has invited us to write a brief foreword focusing on this point, since we have been researching and writing about the empirical evidence for the afterlife for almost thirty years.

Spontaneous after-death contacts between people who have no special psychic abilities have been studied scientifically since 1882 when a survey was conducted in England. Altogether 32,000 cases were recorded, 17,000 in English. It was published in Volume X of the Society for Psychical Research *Proceedings* for 1894 (Sidgwick, Johnson, Myers, et al., 1894). Further studies were carried out by the American Society for Psychical Research and by the French researcher Camille Flammarion who compiled thousands of cases in his books *The Unknown* (1900) and *Death and Its Mystery* (1925).

Since that time, after-death contacts have been documented in every country. In 1973 a University of Chicago sociologist asked a sample of 1,467 Americans if they had ever felt they had contact with someone who had died. Twenty-seven per cent answered that they had (Greeley 1975). Many other studies found a similar figure.

Recent research shows that people who die make their presence known in a number of ways which the writers of this book outline at the end of the next section "The Journey Begins". Contact is more frequent when there is a strong love link, provided that intense grief does not get in the way. Dr. W.D. Rees, a British physician found that of a sample of widows in Wales, forty-seven per cent had experiences—often repeatedly over a number of years—that convinced them that their dead husbands had been in contact with them (Rees 1971: 37-41). An earlier British survey by Dr. P. Marris (1958) had found a figure of fifty per cent. Dr. Melvin Morse, a pediatrician who has done many studies of death and dying, claims that it is rare for someone to lose a child and not see them again in a death-related vision (Morse and Perry 1994: 135).

There are a multitude of reasons to believe that these contacts are more than wish-fulfillment or the product of the unconscious mind. In many cases the witnesses are scientifically trained people of high credibility and, in most of the reported cases, the person was in a perfectly ordinary state of mind, free from shock or stress. The experiences were totally unexpected and took place in familiar surroundings (Tyrrell 1963:23).

Sometimes the appearance of an apparition involves physical phenomena such as the movement of objects or knocking things off a wall. Sounds like footsteps have been recorded on tape. Apparitions have been observed to cast a shadow, be reflected in a mirror, overturn furniture, leave a scent, ask for a lift, and even sign their name. In her book, *On Life After Death*, Dr. Kübler-Ross reports an encounter with the fully materialized form of Mrs. Schwartz, a former patient, who had died. She writes: "I even touched her skin to see if it was cold or warm, or if the skin would disappear when I touched it."

Many of the recorded cases have been seen by more than one person. In a case investigated by the Society for Psychical Research, nine people living in a house in Ramsbury, England saw the apparition of a man who had died ten months before. They saw him many times both separately and as a group, from February until April. He was always seen sitting at his dying widow's bedside. His hand was placed on her forehead and he was visible for up to half an hour at a time (Holzer 1965: 52-56).

Professor Hornell Hart, in his book *The Enigma of Survival* (1959), claims that between one-third and two-thirds of all apparitions are seen by more than one person.

In some cases people appear in order to save loved ones from danger or give important information. Bill Guggenheim, co-author of *Hello from Heaven: A New Field of Research—After-Death Communication Confirms That Life and Love Are Eternal*, claims he became interested in after-death contacts when he heard the voice of his father telling him to check the swimming pool. He did, and as a result was able to save the life of his young son who was floating face down. Diane Archangel's book *Afterlife Encounters* tells of a mother, Beverley, whose son, Tommy, was killed in an unknown way. After the funeral, Tommy came to his mother in an apparition. He told her to go quickly to a certain corner in Brooklyn where she would find his blood in the snow. She went there and called the police who did a DNA test on the blood and found three eye-witnesses and were able to solve his murder (Arcangel 2005).

So far we have only talked about contacts received by witnesses who were not mediumistic or telepathic and who said that they only had one or two such experiences in a lifetime.

But in every culture there are people like August Goforth, co-author of this book, who claim to be able to see and hear spirit people often with as much clarity as living people. We know from research that this ability runs in families, is accelerated by difficult or lonely childhoods and is often experienced more strongly after a near-death experience.

Modern studies validating the work of mediums have been carried out by Professor Gary Schwartz at the University of Arizona, by Professor Archie Roy and Trisha Robertson from the Scottish Society for Psychical Research, by Dr. Julie Beischel and her team at the Windbridge Institute, by the University of Virginia and by the Institute of Noetic Sciences.

And far from the old idea put forward in religions that we should not be "calling up the dead" we learn that those in spirit are very keen to contact their loved ones to tell them that they have arrived safely. They tell us that death is nothing to fear and that they have gone to a world which at first is just as solid as real as this one. In fact, they tell us that to them our life seems unreal. They are met by family members or friends and taken to live in houses with furniture and gardens and begin a rich and rewarding life. Time is different in the afterlife and for them it seems as though we are not separated. They tell us that when we sleep we visit them in their world and that, although we miss them, it is important to them that we go on with life and not get lost in grief. Our relationship with our loved ones is different, but it still continues.

We have learned that organized teams of spirit scientists and philosophers have been behind attempts to improve communication with the living since at least the 1850s. Part of the reason for this is to reduce grief and fear of death, but a larger part is to give guidance to living people about the purpose of life and the danger that our current way of life is posing to the planet.

Currently teams of scientists in the spirit world are working very hard to establish new methods of communication between the dimensions using electronics. Research on the creation of a "soul phone" is being undertaken by Professor Gary Schwartz who is working with mediums and a huge team of Risen scientists at the University of Arizona. There are astral level Instrumental Trans-communication stations relaying messages from children who have died to their parents in Brazil, Italy, Portugal and Germany. Dr. Craig Hogan and his team from the Afterlife Research and Education Institute are working with a Risen team to create a North American station.

So there is nothing in this book which is not totally consistent with modern afterlife research and with what we know of the efforts of teams in Spirit to assist the evolution of those who are still incarnate.

One of the many things which is special about this book is the way that it provides a roadmap for those who are experiencing grief, which is presented in all its raw intensity. Along with many wonderful insights about the challenges of inter-dimensional communication, August shows us that he is someone who really understands grief and, what is more, values its transformative potential if allowed to run its course.

The book presents us with a wonderful example of how grief can be transformed through a continuing relationship with a partner who has transitioned, something which the field of grief counselling has only recently started to recognize. August writes:

> "People often form a new relationship with their partner after the partner has transitioned and their shared grief has eased. I'm far from lonely without Tim being here in his body, or demented in some way to prefer this ethereal relationship to the security that companionship with an embodied person might seem to promise. Because of our work together we have managed to become more alike in vibration, and this acts as an attractive force—a resonance—that transcends the usual boundaries between our states of existence, and brings us closer. This force is even more effective when I'm asleep and able to move about in the astral realms, free of the confines of a dense material body. It's then possible to experience the embracing and merging of mind and soul and be much closer together. … Tim sees and understands more from his Risen perspective, and so can accept me in more evolved ways and without judgment, which can only strengthen our togetherness. We're both in awe of the fact that our relationship and communication are real, and there's mutual excitement about eventually being physically together again, side by side in the same world. I know that my transition is inevitable, and often it feels like I'm a four-year-old waiting for Christmas."

The authors claim that one of the main purposes of the book is to enable those who are still "embodied" and those who are Risen to understand that ongoing contact between loved ones on different planes is possible and to guide them on how to achieve it. And they say that the book has been carefully orchestrated by groups of higher intelligences to awaken latent abilities.

For this reason Tim suggests that people read the book from the beginning, because "every chapter has been designed to gradually lead people through deeper highly vibrating concepts." They caution that this is not a book for "professional skeptics" but will resonate most particularly with "those who feel drawn to the subject in some way, however slight, however wary."

Together August and Tim have created a timeless classic full of valuable insights which is a wonderful addition to the field. It is a beautifully written book full of subtle insights about love, grief and most of all, survival beyond death.

Victor & Wendy Zammit
A Lawyer Presents the Evidence for the Afterlife and *The Friday Afterlife Report*
www.victorzammit.com
New Zealand, 2017

THE JOURNEY BEGINS

Do not require a description of the countries towards which you sail.
The description does not describe them to you, and tomorrow you
arrive there, and know them by inhabiting them.
~ Ralph Waldo Emerson

Envision, with your mind's eye, a world where poverty is impossible and abundance unavoidable. Because there are no needs there is no necessity to work. There is instant access to infinite sustenance, clothing, and shelter, and anything else you might desire. This will be so for everyone there, for these elements will be available to all. Hence an economic system of any kind—which implies lack—will not be needed in this world. None whatsoever—unless you might want it for yourself. The same will hold true for any social, psychological, political, scientific, and religious systems, which all inherently embrace presumptions of need. Your environment—the weather, the light, the mode of transport, and your home—will be what you choose them to be, continuously reflecting your personal consciousness.

Everyone in this world is free to do whatever they like and as much or as little of it. Work is play, and play is work—they are indistinguishable from one another. You may work and play, live and love with those who are most like you, for in this world the Principle of Affinity is the guiding force of relationships. Those who are not like you will be with others most like them.

Most refreshing and relieving of all, there is no judgment or criticism in any way in this world, no matter how much we may think we deserve it. And if that should be the case, we would be judging only our self and not prevented from such a desire. The Principle of Affinity will convey us into an environment that reflects our self-judgments, while allowing for relationships with others who see themselves in various supporting roles that reflect our decisions about our self. Although nobody will attempt to interfere with our judgmental intentions toward ourself, there will always be observant, compassionate guides waiting to respond to the slightest request for help to release such intentions.

Because we will be able to perceive that there is love freely available to all in this new world, the usual distortions from lack of it will not exist, and any enduring falsehoods will vanish quickly when we allow ourselves to fall into love's awaiting arms. This falling into love will be as easy as breathing, for we are designed to self-correct through change—that is, through intelligent transition. Death is also "corrected" through this loving process of transition, from which we will emerge and arise anew.

What would such a world be like compared to where you live now? What would *you* do in such a world?

"If only such a place existed," many will sigh with dim weariness.

Such a world *does* exist. This other world awaits each one of us at any moment. It exists even now. We all already know this Home with great intimacy, for whenever our body sleeps and sometimes when we daydream, we visit it and all those whom we love. We have been leaving our bodies to travel in our spiritual body to this other world, this home, since the day we first arose upon the earth. Very few of us remember these travels upon awakening back into our terrestrial bodies, so heavily does earthly life weigh us down. The sheer density of our physical body filters out the greatly finer vibrations of such memories. If we could remember even just a little bit, our life would be tremendously lightened by the awe of such experiences, and further comforted by the sureness that the day *will* come when we will take our last step away from this earth, never having to return.

We will each enter a final terrestrial sleep of some kind as we begin our transition. Upon awakening we will arise into a new life—not beneath another earthly sunrise, but into a new, light-filled world—our True Home—where joy, not fear, will be the ground upon which we will move and have our being.

We will have transitioned into a Risen One.

Undoubtedly, there will also be much laughter, as we wonder how we could have possibly feared the final earthly sleep that was given the terrifying epithet of "DEATH."

The authors of this book have a simple yet grand wish for you—that you will no longer think you must fear what so many imagine as the "final silence." *Every thing has life*, and because there is nothing *but* life, there is no silence anywhere. The very structure of the Intelligent Universe is light and music—singing, talking, and laughing. Life is real and death is not, so there is nothing to fear unless you fear life's light-filled music. Death is not the end to life but another beginning, another birth. It is a door, a passage to more life, more than we could possibly imagine. And even though we are irreversibly immortal, we will *never* be able to imagine it all.

Everyone involved with the orchestration of this book can confirm that by intentionally and consciously reaching out in various ways, *anyone* still on the earth can make contact with those who have survived the final sleep and are now living in a Risen world. And that it is possible to continue to share our lives *now* with the Risen, while we are still here on earth. Equally miraculously, when we on earth diligently strive to make contact, the Risen will also feel motivated to strive and succeed to share their experiences with us. Through these cooperative efforts, all involved can and will experience development, expansion, intensification, augmentation, amplification, improvement, growth, and evolution of life, service, and love—in short, pure bliss. At first, and for an undetermined time, this bliss may come in small doses, but it is the only real healing balm for grief. As grief lessens, the balm of bliss intensifies.

Human suffering becomes transformed when viewed through the new lens of knowledge gained about survival beyond death. As the light of conscious awareness is turned upon the alleged darkness, it will be seen that the negative things are actually positive, waiting in the shadows to be revealed. Some of this new knowledge appears majestically and quickly, but much of it is so subtly measured that sadly it's often dismissed long before it fully arrives.

There are those on the earth who contend that human fear and pain are "illusions" of some sort. This might make sense as certain truths on greater spiritual planes. Yet how many among us have grown to such advanced levels of being while having to move and breathe in our daily lives on earth? It is appropriate to say that for most of us, an inseparable part of the human experience is the pain that emerges from having human bodies. For most people, bodily discomfort and emotional worry often result in more complex and persistent forms of pain and fear, causing us to feel helpless, hopeless, and demoralized, which together comprise the experience of earthly suffering. Perhaps while we're still on the earth we may eventually be able to learn and comprehend enough about the continuous flow of universal grace, which, as all religions have said, will undo our suffering. Let us accept that we are good enough as the human beings we are right now, honestly and courageously acknowledging our pain, as well as our beliefs in hopelessness and hopefulness, which are two sides of the same coin of fear.

Hopelessness, a helpless feeling fed by fearful memories of the past, diminishes when we become open to help from people in the present around us. These people can be not only those on the earth, but also those who have risen beyond the earth. Helplessness diminishes when we, including the Risen, become helpful to others—also known as *service*.

Hopefulness is a feeling that obtains its sustenance from the energy that we put into the non-existent future. Hope acts as a distraction to keep us out of the present, and the fear connected with it shows itself as worry. Because the future and the past do not exist in the way the present does, both hopefulness and hopelessness are not *here*—they are nowhere in wakeful reality. Fear needs increasingly larger amounts of worry in order to survive, and will drain us of the energy needed to sustain our physical body in the present. The fear will continue to feed off the mental and spiritual energy otherwise needed to feel present, eroding our ability to be aware of the thrill of one's spiritual body as it permeates the physical body.

The only place to be is where we are—*the present*. This ancient fragment of mislaid information is one of the most important aspects of human spirituality to re-emerge in the early twentieth century. Many are now familiar with the notions of "be here now" and "don't worry, be happy." These concepts have been clearly held before us from every spiritual worldview for many thousands of years, such as the Bible's suggestion to "consider the lilies of the field."[1] Now, just inside the gates of the twenty-first century, we are beginning to return to the understanding that *we* are the lilies of the field. There is also increasing awareness by scientists and non-scientists that eventually we will come to consciously experience that we are the *field* as well.

In spite of this simplistic speech about past, present, and future, time is more than just a concept—it appears to be a fact for those of us living on the earth. If we want to live as a human being on this planet we have to be able to experience the appearances of time, as informed by our physical and spiritual senses. The physical senses tell us about the present as it emerges from our experience of physical being, while the spiritual senses infiltrate, enrich, and extend this sense of being even further beyond the body. Our physical senses can tell us nothing about the past or future, so what we might believe to be sensations of the past or the future are really thoughts informed by memory—and memory is only of the past.

---

[1] "And why take ye thought for raiment? Consider the lilies of the field, how they grow; they toil not, neither do they spin: And yet I say unto you, that even Solomon in all his glory was not arrayed like one of these. Wherefore, if God so clothe the grass of the field, which today is, and tomorrow is cast into the oven, shall he not much more clothe you, O ye of little faith? Therefore, take no thought, saying, 'What shall we eat?' Or, 'What shall we drink?' Or, 'Wherewithal shall we be clothed?' For your heavenly Father knoweth that ye have need of all these things . . . Take therefore no thought for the morrow: for the morrow shall take thought for the things of itself . . .". — Matthew 26:28 (*KJ*)

Our spiritual senses operate on non-visible, non-tangible levels, in non-physical circumstances. Because the appearances of time have different qualities on non-physical levels, we have senses that can experience non-physical time, which is also *spiritual time*. These "extra" senses are similar enough to those of the Risen that we can sometimes share sensations and experiences with them.

Those who have left the earth via the transitional process and are now Risen also experience time as informed by their senses. Like us, they are in the present but are also exquisitely aware that they are in an eternal state of being, an existence outside of the appearance and effects of our earthly time—or timelessness. Time exists in a certain way for those on the Earth and in a different way for the Risen, who can experience time as ever present and everlasting.

It is possible for a Risen sense of time to be experienced by those who are still on the earth. We ourselves can assist this process by finding our own sense of calm presence and then directing this heightened, expanded, and receptive sense toward the Risen. Like a child waiting for fireflies to appear in the twilight, the naturally heightened state of a Risen mind can perceive our mind reaching out—and then move forward and reach out to touch us, while stepping into our space of expanded receptivity. Depending upon our openness and persistence, we may be able to feel their thoughts and their presence. We might even connect and touch, remaining together for a few brief but unforgettable timeless moments.

Feelings of suffering and grief begin with and are fed by thoughts, which are a function and result of something this book will refer to as the *ego-mind*. The thoughts may be so deep, so subtle, or even wordless that they are hidden from our conscious awareness. The combined presences of the earth-embodied and the Risen can become time*less*, and thus powerful enough to dissolve thoughts and thereby release feelings of suffering, which is healing. There is much assistance awaiting us from the Risen, who have ways to help us find this place of timeless power. They can show us that consciously becoming aware of our sense of internal presence is a way out of suffering, and they can help us stop expending energy trying to flee to the past or to the future. With Risen assistance we can become enabled to discover firsthand that the idea of being alone with nobody to help us is but a slight misunderstanding.

As we continue to progress together with our Risen loved ones, it becomes possible to discover that both worlds, and indeed, many worlds, interact together with the greatest of ongoing intimacies. These interactions have been happening all along, ever since the day we entered this particular material realm, and will continue to do so when we finally leave and move beyond it. This all may sound paradoxical, mysterious, and even mystical—because it is.

The Risen orchestrators of this book acknowledge the tragic feelings of those who are temporarily but still so tangibly left behind on the earth. Not one of us who lives on earth can escape the experience of loss and grief. Human reality is within those still embodied as humans on the earth. Loss and grief are part and parcel of human reality and yet are very divine and inexplicable gifts—to not be able to experience these things would not be human. Yet we can learn and grow to experience that even while the bodies of our loved ones are gone, their reality is still *here*—not in the past or in the future, but in the *present*. They have not gone away—they merely seem less accessible for a little while. The human reality that was within them is still within them but in a new and exciting way. They are waiting for us while we are still in our reality, to join them in their realities at any time.

Tim, one of the many Risen co-authors of this book, has shared on several occasions that he's noticed that many embodied people will try to comfort someone in their bereavement by saying something like, "They're still in your heart." They might even bring their hand up to hold over their own body's heart, as if to indicate that the loved one is in an actual physical place. Tim asks us to consider that in making this kind of physical gesture, we are intuitively demonstrating that we are aware on a very deep level of the actual reality of what we are saying. Just as we are in a physical body and in a physical place, so, too, are our loved ones. Those who are passionately connected with their Authentic Self will know that there is this great mysterious truth going on right in our own bodies. All of us can connect with this experience in some way.

When a person leaves their body—when they "die"—they are still in that place of mysterious truth, but without the material body. We all have another body of higher vibrating substance that we usually cannot see, but can often feel. If we are able to consciously go to that place of mysterious truth within us, and we can feel and become consciously aware of the space we call our heart, then we are also able to feel and be aware of the disembodied person's space, their heart. *The feeling is the connection*—the corridor of opportunity through which we can travel and then be with them, to commune together in a combined heart space.

The experiences found in the following pages are shared endeavors between the Risen and the Yet-To-Rise. Many of the events are about the transformation of grief into many things, including joy. This transformation gives all involved greater access to one another. Whereas before our grief might have been draining the life out of our living, we will have opportunities to experience and subsequently understand that there is no such thing as death. This will allow us to put joy back into our living, which is the meaning of "enjoy." Many these days seem to think that they should be getting joy *out* of living, but they have it backwards. Joy is something we put *into* living, for we are the channels for this ever-emerging energy, which is also our Source. That is, the Source is not only in us, but we are the Source. We are the fountains through which the waters of life flow. We are the lilies and the fields and the ground from which all being and awareness of being arises and manifests.

Those who turn their minds toward outflowing joy into their earthly experience will come to know a continually new and greater serenity in life and in living, as well as realizing that a joyful reunion with their loved ones is unavoidably inevitable. There is even comfort in knowing that if, for whatever reason, we cannot allow this outflowing to happen now, it will eventually happen in *another now*.

The Risen ask us to contemplate a spiral as we journey through this book. The spiral is an ancient emblem of life, transcendence, and eternity, running deep through all earthly cultures. It evokes deep relaxation and calm. It is revealed as a living symbol throughout Nature—in pinecones, the petals and seed heads of flowers, the arrangement of leaves on a stem; water spinning in a whirlpool, the shell of a snail, the winds circling the earth; the horns of a goat, the coils of a snake, and even a head of cauliflower. Stars, galaxies, and people dance in waves of living spirals. Spirals are found throughout our body—in the proportions of its components, in our fingerprints, in the movement of the blood as it travels through us, and in the pattern of the hair on our heads. The very strands of our DNA intertwine in an animated spiral.

Life is also a spiral—a sacred relationship of matter, time, and space that leads to a continual transcendence of them. Life's presence and actions are its own evidence—of itself and of its immortality. The center of life's spiral is the center of the Self as it moves through eternity, never the same at any moment, yet never losing the essential spirit of its Origin. Life is the Original Spirit.

The spiral often seems to be a maze, an icon of the life journey of a human being, seemingly struggling alone along an unknown path, while trying to discover its center. Many of us will spend a lifetime worrying about whether we are journeying toward or away from the center.

For those of us still earth-embodied, our spiral path will change. In fact, it simply cannot exist without change, for the spiral of all life is a process. Upon our transition to places of existence beyond this planet, our journey will transmute into a new and more intensely living motif. We will each begin this transition in our own unique way, and then we will awaken as a Risen One into a new world. Instead of continuing to manifest as a seemingly isolated island encircled by a sea of unforgiving loneliness, a new life-spiral and a new way of being will emerge. As these new beings, we will rejoin all whom we have ever loved and who have loved us, including many old and new friends and lovers. We will emerge as an integral part of an infinitely spiraling community of like-minded others, to dwell in ever-present joy, learning, service, and love.

SIGNS OF RISEN CONTACT

Intermingled with our physical body's senses of sight, hearing, taste, smell, and touch are other senses sometimes called "extra" senses, but which are not extra at all. These are our spiritual senses, which belong to our spiritual bodies, which interpenetrate the same space as our physical body. For most people the spiritual senses are barely detectable and are often undernourished from lack of education, awareness, and attention.

You have been drawn to this book by your spiritual senses. Your spiritual bodies can sense things that usually evade the physical senses, including very particular "somethings" interpenetrating the physical space of this book you are holding in your hand. As the physical senses communicate messages from the physical world about us to our brains, our spiritual senses bring us messages from the spiritual worlds to our minds and hearts.

You have most likely received communications from those who no longer have a physical body. Your spiritual senses informed you of being touched, seen, or spoken to in certain ways by a Risen person. These experiences are common for many people, regardless of their beliefs or understanding. The Risen can contact us in countless ways. One of the things this book will help with is to enable you to begin to familiarize yourself with how your loved ones attempt to reach you. Later on you may find yourself joining with them in devising your own unique and brilliant ways to connect and communicate.

Following are just a few of the many ways you might have spiritually sensed Risen contact or their messages, but were never quite sure if you could believe them—at least in the way you feel you can believe your physical senses. Some may be quite familiar to you already. By the end of this book, you will have gained an increased understanding about the ways and means of the Risen, which can be best described by the curious concept of "orchestration."

- ℭ Finding yourself spontaneously having a conversation with someone you know is "dead" but not realizing it until a few moments have gone by, and then you dismiss it as "talking to yourself." Here's a hint—you were responding to a conversation that *they* started.
- ℭ Feeling a sudden and overwhelming emotion—sadness, joy, peace—when thinking about someone who has "died."
- ℭ Feeling breezes, tickling sensations or "cobwebs," or pressure about your face, especially near the eyes and on the sides of the head near the temple, when thinking about the "dead" person. Sometimes the pressure manifests as discomfort or even headaches.
- ℭ Feeling these sensations after you get into bed at night and turning out the light, whether or not you are thinking of anyone in particular.
- ℭ Seeing tiny points of white-blue "sparks" after the lights have been turned out, or while sitting quietly in the dark or in low lighting.

- Feeling sensations on your hands, such as breezes, tickling, or pressure of some kind, especially when writing or thinking about writing.
- Hearing your name called as you're falling asleep or waking up, or when you're alone.
- Awakening from a dream and firmly convinced it was no ordinary event, and perhaps even more real than waking life.
- Hearing music or nature sounds, like bells or birds chirping, or choirs singing, just as you're falling asleep or while daydreaming.
- Feeling as if someone is watching over and guiding you.
- Feeling someone place their hands on your shoulders or embracing you from behind.
- Finding strange and often undecipherable messages on your answering machine that sound like a mixture of voices, music, static, and other noises and feeling reluctant to erase them.
- Briefly but repeatedly seeing total strangers who look like your loved one in breathtaking ways, but often in ways only you can see.
- Coming upon a book that seems to contain messages that were written directly from your loved one to you.
- Hearing a song on the radio at a specific time that seems as if your loved one ordered it especially for you, or turning on the television and the program seems to be speaking directly to you about something related to you and your loved one.
- Timepieces stopping when they shouldn't.
- Light bulbs dimming or burning out around the same time you're having strong thoughts and feelings about your loved one.

If you've experienced any of these things ask yourself, "Is it possible it could actually have been real?"—and—"Do I want more?" If you feel a rising excitement somewhere inside you when you ponder these two questions, know that your spiritual senses are beginning to vibrate faster, and that this raising of vibration brings you closer to the place where your Risen loved ones are right now. Most likely some of them are right here with you, reading along and encouraging you to keep going.

Know also that both fear and excitement arise from the same feeling. One brings you closer to love and adventure, while the other takes you further away from them. Your loved ones, who are in a spiritual body like yours, but in a physical body unlike yours, sense your growing excitement, and are not afraid. Let's begin to look at these strange and wonderful implications with them.

The journey begins.

The great and sad mistake of many people — among them, even pious persons — is to imagine that those whom death had taken, leave us. They do not leave us. They remain! Where are they? In darkness? Oh, no! It is WE who are in darkness. We do not see them, but they see us. Their eyes, radiant with glory, are fixed upon our eyes filled with tears. Oh, infinite consolation! Though invisible to us, our dead are not absent.

I have often reflected upon the surest comfort for those who mourn. It is this: a firm faith in the real and continual presence of our loved ones; it is the clear and penetrating conviction that death has not destroyed them, nor carried them away. They are not even absent, but living near to us, transfigured: having lost, in their glorious change, no delicacy of their souls, no tenderness of their hearts, nor especial preference in their affection. On the contrary, they have, in depth and fervor of devotion, grown larger a hundredfold.

~ Attributed to a sermon by Karl Rahner, FSJ

WORLDS WITHIN WORLDS

"The new life is so crowded with overwhelming surprises, so fruitful of charming distractions, so beautifully bewildering with unimagined pleasures, so tender in its diverting sympathies, that even earth's purest conceptions are certain to be shattered and carried away, and the perfect God-design leads us gently forward into the fullness of our unanticipated joy."
~ Aphraar, a Risen One [2]

I have the great, good fortune of living on the edge of the only remaining tract of primæval forest in one of the largest cities in North America. There are enough trees there to go for long walks without seeing too many people at most times of the day, and should I feel the need I can plunge into the city's collective richness of humanity, art, and culture. Wherever I go, wherever I am, there are worlds within worlds.

Sometimes I go for a run in the early evening just as the sun is setting—when light, air, and sounds are mixing into that most illusive, peculiar hour of time called *twilight*. It's seldom that I don't find something unusual at that time, things that the forest elementals have dropped in their hurry to get home before dark. Their odd flotsam and jetsam tell stories only the færies would appreciate in their alien ways.

While out on a run one particular Indian Summer evening, I came upon an unusual goblin's treasure. A tiny, coiled dead snake, flattened like *découpage* on the path—a very strange sort of charm. In my many years here I had never seen a snake in the woods before, alive or dead. This one was a scaly fingerling only four inches or so long. It brought many questions to mind. Was it a baby snake or a grown one? Do snakes even have babies at this time of year? What on earth happened to it? Why should I see such a thing *now*, and in such a way?

---

2 Robert James Lees, *The Life Elysian* (Leicester, U.K.: Eva Lees, 1905), 17.

The footpath is narrow and for walking only, so a car couldn't have done this. It was like the rural legend I heard years ago back in the Appalachian Mountains where I grew up. A group of teenagers, out for a spin in their pickup, came screeching around the corner where the deserted coal mines began, and barely avoided careening into a massive hunk of metal smack dab in the middle of the road. It turned out to be a car, only it was flat as a pancake, as were its occupants. Local folks always ended the tale with, "*And nobody ever found out how or why.*"

The snakeling before me was coiled in a circle, with a smaller coil in its middle, its mouth touching its tail. The body was still flexible as I gingerly peeled it away from the hard dirt path with a small stick. I felt that I was being watched from the darkening undergrowth by eyes that neither blinked nor wavered, following my every movement. I gently placed the little body beneath the layer of oak leaves that covered the forest floor. As I relinquished it back to the earth, I regarded with interest the few argumentative ants still clinging to what would certainly become a gourmand's myth in their city.

Feeling that I'd probably never find out how or why, I breathed a small prayer of safe travel for its snakey soul. Brushing my hands off on my shorts, I continued my run to the top of the long hill I had been gradually climbing. The early autumn evening was still clinging to the heat and humidity of one of the hottest summers I'd known, and I was dripping with sweat as I slowed to a halt for my mid-way rest. This was the highest spot in the forest, a small clearing where I always stopped and let the sun warm my bones in the early morning, or watched my breath turn to mist in the cooling dusk. It was here that a very ancient, twisted and crusty crabapple tree has set its roots, probably for well over a century, still reluctantly putting out leaves and increasingly smaller bittersweet fruits each year. I had come to regard it as a kind of special friend. It's also a bit of a mystery, for I've never been able to figure out how or why there should be such an anomaly in the midst of an oak and beech forest.

Leaning against the rough bark of my friend, I peered up through its branches silhouetted in the early evening sky, which was beginning to dim from turquoise to indigo, turning the air into what I thought of as *gloaming*.

And then I felt the quality or the tonality or the *something* of the world around me alter in that familiar way I'd experienced before. I didn't need to turn to know that Tim was there, stepping out from his world into mine.

"*Gloaming*—that's a good word," he chuckled quietly, his speaking easily distinguishable from and yet somehow part of the rising chorus of crickets who were also just stepping out for a good time of evening song and dance.

Tim, ever the collector of words, never seemed to be very far away, even if I wasn't aware of him. When caught up by my own body's insistence that its material world is the real and only one, I don't always instantly recognize his comments and musings as separate from my own inner chatter. "Was that you, then, when I felt something watching me?"

"Yes, 'twas I."

"And the snake?"

"We shall never know how or why."

"Always the wit." This was our private joke about how the letters of his name could be rearranged. It seems so terribly long ago when we first did that.

"Coming up on fifteen years now, your time, Augie." When he had been alive, Tim had never known me by the name "August." Nobody had, for that matter—at least in *this* world. Other Risen Ones, who had been close friends long before Tim's transition, had bequeathed me the name "August." Tim uses it often, sometimes kidding me gently by shortening it in various ways, because I had never approved of nicknames very much. And yet he teases with an amused and warming love that is familiar and reassuring.

"*When* I had been alive? So I'm *dead* now, Dear Heart?"

"Of course you're not dead. You're just pretty sensitive for someone without a body."

"You're just picking on me, Aug. You know I still have a body. It's just different than the old one I had and the one you have right now. Anyway—what about our book? Still want to do it?"

"As long as you're doing it with me, then yes, I do. It's an intriguing idea, but remind me why we're doing it."

"It's time."

"That's it? 'It's time?' I thought you didn't have 'time' *there*? Typical. You spirit people can be so enigmatic."

"We can be enigmatic, but never typical, Aug—you know we don't waste words. I'm talking about 'time' in terms of the present. Remember the saying, 'No time like the present'? That's all we ever have—the present. And hey, you're a spirit person, too, you know."

"Ok, Tim, I should know better than to try to ask for too many details at once, much less argue with you. So where do we begin?"

"How about at the beginning?"

I rolled my eyes. "There is no 'beginning!' You know this, Tim, having just reminded me that there is no 'time'."

Time. What do we really know about it? No matter how far I look back to some event in time I experienced, there always seems to be something before that, at least in my memory or from what others tell me. This certainly *seems* true to me, at least from a human perspective. Tracing each event back, it becomes a cause and then each cause becomes an event before that, and so on, *ad infinitum*. This eternal process has given rise to countless scientific and religious theories and endless beliefs about how we came to be here.

"Well, August, that's a subject pretty much left alone for now, just like that little snake. Anyway, I'd say we've already begun, wouldn't you?"

Indeed, we had already begun, within that very living moment. But where this particular beginning exactly started, I will never be able to say with any certainty.

The air had become noticeably cooler—Autumn was finally arriving. I looked up and was startled to see a few stars. Somehow day had changed to night in an instant and it would be too dark to run the two miles back. I'd have to walk home carefully through the shadows. Where had the time gone? It seemed like we had only been talking for a minute or two.

"Like a snake coiled upon itself, so doth time."

"You know something about that snake, don't you, Tim?"

But he was gone, and as the Risen go—without drama, sparks, bells or whistles—*usually*. Gone, but not away—far, but not forever. *There*, but not *here*. I sighed, a mixture of serenity tinged with an unfathomable sadness, knowing that it would be some "time" before I could finally and at last be *there*, as a Risen One, fully sharing life once again with the one I want to love forever.

TIM SPEAKS

"There came a time when the risk to remain tight in the bud was
more painful than the risk it took to blossom."
~ Anaïs Nin

66 Greetings to you. I'm Tim, here to welcome you as you join us on the journey we're undertaking within the guise of an earthly book. I'm no longer on Earth but have transitioned into a new body and a grand, spectacular world and life—I am *Risen*. I'm still the same person I was but also very, very much more. The name I used while embodied was Timothy Gray and I'm utilizing that name here as well. But I also have other names now—symbols, really, to represent my spiritual expression, which changes constantly. Change is the constant, the nature of all existence, at least for those embodied on the earth and for those who are Risen like me. Even the nature of change changes, depending on who perceives and from where the perception arises. My other names are not the kind of symbols that can be transcribed into terrestrial language, so it's most convenient to use my old earthly name here. The name 'Tim' is also still deeply meaningful to August. Its resonance helps us maintain the remarkable connection we now have and want to continue having until he can join me on the level where I am, when the moment arrives for him to make his own transition to a Risen One.

"It was at the request of several highly vibrating Risen Ones that I suggested this little project to August, who assented right away without even knowing just what he was getting himself into. This book will take much of its shape from the countless dialogues and other conversational experiences that August and I have had for almost fifteen years. Because they are real conversations *and* living experiences as well, this book is itself a real and living manifestation. I will also be speaking in the present to him and to you, the reader, as these pages unfold.

"One of the main purposes of this book is to assist others in enabling themselves to realize contact with the Risen. Many readers will probably try to start with just any chapter or pick selections at random. This approach might give one some interesting thoughts, but resonance will not be affected sufficiently to enable the increase in the vibration levels needed for Risen contact. Every chapter, page, and sentence has been exquisitely orchestrated in a particular Risen manner that will lead one through carefully simplified ideas—guided suggestions, really—and on through to deeper, higher vibrating concepts. Most readers will not even realize this happening, and so it is strongly recommended that they begin at the beginning and not worry about it, just as August and I did.

"Ok, I've gone on enough for now—your turn, August."

"You're absolutely right, Tim, I had no idea what I was getting myself into when I agreed to this 'little project'—although I might have thought so at the time. I also want to confirm that you are still very much the same person I knew when you were on the earth, but that you are also even more of the same person, and more than I ever knew or thought possible."

"I will take that as a compliment, which I know it is, Augie."

"It's definitely a compliment. Now, let me have my turn, I have a good deal to say."

"Then onward, ho! I've said my piece for now, so I'll step back and observe. But don't worry, I've plenty more for later."

August Auberon Goforth is the name I was given by Risen mentors when I was a child. Although this name might seem to be obviously meaningful in certain ways and on certain levels, other connotations go far beyond the usual known earthly ones. I've never used these names with those who are here with me on the material plane. The meanings and the multileveled ways in which they are intended would have no relevant significance to those relationships. Even *I* don't yet comprehend all the subtle intentions in these names, and most likely won't until I myself have fully transitioned into a Risen One. Although Tim sometimes uses the name given to me by my earthly parents—for it still remains a meaningful connection between us—he also calls me August. I resonate and identify with this name on a very deep level. For this reason it is appropriate to use this name as one of the co-authors of this book—especially as all the other authors are Risen Ones.

I use my Risen name here, and not my earth-born one, for other reasons, including the fact that I'm a psychotherapist. Some of my personal information is highly essential to the intentions of this book but needs to be adapted for the sake of privacy—mine and that of my therapy patients. It is crucial that they have a safe and confidential space, psychologically as well as physically, from where we can carefully address their issues of healing and growth.

I never intentionally use my mediumistic abilities as part of the process of therapy sessions. Nor do I work as a professional medium, giving readings for others as a means of self-employment. This is a professional bias as well as a personal choice, and my example may serve as a model for other therapists and counselors who might be misguided to inappropriately use mediumistic abilities in their practice. The services that I fulfill with my mediumistic abilities are required in other ways, including my participation here.

There will be an eventual evolution of humanity, as enriched by Risen contact, whereby the various human therapies will all successfully utilize mediumistic gifts for healing. Intrapsychic, that is, intuitive, psychic communication between individuals, is unavoidable in any human relationship, including one between a therapist and a patient. Each therapist will perceive intrapsychic experiences in different ways, specifically and generally—as insight or hunches, as transference and countertransference, or even as coincidence and synchronicity, and may be able to effectively use them within or without certain theoretical structures.

Tim and many other Risen Ones have collectively constructed this book in certain ways to ensure that my privacy will not be invaded in any way that would be detrimental to my life, or to the lives of those with whom I work. I have learned to trust and accept Tim's views on many matters, and we are additionally guided by Risen Ones far advanced in wisdom. It is because of this trust that I whole-heartedly agreed to Tim's decision to retain his own name as it was while on the earth, although it has been an oft-visited subject of differing opinion between us.

Some may react to my not using my earthly name by assuming that it somehow detracts from the believability of what this book is about. But this book is not about trying to change beliefs, much less to prove that I was born. Beliefs can be altered, amended, transformed, and discarded, but any such changes are best left up to each individual's choice. As it will be shown, the choosing of beliefs is a major factor in one's transition to the Risen condition.

My many years of personal experience and research indicate that even when authors have supplied their birth name, it's had little or no influence on others' beliefs about the subject of survival after death. Throughout the existing literature of the nineteenth, twentieth, and early twenty-first centuries, people outstanding in a great diversity of professions, including highly degreed and respected scientists, have loaned their names and reputations to books and research about the subject of survival after death. It's clear that they all discovered in some way that skeptics need their skepticism. A lot of time and energy has been fruitlessly spent in trying to convince individuals who simply were not interested in admitting that the fact of survival is more important than the fiction of their ego-minds. Yet even this will change as more and more professionals come to their own personal spiritual discoveries, and as the world continues to grow increasingly comfortable with the realization that we all survive death.

Not everyone will embrace all the information we share. My experiences and those of Tim's do not make us authorities in anyone's life other than our own, and even *that* may be an assumption. Perhaps it's more appropriate to suggest that our experiences can teach us to let go of certain postures that might otherwise keep us from evolving into greater awareness. Truly every person is writing their own book by living their own life, whether or not they are consciously aware of it in this way.

Tim and I share our experiences with you as inspiration, but not to make you feel as if your life should be like ours. In our own way we are skeptics, too. It might be surprising that Tim, who is Risen, would still be skeptical. But just because he's Risen doesn't mean that all has been automatically revealed to him or that he buys every idea that comes along.

"Exactly, August. It's inaccurate to think that because I've made my transition to a Risen state I'm somehow ahead of the game and have greater abilities and powers than those still embodied on Earth. Especially in the beginning of my new Risen life, I was no more able to contact you than you were able to contact me. I had to first become aware that such a thing was possible and then I had to struggle with believing it was possible, and then I had to work and study with great diligence to *make* it possible. Much of what I was told seemed unfeasible or beyond my capabilities. Even when I was informed that I had finally achieved mental contact with you, I still doubted it. I didn't have enough experience, and until I did I was acting on blind trust."

"Thanks, Tim, for putting it in a way that brings the Risen and the yet-to-Rise closer. You and I are alike in many ways."

"Also, Aug, while there's potential to help bring the non-Risen together in their own material realm, we can also assist Risen individuals to become more resonant to each other in their Risen environment. You've learned about after-life communications because of what others have shared with you—personally and through books, for example. In the same way, I've also learned from other Risen about similar matters. In turn, you will share what you've learned with those on your physical plane, while I'll share with those Risen who wish to know about the possibilities of contact and communication. We will be joining a very long line of tradition and service on both sides through these efforts. But just being Risen doesn't automatically bestow instant knowledge and abilities on a person. Everyone arrives here with endless questions, as well as different degrees of confusion and understanding."

Tim and I tend to question everything we don't understand, while striving to remain open in order to be there when the answer shows up. Sooner or later it always does, recognized or not. Hopefully we *can* recognize it, and especially to remember to keep a sense of humor while struggling with our wanting everything our own way right now. As a Risen friend once remarked to me, "Humor is the universal polish that keeps the personal tarnish away."

Like most theories, a lot of things we will say will look wonderful here on the page, but being able to actualize any of it beyond paper is not a certainty. The reality of what we're going to share goes far beyond the physical confines of pen and paper, which are manifested physical expressions of time and space. In spite of my achievements in contact with the Risen, the answers to many of my questions rarely come easily or quickly. It might seem as if it should be easier for me to just ask Risen Ones for advice and then get an immediate answer. But an evolved Risen Person will *never* tell me what to do. They may guide me with suggestions, counseling, and even an occasional hint, but they will never directly insist that I *must* proceed in a certain way. There are, of course, exceptions. But not even Tim, in his undying love for me, has yet to bend this rule, sometimes much to my frustration. The Risen will remain firmly silent but steadfast in their support of whatever choices we make for ourselves. They know that not thinking for ourselves gets us no further than the ends of our noses. And there is *so* much more beyond our noses.

Sharing our lives and experiences is how Tim and I wish to open up to each other and to others, who may then respond by opening up to their own selves and to others. We can all experience the taking in of more truth and mystery. From there we can increasingly expand, individually and collectively, as we move together through the never-ending universe, which is also continually opening up and expanding. This personal and universal expansion makes us all givers and receivers of gifts. Gifting is what it's all about.

There is another reason for refraining from attracting inappropriate attention to my private life. It arises naturally from my life as a contemplative, which I have inwardly led since I came to it, or it came to me, as a young adolescent. It is out of this same, ever-flowing fountain of contemplation that my intuitive and mediumistic senses have evolved—the innate knowing that arises from my soul's connection with the earth's spirit, as well as that which has its eyes and ears ever attentive on Original Creator Source. These connective perceptions of a contemplative self neither need nor seek worldly recognition. The only seeking involved is that of an attentive awareness that is open to serving others. This expression of openness is what attracts the higher light-filled vibrations of the Risen, and is a mirror of delicate clarity that must not be clouded by the dust and grime of celebrity.

This book was developed and granted directly from many Risen worlds, from where those who have never stopped loving us freely and willingly share their combined wisdom with us from their greater Risen perspectives. Their continual loving revelations tell us with total certainty that no matter how much we might want to, we shall never die, and that however lonely and isolated we see ourselves, we are never without support.

Tim and I assure you that this book is not a work of fiction, and ask that you keep your mind open to the very astounding things we will present. Much of what we report actually occurs as we write, making it a living work-in-progress. When we finally run out of things to say it will be only because we are following the natural ebb and flow of the tides of living, and have reached a temporary fulfillment in our endeavor. Along with us, you will most certainly see the end of one trail merging into another, reflecting that all of existence is a spiraling adventure that is open-ended, never finished, and undying.

THE RISEN

Tell all the Truth but tell it slant —
Success in Circuit lies
Too bright for our infirm Delight
The Truth's superb surprise

As Lightning to the Children eased
With explanation kind
The Truth must dazzle gradually
Or every man be blind —
~ Emily Dickinson

A little later after my encounter with Tim in the forest, I was back in the coziness of my home. The cat was snoring with little quacking noises by the gently flickering fireplace. I thought about Tim's comment that I'm a spirit person, too. It's true—we're each a spirit person while on the earth, wearing a material body needed for the time we're here.

As an individualized manifestation of Original Creator Source, our spirit needs a form or body to navigate certain environments. As embodied, spirit energy beings on the earth we actually have more than one body, each interpenetrating and integrated with one another. A body is any form through which the individualized self moves and functions on some level. A soul is also another kind of enlarged mental body which encompasses this self, participating in life simultaneously with other souls. Original Creator Source Mind is the infinite, underlying source of this enlarged soul self. All minds are participating simultaneously with one another, as united and sustained by the same Spirit.

Our material body is needed by our spirit while on the earth as a diver or an astronaut needs a life support suit to explore the depths of oceans or space. We also have an etheric body that interpenetrates the material one. It's usually hidden from our physical senses, so we're basically unaware of it. This etheric body could be thought of as an energy form that connects our physical body with the third one, the astral body. We travel in the astral body when we leave the physical body during sleep or when it has been injured by physical or emotional and mental trauma. Our astral body will also be the first of many that we will wear in those places in which we find ourselves after the physical body has expired. After an earthly death, the etheric body may still cling to our spirit energy for awhile, depending on many factors, but it will eventually dissipate and then the astral body will be free to leave the earth for good.

While living on the earth our primary conscious experience is informed by the senses of the physical body, which is the densest of our bodies—so dense that we experience it as material and made of matter. This matter is so compacted from its slow vibrations that the Principle of Attraction on earth is based on some of the gravitational forces that are generated by this matter—or more aptly, generated *because* of matter. As this suggests, there are several kinds of gravity, which some scientists have suspected and are investigating.

In this book, we will say "principle" where modern scientific and other societies would automatically use "law" when attempting to speak of the so-called "inexorable events of manifestation observed in Nature." It is crucial to state clearly and plainly that "law" is a concept of human social origin. It implies observed boundaries, restrictions, judgments, rewards, and punishments, any of which can and do change at any time. Nature's forces inextricably include each of us, as revealed by manifestation. The idea that they are rigidly determined and inflexible is a supposition that denies the divine primal gift of freedom. Laws are based on human, earth-bound collective observations, which are organized and followed according to the collective ego-mind. While "principle" does not quite give the true flavor of the collective Risen concept, it is more open and flexible than "law." "Principle" alludes to the kind of attitude or stance from which the expanded observations of the Risen are made and where beliefs are seen for what they are not.

The day will come when we'll no longer need our physical form, the densest of our bodies, and it will be shed like an old winter coat. Left behind, it will be broken back down into the basic elements that constitute starlight. The old garment will be reabsorbed into the earth as well as released into the cosmos to be used again in other ways. As an individualized spirit we will continue on in a state that can still be called "embodied," but in the far more subtle and highly vibrating astral body. We will move on and into a new season of life, a place or condition the Victorians quaintly called "Summerland" and some Native Americans might have called "The Yearned For Good Hunting Ground." Almost every culture on the earth has its way of describing where we find ourselves after we die. We say "almost" because the culture of our highly technological and materialistic modern society has left barely any room for such a concept. Yet a spiritual revolution appears to be occurring now, re-opening our lives to ancient understandings.

As Risen, we won't be dead at all, but more alive, conscious, and aware than ever before. We'll be free of the immense gravity and spirit-numbing effects our materially dense earth bodies had been continually bearing upon our spirit. We will learn to move, live, and love in the astral body we had been carrying all along within our densest material one, and which had been evolving—or not—according to how much we focused on its evolution. When we arrive at our new place of living, generally most of us won't be very far in our consciousness from the earth plane, mainly because we didn't focus much or even at all on the spiritual care and growth of our astral body.

It's usually easiest for the *newly* Risen to be able to communicate in some way from this particular astral environment with those still in their earthly material bodies. How subtle or dramatic the communications are depends on several things. Some of the considerations include how intensely the newly Risen want to communicate with those still on the earth, on their acceptance and belief that it is possible to do so, on the developed abilities of everyone involved, and if they are ready to receive assistance. Tim can explain more about this later on.

"I can certainly try, Aug, but it's going to be very interesting trying to explain it in ways embodied people can understand."

"Yes, Tim, it can get quite knotty as I know from experience. It's easy for me to talk with you from within, but to convey this conversation to the outside—well, I'll do my best. It's an ongoing learning process for me. What you and I do is so much more than simply carrying on a conversation. There are many subtle senses involved in this kind of communication."

"And, as you've discovered, Aug, the five wonderful senses that help you get around in your terrestrial world can actually be hindrances if you want to navigate in the Risen one. Spiritual sight and hearing are abilities to see through and past all earthly forms, forms that embody and express or outpicture those ideas that are symbols of your material existence. The spirit within you is trying to express itself to the consciousness of the spirit of everything else, but the material earthly senses are too dense and low in vibration for them to be aware of the finer, higher vibrations."

"Well put, Tim, and I must add that not being able to use my earthly senses in their usual ways to communicate with you is frustrating as well— although I've learned from our experiences that these earthly senses *can* change in some way or become enhanced or even evolve."

"There are Risen who actually study this kind of process, or so I've heard but I know little about it—yet."

"So perhaps we'll find out more about such things as we move forward together. Do you feel that you experience such changes for yourself, Tim?"

"Absolutely, August, but it's as mysterious to me as well. Talking about it makes me want to learn more, and I will certainly seek out assistance. When I was on earth, I could drive a car perfectly well but couldn't automatically tell you much about the mechanical processes taking place. Or when I was sick I could tell you how I was physically feeling but would have been unable to explain much about the medical reasons for those feelings."

Since the conscious realization of my mediumistic sensitivities, and the acceptance of their reality, I've come to want to know as much as I can about them and become informed about the process. Being a voracious reader and an academically inclined person with a bent for research, I've gathered many books, articles, pamphlets, recordings—anything I could find on the subject of survival after physical death. Tim is also a bookworm and has greatly helped me in finding things, often in very ingenious and surprising ways. Some of the several hundred references I now have were printed over 150 years ago, and it's fascinating to see how people struggled then with finding ways to describe their experiences in much the same way as I do now.

For example, Stewart Edward White, (1873–1946) a well-known American author and historical novelist, recorded between 1919 and 1936 his wife Betty's meditative "excursions" into another dimension in *The Betty Book*. He designated her incorporeal contacts, "the Invisibles." Although he accepted their intelligent and distinct, albeit disincarnate presences, he was never able to identify their actual source. When he asked them about it they unwaveringly insisted on complete anonymity. So he wondered if Betty was tapping into her subconscious or into some stored, accumulated information of humankind that existed in the shared universal unconscious. The Invisibles refused to give any clues, citing the subject as irrelevant to their work. They also avoided giving any opinions or advice on everyday matters.

The Invisibles explained they wanted to come to the translator—to Betty—but the denser conditions of earth dulled and confused them. They decided instead to teach and guide Betty into greater areas of awareness outside her own bodily experience and its habitual consciousness, and to enter *their* conditions and be able to report back. This sort of "reverse engineering" has also happened to me in certain ways.

Arthur Findlay was another well-known and prolific writer and researcher into psychic phenomena and mediumship in the mid-twentieth century. He labeled those in spirit as "Etherians." He saw the etheric body as a duplicate of the physical one and that death was simply the separation of the two from each other. Our individuality was retained and our minds continued to develop even more rapidly, but in new surroundings. He stressed that those in the physical body cannot see those in the etheric body, as our physical sight and touch are too confined to sense the higher vibrations of Etherians.[3]

---

[3] Arthur Findlay, *Where Two Worlds Meet* (London: Psychic Press Limited, 1951), 24.

Both these writer-explorers have deftly explained their experiences and their understanding of them in ways that often come very close to my own. Although "Invisibles" is an apt descriptor for how most people experience them, it sounds too plain to me and even a bit silly, as it brings to my mind the Invisible Man, who actually had a material body and was not disembodied at all. "Etherian" has an interesting, otherworldly feel to it and we are, after all, talking about another world. Still, at least for me, it sounds somewhat old-fashioned. As for the term "spirit," I really can't use it as a distinctive label since we're all spirits.

"Aug, you can only be so politically correct."

"Ah, my dear Wit! I'm not surprised that you decided to comment just now." It seems that Tim is often aware of my thoughts. But he never invades my privacy, although there is very little that we keep from each other at this point. I trust him completely and have never felt him to be judgmental about thoughts I consider particularly private. He has ways of determining when I need my thoughts to stay private and when it's ok for him to join me. It's somewhat similar to how one person, if sensitive enough, can tell when another person wants to be alone, even though they don't say anything. Similarly, I can hear Tim's words or more precisely, discern his thoughts, and even feel his feelings. It's as if we "think-feel" in the sharing of our conversation, although normally I cannot see him except for an occasional clairvoyant glimpse. When we talk together there is a very distinct emotional event happening and flowing, as if we are immersed in a pool of feelings that are uniquely familiar to our relationship—just like close friends or lovers might experience. Because of the intimacy of such communication between us, I often refer to it as "communing."

"Tim, it's true that one can only be so politically correct, but labels can be liberating as well as confining, depending on how we utilize them. Labels are part of our process—it's an 'Earth thing.' It seems to be a necessity although perhaps a temporary one. This process of defining things never stops—it becomes a process of *refining* for us. The evolution of new ideas, of new consciousnesses and new expressions of light doesn't appear to end here on earth, but to continue on forever."

"And so will you, I see, until you find this label you're looking for."

"Well, relax, as I've been using it, because you already gave it to me. You've been referring to yourself as 'Risen' for as long as I can remember."

Joa Bolendas, a modern Swiss visionary and mystic, has also had intimate conversations with the "dead" for many years, along with the entities sometimes referred to as angels. Her conversations with people who are no longer in their earthly bodies reveal their experiences. She once asked them what their "substance" is. They answered her with the following—

"It is a substance of spiritual energy, a substance of light,
Unchangeable light—
Which is the same as energy.
The risen human remains a created being linked with God's Spirit.
The flesh, the earthly covering and clothing, falls away."[4]

"The risen human" is an exquisitely beautiful, evocative expression. "Risen" or "Risen One" is immensely appropriate for a twenty-first century exploratory discussion about our loved ones who have gone on before us, and who have risen elsewhere and continue to live and love us from that place.

"Hey, August, wasn't there some comic book super-hero named 'The Spirit' when we were kids?"

"Yes, Tim—you probably pretended to be him when you were eleven."

"Actually, that was Tonto."

"That's very interesting, Tim. And how do you identify now?"

"Behold before thee—a Risen One!"

"And a thing of beauty, you truly are, Tim."

The expressions *Risen Ones* or *the Risen* will be used primarily in this book when speaking about discarnate—or disembodied—persons. "Spirit" will also be used from time to time, which many people today use in a kind of generic way, such as, "I was aware that Spirit was never far away" or "I left the matter up to Spirit, since I didn't have a clue about what the hell to do next."

The knowledge that we're in possession of more than one body at the same time is profound and ancient. Down through countless eras, virtually every culture's spiritual system has conceptualized these multi-bodies in various ways—from how they appear to the spiritual senses, to what they can do, and to how many there are. This speaks to the miraculous gift we each have to manifest those unique realities that best express our individual experience.

There are at least three bodies we each possess while on the earth—our densest material body, and our less dense etheric and astral bodies, all inter-penetrating one another. In the West there have been different perceptions about which body is subtlest—etheric or astral. For some people it seems to be important to precisely delineate them as separate, subtle bodily experiences, and for others it's more a matter of awareness of one's unique situation.

For our purposes here and for simplicity's sake, Tim and I will usually refer to the subtle body experience as astral or astral-etheric, even though there is often more than one subtle body involved. The interpenetration of these

---

[4] Joa Bolendas, *Alive in God's World: Human Life on Earth and in Heaven* (Great Barrington, MA: Lindisfarn Books, 2001), 46.

bodies is not a static condition but an evolving one that undergoes important changes and reflects one's own personal growth.

Joa Bolendas also received a lovely description about what remains when the earthly body falls away—

> ". . . *eternal light in human form remains. This body of*
> *light lives! God's Spirit is in it. The people of light are*
> *noble and fulfilled when integrated into God's kingdom."* [5]

Even while we are in these material bodies on earth we are still "people of light." When it is time, we will shed our material body as if removing worn-out clothing. Our material bodies are designed to be so dense because otherwise our spirit bodies could not be contained—it takes a great deal of density to hold them to the earth. Although also literally made of light, our heavier earthly bodies are cloaking us in "denser light," opaque enough to be called shadows. When the shadows fall away we will stand revealed as beings of light.

As beings of light we continue on endlessly—our immortal experience. *This realization is of immense importance,* for we are literally having our immortal experience *in this very moment.* Immortality doesn't begin *after* we transition to Risen, but commenced when we first arose on this world, fired into life with a Divine Spark, to awaken and breathe and move up and out into this world, our earth. When one not only mentally accepts this realization about our immortality but is able to gain awareness of it and then *feel* the realization of it, life is experienced with much less fear and much more freedom. It is spiritually imperative to understand that besides having the experience, we must be able to observe the experience, to participate as observers, and to especially become aware of it by feeling it.

Many Risen Ones have told me, and I myself have experienced, that there are many more finely-defined bodily experiences than just the three—they're actually infinite in number. Also infinite are the geographies in which we might find ourselves upon shedding our earthly woolens. These geographies inter-penetrate one another just like our subtle bodies. Everything and everywhere is able to share the same space with everything else. Our loved ones are not off somewhere over the rainbow or separated from us by unimaginable distances of light years. They may be even closer to us now than when they were in their denser material body. As mentioned earlier, it's not that they've left us, but that they seem less accessible. It is the density of our earthly body with its physical senses that affectively shields us from directly feeling their closeness to us.

Unlike the earth's primary principle of attraction based on various forms of physical gravity, the principle of attraction in the non-material Risen reality

---

[5] Bolendas, 47.

is based on "like attracts like." Upon casting off our earthly body we will find ourselves with other people very much like ourselves, and in environments we personally and collectively find comfortable. Depending upon the density of our mental, emotional, and spiritual substance, we will naturally gravitate toward those people who are most like ourselves. This process takes place under the Principle of Affinity and the Principle of Resonance, which Tim and I will speak about in detail further on. To repeat—while some people refer to these Principles as "laws," the Risen prefer not to, as a law is a human concept that carries millennia of race connotations of right and wrong or justice and injustice. Principles of Spirit simply do not recognize a binary—all *is* one.

People who are spiritual opposites definitely will not attract one another in the Risen geographies. I have heard many stories about the surprising discovery of who *is* most like us—often they're not who we'd expect. As some might intuit at this point, the Principle of Affinity is but a very small facet of the Unprincipled Principle—love, the ultimate energy.

"Spiritual substance" means literally that—a substance that is of spirit and also *is* spirit. In this book we will not use "spiritual" in the way it's heard most of the time on the earth. That is, as a kind of qualitative description that means a person is good or better in some way, connoting moral achievement or superiority over self and others, or something that we aren't now but will later become. To use the word "spiritual" in such ways is a materialistic interpretation and a judgment about how we perceive and compare our own behavior with that of others. Humans are the ones who have laws about spirituality. These laws, which are ideas or beliefs, can continue on into the afterlife, but will still be human-defined as well as limited and limiting.

One does not have to be a good or moral person to be a medium and discern spiritual forms and places anymore than a minister, doctor, or a scientist needs to be ethical in order to do their jobs technically well. The tools are there to be used and it's up to us to determine how we want to use them. We can become more loving, compassionate, and evolved through our experiences, which is another way of saying that we are able to be more open to more love. The more refined we are in the areas of compassion—astrally as well as physically, as well as the more skilled—which takes a lot of curiosity, practice, and maintenance—the more capable we can become at establishing communication with those Risen who are also focused on their self-evolution.

Tim and I cannot present a set of precise lessons for mediumistic experiences. Each person on the earth already has a built-in set of instructions, completely unique and awaiting self-discovery. As touched upon earlier, this book has been orchestrated by the Risen to evoke a gradually increasing resonance of the spiritual bodies of each reader. As one moves through the book, visible and invisible material will excite the spirit energy, which will reveal itself in particular ways to be interpreted by the bearer of that energy.

The Risen intend this method to enable our fellow spirits to transform this quickened energy into the excitement brought on by the chance to discover their own personal, unique, and incomparable spiritual reality. Because the way lies within each of us, it is ultimately up to each person to discover how to use the energy of love in ways that best serve them and their universe. And there will be as many ways as there are individuals and universes.

As a spirit we each communicate with other spirits, embodied or otherwise. It helps to be open to the unexpected. Everyone can and does communicate with the Risen, whether or not they consciously accept it. Your awareness may expand as you continue to read, perhaps to where you might become consciously aware of something very new and very interesting taking place. *This will be an ongoing, accumulative process.*

There will be certain points in this book where it will be particularly important to not let yourself become discouraged when you read something that doesn't make immediate sense. To help you stay grounded and remain open when particularly challenged, the following phrase will be placed at junctures the Risen have deemed exceptionally significant.

~ 1 ~

These words may not make conscious sense at this time,
but my spiritual senses comprehend and retain
this knowledge for Authentic Self.

Even this phrase may not make much sense right now, but eventually it will, as you read on. You may want to revisit and ponder these junctures again later on, so each is numbered and visually easy to locate.

We are offspring of Original Creator Source, divine inheritors of limitless abilities and cosmic understanding. Yet our current knowledge is that of earthly children. From here, we now move forward with trust, patience, and curiosity—all childlike qualities, and gifts that will serve us well.

SPIRIT & SCIENCE

"Science alone of all the subjects contains within itself the lesson of the danger of belief in the infallibility of the greatest teachers in the preceding generation . . . Learn from science that you must doubt the experts. As a matter of fact, I can also define science another way: Science is the belief in the ignorance of experts."
~ Richard Feynman

"A child of five would understand this.
Send someone to fetch a child of five."
~ Groucho Marx

My journeys into the strange and breathtaking Risen worlds have gifted me with many experiences that are profoundly mysterious and often resist explanation. "Explanation," a word meaning, "to make clear," is sometimes used in English in opposite ways. We want an explanation to expand our understanding of something in order to keep it in existence, so we can continue to study and learn from it. At other times we might seek to explain something in order to minimize or dismiss it entirely—to explain it away. By shining the light of attentive awareness on something, we may come to see that there's nothing there. On the other hand, it might be seen that there's a lot more there than had been thought possible.

Some people are Skeptics with a capital **S**. These Professional Skeptics feel it's their job to remain closed in their minds and hearts while retaining the right to question anything. Many of them include scientists, who represent a very small minority of humanity on earth, but have been placed on pedestals that raise them above the majority. This misapprehension disempowers the majority, disabling them from assessing their own valid experiences of personal reality. Science has given us brilliant advances in many aspects of human living, but not without a lot of trials and errors. The facets of truth that science presents as dogma are often successful in creating distractions from those with alternate viewpoints. Yet scientific history consistently reveals the inevitable result of radical exchanges of such dogma. Former universally accepted and supposedly proven axioms are continually replaced by new discoveries, which are then made formal by a collective agreement of this minority. Such has been the course of mainly Western science as it has evolved on earth. This is finally changing as science rediscovers the idea of the energy we call *spirit*. Science is wonderful, amazing, and necessary, and can provide a certain amount of insight into our existence, but not all. Given the amazing changes in our scientific world-views over the past one hundred years, can we truly think we can now put a cap on what is to come in the next hundred?

Earthly, western scientific methods are not derived from Nature, but from human minds that see themselves as separate from it. But it's not the only way of thinking about things. If something can be seen, held, heard, smelled and felt, then scientific measurement can be applied. If they're too subtle to be detected beyond the senses, then they're beyond known scientific methods.

The materialistic reductionist models of Western science have attempted to govern humankind's world-mind for the past two centuries. This is particularly exemplified in the dominant Darwinian life-models. These reified theories have been less concerned with subjective value issues, focusing primarily on objective experiences manifested by those human senses that can be used to physically see, hear, touch, smell, taste, and measure. Traditionally, materialistic science has sought to gather, weigh, measure, compare, and ultimately predict and control aspects of our existence, even if no understanding of the phenomenon is ever gained. Value is seen in terms of who can predict with the greatest accuracy, and thus who will have the most control. The Global Madison Avenue, or the world of advertising, uses materialistic science to assign value to whatever market they wish to control, including their primary target, the mental market of the masses—the collective ego-mind. One does not have to look too deeply to reach the conclusion that most of our modern societal beliefs—and worldly ones as well—are created, maintained, and controlled by the collaborative efforts of the media and the Global Madison Avenue. Imagine what might happen if the same energy from the efforts placed into creating and selling fossil fuel-burning cars was channeled into communication with the Risen.

"I'd like to add something here, August. There are Risen Ones who were business people on earth and worked in advertising and marketing. Many of them still maintain a strong interest in those areas, and some seek to do service for mankind by trying to find ways to utilize the energies in the way you just mentioned. But they realize that their earthly counterparts might try to capitalize on any opportunity and aspect of Risen communication possible. This would be primarily for their personal earthly monetary and worldly interests, but not necessarily for the sake of furthering humankind's spiritual evolution. However, true to their own peculiar genius, certain Risen 'business people' are capitalizing on their earthly peers' predilections. This is why there have been a lot of recent movies about the afterlife, and mediums are now appearing with their own books, workshops, television shows, websites, and the like. In fact, these earthly technologies are being used by the Risen 'business people' to get as much information to the most people in the shortest time for higher aspirations. There are those business people on earth who are genuinely interested in promoting these things as a service toward furthering human spiritual evolution. Even those who are not interested, believing they have no spiritual beliefs and are only in it for the money, are actually coming into contact with higher vibrations, which will invariably have an effect on them, however small. Now what do you think about *that*?"

"Frankly, Tim, I'm astounded at the irony of it. This is an example of a spiritual paradox if ever I heard one. What will come next?"

"Well, don't be surprised if some of your earthly business corporations try to drag our higher efforts down to their level."

"What do you mean?"

"First there will be fan clubs for mediums, then action figures and lunchboxes. And the grocery shelves will feature 'Ghost Toasties' cereal ('Put A Little Life Back In Your Mourning!') The sports industry will promote basketball sneakers that let you jump higher than the astral planes. And of course there will be vitamins to promote healthy etheric bodies."

"Tim, now you're scaring me. And I suspect you're more than half-serious. But let's discuss yet another scientific viewpoint that *does* allow for survival after death, if not spirit vitamins."

"Ok, I'll be quiet for a while—carry on."

"Thank you, but please don't wander too far."

Noetic Science has gained attention in this early twenty-first century particularly where studies of the mind-body are involved. It is specifically concerned with qualitative values while less concerned with the quantitative features, although quantity still has a natural validity. This science seeks to gain understanding about the purpose of subjective experiences while suggesting holistic models that can link and include even reductionist models.

Appropriately for this book, the word *noetic* is from the Greek for "intuitive knowing." While materialistic science is a process of discovery, noetic science is one of *recovery*—recovering that which we already intuitively know. This is not to say that materialistic scientists are discovering new things. Rather, the nature of their discoveries is that they are *uncovering* things which lead to intuitive knowledge. Who, where, and how we are at any given present moment will determine the uncovering process—which often seems more like a recovery process. One might wonder if our lack of knowledge about what makes Nature tick is an indication of ignorance or just confusion. Ultimately, as we will each gradually come to see, everything in the universe is already here, just as we are. This visionary experience appears to be ongoing and unending and is becoming more frequent in many fields of present-day science.

And yet, we *do* need skeptics. There are scientists who maintain a healthy measure of skepticism *about* skepticism, and remain open while questioning. This openness has led to emerging, revolutionary scientific models, such as R. A. White's *Experiential Paradigm*.[6] Inspired in part by psychologist Abraham Maslow's classic work on cognitive-being and his insights from what he called exceptional "plateau" or "peak" human experiences, White asserts that there's a form of knowing that can only come from having been immersed in a particular experience. This means that the worldview of a medium can only be objectively analyzed after the *analyzer* has also subjectively experienced it. Mediumistic experiences often take place outside the constraints of space and time and therefore may pose serious challenges to those scientists who have always relied on such matrices in their laboratories.

Maslow saw the Western worldview as typically deficient in its perception, due to limited judgments resulting from researchers not sharing the experience of the subjects they study. In science this results in a kind of "single vision." But having similar experiences to those they study could result in "double vision," where the world can be seen from inside the experiential paradigm *and* from their own limited viewpoint as well. This would be like first being underwater, and then mentally re-experiencing what it was like after being back on dry land. Hindu scriptures express this experience as "That Art Thou."

The notion of Intelligent Design, which has emerged in the last ten years and challenges the currently dominant Darwinism models—along with the positions of self-organization and theistic evolution—is guided by the subjective wisdom of intuition. Although this is not the place to discuss these models, there is plenty of brisk debate presently taking place.[7] In a later chapter on reincarnation, Tim will lightly touch on some Risen theories of life that appear to reflect some of Intelligent Design's inspirations.

From within a mediumistic experiential paradigm—paradigm meaning "model" or "prototype"—the individual and her universe are both experientially known as "spirit." This spiritual universe, or the Universe-That-Is-Spirit, consists of those worlds that have largely been beyond our modern twentieth and twenty-first century earthly physical experience. These worlds simultaneously interpenetrate our own physical world, and cannot be intellectually grasped within most modern scientific constraints of measurable

---

[6] Rhea A. White, "Exceptional Human Experience and the Experiential Paradigm," *ReVision*, 1995, 18(2): 18-25.

[7] William A. Dembski and Michael Ruse, eds., *Debating Design: From Darwin to DNA* (Cambridge University Press, 2004).

space and time. Intellect, a child of the mind, is gifted at comprehending the material things of the earth. But Spirit is accessed experientially, inspirationally, and intuitively—that is, noetically. Spirit most effectively interfaces with Spirit. Know Thyself. Thou art That.

Spiritual awareness, like science, requires diligent questioning and participation. Simply accepting something because one is told to believe it is not equal to experiencing it. But once we experience something, we have begun to know it. Upon greater and fuller experiences of experiential knowing, we begin to have faith. From there, wisdom arises from the event and this faith becomes an integral part of our present awareness.

While giving due credit to the necessity of healthy skepticism, this book does not address the needs of professional skeptics. As Tim has pointed out, it has been orchestrated by many, many Risen Ones to evoke and inspire various levels of resonance and deeply intuitive responses from the reader, skeptic or not. This will be especially effective for those who are either working through or have worked through their fears and doubts, and feel drawn to the subject in some way, however slight, however wary. A scientist and a non-scientist may not think they're looking for the same thing, but the shared desire to understand will likely bring them into contact with one another in some way.

All human seeking brings relatedness to our collective understanding about our universe. Along with the Higher Risen who are orchestrating this book, we would like to share a little bit of what we've encountered where science and the Afterlife are concerned, as permitted by our limited understanding. Various discoveries and ideas of modern science have helped me in achieving a more conscious understanding of my spiritual adventures, and at the very least are provocative and stimulating. Tim's experiences often reflect mine, although from different perspectives. The following brief discussions about particular scientific explorations, which were brought to my attention by the Risen team who are behind this book, are meant to aid the reader in achieving a better understanding of the more astonishing things we will share later on. While most earthly scientists involved with these particular topics might be very reluctant to apply them to spiritual ideas about the Afterlife, we will bravely—but briefly—explore some possibilities in this and other chapters.

75 years ago, scientists became aware of "dark matter," and in 1998, of "dark energy". While they exist, they can't be seen. "Dark" is a misleading label, since we *can* see things in the dark, if not with direct vision then with the aid of such things as infrared instruments. Believed to have no atoms and so unable to interact with ordinary matter via electromagnetic forces, this energy can only be detected indirectly, although it apparently has mass, as revealed by its gravitational effect on visible matter. It passes through Earth—and us— every second. Scientists believe they have determined that it's the dominant substance in the universe, and various theories suggest it's at least six to ten

times more prevalent than all visible material. If visible matter is just 10 percent of what we can see, then what is the other 90 percent? Is dark matter/energy also spirit energy? The Risen response is, "Yes, and a whole lot more."

Scientists from many disciplines have now begun to explore this substance of spirit, which they'll probably continue to refer to as some kind of "dark energy-matter." One of the two main and broad hypothetical categories that scientists have placed it in predicts it to be small elementary particles which are not charged and are therefore invisible. The other category suggests that it might be material that is somehow related to black holes, where objects do not emit much or any light.

The first category of thought concludes that these particles are not charged and can exist at the same time and in the same place with charged particles. This sounds very much like the idea of the interpenetrability of spirit bodies and spirit geographies.

Quantum mechanics, the basic principle underlying modern atomic physics, attempts to describe the behavior of that matter which we can see and feel. Subatomic particles, the fundamental pieces of matter, are understood not as solid substances but as "packets of energy" interacting with each other. This interaction is movement, and charged in such a way to produce electric fields. These packets of energy are actually light—or photons—and their movement is the behavior. The moving charges produce magnetic fields, and accelerating moving charges produce electromagnetic waves—meaning light—and therefore charge would be responsible for vision.

It is believed by some that quantum mechanics demonstrates that charge is the force that binds atoms. This force is responsible for how atoms behave and for their chemical properties, enabling us to see objects. A particle's charge prevents it from occupying the same space of another charged particle, which is perhaps why we feel objects as solid. All our complete sensual experiences of the outer world would be due to the property of electric charge. So if a particle has no charge we would not be able to sense it in any way and it would also be able to pass right through detectable matter.

A particle of dark energy-matter seems to have no charge, and interacts with itself through some as-yet-unknown force. This goes far beyond our present knowledge about the universe. If there is no charge, there are no electromagnetic waves and so no visible light. So these particles can't be seen in ways we currently use. The lack of charge would not prevent these particles from occupying the same space of a charged particle. Hence we have the possibility of substances, forms, people, planets, entire galaxies and universes interpenetrating one another, and simultaneously existing in the same space.

Yet dark energy-matter apparently has mass, as it exerts a gravitational force upon visible objects which also have mass. Further, it seems that all of this dark energy-matter existed before the Big Bang, or whatever the event was that science believes brought charged, visible, solid matter into existence. In other words, although the Big Bang may be how our visible material bodies were created, the substance of spirit existed before this event.

For millennia, mystics and mediums have shared their experiences of the subtle astral-etheric realities, perhaps experiencing dark energy-matter. Having gained a self-awareness of their own subtle bodies and subtle senses, they are able to see, hear, touch, and take part in realities—or fields—that interpenetrate our material one. To the extent that they could find the language, some have recorded their journeys into the astral worlds, attempting to describe the nature of the corresponding bodies we all have in those worlds. Persian mystics of the twelfth century were particularly adept at exploring spirit worlds, and certain parts of their literature will be examined in Chapter 13— Mundus Imaginalis, as our Risen discussion is built. The notion of "fields" will be expanded upon a little more in Chapter 15—Psychospiritual Amnesia.

Even this relatively mild scientific discussion might seem daunting, but keep in mind that this material is presented to aid in raising the spiritual vibration of the reader. Understanding will occur as a natural part of the process—if not on the conscious level then on other levels of consciousness. Any understanding will be valuable and will be utilized by your spiritual self.

~ 2 ~

These words may not make conscious sense at this time,
but my spiritual senses comprehend and retain
this knowledge for Authentic Self.

Something now occurring on a planetary scale seems to be showing us that one does not have to be a mystic to have an experiential awareness of the unseen. Everywhere, people are coming to realize in their own ways that we not only all co-exist within what we'll now refer to as spirit—instead of dark energy-matter—but that *we* are actually made of this spiritual substance. We simultaneously exist as and in this spiritual substance. We are the lilies and the fields and the ground. Since it seems to have existed before our charged, visible material universe, it appears that our very foundations of being are in Original Creator Source, of which we are an inseparable part.

FIVE

TRANSITION, FORMERLY KNOWN AS DEATH

"Very likely it is difficult to believe or realize existence in what is sometimes called 'the next world'; but then, when we come to think of it, it is difficult to believe in existence in this world too; it is difficult to believe in existence at all. The whole problem of existence is a puzzling one."
~ Sir Oliver Lodge [8]

Our experiences and the knowledge we've gleaned from them and then present won't always appear straightforward and simple, and most certainly will be challenging. Many will be unable to comprehend what Tim and I seem to easily share, finding our language frustrating and even nonsensical, like the exotic quantum world. Yet others will be able to connect with us in their own way.

~ 3 ~

These words may not make conscious sense at this time,
but my spiritual senses comprehend and retain
this knowledge for Authentic Self.

To write this book, we must use words. To use words, we have to speak in terms of time. Time is one way in the geography where Tim is, and different in the time-space where he and I commune. Our combined sense of time is less familiar to one another, so it's often tricky but stimulating work to find common ground. Those of us with earthly bodies are walking paradoxes, existing in at least two different dimensions that differ in time yet at the same

---

[8] Oliver J. Lodge, *Raymond or Life and Death* (New York: George H. Doran Company, 1916), 308.

time. Our material bodies are aware of earthly time, as affected by physical elements of light, darkness, seasons, and weather. Simultaneously our bodies also contain the etheric body and the evolving astral body, each with a time-nature of its own. It's often easier to connect with Tim's astral awareness from the awareness of my astral body than from my physical body, because we both have an astral body. But because he no longer has a material body like mine, it's far more difficult for him to connect with my material body awareness.

Tim and I often share a wordless awareness. Many of us know what it's like listening to a song without words while still being able to understand the complex emotional content that the composer sought to convey. We might even be able to hum a few bars to someone and convey the song's meaning. This "song without words awareness" describes rather well many of my communication experiences with the Risen.

Songs *with* words are also powerful and often utilized by Risen Ones to speak with us. Once, Tim communicated to me through a friend who is also a medium, and his ability to maintain the energy needed for further contact suddenly began to fade. I was disappointed that Tim had never said "I love you" during the reading. But as the energy faded he played a song in the background of my friend's clairaudience. Neither I nor the medium knew the song very well, only that it was popular when we were teens. When I looked up the complete lyrics, it was just as if Tim had written the words himself, with personal references that "coincidentally" had intensely personal significance for me. Somehow, he was able to brilliantly find just the right lyrics that would finish speaking for him because he couldn't stay long enough to say them directly himself. And—the song ended with the words, "I love you."

Language *seems* to define the concepts it seeks to express, yet it already has built-in prejudices and predispositions, and so people's pre-concepts will limit the language. An inability to understand what others say does not mean we're unintelligent or not good enough or not enough of something. If non-understanding or even misunderstanding has any significance, it's the encouraging indication that there is further space ahead for exploring as well as a need for continued attempts to engage in communication.

Human beings take for granted the wondrous but still greatly limiting and easily misleading symbolic system of words we use to communicate with each other and with our own inner selves. Like our bodies, and like this material world, words are dense with meaning, often with multi-connotations that are seldom agreed upon by the same two people. For instance, if someone from the megalopolis of Los Angeles says "traffic," it won't have the same qualitative meaning for someone from a town of three hundred people in Kentucky, or from any other place for that matter. Subjective words like *sad, happy,* and *depression* become even more individualistic and problematic.

Consider an island paradise. Somebody can talk to you at great length about its magnificence, and you could read many books about many island paradises, but until you actually go to one you will never be able to truly say you've experienced it. Hearing about its lovely qualities may inspire you to visit one for yourself, rather than just accepting a second-hand account. This can also be said about our *beliefs*, which are acceptances of others' second-hand accounts—or hearsay—without our ever having actually experienced them. But once we've experienced something for ourselves we no longer have to believe in it, because we now *know*. Having empowered ourselves with experiential knowledge, we are then in a position to choose to change or let go of beliefs. This knowledge may contain truths for one that might not be so for another. We are each a universe unto ourselves, and each in a different place at any given moment, in any given time. Truth looks different from different places.

The word *paradox* will be a particularly useful concept to keep in mind while reading this book.[9] A paradox can be defined as a seemingly contradictory statement that nonetheless may express a possible truth, such as "doing nothing is more tiring than working all day." This is something we've all experienced, and it makes sense in its own way. However, it won't really make sense unless we've actually experienced it. Tim and I will do our best to try to define certain words and phrases used to describe our experiences, but we will often have to let the experiences communicate for themselves.

By sharing our experiences, which have been more splendiferous than any earthly island paradise could ever be, you might be inspired to seek your own experience. You may recognize that you've had similar experiences and thus find support and validation. Equally valuable will be your own intuitive experiences, which, for better or worse, are very often paradoxical to others and even to you. This book is especially for those who are ready to hear and accept ideas that challenge long-held beliefs.

Tim and I passionately want to share that there is no such thing as death. *There is **only** Life*—infinite varieties, forms, qualities, and expressions of it. What the majority of still-embodied people fear as "death" is simply a transitional phase from one quality of life to another. Transition literally means "passage from one form, state, style or place to another." Any state of consciousness is a state of transition toward another state of consciousness, which means this is a never-ending process of our irrevocable immortality.

"Death" is not an ending, but a transition of consciousness, just like falling asleep and then waking up. From hereon, then, we will use the concept of *transition* for the great and wondrous event formerly known as "death."

---

[9] Or "a pair of ducks," as Tim likes to say. – *AG*

SIX

THE FABRIC OF BEINGNESS

God grant me the serenity
To accept the things I cannot change,
Courage to change the things I can,
And the wisdom to know the difference.
~ *The Serenity Prayer*

The encounter in the forest I shared earlier is fairly typical of how I often experience Tim's presence. I'm very much awake, and consciously aware of my physical body in its physical world. This awareness of the physical becomes expanded by a deepened inner awareness of emotions and thoughts that words can seldom adequately describe. As Krishnamurti maintained, such awareness is observation without condemnation—that is, without making any judgments or decisions about what is observed. As a spirit-medium I am not just some sort of passive conduit through which information gets channeled. It's more accurate to say that I discern, connect with, and assimilate the information I attract and which attracts me. Therefore I'm an active, consciously aware element of this dynamic process.

I might join further in the process by responding in some way, and so a dialogue may begin to develop, a communing of like minds and spirits. This can happen anytime and in any place, while awake or sleeping, while sitting on a park bench, or even while conversing with other embodied persons.

Many worlds overlap, including Tim's and mine, interwoven into a continuously expanding, complex, and indescribable fabric of beingness. As an integral part of this fabric, I have a definite self-awareness of *being* this fabric. While this fabric of being has textures, colors, and intelligence that are its own, it's still a part of the greater universal structure. Human beings usually depend on their own logic for understanding the world which we think we have in common. When people have wanted to share experiences of mystery, analogy and metaphor have frequently had to be utilized—mainly by mystics and poets—to try to convey the experience of what can only be referred to as *other*. My experiences with Tim are real but are also mystical, and any earthly language proves difficult to use as a mode of communication, although we will strive to do our best to share these experiences.

Initially after Tim's death, I can't recall having any awareness of him whatsoever—only my own isolated shock and grief. Later on I would have occasional wistful thoughts about him and about our past together, but I really didn't like to think about it for too long. We had separated under confused and painful circumstances, exacerbated by my problem with alcohol and by his secret that he had become infected with HIV. Rather than tell me about his health situation he chose to end our relationship, abruptly and without any explanation. Rather than admitting to my own disease, I also went into denial and chose to accept his evasion—for a while.

Within two short years his HIV escalated to AIDS. Terribly ill, his body became eroded from the intense and radical medical interventions he endured. It became too weak to withstand the accumulated treatments that were being used to control his increasingly unendurable pain, and he transitioned during a deep sleep on what must have been the worst Christmas Eve ever for his family. They had encouraged me to go visit my own family over the holidays, assuring me that I would be notified if his health changed in any significant way. I agreed to this, knowing the great stress they were all under and not wanting to add to it. But for some reason, they were unable or unwilling to call me when he died. I didn't learn about his death until two weeks afterward, and then only because I had called his family to see how he was doing.

The shock that I felt over this, as well as the enormous sadness, grief, and anger around his undeniable leaving were dampened and pushed out of the way by my own personal treatment for pain—alcohol. The feeling was of a greater distance, a deeper abyss between us than ever before. I was no more aware of him or other Risen Ones than I was of my own spiritual yearnings for contact with the person I had once thought would be with me for the rest of my life. I now know that this inability to access such contacts was there for several reasons, but the main one was that I had been using alcohol for so many years that I had become emotionally and spiritually dependent on it, which greatly dampened any mediumistic abilities.

Being alcoholically high intensified my inner, intuitive world—alcohol is called "spirits" for a good reason—but its toxic effects kept me too ill to have consistently conscious contact with people in spirit. Life functions are suppressed by this poisonous substance, and enough will eventually kill the body. A deeply alcoholic state is akin to a kind of false labor. The spirit starts to feel that it's time to leave, and so a lot of the symptoms of transition begin to occur, including unconsciously seeing, hearing, and feeling astral presences.

Abrupt cessation of severe alcohol addiction without medical supervision may allow these presences to break into the conscious awareness without warning and without control, commonly known as *delirium tremens*, or "DTs." The attempt to stop taking in alcohol without the controlled monitoring of professional medical attention could result in death. I would be fortunate enough to never reach that point.

My drinking greatly compromised my sleep state as well, bringing vivid, painfully intense dream events that were quickly lost upon awakening, or else just merged into muddled memories. I would have dream experiences that were so overwhelming that they'd exhaust me for days. Addictions are not uncommon among mediums, who often struggle with strong attractions to food, drugs, and alcohol. This shows the very real physicality involved in the great expenditure of energy that occurs as a result of their abilities. A medium may also struggle with sleep and weight problems brought on by energy drains due to poor attendance to proper physical and spiritual health needs.

Some disincarnate people refuse to relinquish their earthly lives. Instead, they choose existence on low spiritual levels that are so close to our terrestrial plane that they can directly influence a medium's thinking and behavior— especially one using drugs and alcohol—by utilizing their prey's material energy to enhance their own. If someone had addiction issues in physical life and didn't deal with them successfully before his transition, he will still have to deal with them on the other side. Although he'll continue to carry the essence of the addiction, he'll no longer be able to experience it in the same physical ways. Unfortunately, some newly discarnate people discover that they can still receive a kind of mental high if they hang about addicts on the earth plane—to whom they are attracted like flies to rotting food—and they will invasively merge with them while the addict is using or passed out.

Gratefully, there was a determined and continuous campaign amongst the Risen to gently but insistently bring me to sobriety. This campaign culminated in one powerful event, which resulted in my alcoholic compulsion being lifted in literally a few seconds. Medical literature refers to this as a "spontaneous remission," rare and seldom reported. An intensely personal event, I will share only that it has been, so far, the greatest spiritual event of my life. It marked my own transition on this plane from a helpless, unhealthy human being to a new life of greater consciousness, where I've come to know a more authentic and intimate reality in this body. There's now a new awareness to bring to each day as well as a growing, compassionate self-acceptance—also known as serenity.

My beginning recovery from my addiction also marked the commence- ment of a great and wondrous journey, and the discovery that I was far less alone than I had ever imagined. As I began the retrieval of much that had been lost or hidden for so many years, I had no inkling that Tim was still very much alive and was already on his way to find me.

CONTACT

"The true type of seeking for spiritual contact is of the type that does not reach, but which expands to receive. You are in contact if you open out your spirit. You do not reach for it, it is with you always. But if you reverently and whole-heartedly open your heart to it, you get it."
~ Betty White, with Stewart Edward White, *The Gaelic Manuscripts* [10]

A year of sobriety had brought me into a new form of living, clear-headed but still stumbling a bit from the reality of life without alcohol. I often didn't feel physically well, and my body continued to detox on many levels of being. The solitude I had spent for so many years with a bottle were now spent with my sober self, as well as with my two cats—Bridget and Oolong—my children, companions, and teachers. At the advanced age of sixteen, Bridget was becoming increasingly frail. I was grateful for being able to truly be there for her in sober ways as her health began to fail.

I used my time for long periods of introspection about the past and then letting it go, while becoming more familiar with my present. I journaled, exploring and recording thoughts and feelings, especially dreams. I was sitting in this very same chair, typing away on the computer about something I can no longer recall, when Tim made his first breathtaking re-entry into my world.

We had first met through a mutual friend, and after a few months of hemming and hawing, eventually got around to dating. Within a year we had become a couple. When embodied on the earth, Tim was what I can only describe as "A Character." Tall, well educated, and exceptionally handsome with classical features and gorgeous, dark brown wavy hair, he had a keen

---

[10] *The Gaelic Manuscripts* was never properly published, and unlike the Whites' other books, was intentionally not copyrighted. Hence few printed copies exist, besides those passed from person to person and the few hundred copies White had mimeographed. Now, thanks to modern technology, this book has been reprinted with free access on the Internet by the Glastonbury Archive at http://www.isleofavalon.co.uk/GlastonburyArchive/gaelic.

intelligence and a bizarre sense of humor, along with an interesting infatuation with drag, which somehow all went together just right. A writer, editor, drama critic, and photographer, he always had invitations to parties and event openings and we had great fun attending them together. He was outgoing and unselfconscious, whereas I often preferred to remain the wallflower. But he always helped me forget about my shyness and to feel at ease amongst strangers. Our relationship was more like two young mischievous boys sharing a private magical joke, instead of a predictable, respectable pair of adults. We had a great love for books and reading, especially words and languages, and took childish delight while lying in bed at night making up silly names for people, and planning children's books and board games. Tim had a flair for the unusual and quirky and yet seemed so down to earth, especially when he was cooking some new organic food recipe he'd make up on the spot.

Sometimes he was moody and distant, or unpredictably remote and even unkind to me. Perhaps that was also part of my addiction problem, which could distort my perception of others' behavior. Then he would suddenly surprise me with a totally unexpected display of attention and affection, memories I intensely cherish. But it would have never occurred to me that he would somehow find a way to surprise me after he had died.

It happened suddenly and vibrantly, like a silent firecracker. One moment I was typing away, oblivious to anything other than my own thoughts, and then something, a movement perhaps, caught my attention out of the corner of my eye. I automatically turned my head to glance in the direction of the bed, which was just to my right and only a few feet from me.

And there was Tim—sitting on the bed, a huge grin on his face, his legs crossed at the ankles and hands calmly folded in his lap! Startled out of my wits, I screamed—who wouldn't? Books crashed to the floor as I sprang to my feet. In the same instant that I screamed, he was gone. No *POP* or fading away—he was just suddenly not there. But his appearance was long enough to turn my world completely inside out, and set in motion an adventure I never could have conceived on my own—and one that is far from over.

Afterwards, I just sat in my chair, staring at the space on the bed where I had clearly seen someone sitting—someone I hadn't seen since his death over two years ago. Eventually I got up and slowly wandered around, dazed but excited. *What was going on?* Everything looked the same. There were no ghostly sounds or strange lights, no scent of roses. Did insanity always appear so normal? I closed my eyes and could see a kind of afterimage of him—he had been wearing blue jeans and a red and blue flannel shirt. I didn't even question if what had happened was real—I just knew it was. Sleep did not come that night, as I was stressed out from wondering if he would return, and desperately hoping that he would. But he didn't, and I couldn't shake the feeling that something familiar was going on. And indeed, there was.

This was just like the times when I saw Risen Ones as a child, although it took a while for me to realize this now as an adult. It seems as if the child part of me could accept Tim's appearance without question and yet another part of me, while not at all skeptical, was thrown into a vacuum of some sort, unable to link it with the material world around me. I kept this event about Tim to myself for a few days before talking about it to a friend and then a month later to my intensely interested therapist. With great depth of nonjudgmental compassion, both simply accepted that something very unusual had happened.

Support like this was significantly instrumental in allowing me to move through this experience, rather than staying stuck by fear in all its countless aspects. Unlike the childhood spirit experiences that were usually minimized or ignored by an adult society unable to tolerate them, I was now being given the chance to share these experiences with other persons who were willing to allow for the possibility of such things. This was like rain falling on a tiny seed of unlimited potential, waiting for light and sustenance to awaken it from dormancy. This nonjudgmental acceptance by other human beings helped keep me from judging myself, from isolating, and to remain open for more.

Eventually I came to see that even while my alcoholic life had become unmanageable, loved ones from the Risen Side had been readying me for this experience with Tim—mostly when I was asleep and so more manageable. During that time, I was instructed how to let go of doubt and open my inner self to embrace an enlarged idea of reality in all its endless forms, no matter how unusual they might be. Tim's return was proof of one such reality, which revealed and confirmed a great personal and universal truth to me—we really, truly survive that which we think of as "death."

Certain abilities of mine describe the experience of an "intuitive medium." Most of us in the twenty-first century are familiar in some way with the phenomenon of channeling, and, to an increasing extent, that of mediumship. They seem to be compared rather than contrasted to one another these days. Channelers are individuals who, for various and often unapparent reasons, are utilized by other consciousnesses usually outside three-dimensional awareness, primarily for teaching and inspirational purposes. The channeling entities are usually from higher levels of evolved intelligence and compassion. Because they're without material bodies, they're primarily interested in temporarily utilizing someone else's body, by borrowing their brain and voice, thus enabling them to speak to embodied beings. The channeling entity is almost always seeking to impart spiritual information, and often has never been human, in the sense of having lived on Planet Earth. Of course nothing is written in stone about this and any and all possibilities are endless. While in an altered state of consciousness—or trance—channelers may be completely unaware of the experience as it's happening, while others are more or less aware of what's going on through their physical and spiritual senses.

These conditions of awareness are similar for those individuals who are often called mediums. Some mediums are completely unaware of what's happening around them when in contact with non-bodied persons, and have little or no memory of the event afterwards. There are also mediums that can maintain total conscious awareness of what's going on. Truly evolved Risen Ones who wish to communicate will not seek to control a medium in any way, except in very rare instances when no other way is possible to deliver an important message. Controlling a medium utilizes a universal principle where the active always organizes or controls the passive. Unfortunately this has an accumulative, disintegrating effect on the medium's physical state of health. This is not to say that those mediums who allow themselves to have a controlling Spirit are wrong or misguided, but simply that there are consequences for submitting to the higher vibrating, active power.

Those Risen who are of the highest spiritual vibrations prefer to give their messages through impressions, whereby their astral body facilitates communication with the astral-etheric body of the embodied person. From there the communication emerges from the medium's underconsciousness into the area of the more objective interpreting consciousness. To the inexperienced these impressions may seem little more than vague thoughts of one's own. For those who are exceptionally sensitive and more experienced in psychic matters, what comes into their consciousness is quite obvious, often floating to the surface in nearly complete sentences, like streams of bubbles floating from the bottom of a lake to the surface. For the even more sensitive, and as influenced by the universal Principle of Affinity, or Like-Attracts-Like, the communication can be an actual conversation. This experience mirrors that of Tim's and mine, where the conversations are silent to the majority of other embodied persons but audible to us.

The discarnate beings utilizing a medium are almost always humans who once lived on earth. They're usually friends and family and sometimes strangers seeking to send a message to a loved one. Often the strangers turn out to actually have some sort of connection, however distant and unexpected. These spirit people, or newly Risen Ones, are interested in maintaining contact with us since their recent transition, primarily to reassure us that they're alive and ok, and are closer to us now than we might be capable of believing. And not much more than that, for they're really no wiser or more spiritual or saintly, just because they made the next natural step in the course of their evolution. Greater maturity and wisdom-awareness don't get handed out like diplomas simply for leaving one world and entering another.

Not everyone is necessarily interested in contacting those left behind on the terrestrial plane after their transition to the Risen state. For one thing, it's very difficult. And for another, the heightened reality of the Risen experience is so intense that many individuals quickly lose interest in earth and even forget they ever had a life there. Tim and others have told me that there are Risen who believe that their earth experience was all a dream—or a nightmare—from which they simply woke up. There are groups of Risen, including those who were once scientists on the earth, who maintain adamant skepticism that such a place as earth ever existed. When compared with their present reality, it simply doesn't make sense to them and so they challenge others there to prove the existence of such a crazy-sounding place as "Earth."

Because relatively few Risen individuals are able to connect and communicate with those of us here on the earth plane, our terrestrial existence becomes supposition and theory to many there. In a similar way, as a mother can completely forget the pain of giving birth to her child, we may quickly forget the suffering endured during our earthly existence, once we are secure in the knowledge that we have permanently moved to a far better state of existence. The past and all the suffering it contained fades very quickly when there is no linear time and only awareness of the Eternal Present.

Even those Risen who want to stay connected with loved ones on earth can rarely make contact. It's very problematic to achieve, and must be learned by studying, understanding, and utilizing advanced principles of physics and psychology totally unrealized on earth. If it were easy, a lot more of it would be happening. But as the twenty-first century unfolds there is increasing evidence of more and more Risen communication occurring globally. And not just through human mediums but through the use of non-human mediums as well.

Computers, telephones, televisions, and other forms of modern technology are increasingly being utilized by Spirit, resulting in Electronic Voice Phenomena (EVP) or Instrumental Transcommunication (ITC). There are special Risen facilities or "centers" that specialize in the complex technology and spiritual evolution needed to achieve inter-world communication. This Risen technology has been advancing with ours all along—*much* further along, actually, utilized by teams consisting of the many sophisticated specialists needed to make it happen. Most of the work regarding interdimensional communication is done by the Risen. On this side, mediums and researchers basically end up sitting and waiting, having few technological means to match that of the Risen. Even so, Risen Healer-Scientists hope to eventually achieve great results by joining their technology with ours. Tim will share some of his own experiences with this technology later on.

When utilizing a human medium as a receiver-interpreter, the Risen often try to explain what their life is like. Like most people, they want their loved ones to know how they're feeling and that they're alive and well. They want to share their experiences, just as we would call a friend on the phone to describe some fantastic foreign country we're visiting. In just the way that feelings precede the words we then use to describe these feelings, a Risen One will utilize our emotions to evoke symbols and words that are familiar enough to the human medium so they can be interpreted, and which the medium can then relay to others. The symbolism may take shape intuitively as feeling and impressions, as well as mind-pictures, inner sounds, smells, tastes, and memories—all ways in which we also sense the physical world around us.

Our minds are extraordinarily skilled at making connections and often the pieces come together like a puzzle. The more educated a medium is about a particular subject, the better he can recognize that particular type of material and put the pieces together. If a serious Risen mathematician wanted to relay information on the work she's continuing to do in her new life, she might not want to utilize *me* for that, as I'm severely lacking in mathematical knowledge. But I'm educated in the arts, religion, natural sciences, and psychology, which makes me quite accessible as a source for symbols associated with those areas.

The communicating Risen One draws on the medium's intuitive senses of feelings and symbols. They then cooperatively find words in the medium's memory bank where the recorded sum of his life experiences resides, as well as where the human collective conscious can be accessed. Feelings evoke words and the words evoke feelings, which again evoke more words and again more feelings, thus causing a stream of connected communication to begin flowing.

While our human physical senses involve light and sound—which are physical vibrations—there is also a non-physical vibratory hearing and seeing taking place through our spirit's eyes and ears. Due to a complex process involving higher vibratory rates, some mediums can see and/or hear the symbols of Risen Ones, or even the Risen themselves. This ability to see is often known as "clairvoyance"—or *clear seeing*. The ability to hear is known as "clairaudience"—or *clear hearing*. "Clairsentience" is *clear sensing or feeling* and evidenced by such physical feelings as cool breezes or tickling, "cobwebby" sensations on the skin or on top of the head and hands, or as a pressure around the forehead. Clairsentience also takes place on inner levels, activating strong emotions that may then evoke corresponding physical sensations.

There are marked differences between clairvoyance and visualization. Visualization is a function of imagination, a human faculty that is a perceptual form or aspect of thought. When inner visualization occurs during imaginative thinking, one does not see things in the same way one would with the outer eyes as they interact with their material surroundings. Visualization is not a developmental visual skill like eyesight, but a *form of thought* that produces impressions. These impressions then stimulate the brain to seek and find within the memory those past experiences that are similar to the impressions.

These memories could be thought of as a kind of Braille impressed upon the molecular structures of our brain. When we "touch" the impressed memories with our mind's awareness, the emotions connected with them are activated. When felt, the emotions evoke symbols, which also involve memories, which we are then able to "read" and interpret.

It may sound paradoxical, but we can't actually see what we visualize. Braille is an apt comparison because it's used without vision—without light—to read something. Visualization does not involve the use of light except when it becomes enlightened. Enlightenment involves actual light, which is spiritual light that is vibrating on a much higher level than earthly material light. The nature of spiritual light is to bring a new vision that clearly reveals formerly hidden aspects, which then brings about understanding. When visualization becomes enlightened another type of seeing occurs altogether—*clairvoyance*.

The literal meaning of clairvoyance is "clear seeing." When the physical eyes are closed one sees not with the mind's memories alone but also with the mind's eye. This inner eye, also known as the "third eye," is a spiritual sense organ that has yet to be confirmed by modern science, but has been acknowledged by ancient sciences and spiritual teachings. It interpenetrates the physical body's pineal gland, and is its spiritual counterpart. The pineal gland nests in the back of the midbrain above the cerebellum, and chemically regulates levels of sleep. Like the material pineal gland, which is sensitive to physical light, this spiritual organ is activated by spiritual light, which vibrates at a much higher rate than physical light and is considered to be the connecting link between the physical and spiritual worlds. For some individuals, clairvoyance can also take place with the eyes open. Think of it as the times when you are staring off into nowhere—your eyes are open but your inner eye is looking at something nobody else can see. For most modern humans the sensing ability of this spiritual gland is completely inactive.

For some, however, this light can become activated by various consciousness-raising practices, and by allowing certain beliefs to be altered and adapted by one's spiritual experiences, thus becoming more open to information arriving from spiritual levels. When the eyes are closed and the ego-mind brought to quietness by gradually reducing inner interference—or the noise of thought—the emotions are also simultaneously slowed and halted. Then one can begin to see actual, real scenes, landscapes, and people from within. It would be as if one were literally watching a movie with the eyes closed. When the seer tries to analyze, judge, or react to what is being witnessed, the emotions become activated, causing the vision to disintegrate and fade. The vision will then be stored in the memory as impressions.

By resting in the quiet space of aware, conscious non-interference, more will become clear as the material world's veils diminish. The light of the spiritual planes dissolves these veils, simultaneously bringing spiritual objects into clearer focus. When higher forms of Authentic Self emerge into the consciousness, so, too, will higher forms of spiritual emotion arise. These evolved emotional energies will act as catalysts, enhancing and further enlightening existing otherworlds, whereas ego-generated feelings will interfere with the act of clairvoyance and bring the awareness back to earth.

Clairaudience and the other clear senses also reflect spiritual realities in direct, localized ways, enhanced by evolved emotional energies. My first contact experience with Tim was direct and localized, but not clairvoyant. It was on a very different order, best described for now as an "association of spiritual and terrestrial energies"—something physical and yet something more.

Visualization occurs within one's self-concepts of past and future. Clairvoyance, however, occurs within the individual field of mindful awareness of the present as it intercepts the awareness fields of other beings and worlds.

To understand this, try to visualize something while not identifying with any inner feelings that generate thoughts. That is, suspend thinking while trying to imagine something. In order to function, the act of thinking needs our memories. Detaching emotional connections will disengage the ego-mind's grasp and its cache of memories, and one may then enter an altered state of being-without-words. If anything visual appears, either with the eyes closed or open, then clear seeing or clairvoyance is occurring. The vision might be indistinct at first, but with determined yet relaxed practice it becomes clearer.

At first we might see only "static" or swirling energy behind the closed eyelids. But continue to keep the attention focused on whatever's there, without trying to label it like we do when trying to see shapes in clouds. Labeling or responding to what we're seeing, in any way, will stop the process. By finer tuning—meaning by staying focused without thinking—one's vibrations are raised. The static will then seem to slow down and coalesce, and with practice, will be seen to begin to form. Pictures will first start to appear as projections upon the blank screen of the mind. Eventually, and from within the space of one's quiet, open awareness, the screen itself may dissolve and then resolve into moving, holographic environments one can astrally enter.

Conversely, if something is sensed but can't be seen by the mind's eyes, then visualization is occurring. Visualizations are conceptual impressions and nonlocal, meaning they're ambiguous, fleeting, and hard to hold onto. They arise from emotionally-driven responses that originate in the body-ego-mind relationship. This relationship manifests as the *simulate self*, which will be explored more in a later chapter. For now, it's sufficient to say that emotions cast shadows and misdirect Authentic Self's attention from underlying realities.

~ 4 ~

These words may not make conscious sense at this time,
but my spiritual senses comprehend and retain
this knowledge for Authentic Self.

If there is suffering on a mental level, the ego-mind utilizes this mental energy to take the mind out of the present, and manifest visualizations with originations in the past. Physical pain is also used by the ego-mind in this way. If the mind-body is in enough pain, a kind of transcendence occurs, causing a dissociative experience whereby the ego-mind is disabled, and true *clear-seeing* arises. This is often what's happening when people on the edge of death report seeing and hearing things that are beyond the physical senses of others.

Imagination has its own valid reality, and is actually a key that opens doors to clairvoyance and other extra-sensual experiences. This particular faculty of perception will be explored later in its own chapter. Keep in mind that resonance is slowly and carefully being increased here and now, as one reads.

Certain Risen Ones can be sensed and later even regularly recognized by "signature manifestation energies" within various ranges of clarity. A medium may see other people's auras only when a Risen One's energy is within her range of sensing, while others can hear higher-pitched sounds, distant voices, laughter, or music. Such visual, aural, and emotional messages may be sensed internally by mediums through their minds, or less often as projecting on the background of the immediate environment, where they are then sensed externally. These "extra-sensory" experiences may then allow the medium to convey information back to the Risen, thus becoming a dynamic rather than a single-sided process as inter-astral communication begins to take place.

Our loved one's name is what we most often yearn to hear from a medium. But sounds, especially names, are exceptionally difficult to hear for many mediums, inwardly and outwardly. Names aren't usually connected to a color or sound when we use them with each other on earth, but a Risen One may resort to using these elements as a strategy. For instance, a red truck will be shown to the medium because your Uncle Red is trying to be acknowledged. However, the truck itself may cause confusion if he didn't have one. But if he happened to have a red house, the Risen One might try to project that particular symbol into the mind of the medium, which the appropriate person would most likely recognize.

Why can't the Risen just simply say their names, for pete's sake? Because light and sound move at a highly faster, finer rate in the Risen environment, so a medium may catch the sound as it zips past his spiritual ear—and not much more beyond that first sound. "Mandy" might sound like "M–ee" to the medium. It could be Mikey, Mindy, or Murphy. If everyone involved in this effort insists on pursuing this, then a great deal of ingenuity will be needed to continue. The Risen One might present the symbol of candy, which rhymes with Mandy. But maybe showing a piece of candy further complicates matters, as not every medium eats or thinks about candy, or candy might mean something to them that takes their mind in a different direction. Still trying, the Risen One may cause a sweet taste to appear in the medium's mouth but again, this might not be interpreted as "candy" but something else entirely. A medium who is adept around medical matters might interpret it as "a sugar problem," i.e., diabetes. Needless to say, this all takes up a lot of time and energy and can cause more confusion than clarity. This was especially true in the early days of séances when hours would be spent while the Risen Scientists would cause "raps" to occur—one rap for "A", two for "B" and so on.

Experienced Risen Ones will forgo wasting time and energy on a name, hoping that other details and the feelings they evoke will be powerful enough to validate their identities. A medium must be exquisitely sensitive to intuitively understand where the Risen One is trying to lead. There is great discipline involved in serving as a medium, for one must be able to keep the mind quiet, like a still pool of water in which the slightest movement can be clearly detected. Muddying up the bottom can be hard to avoid.

It's not uncommon for many Risen to accompany the communicating Risen One. These individuals are experienced communicators who do service by teaching and aiding newly Risen communicators who are learning this challenging skill. A few have even been mediums while on the earth. Although it might seem that there is only the medium and the loved one involved in the communication, it is quite typical for there to be *hundreds* of Risen participants. Some perform special technical tasks involving Risen physics, electromagnetism, chemistry, and other sciences, the likes of which have never been seen on earth, and which enable the process for just one reading. Others are there to prepare the material space around the medium, clearing it of unwanted energies while raising the vibrations of those present. Still other Risen are present in psychological capacities, influencing the psychic atmosphere so that there is emotional peace and calm and to lessen any fears. There are those who are observers, whose focus is to gather information for further analysis and experimentation. They are there in the common interest of service to all, working quietly in the background to avoid causing distraction.

When it becomes known that a medium is in place to be of service, especially for a public reading, I've clairvoyantly seen many thousands of Risen Ones immediately assemble at a kind of ethereal amphitheatre manifested to observe what's considered a rare event. Sometimes they gather on a large hillside or in a large structure, the architecture of which is impossible to truly do justice to with a physical description. Such gatherings are rare because the denial of an afterlife is so strong in this world and formal communication attempts are far apart and few between. This is why our Risen loved ones and friends often become quickly frustrated and give up trying to contact us.

Yet sometimes there are exceptions.

"Meaning me."

"Meaning you, Tim."

SMALL MEDIUM AT LARGE

"It's as though," Daily Alice said, "each day is like a step, and every step takes you further away from—well, from when things made more sense. When things were all alive, and made signs to you. And you can no more not take a step farther away than you could not live through a day."
~ John Crowley, *Little, Big*

Tim and I have deep, intimate conversations, sometimes speaking on several levels at once—even now as I write. Occasionally there are others speaking to us as well—sometimes one at a time, but oftentimes simultaneously. I know from experience whether it's someone Risen or my mind talking to itself. There are specific physical sensations, such as light breezes blowing across my face and hands, or internally hearing music or birds singing, and as well as feeling energy about my head that tickles a great deal. There are also inner emotions of warmth and security as Tim and others embrace me on many levels of being.

Talking with another person that we can't see is not such an uncommon thing. In fact we do it every day in these modern times. When someone calls on the telephone, we speak with a disembodied voice that we assume belongs to someone we know because it sounds like them and they say things nobody else knows. Therefore they must be who we think they are. Yet what makes us so sure it's really *them*? Do we ever question their identity, or stop the conversation and say, "Wait a minute, let's have some proof here, how do I know this is really you?" Of course we don't. As children we were taught to believe that we were talking to a real, albeit invisible, person. And yet few of us were given any explanation of what was really going on or how it was done. And we think nothing of carrying on long emotional conversations with someone's voicemail, which has no intelligence, cannot hear or reply with understanding, and can only mindlessly repeat back what we say.

A scientist might say that at least the telephone can be scientifically and reasonably explained, but ask that scientist to explain exactly what the electricity is that allows us to use the telephone. She will have to admit that science has no clear grasp whatsoever about the answer to this, and so it stands revealed that all we do know is how to use it. What and why electricity might be is anyone's guess. Yet this lack of a clear answer does not cause humanity to avoid using the phone.

Consider the conversation carried on with someone via "instant messaging" on the computer. Do we ever wonder how they're doing that? How are words appearing before us without anyone visibly there typing? The words certainly seem intelligent, whoever is typing. Or not, as the case may be.

When using our technologies, we automatically accept these invisible people and their disembodied voices and messages as real. They communicate through television, emails, answering machines, and radio programs, all things accomplished by ways and means that are mysterious to most of us. Few of us know or care much about electromagnetic waves and impulses, or question how it's all done. We use only two of our physical senses, hearing and sight, to verify and validate the reality of these communications. How is it that a voice coming over the wires or even as a visual message in an email can cause us to feel loved or loving, safe or angry? Would we feel any differently if we could somehow feel people touch us during these conversations, or if we could smell their perfume? We might question the content of the messages, but nonetheless would accept them as part of our reality.

If the conversations we had as children with the Risen were acknowledged, validated, and encouraged by the grownups in the same way as with these technologies, we would have grown to automatically and instinctually know when we're talking with real people or with those in spirit.

So it makes one wonder, why all the serious and sometime hostile denial about the idea of people intercommunicating in yet other mysterious ways? We believe in the power of electricity and act as if this power is limitless. We also believe in the power of love but are acting as if it's limited when we deny the fact of survival. Tim and I leave these issues for you to ponder and decide on for yourself, with an additional suggestion to consider. Besides physical hearing and sight, communications between corporeal and incorporeal people often *simultaneously* utilize the senses of touch, smell, taste, and especially emotions. This suggests that something is occurring on much more sophisticated levels than any of our present technologies on earth.

The experience of having communicative relationships with people beyond the terrestrial plane has been part of my life as far back as I can now remember, and well before I could talk—which is fortunate, since nobody might have believed me even if I could have talked at that time. I believe that my experiences were on a much more intense level as a child than they are now, but I've experienced that this intensity can be recovered. As is often the case, such abilities appear to fade as one grows older, or they at least change into less tangible, harder-to-access forms. This may be due to some sort of physiological reaction from aging or even sociopsychological factors and events, such as the cultural belief systems that are assimilated while growing up.

Many of us have seen children talking to the empty air and playing with imaginary friends. A newborn baby can often be seen watching and listening to something beyond our adult sense perceptions. Unfortunately, at least in our Western, Eurocentric society, when children attempt to integrate these experiences into their gradual entry into society by sharing them with adults, they are usually dismissed immediately, and sometimes ridiculed or ignored. If they keep it up, there are reprimands and even punishments. Thus their precious experiences, which are devalued, belittled, and marginalized, become neutralized by the enforced belief systems of others.

What could children be experiencing? I can tell you about some of my own experiences, as I was fortunate in not being successfully neutralized.

According to my parents, they noticed that I would play alone very happily for hours, sometimes talking aloud to my invisible friends, and at other times sitting in enraptured silence, seemingly watching and listening to something going on that they couldn't see or hear. I was probably around the age of three and learning to talk fairly well when it was deemed I was old enough to sit at the supper table with my parents. Shortly thereafter I began insisting that they bring more chairs and set more places for "them." Amused by their first-born's precocious behavior, my parents humored me. But if they forgot the extra places, which of course they inevitably did, I would get upset and quickly become quite demanding and even angry about the situation until they gave in.

Perhaps they just put up with me out of parental love or were hoping that it was a passing phase. But when I became old enough to accompany them to restaurants, they ran into a problem—other people. It was not much trouble to set a few extra places at the table at home, but it simply would not do to expect the same of a restaurant staff. By then I was used to being accommodated and so I'd protest long and loudly, hurt and crying because of the mistreatment of my friends. Why, they wouldn't even so much as hold the door open for them when we came into the place! My folks were very quiet, private people and I drew far too much attention and public embarrassment their way. After one or two more of these events my parents decided to use baby sitters, who have their own tales of the night to tell.

My parents seemed to gently dismiss these matters, sometimes within my hearing range by exclaiming, "What an imagination he has, such a sensitive child!" I heard these discussions as being said in a positive, affirming kind of way and so I saw no reason to feel that I was anything other than ok. When finding themselves having to explain my behavior to their friends or strangers, they would qualify it in a slightly different way—"He's just over-imaginative" or "He's pretty sensitive." Still, I never detected a negative tone in their voice that said I was a bad person for my behavior. In fact, I thought that using words like "pretty" or "over" was an excellent thing, because it meant something extra or even better.

Many years later my Risen friends revealed to me that in reality, my parents *were* trying to discourage me but without being too harsh, for they did at least recognize how sensitive I was to criticism. I might have felt negated and diminished if it weren't for the fact that there were Spirit People who were there to immediately counter anything negative said to me with positive, reassuring remarks of their own.

"Spirit People? Why do you call us that?"

"Then how about, 'the materially challenged?' You already got me for trying to be too politically correct earlier. Maybe I'm just trying for a little variety and a change from Risen One or Etherian."

"If you were here you wouldn't call yourself a spirit person."

"So then tell me, what exactly do people call themselves there?"

"People, of course, what else?"

"Well, I figured that much already, but I still stand corrected. Can I get back to my story?"

"Please continue, Dear Heart."

So it seems that somehow I wasn't completely disabled by the usual early societal pressures to conform. My grandmothers, who each had special abilities, also had an influence on my path. My Irish grandmother was quietly known for automatic writing, which she expressed in the form of simple but beautiful prose poems. She was very private about them and kept them mostly to herself in her journals. My English grandmother was part of a long line of psychic women who knew things like healing charms. This was also considered private and not discussed openly in the family very much. Her husband, my grandfather, had his own abilities and was the official water-diviner for the small village where they lived. For some reason his talent was not considered unusual, other than the fact that it was rare and valued by his neighbors. I remember my grandfather taking a few of us grandchildren, all very young, out into the yard to test us for the same ability, giving each a forked stick to walk around with—but none of us passed the test.

I have other memories of sitting in a highchair at the table at the house of these particular grandparents. There were always at least two adults, sometimes more, who never sat and ate with us or talked, but instead sat in chairs against the dining room wall. They were often still in their coats, intensely watching us talk and eat. I noticed that nobody ever talked to them, nor did they speak with each other. But when I would catch these silent watchers' eyes, they'd smile and their eyes would light up. Sometimes they'd give me a wink, making me laugh out loud. You've probably seen babies suddenly start laughing for no apparent reason, although right away any adults around them will egotistically assume the child is trying to communicate with them.

These same "quiet people" also accompanied my grandparents when they visited my parents' house—they even came for Thanksgiving. It wasn't until many years later that I asked my parents about the identities of these strangely behaving relatives. They had no idea who I might have seen, and by then, having become rather hardened by worldly difficulties, had lost much of their own spiritual innocence. I was dismissed with "you must have been seeing things," in an amiable, joking way. Not to be deterred, I finally found some old photo albums in the attic, and with some further careful questioning, discovered that the people I had seen were aunts, uncles, and distant cousins who had transitioned before I was born.

I was barely two years old when my Irish grandmother made her transition, but I continued to develop a relationship with her as I grew. I was an only child at that time and spent a great deal of time by myself—a valuable experience, as I still find myself to be very good company. I had an old platform rocking chair in my bedroom—the kind that rocks on springs while the base remains stationary. It was obviously made for a small child as it fit me perfectly until I was about five years old. But I didn't sit in it too much in case the beautiful blue lady wanted to sit there. My greatest recollection of her is that she glowed with a gentle blue light, and it made me think of the votive candles at church. She never spoke while gently rocking. I can still clearly see her sitting there glowing and smiling, watching me while I played with toys or looked at books. I never felt frightened or the need to interact with her. She exuded such a sense of peace that I played quietly and contentedly while basking in her presence.

At some point in my adolescence, and possibly due to the hormonal insanity of puberty, I lost the ability to see the blue lady—she just faded away. But I was developing greater intellectual abilities of self-observation as well as increased intuitional and contemplative capabilities. I began to experience her more from a place of within, and less from without. The blue lady was, of course, my Irish grandmother who was watching over me. But I've often wondered—how did she ever fit in that tiny chair?

Many mediums these days can be described as "mental mediums" because the communications they receive take place primarily on mental levels. Mental forms from the Risen draw near or enter their minds, which their physical brains then try to interpret into spoken or written words. Because many varying factors are often impossible to control or predict, transmitted mental messages can be quite difficult to interpret. The Risen must lower their higher vibration in some way in order to make sense on a human level, while mediums must raise their own vibration. Because many mental mediums are also gifted intuitively, they can access and comprehend messages on the deeper levels of the subtlest of feelings. These feelings carry much information in multi-leveled ways. Having a rich life experience and being knowledgeable about many different things is also very useful for mental-intuitive mediums in their work.

My mediumistic abilities are primarily mental, with an exceptionally strong emphasis on intuition and an additional factor that could be called "spiritual inspiration." A formal definition of intuition is "the act or faculty of knowing or sensing without the use of rational processes; immediate cognition." Other definitions might include an instinctive knowing, an insight, an inspiration, a second sight, a sixth sense, a premonition, an impression, a hunch, a funny feeling, a nose, or immediate knowledge springing up from within. Ernest Holmes defined it as, "Intuition is Spirit knowing itself."[11]

One of my personal definitions of intuition is that it's a form of communication with Authentic Self—a metaphysical and mystical experience. I see it as a kind of prayer-without-words, where information from those *beyond* Risen dimensions reaches me through spiritual inspiration. Awareness of such intercommunications depends upon the degree of our receptivity. Intuitive experiences may be brief and fleeting, but we can learn how to extend them to be in prayerful thought and communication for greater lengths of time.

A highly useful term appropriate to mediumship is *discernment*, where the medium utilizes mental faculties, hand-in-hand with intuition, in order to arrive at a place of penetrative insight. Discernment takes interpretative aspects to higher, fuller levels of intuitional knowledge. At these levels the medium's insight into spirit realities can be most penetrating, indeed.

I also have tendencies toward physical mediumship, something much rarer in modern times, although there is evidence of it increasing again as the twenty-first century unfolds. This is where actual physical manifestations of Risen energies materialize, usually in the physical presence of the medium. Certain Risen Ones are able to make themselves known in more direct material ways, from appearing on the earth plane in a visible, tangible body, to other materialistic phenomenon involving energy in the forms of light, sound, and other physical elements. Tim and I have been involved in several Risen experiments concerning physical manifestations, and it will give us especially great pleasure to share about these experiences.

It can be quite difficult to give exact explanations about what one's own mediumship is like. I've done much research about the experiences of others and often refer to a large personal library I've amassed on the subject. Many of the books were written over a century ago, and each person who shared about their experience had to find their own way to explain it.

---

[11] Ernest Holmes, *The Science of Mind*, p. 113.

Many mediums can sense on various levels those who have recently transitioned and are still rather close to our earthly plane. Frustratingly, it appears that I am *less* able to do this. My physical, etheric, and astral bodies apparently vibrate at a particularly higher-than-average level. Not really much more than normal, but appreciatively enough so that my perceptions are expanded *beyond* the closer earth planes. I can often sense but not always clearly understand those in Spirit who are still relatively close to the earth. They actually have more luck by joining me on the astral planes during sleep and sometimes during trance where we can communicate more easily. This heightened sensitivity enables me to commune with those who have passed on to astral planes far beyond our earthly realm of existence, and even beyond Risen geographies. I use the word *commune* instead of communicate because the experience is much more than just having a conversation with someone. It's a sharing and merging of presence, of mind and spirit in an integrative way that goes far beyond mere dialogue.

When I initially realized my strange limitation, my first thought was that I should immediately begin to work to correct it. When I asked for help from Spirit in this, the wiser beings watching over me advised, "There is no need to move toward a place from which others are striving to move away." They emphasized that the usual basic psychic phenomena that are more obvious to us are meant to be only temporary "side effects" of the growth occurring, and eventually must be left behind to allow further growth of a higher vibrational nature to occur. So I was not limited at all—instead, I was already able to travel about less burdened in the higher areas of the Risen. But there were inherent physical side effects as a result of this increased facility. There were also consequences to Tim's and my willingness to join in a concerted Risen effort to explore and experiment with what they called "inter-astral contact," which we'll discuss later on.

After we make our transition to the Risen state in those astral planes which are still relatively close to earth, there is no telling how long we may reside there. The transitional process on earth seems to be directly reflective of a greater universal transitional process. So there will come a time on the astral planes when we will transition to yet another more finely vibrating state of existence. This process apparently continues on in varying ways forever. The particular Risen Ones I tend to be in contact with have risen further beyond our planet's astral planes and no longer have the same kind of astral bodies they once had. Their present bodies vibrate at a very high level, and because of this they cannot get close enough to earth to be able to communicate well with many mediums.

Nevertheless, they sometimes try to get close, in spite of the great discomfort it causes them. I've heard the experience of descending to the lower vibrating earth levels described as suffocating, airless, dark, and claustrophobic.

Should they want to communicate with someone on earth and avoid such discomfort, they'll have to utilize a Risen medium from within their own geography. In turn, this upper-astral medium, who usually had a human existence on earth, utilizes the medium in the lower astral area closest to them, who can then hopefully reach a medium here on earth—truly a long-distance call. The Risen continue to explore and experiment with their technology to contact earthly mediums in ways easier than this "astral pony express." Labels like "higher" and "lower" are not descriptions of distance in the various astral levels, as we on earth understand time and space, but are meant as reference points of vibration.

Sometimes these higher astral beings are able to utilize my abilities. These are individuals who have moved beyond the need for communication that uses symbols and instead share information directly, mind-to-mind. Because of their higher state of consciousness they no longer utilize human symbols, and so there are no words for much of what I discern when in contact with them. A great deal of mystical writings, spiritual poetry, art, dance, rituals, and some channeled materials are the result of such higher intuitive and inspirational mediumship experiences. These forms of experience seldom make a lot of immediate concrete and rational sense. Yet they somehow manage to convey a rarified energy in the form of refined thoughts and emotions to the medium, transporting the ordinary mind to higher states of consciousness. I experience these higher states of consciousness when in contact with these particular Risen Ones, but often can't even begin to put this experience into words—an ongoing learning process for me.

In order to make a connection, sometimes I must utilize the gifts of those mediums that are closer in vibration than I am to the astral planes nearest earth. In the beginning there was a lot of confusion and frustration for me when trying to connect with someone close to the earth plane. It didn't make sense why I should have so much trouble with something relatively simple, while I could easily connect with much higher vibrating beings. It was a friend, also a medium, who finally realized what was going on when she saw that I was using her vibration-raising exercises in the opposite direction. She would sometimes raise her vibrations in order to reach those in the astral by envisioning walking up some colored stairs in a particular order. Yet I kept reversing the color of the stairs, and she finally saw that I was actually trying to lower my vibrations in order to reach the level she was raising to. This "higher level mediumship" might sound very grandiose. But in truth, and not to devalue my inspirational experiences, it has been maddening for me because the people I most often want to get in touch with are those who are closest to the earth plane, not some far-off distant entity in another dimension.

"Maddening for *you*? Good lord, August, how do you think it's been for *me*, knowing that you can get in touch with people far beyond the earth, and then it turns out that these people exist on planes *I* could never get to in order to meet *you* there! When I could finally get to a place where I could feel you, and then see and hear you, you might as well as have been blind for all my shouting and waving."

"It's not as if I wasn't trying."

"That's very true. Once you accepted the subtle signals, they became increasingly more substantial as your belief system changed and adapted. Then when you were able to realize that I *was* real and alive you took off like lightning, trying to learn as much as you could about it all. Once you got going there was no stopping you. And your efforts to move forward made it so that I had to move forward, too, if I wanted to keep up with you."

"Funny, at first I thought it would be the other way around, Tim. Since you were the one who actually transitioned, *you* would be more knowledgeable about all this and somehow more capable."

"But just dropping the earthly body and moving to a new plane of consciousness didn't grant me some kind of special dispensation or bring supernatural insights. I found I still had much to learn, and a lot of it would have been easier to do while on earth."

"Why is that?"

"On earth you have a special relationship with a thing called 'time,' which gives a particular structure and order to your material living experience. This order is the process itself, and follows a kind of 'template' for a human experience on the earth. Within this particular structure of time the things learned are enabled to become substantiated—that is, they become realized and so become part of you. Those parts of you *are* you, and these realizations come with you when you transition to the Risen state. We can achieve some of those realizations as Risen, but we don't have time to use as you do. We have our own version of time, but it's less structured and more flexible than yours, and only appears when we're manifesting a particular pattern, or have an awareness of the structure of an activity or event."

"It sounds like the differences are between psychological and chronological time. I'm getting a very strong inner sense of what you're talking about and it really is very interesting. But we kind of drifted away from the original subject about mediums."

"I noticed that we tend to do that a lot. I find this kind of stuff very stimulating."

"It greatly interests me as well, so hopefully we'll get back to it."

As an intuitive or inspirational medium, this inner experience is intensely magnified and expanded for me and seems to have unlimited potential. It's so silent and invisible to anyone else that nobody would ever have any idea that I am experiencing anything out of the ordinary. These experiences go on all the time and I've had to learn how to shield myself from such higher vibrations in order to just move and interact as an embodied being on a physical plane. If I forget to shield, my body often reacts with headaches and deep fatigue and I may become physically uncoordinated. My inner bodies seem to handle it just fine but my denser material body often has issues, and I have to listen to it when it says stop, drink some water, eat something, or get sleep.

The importance of rest and sleep for healthy earthly lives should not be ignored. This is especially true when we are dealing with not just the higher energies that come from contact with Risen Ones, but with the energies that accompany the process of grief. Grief is often the primary experience resulting from someone's death, although we are capable of experiencing a great deal more. Too often we are not allowed nor do we allow ourselves to fully experience grief, which is a natural part of human earthly living. When accepted as a gift and treated with great care and compassion, grief can become transformed. Depending on how we choose to use it, our grief can shut us down or it can transmute our very being, opening doors we had previously believed to be shut forever.

NINE

GRIEF TRANSFORMED

"To spare oneself from grief at all cost can be achieved only at the price of total detachment, which excludes the ability to experience happiness."
~ Erich Fromm

"Death is not extinguishing the light; it is putting out the lamp because the dawn has come."
~ Rabindranath Tagore

Grief is an inescapable aspect of our human experience. Part of the great mystery of life, it is a portal to greater unknowns. It is not a mystery to be mastered, but a doorway to be opened and entered.

The fear of pain can overwhelm us, even for fleeting but seemingly unending moments, preventing us from crossing grief's threshold. No one will be exempt from the grief experience during an earthly life—nobody can avoid it. The feelings of loneliness and abandonment will never be adequately described, as those left behind wonder how and even *if* they will survive the desolation and isolation that has descended upon them. Because grief is difficult for us to express in this modern age, the natural process of this exquisitely human experience may never be allowed to fully unfold into its glorious intent.

Each "death," each transition, is a major life event, sometimes dropped like a terrorist bomb into the midst of our existence. Or it may open up beneath us like an earthquake, our grief placing us at the very epicenter. Aftershocks continue outward, each one resounding with the explosive force of the original event, expanding and then returning as imploded echoes, gigantic tsunamis or smaller tremors, each one separated and cushioned by unpredictable periods of silence. As the mind shuts down, the silence is not always peaceful, but resounds with deafening echoes of the original explosion.

The event also launches cycles of waves that swell and recede, ebb and flow. There is something new here that now uses our life for its own breathing. We seem to float helplessly on a depthless ocean, struggling to keep from sinking. The cycles' momentum may slow down over an indeterminate period of time, causing us to sleep too deeply, or be kept awake by haunting memories. The slowing down feels depressing to the body, and the ego-mind uses this feeling to justify uninvited dark and dismal thoughts. These thoughts collapse into remorse and guilt, holding us fast like an anchor caught in reefs of despair. The cycles grow increasingly heavier and slower, encrusted with crystallized memories. We become trapped in a frozen hell of numbness.

But these cycles, which are part of Nature and so part of us, cannot be interrupted without consequences. They are meant to carry us *away* from the event, supported by waves on an ocean of unlimited love, not of endless grief. These waves of sadness carry us to new waters, geographies, and life experiences, and to expanded understanding and awareness that we are always safe, and cannot die. This supportive ocean of love is Creator Source, and It will wash away the old to reveal the new. If we allow ourselves to surrender to the process, our grief can carry us to the mental and emotional shores where our loved ones, once thought lost, await us. Surrender is not submission, which is defiance that puts up barriers. Rather, it is an agreement to put down the weapons against grief. One can always pick them back up again if needed, but the only place they can be aimed is at one's self, wherein the grief resides.

Recognizing that we're engaged in a cycle of grief is also part of the surrender. Conscious and aware recognition of how earthly time works in these cycles becomes a self-empowering tool. In the early days of bereavement, we may feel disengaged when the cycle is at a low point, and little or no movement is felt from within the "stuckness." But we shouldn't use the down time to try to shift things by doing something. This time is for non-doing, non-thinking, and for rest. The body and mind are in recovery mode during this period. Arrangements should be made to not be working for at least a month or more if possible. Some, in their loss, may feel an urgent need to quickly return to the structure of work because their life's structure has fallen apart. But this return will bring only temporary relief, and is actually avoidance of the greater need of the soul to heal and rebuild, through the experience of new growth.

Sleeping and eating are essential and must not stop. If sleep will not come or stay, it's best to consult a medical advisor about temporary medication. Because grief is a very watery process, plenty of the purest water must be taken in to replenish lost fluids. Quiet support by trusted others, close by and in contact by phone, letters, and email is also nourishing. This time may be also well-spent in the sequestered safety of a therapist's space. The therapist will know how to help you thoughtfully and carefully use your time of healing.

During these quiet down-cycles, we can let the feelings of grief arise, like bubbles trickling up through a muddy lake. These bubbles will stir up a lot of cloudy stuff before the waters begin to get clear again. There may be large pockets of sadness or enormous rushes of despair and even rage—let them do their work by letting them pass, knowing their energy is finite and malleable. These feelings are the aftershocks felt within one's own body. Although they are real, they are not signs of weakness, sinfulness, or insanity. It's all humanly normal. Pay attention to the breath—breathing through the mouth will intensify feelings, while breathing through the nose will calm them.

These down-cycles are the time for quiet respite—let yourself rest. Don't permit the mind to dwell on any particular thoughts. Rather, with the eyes closed, let a spot of sunlight shine on the face and on the heart area—warming with a gentle glow—nothing more. Sunlight is deeply healing.[12]

It's advantageous to seek help from the Risen during the down-cycles, including from your transitioned loved one. Worrying that they're in pain or in a bad place is counterproductive and works against the cycle. It's safe to say they're in a better place than before. If you can't convince yourself of this, say the following blessing during the down-cycle: "[The loved one's name], may your soul rest in peace, and may everlasting light shine upon you." Continue to invite Risen Healers to assist your own healing. Say: "May all those who are interested in my welfare and that of the Universe, assist me now." Allow yourself to relax into accepting that your request will be answered without fail. Relax, and rest.

When the cycle begins to turn upward, the time has come for doing—but not much—in fact, very little. Walking or sitting quietly in nature is especially grounding and really quite enough. When we hear the sounds of birds and insects, or the leaves rustling in the wind; feel mist and rain on our face, or watch clouds slowly cross the sky; gaze at the incomprehensible majesty of the stars at night, and inhale the scents of water, air, earth, and plants, the most ancient part of our brain is stimulated, bringing us back into contact with our primordial race origins, and grounding us in its ancient foundations.

It's best to completely avoid alcohol and other substances, but watching old TV movies and eating comfort food is not a bad thing. But too much is not healthy either, and may stimulate addictive tendencies or result in hangovers in the form of nausea, headaches, confused thinking, absence of mind, lethargy, and physical depression. In turn, these affect the mind in similar ways, swinging the body back into the next down-cycle too soon. Continue to rest during subsequent down-cycles but engage in slightly more energetic healing exercises—listen to meditation tapes, for example.

---

[12] This is not to be misconstrued with Surya Yoga—or sun-gazing—a practice that should never be attempted without proper information, training, and an appropriate guru. Regardless, keep the eyes closed and don't forget the sunscreen. – AG

The main thing to remember—which is not often easy in the midst of pain—is that there is usually what feels like a delayed reaction between one cycle and the next. We are in a physical body of matter which exists within terrestrial time, and so "time matters." A more accurate way to say this is, "matter is timed." During the down-cycle, the physical body has cycled to a state of quiescence. The astral-etheric spirit bodies are then less inhibited from responding to various healing approaches, even such gentle ones as the sunlight exercise mentioned above, for the sun will slightly raise the body's vibrations. The response of the astral-etheric bodies also takes place in the form of increased vibration. This increased vibration, however slight, expands one's receptivity to the Risen, who are naturally of higher vibration. Laughter also raises one's spirit, and it's a very good sign when a sense of humor peeks through the clouds.

Because of the seeming delay due to the timing of physical matter, little or nothing will appear to happen as result of any healing interventions. There is no immediate appearance because healing is first taking place within the astral-etheric bodies, which are usually beyond our physical sense perceptions. But as the down-cycle begins to swing into an up-cycle, its momentum will increase, enhanced by the spiritual healing. The up-cycle will occur faster because of the healing attention during the down-cycle, and both cycles will grow shorter and less frequent. As the spirit's health improves, the body's health will follow. When it's time for a down-cycle, it's easy to forget that one actually felt better just a little while before, and fall back into old negative response patterns. If we look at the things we're still managing to achieve in spite of how we feel, we may realize we're doing better than we thought.

Grief is as much about surrendering to our physical and emotional feelings as it is about talking about them. We must allow the emotional experiences to be, even though they may feel neverending. This feeling of endlessness could be reacted to with fear and its own endless forms of defensiveness. Or we could instead respond to this endlessness—which is the awesome feeling of eternity—by embracing it, gently at first, until its coldness gradually becomes warmed and familiar. No longer felt as a threatening presence, grief transforms and evolves into a feeling that is accepted as part of one's self. It's like taking an abandoned and shivering kitten and putting it under our coat to keep it safe and warm, instead of ignoring it and leaving it to deal with the harsh elements of life all on its own. Unkindness is never necessary, especially to oneself.

Whether or not we describe the leaving of a loved one as "death" or "transition" the fact remains that for most of us, these people appear to no longer be with us, and this seems to be final and irrevocable. Even when joy and anticipation are measured in with the sorrow, there is still the immeasurable pain that falls and remains upon our shoulders like a heavy cloak, often for the rest of our earthly lives.

Ignored and unresolved anguish will stagnate, harden, and fester. This growing wound will then begin to devastate our life from within, and from there our life's energy will spiral downward. The same will happen if grieving is given too much energy. If we focus exclusively on our grief, it may gain an ever-increasing momentum that generates agonizing guilt, which becomes nearly impossible to stop. "What ifs" and "I should haves" will appear and grow like fungus in our very heart and bones.

Grief can be so darkening, so deafening and mind numbing that we might not be able to see or hear those around us—embodied or Risen—who are asking us to let them in to help. Neither would we be able to ask for their help. We certainly wouldn't be able to experience any awareness of our Risen loved ones who are near us while we are cloaked with feelings of light-sapping futility. The Risen are *very* aware of our intense suffering and our feelings of loss. This loss is not the same for them, for they have gained the self-knowledge that they are alive. By focusing on beliefs that grief should be ignored or negated, we deprive ourselves of opportunities to center on and attend to the advanced form of the reality of the Risen.

If we promote our negative beliefs about grief strongly enough, the resulting feelings *will* reach out and connect to our Risen loved ones, but in negative ways—usually by exerting a feeling of pulling them back to the earth. This pulling feels dark and depressing to them, especially because the earth is no longer their natural habitat—it may even hurt them. In the early days after his transition, Tim once described this as if I had a headlock on him while we were trying to walk together along a beautiful path. Letting go of Tim did not mean he was then going to leave. He just wanted to be able to be with me on his own terms, so he could stand up straight and enjoy our togetherness while seeing the sights.

Grief is temporary because it transmutes to something higher and finer. Yet there is a paradox about this. Even transformed, grief does not completely vanish, for it becomes a permanent part of our life while we're on earth. The *quality* of grief may be different for those whose understanding allows them to accept that their loved one's absence is transitory. If this is accepted, it's possible for the experience to transform into something less sorrowful and more affirmative. From there, the experience moves into realms of higher spiritual qualities. The new inner conditions allow for more openness and less fear. Outer conditions will often change to reflect the inner transformation. When not held back, grief moves through us. This will have the equal, balancing effect of moving *us through it*, as if it were a door. We will be enabled to commune with our Risen loved ones instead of feeling isolated from them. We learn firsthand that they have not really left us but are simply less accessible at times. Thus empowered, we can also begin to communicate and live more authentically with our loved ones who are still with us on earth.

I've learned I can let my feelings work for and not against my transitioned loved ones by finding a way to be happy for them. In doing so, I grow to become happy *with* them, which allows me to forget my own self-absorbed loneliness for a little bit. It might seem obvious here, but not feeling lonely, even for a little bit, actually feels better.

The Risen experience an expanding joy from being who they are and where they are, and may want more than anything to share their wonderful new fortune with us. There really is no need to fear that if we think we are letting them go, it means that we'll never see them again. They would never leave us— it's as simple as that. Think of letting go as if you're releasing a bird so it can fly as it's meant to do, and not imprisoning it in your hands, where it would only languish for freedom. Think of it as letting a small child learn to crawl on its own so that it can learn to walk, while it laughs in delight and pleasure at seeing how it can move freely through its own volition in its new world. We are all such children with dreams of dancing and flying to our own music.

There is no more powerful earthly story than that of death. Every story begins with "once upon a time" and every story has an ending—which is really another beginning. Stories must be told or else they become secrets, which eventually eat their way back out. And then they're hardly recognizable as they become exposed, and treated as painful evidence of something unnatural. Trying to keep them from coming out will result in their implosion, which sets up a resonance that attracts negativity like iron shavings to a magnet.

Grief is the main human response to death, and can keep us apart rather than bring us together. Our Western culture perceives death through a lens of suffering rather than one of healing and joy. Because most of us have had some kind of grief experience, a commonality exists that allows us to join with others in discussions about our suffering. We need to tell and re-tell our stories, for that is how a true transformation of suffering is accomplished on the earth plane. Tim and I share our stories with you so that there may be a gradually increased understanding of this process, from which validation and strengthened confirmation of your own experiences will arise.

When some of my still-embodied friends and I get together, we sometimes feel compelled to re-tell our personal stories of loss. At times, there's a bit of underlying inner guilt that chastises, "They don't want to hear it *again*." Yet because we love each other and there is great trust in the safe-holding of our friendship, we've realized just how important it is that our stories are told over and over and over again. We experienced that our narratives changed over time. More details emerged, connections were made, and flashes of insight sometimes appeared. Our tales of death were revealed to be novels of life, unsolved mysteries much stranger than fiction. And we noticed another miracle—we enjoyed telling our stories. Somehow in the telling, joy quietly found its way back into the chronicles of our lives. Here is grief transformed.

Undeniably, grief may be frightening and take us to places of seemingly no return. Our culture urges us to move away from bereavement as quickly as possible and not take too long a look at it, and certainly not to talk about it. But we *must* look at it in order to understand what is happening, and we *must* talk about it in order to shift the energy of understanding in a new direction. In order to do this effectively and to move toward a shared understanding, we begin with what we each already are—Authentic Self.

Few of us are aware of Authentic Self, and so we'll have to start with what most of us *think* we are. In this book we call this misthought "the simulate self." Generated by the ego-mind, it needs us to be frightened by grief while it continues to cultivate feelings of ever-deepening separation from our loved ones. This feeling of separation is also simulated, and will fade away into nothingness as we disconnect from the simulate self, and eventually reconnect with our true essence, Authentic Self.

EGO-MIND & THE SIMULATE SELVES

"If the doors of perception were cleansed, everything would appear as it is, infinite."
~ William Blake

> "We have met the enemy and he is us."
> ~ Pogo

> "Vast emptiness, nothing holy!"
> ~ Bodhidharma

W illiam Blake's words speak of perception from a timeless and changeless point of conscious awareness of Authentic Self. They are paralleled by Pogo Possum's earthy swamp wisdom, hinting to look with honest humility at who we are versus who we think we are. Bodhidharma exclaims at what is revealed beyond the gates of ego-mind.

There are vast differences in the world when seen *through* the eyes rather than *with* the eyes —

> "To see a World in a Grain of Sand
> And a Heaven in a Wild Flower,
> Hold Infinity in the palm of your hand
> And Eternity in an hour. . .
> We are led to Believe a Lie
> When we see not Thro' the Eye
> Which was Born in a Night to Perish in a Night
> When the Soul Slept in Beams of Light.
> God Appears & God is Light
> To those poor Souls who dwell in the Night,
> But does a Human Form Display
> To those who Dwell in Realms of day."[13]

It is the intention of those Risen who are orchestrating this chapter to stimulate the recognition and awakening of the feeling of the reader's

---

[13] William Blake, *Auguries of Innocence.*

Authentic Self and of Original Creator Source, and to begin the realignment of the ego-mind's processes.

The material presented here is meant to be an in-depth guide to those who want eyes to see and ears to hear the Risen, and to converse with them.[14] We apologize for the peculiar denseness of the detailed and involved language that follows. This is largely due to its being deeply channeled and intuitively extracted from Higher Inspirational Sources—including Tim, who is studying the ego-mind phenomena as it relates to transition from not-Risen to Risen.

There is a kind of manual, our own "self-help book," that resides within Authentic Self—the Risen will be guiding the reader to find it. To begin the process of recognition, the subject will be approached slowly and incrementally, and repeated in different ways to carefully impress the awakening mind of the slumbering Authentic Self.

~ 5 ~

These words may not make conscious sense at this time,
but my spiritual senses comprehend and retain
this knowledge for Authentic Self.

The ego-mind is an obsessively opinionated, decision-making psychological component of the earthly mind-body. *All* thought arises from its mentality, generated to manifest physical forms and experiences on the material plane. Simultaneously, it outwardly projects judgments about our mind-body's perceptions and its environment into our inner space, and onto the bodies and environments of others. This projection is the *simulate self.* When the feeling of Authentic Self has awakened, all thoughts can be observed, accepted, shelved, or dissolved from a consciously aware stance. But until then, the ego-mind is in complete control of any rising thoughts.

The language of a malfunctioning ego-mind is tribal and therefore fear-based. It subscribes to judgmental concepts that use words and phrases such as "exclusive," "special," "restricted," "fashionable," "better than/less than," "best/worst," "superior/inferior," "evolved/degenerate," "elite/common," "chosen/damned," and "new and improved." Gossip, complaint, and criticism are its food and drink. It is motivated by fame and recognition, and fueled by envy and competition. Insatiably seeking entertainment, "gleeful" and

---

14 "God has given them a spirit of stupor, eyes that they should not see and ears that they should not hear. . ." (Romans 11:8). Here, "god" means "the god of our mind," i.e., the ego-mind. – *AG*

"gloating" best describe its sense of humor, which is delivered with jealousy, sarcasm, and resentment. The ego-mind loves competitive contests. It enjoys attracting and manifesting disasters.

The ego-mind is future-oriented—it cannot wait, and it worries. It worries about worry. Its language, couched in suggestions, generates anxiety attacks. The ego-mind will seize upon the body's minor aches and escalate them into mental terrors and fantasies about disease and death.

The ego-mind prefers to begin speaking with "I think" and "I believe." It developed the ritualized practices of "say please and thank you" and "I told you so." Co-conspiring ego-minds are responsible for the inventions of money, business, politics, capitalism, socialism, spectator sports, organized religion and other forms of war games; journalism, art criticism, bumper stickers, body dysmorphia, racism, sexism, homophobia, genderphobia; so-called "reality" shows and other Nazi-like experiments; as well as the destruction of the rain forests. The Internet has been co-opted almost entirely by simulate selves. The collective ego-mind's greatest desire is to achieve a Global Madison Avenue.

Awakened Authentic Self, while outwardly aware of these insane aspects of the simulated world around it, remains inwardly undisturbed and at peace.

Few earth-embodied Authentic Selves are consciously aware of the psychological component of their mind-body-spirit, also called the psyche or soul. The vast majority of people are moving about in the world with the ego-mind in the driving seat while they sleep in the back, occasionally and briefly waking to look at the scenery passing them by, but then quickly falling back into hibernation. The ego-mind's driving is compulsive, habitual, and irrational—it's mad as a hatter. Its ever-increasing neuroticism is generally uncontrollable because of our ignorant somnambulance. As a species, we have relegated it to our underconscious, from where it secretly dictates most, if not all, of our mental direction. In other words, it completely controls our world.[15]

The ego-mind's development began very soon after the dawning of human consciousness, and so is the most ancient source of human-generated deities. A more detailed etiology of the ego-mind and the simulate self will be presented further on.[16]

Because of the unlimited energy permitted to the ego-mind, the simulate self is able to present and maintain the *semblance* of a self-aware consciousness. In effect, this simulacrum or imitation manifests its own kind of form, and

---

[15] *Underconscious* is used here instead of the classic "unconscious" because there is no such thing as "unconsciousness." It is, perhaps, closer to the concept of ancient cultures generally known as "the underworld." – *AG*

[16] Exploration of these components, here called "the ego-mind" and "simulate self," has been presented in different metaphysical ways in various writings in the past two centuries, notably as "the kundabuffer" by Gurdjieff; "the physical mind/goldfish bowl" by Mirra Alfasa (also known as "Mother"); and more recently as "the ego/false created self" by Eckhart Tolle.

simultaneously, a projected, perceived environment for this form. This environment arises from the multitude of anxious thoughts we allow the ego-mind to generate and amplify, drawing from the vast expanses of energy circumscribed by our fear and trembling.

A therapist who is present in some way as her Authentic Self is there to converse with the sleeping Authentic Self of the patient, until some awakening dialogue begins to occur. The therapist also continues to awaken due to her own conscious participation in the process. Often the patient literally falls asleep during these dialogues or lapses into a shutdown of mental processes, such as short-term memory failure, a kind of dissociation that Tim and I call "psychospiritual amnesia." Therapists are also not immune to this ego-mental stupor, so unless a therapist is consciously aware of her Authentic Self at some level, it's more than likely that the "treatment" is an ongoing dialogue between at least two simulate selves.

The label "false self" has been utilized mainly by psychoanalytical and ego psychology models. Related terms, such as ego strengths, transference, countertransference, neurosis, conscious, unconscious, super-conscious, and so on—which presume to be about treating Authentic Self—are actually but obliviously referring to the ego-mind.

The word "false" usually brings up the idea of something bad or unhealthy. This idea suggests that this "other self" is not only malevolent but that the assumed personality is inherently wicked or sick, and that the authentic person beneath the personality needs to be controlled, changed, healed, or eliminated. Because of the inferred relationship, there is usually an attack on one's own mind-body or that of another's in some way.[17] This violence is directed or self-directed toward the false self while actually impacting the pathologized real person.

As guided by the Risen, to avoid strengthening established negative connotations, the false self is relabeled here *the simulate self*, as associated with the ego-mind. The terms simulate self, personality, character, and identity can all be exchanged for one another without loss of meaning, being analogous in their illusory concepts, actions, and affects and effects.

Acknowledging the existence of the ego-mind and the simulate self begs the question, "What, then, is Authentic Self?" The ancient dictum "Know Thyself" is the open-ended answer. Once the question has been raised, the answer can be revealed only as truth reveals itself through our individualized Self of Authorship and its various states of conscious awareness. These states

---

[17] Our mind-body can be said to be "energy." Earth scientists have seen, albeit from limited ego-mind perspectives, that all is energy, which cannot be destroyed but only manifested differently. This confirms that creation is finished and complete. "Manifesting differently" is experienced as change, and is *transition*, as well as *transformation*. It is transformative transition, or *mutation*. – AG

of awareness are experientially known through vibratory sensation, which is *feeling*. Krishnamurti maintained that "truth is a pathless land." The core Authentic Self will inevitably recognize the feeling of its pathless truth in its various states, thereby recognizing Itself as an immortal individualization as It moves inwardly from any felt point of "now," forever onward.

The simulate self fabricates, presents, and maintains a "personality" or "character" in order to appear real and to appeal to others. It assigns the greatest importance to itself regarding the affairs of the world. It is extremely valuable to keep in mind that our personality is an illusion and not who we are at the core of our immortal existence.

Our simulate self and the simulate selves of others will support one another's personalities in order to keep the illusion of personality sustained—"flattery will get you anywhere." The ego-mind convinces us to make the simulate self our primary identity, so whenever our ego is threatened we are influenced to believe that Authentic Self is threatened. However, being immortal, Authentic Self has nothing to fear.

It's fairly easy to see the inherent negativity in a personality—especially when it's someone else's—or when feeling threatened by another ego-mind's presence. It is a relentless suggestion of the ego-mind that we let it take the reins of Authentic Self's mind processes. Once we agree to this, it can then fulfill its agenda that everything would be easier and better if we just forget that it exists, and let it continue in its delusions while concealed in our under-consciousness. We are then permitted to carry on our lives in complete unawareness of it. Most of us end up agreeing to this conspiracy with little or no questioning, much less with any conscious awareness of the situation or of ever having made any such agreement.

The simulate self resides in our material body's mental areas. The core, true self, or Authentic Self, dwells within the *non-mental* areas of our interpenetrating material, etheric, and astral bodies. Although the ego-mind is always seeking to condition us, Authentic Self does not seek to condition, nor can It be conditioned.

Authentic Self does not think or have thoughts. It observes them as they arise from the ego-mind, which is contained within the infinite space of Mind. Mind is also *imagination*, an aspect which is neutral until activated by a particular emotion or thought. As unaware beings whose lives are dictated by the ego-mind, we sustain the false belief that *it* is Authentic Self. This grants the ego-mind the power to rule our body, our imagination, our environment, and our life by its thinking and in any way it so chooses.

A perceived projection is a presumption of reality, giving rise within the mind of the ego to the illusions *it* thinks we should experience as "the world." Thus, "the ten thousand things" of this manifested world are projected and named by the ego-mind.[18] It will unfailingly and skillfully use the illusion of any form of presumed, perceived loss—grief, fear, sadness, anger, regret, anxiety, nostalgia—to keep us from connecting with and awakening to true, present reality. Awareness of our immortal existence—our true presence—within an infinite universe of experience reveals that "loss" is only a thought, an idea with no base in authentic reality whatsoever.

The presumption of loss arises from lack of experiential awareness, which is misinterpreted as actual lack or "less-than" and even misconstrued as "more-than." Lack of experiential awareness arises from fear and anxiety, which are generated by the ego-mind to maintain the projected illusions. This is a circular and repetitive cycle. This circumscription of the life experience also projects an illusory *edge*, beyond which is a presumed unknown, which serves as a threatening presence—also illusory—to keep us from exploring beyond our prison's perimeters. The Risen are to be found beyond such perimeters.[19]

~ 6 ~

These words may not make conscious sense at this time,
but my spiritual senses comprehend and retain
this knowledge for Authentic Self.

The ego-mind detests and resists change of any kind. Change signals transition, which suggests the idea of death, and so the ego-mind continuously uses fear to keep the status quo. Yet change is how mutation comes about, and mutation is how a manifested universe allows us to creatively progress from one state of being to another, while simultaneously *being* that experience, that is, a conscious, Authentic Self-Awareness.

"True reality" does not mean true in the sense of a straight line or a path that never swerves or alters. Rather, the *truth of Reality* unceasingly emerges from the ever-mutating ground from which our manifested universe arises. Authentic Self is the ground from which the feeling of "I Am" unceasingly emerges, and is both dimensionless and all-dimensional, depending on the amount of awareness in perception. This point of emergence is one's

---

[18] "The Tao that can be told is not the eternal Tao.
The name that can be named is not the eternal name.
The nameless is the beginning of heaven and Earth.
The named is the mother of the ten thousand things."
~ *Tao Te Ching, Chapter 1*, trans. Gia-Fu Feng & Jane English, (New York: Vintage Books, 1989).
[19] See *Appendix* for more discussion about *the edge*.

experience of being. Truth can *appear* to be contracting or expanding, like breathing; on or off, like a light bulb. While the reality of Primal Creation does *not* contract and expand, or blink on and off—that is, change—our *awareness* of reality changes. As Reality, Creation is finished—it needs nothing more. Concerns and issues about "more than" or "less than" are therefore pointless.

Change is the vehicle for creatively moving about and within Reality. When sensed, distance and space combine to manifest the sense of movement, simultaneously manifesting an experiential sense of time. Connecting with true Reality, or even the beginning awareness of a projected edge against Reality, would initiate a weakening of the simulate self's structure, contributing to its possible dissolution and reintegration into something larger, even while Authentic Self is still earth-embodied. The dissolution of the ego-mind and its simulate selves is inevitable, which the ego-mind correctly understands and greatly dreads as its own kind of death. It also instinctively understands that it will become severed from all its relationships with the material world when the individualized Authentic Self transitions to a state where a different kind of embodiment is experienced from the current one. The refusal to accept the instinctual knowledge of its own death and any related references to death is the base element of the complex ego-system known as *denial*.

Change, or *mutation*, is the means of continuance for material expression of Authentic Self. For the ego-mind, mutation forewarns an ending, or death. *Transmutation*, or mutation to a Risen state, is the ending of the ego-mind. For Authentic Self, any ending contains the experience of the next beginning, and the next, and so on, forever. The construct known as the ego-mind has learned how to convince us that its sense of ending is erroneously our own. This feeling is not authored by Authentic Self and so is inauthentic to us, which we feel as a discomfort. This discomfort is little more than psychic effluvium, but because of our agreement to live by the rules of an inauthentic personality, we accept its idea that this feeling is something called "fear" and that we should act in a prescribed way when sensing it.

Since our personality loves to own things in order to appear real, fear can be difficult to release. Using this fear like a gun at our head, our ego-mind takes us hostage. It demands and is given so much *carte blanche* energy that it could be said to have a mind of its own, the mind which used to be fully ours. This entity-like energy will do anything to survive.

Although the ego-mind is not us, it *resembles* us, emulating our body's built-in biological drive for survival. The experience of grief will be often used as an example in this book, since it embodies, literally and metaphorically, so many forms of assumed loss or less-than. The deepest aspect of grief is an angry sadness, which can underscore a human life for its entire earthly existence. With grief as its weapon the ego-mind may weaken us to the point where our body will no longer sustain our spirit. There are people who have died of a broken heart. Like an enraged, spoiled child, the ego-mind can conduct a tantrum of such proportions that it will find a way to cause life energy for the body to be withheld, because somebody (some body) must be punished for the injustices inflicted upon it and upon the other body it believes it owned.

The ego-mind is inherently suicidal. Murder is seen by it as a justifiable act—rather than as suicide—because the ego-mind cannot understand that all individuals are connected as one through One Creator Source. In bereavement, the loss of a loved one taken by "death" would be perceived as the injustice. It was the ego-mind that wrote and promotes all variations of the wedding vow, "until death do us part." This gives further insight to the ego-mind, which seeks control through a delusional agreement called "a promise," which is held to be "sacred" and "unbreakable."

Even as an awakening Authentic Self, we cannot help but miss our loved ones, terribly and painfully. For most of us, this pain cannot be avoided and is part of living in this particular realm of manifestation. We have the ability to learn to accept that everyone "dies," or more compassionately, "moves on." But the ego-mind cannot deal with any reminder that its own particular existence will eventually cease. The fear-sodden and enraged non-sanity of the ego-mind becomes clearly obvious by its plans to survive—even if it means destroying its host, our body, by proving that it is right in its beliefs, hence the illusion of its own superiority.

A Course in Miracles suggests the ego would rather be right than happy.[20] The ego-mind most often insists on both, and is capable of splitting into two mental states in order to hold conflicting beliefs in a way that projects an illusion of one mind. It then continues to split exponentially, resulting in an inner chaos disguised as sophisticated complexity. This chaos, which results from the fracturing into countless simulate selves, is inherently fragile and can quickly fall apart, resulting in a "break down."

The "split," which is actually yet another illusion—being an effect or symptom—is believed to be real. The confusion that results about who or what we are—are we good, or are we bad?—is interpreted as being incomplete or at odds with oneself. Thus we feel compelled to rejoin or "repair" this split by seeking to join with others with the hope that they will rejoin and complete us. We will seek the "right" companion, career, friends, religion, philosophy, or shiny new gadget to fill the "gap" and make us whole again. These things are the false idols we are taught to seek and worship.

The ego-mind capitalizes on the anxiety it generates to fill in the gaps—which are not real and only perceived as such—between the fractured pieces of our self-awareness. It pretends to be "God" and to heal the split and our

---

[20] *A Course In Miracles* (Tiburon, CA: Foundation For Inner Peace, 1985), Text, 573.

feelings of separation by substituting itself, as disguised by the idols, for Authentic Self. In reality, anxiety is multiplied and given residence within us as countless simulate selves, and a constant feeling of groundlessness is the result.

~ 7 ~

These words may not make conscious sense at this time,
but my spiritual senses comprehend and retain
this knowledge for Authentic Self.

When our spirit withdraws from the terrestrial body, some material is absorbed back into the earth, and some is taken up by cosmic rays from the stars. Deprived of a material body, the ego-mind has no further earthly function. Up to that point, supported by cultural hypnosis, the ego-mind believes that only the material world can fulfill its needs. But since the material world is constantly re-manifesting, it can never fulfill the ego-mind's insistence on non-mutation. The ego-mind refuses to accept any change—over which it has no control—and continues to search, to desire, to temporarily find, and then to lose what it finds in a never-ending cycle of no-win games.

From this cycle rises addiction to material things, an automatic resistance to change, and ultimately, fear and hatred of change. This addiction is not in the way one is attached to drugs or other forms of physical or emotional sensation. It is about the denial to understand that all materiality, as a reflection of one's Authentic Self expanding outward, is not real but an illusion—meaning that materiality is temporary and impermanent. This denial must be explicitly maintained in order to achieve the illusory seamlessness needed to support the ego-mind's sense of self.

Although it may seem to be only negative, grief is a residual form of energy that can be shaped by our thoughts and feelings in both negative and positive ways. It is *residual* because it is composed of all memory-feelings which *reside* in the personality fields of the simulate self.

FIELDS

The brain is a tuning system, rather than a device for storing memories. It tunes into or focuses onto invisible, form-shaping fields which are shaped by the resonance between the brain and the energy forms fashioned by the ego-mind—these energy forms are the simulate selves. The resonance is also a form-shaping field which is an imperceptible, organized structure wherein all experience is recorded and stored.[21] These forms are memories, generated and maintained by thought. The fields of personality, which contain the resonating memory-feelings, are further contained within an ego-mind-generated "sphere of existence," which is limited by an *edge* (see *Appendix*).

Authentic Self is not limited by a personality, does not generate thoughts, and therefore has no memories. Regardless of conscious awareness or not, the limitless Authentic Self can access all experience, which continuously occurs within and without time and space. Authentic Self has access to the feeling-memories of the simulate self as well, but usually is not consciously aware that they are forms of energy fashioned by the ego-mind, and so is otherwise convinced that it should take the thoughts, memories, and feelings personally.

When energy is shaped by fear it can manifest as many forms, including grief. The simulate self is the artificial intelligence that shapes the fear generated by the ego-mind. If the energy of grief cannot be transformed or re-manifested by Authentic Self into a lighter form of vibrational energy, its quality may increasingly deepen to an intensified, hypervigilant form. The ego-mind may then alter, intensify, crystallize, or re-express the grief as anger in all its various forms, including resentment, hate, rage, and other such forces that seek to destroy. The ego-mind will even feed upon itself, causing a unique kind of exquisite pain that is the core feeling of all substance and emotional addictions, and to which it compulsively returns again and again, virtually powerless and unwilling to cease its self-destruction.

ETIOLOGY

Etiology is the study of causes. The ego-mind's original and main function is to act as a buffer against the tremendous amount of information coming at us through our physical and other senses. This includes the use of the emotional and astral-etheric senses and energy from other dimensions. This decision-making mental component was designed to be a cooperative effort with the body. Together, as the integrated mind-body, they can make faster-than-light decisions about the information in such a way that Authentic Self can move appropriately about in its material body. Quite early on, the ego-mental part began misconstruing its function as a result of its observations of the body's built-in biological self-preservation instinct. It then withheld information for energy-gathering purposes to enable its own self-preservation. The body's brain was utilized to help shape the form of this energy into that which we call "critical thought." This kind of decision making became separate from the mind-body cooperative, manifesting as judgmental thinking. From the thoughts of ego-mind arose the *idea* of the simulate self. The ego-mind's idea, the simulate self, shapes and joins thoughts into beliefs. The power

---

[21] For a stimulating presentation about morphogenic fields, see Rupert Sheldrake's book, *A New Science of Life: The Hypothesis of Morphic Resonance* (Los Angeles: J. P. Tarcher, 1995).

inherent in thoughts and beliefs is no longer refuted today. The task of the embodied Authentic Self is to re-appropriate this component of thought-belief as the rightful owner and for its own conscious awareness needs.

As humanity moved forward in its earliest development, the ego-mind emerged as a kind of natural extension of the human experience, resulting from natural causes. Because of its intimate enmeshment with the body, which gave it unlimited access to the body's instinct of survival, and because of its decision-making ability, the ego-mind was able to elect to copy this instinct. It is crucial to understand that this copy is not the actual phenomena of instinct itself, but rather an *idea* about it, shaped from the buildup of thought and maintained by a system of belief-fields.

~ 8 ~

These words may not make conscious sense at this time,
but my spiritual senses comprehend and retain
this knowledge for Authentic Self.

ANXIETY

One of the most ancient of cooperative mind-body tasks is to inform the human brain when danger and risk are near. Based on incoming sensory input, the ego-mental component manifests an energy vibration in the body, in the form of chemical substances scientists call hormones, but which most of us call anxiety. The ego-mind uses the brain to shape the energy into a thought to analyze the situation and make decisions about how to regulate the stress and what the body should do next. If the ego-mind cannot or will not make an appropriate decision to keep the body from danger, the body consciousness— the sympathetic nervous system—overrides its authority and uses the ensuing physiological changes from the hormones to move the body to safety.

So while the brain is thinking it's ok to stay, the body's legs are already running in the opposite direction. This is the ancient fight-or-flight response or acute stress response, which the ego-mind labels and promotes as "fear."

Without the ego-mind's interference there would be no fear, but simply some heightened but brief anxiety to stimulate the mind-body to make a quick decision. When the body is safe, the need for anxiety is gone and excess energy dissipates through the breath and glandular emissions, bladder and bowels, vocalizations, and various forms of art. Animals have been observed to assist in this dissipation by rapid wing-flapping, howling, rolling in the dirt, and so on, after the fight or flight is over.

Anxiety is generated by the mind-body and is a natural regulatory component of human existence on the planet. It comes and goes in cycles as intended. As humanity moved further away from the plains and forests, the fight-or-flight response became less of a necessity. The ego-mind continues to retain its decision-making ability to generate anxiety within the mind-body cooperative, simply because risks to the mind-body system still exist, although in less primitive forms. For modern humanity of the twenty-first century it's even less of a survival need, although still a necessary one at certain times.

When we're aware of being in a burning building a particular feeling based in the actual present arises, stimulating us to decide to remove the body, or else fight-or-flight automatically arises and the body leaves on its own. The ego-mind has capitalized on this present-based feeling by labeling it as "fear" in order to generate a second power-weapon, "worry." Whereas fear is based in the present and so is reality-based, worry is future-oriented and so has no present reality base. Hence a person can be in a non-burning building and yet because of uncontrollable feeling-thoughts about fire, i.e., worry, will have to leave the building in spite of there being no risk or danger.

Here is the ground level of a crystallizing mental structure commonly called "neurosis," which can become uncontrollable compulsivity. This compulsivity is often subtle and escapes conscious awareness yet it can be easily identified, such as the inability to stop a musical jingle incessantly repeating itself in the mind, or in private ritual, which includes solitary acts of counting, incessant hand washing, making specific sounds and body gestures, and prodigious memorization feats of sports statistics. These solitary acts are ritualized on more complex scales as ceremonies, which are essential in the transmission and survival of religious organizations.

Such intricate feats of memorization are devised and introduced into ritual and ceremony by the ego-mind and transmitted from generation to generation. Thoughts and feelings reside in the personality fields of the ego-mind as memories. Authentic Self has no ultimate need for memory, as all experience is accessible to Its immortal awareness within and outside time.

When fully aware, Authentic Self can reutilize the weaponry of the ego-mind as tools for its own experiential movement through Reality. When Authentic Self takes back its mind it can utilize a simulate self's talent for shaping thoughts within the previously hidden area of the underconscious. It does this by willfully directing a particular task to be performed which can then be retrieved at a later time when needed.

For example, Authentic Self could request a particular simulate self to compose a paper for it on a certain subject. The simulate self would search its memory fields of all the information it's been gathering non-stop, all the information it has inherited from past generations of ego-mind, and also access merged memory fields of other similarly resonating ego-minds. Authentic Self needs only to wait until it's ready to consciously receive the needed information and then transmit it onto paper or into speech.[22]

In the earliest days of humanity fight-or-flight worked well because it stabilized the level of anxiety quickly and dependably. Because the mind and body cooperated, the level rarely got to such proportions that the process shut down and the person became paralyzed, whereupon injury or even death could result from the system failure. Today, however, modern humanity experiences this system failure on a regular basis—as *panic*.

PANIC

Panic is the result of two actions of the ego-mind. The first is its decision to raise the levels of certain body energy vibrations so that anxiety manifests— not necessarily an inappropriate thing. It turns on a mental alarm bell that warns us away from danger. But the ego-mind has an agenda, which is to engender fear. It then makes an additional decision to *maintain* the anxiety by convincing the body that there is no physical risk at hand, that "it's all in the mind" and so the risk isn't real. This is done totally outside the awareness of Authentic Self. It achieves its goal by suggesting to Authentic Self that if the *feeling* of anxiety is avoided and ignored, then the actual risk can be avoided.

The sleeping Authentic Self receives these instructions as hypnotic suggestions, which coerce It to conceal them within the underconscious, an area of the mind used by a simulate self for covert purposes. At first, the physical mind-body learns how to numb the sensation of anxiety, and then later to completely deaden its awareness of it. The anxiety, however, is still ringing the alarm bell, which never gets noticed and then turned off. Authentic Self actually has some awareness of this malfunction while it's happening, but is usually too sleepy to respond and bring the situation back to the wholeness of Reality. This shallow awareness about the anxiety registers in the simulate self and manifests as neurosis, or worry-about-worry.

The buildup of unresolved neurosis in the simulate self leads to a psychic crystallization known as "paranoia." A neurotic simulate self builds a burning house in the ego-mind through worry, while a paranoid simulate self will mentally inhabit the burning building through fear.

The accumulation of anxiety amplified by the ego-mind's agenda eventually reaches a point we call "panic" and then the natural regulatory system shuts down. The mind-body system is effectively paralyzed by this

---

[22] An unaware Authentic Self would most likely misinterpret such seemingly spontaneous information as "channeling." – *AG*

short-circuiting, which manifests as chaotic body symptoms, such as racing thoughts, rapid heartbeat, trembling, sweating, choking, nausea, faintness, chest pain, and fear of losing control, dying, or going insane. The ego-mind has achieved its goal, which is known to health professionals as "Panic Disorder."

If the mind does not make correct choices to help return the mind-body system to health, then the body will. When anxiety has been internalized so that it accumulates while resisting release—as directed by the ego-mind—the body will shut down to restrict the overall system from further movement. In this way, accumulated mental anxiety and worry transform into depression in the body. Motivation to move through life decreases quickly and so the depressed person may literally be unable to get out of bed, go to work, or experience feelings of joy and meaning in the world. In its insanity, the ego-mind is unconcerned about the mind-body system, and will continue to mentally and emotionally abuse what it believes is its uncooperative slave.

The simulate self utilizes the ego-mind as the source for its own mentality to complete its copy of the mind-body of Authentic Self. It believes it needs to survive indefinitely in order to be a successful simulation. It generates anxiety to get the energy for this survival, and then increases the anxiety in its quest for ultimate power over the sleeping Authentic Self. It denies the fact that regardless of how much power it gains, it will not survive. This denial also often includes an aggressive disdain for the mind-body's "weakness" of eventual dissolution, or "death."

~ 9 ~

These words may not make conscious sense at this time,
but my spiritual senses comprehend and retain
this knowledge for Authentic Self.

A common supposition about our physical senses is that they make us more sensitive to the universe. But because of the way the ego-mind uses the senses, we actually become *less* sensitive of Authentic Self, and *more self-conscious* of the simulate self—thus feeling increasingly separate from others, the ultimate illusion. This split—this additional, simulated self-consciousness—becomes a facet of the body's ego-mind, which uses this aspect to fuel its belief that it is special and separate from others in some way or in every way. Our manifested life may become effectively enclosed in a specialized, windowless and doorless prison of the ego-mind's devising. Yet one always has the choice to strive to remain continually self-aware by focusing one's attention by using the spiritual senses, which the simulate self does not have *nor which it can copy*. These spiritual senses expand our experience as an Individualized Being and are for exploring the universe, our ever-present, ever-expanding home.

The spiritual senses are not resident in the interpenetrating physical and astral-etheric bodies. They are nonlocal in nature, and therefore not accessible to the simulate self. These ultra-fine senses vibrate at a higher rate than the simulate self can detect. It has no *direct* sense of them whatsoever, which is why it cannot copy them. However, it does seem to be able to infer their existence, inasmuch as it copies what it perceives as certain *aspects of behavior* of Authentic Self. These copied aspects are mockeries of the spiritual senses, and often manifest as "psychic abilities" that are much coveted by the ego-mind.

The ego-mind *does* have an apparent and appropriate function—as an analytical holding area that filters and monitors all incoming localized sensory information. It helps decide what the Authentic Self needs to be aware of for basic physical survival, without shorting the mind-body circuits by an overwhelming excess of information. Because of our unsuspecting co-conspiracy with it, and while our brains are shaping the selected energy into thought forms as directed by the ego-mind, the ego-mind inappropriately continues to analyze thought beyond its initial duties. In doing so it attempts to take on aspects of Authentic Self, resulting in an imitation, or a simulate self.

While survival is the ego-mind's prime directive for the simulate self, it is really meant for the physical cells of our temporary mortal bodies, and on a limited basis. It is not intended for the ego-mind's dreams of immortality for the personality of the simulate self. The ego-mind's true function is to serve us while Authentic Self is spiritually embodied. Upon our transition, or "death," the ego-mind's energy is directed elsewhere for other uses, just as the mind-body's cells are re-assimilated back into the elements. The simulate self, which had been fabricated out of that energy, will also *usually* be dissolved in the process of transition, unless very strong emotions continue to sustain it. Such emotions function as a kind of etheric glue, and are particularly sustained by nostalgia, a form of fear. The resulting bond is a cooperative effort, where the still dreaming Authentic Self carries the energies of the ego-mind, which parasitically clings back. In this way the ego-mind's influences continue to bind our spirit to the earth and delay us in becoming fully and healthily Risen.

The experiences of unawakened human beings are multi-layered, con-sisting of complex and dynamic sets of simulate selves, interacting with one another and with Authentic Self. The sensations of gender and sexual orientation are fluid parts of this dynamic complexity, and flow as natural parts of variable biological movement and interaction on the material plane. The complexity never ceases, and is always growing and mutating, sometimes less, sometimes more, sometimes seemingly not at all.

This complexity of selves, of many personalities, means there is not just one simulate self, *but that the ego-mind has fractured into many simulate selves*—into many "-I's-". If we closely watch our thoughts and speech, especially when responding to another person's thoughts and speech—whether or not they are inside or outside our head—it becomes clear that we carry within us many -I's- of an indeterminable number, each with its own traits and opinions. Many are inherited, and others are brought into existence as psychological defenses against the basic erroneous idea of death. There is the -I- of one's career role, the -I- of one's parenting role, the -I- of one's role as lover, friend, enemy, expert, and so on. These could be typed as major -I's-.

There are also countless minor -I's-. These include the sarcastic, the reactive, the self-entitled ones; the opinionated, the resentful, the gossiping and worrying ones. Some are stronger and are leaders which others follow. Some prefer to remain undetected, while others compete for dominance. There are also the "nice" -I's-. We all know the over-cheerful, the do-gooder, the ever-apologetic, the chronic volunteer, the self-degrader. Seemingly benign, these -I's- are just slipcovers hiding the shabbiness of the ego-mind's own agenda.

Close listening also reveals a "committee" of -I's- who control us as if they were a judicial board enacting and upholding "laws." A few are actually more evolved, but most are demonically destructive. They debate and argue with one another, often violently, and compete for recognition and fame. Profoundly judgmental, they continuously harass each other and Authentic Self, determined to pronounce everyone "guilty."

If you've ever "come to" and realized you've been mumbling under your breath, or arguing with yourself, or smiling about a delicious put-down you made earlier, or replaying the boss's congratulations, the next step is to consciously realize that a simulate self was using your brain and body while you, as Authentic Self, slept.

"A big ego" refers to the ego-mind and not the core sense of consciousness. This core sense, or Authentic Self, is partially informed by the ego-mind, which is an aspect of its correct function. Freedom allows Authentic Self to choose feeling-thoughts and the forms of its presentation in the world, while It may rely on the ego-mind component for information regarding this. If our ego-mind believes it needs to survive by being an overbearing, commandeering type, or a self-absorbed, narcissistic personality, or a saintly, helping kind of person, we freely have the choice to believe that these qualities are actually informing the presentation of Authentic Self. Yet these qualities, these various -I's-, are really just so much costuming, masking, and posturing. We carry these beliefs about our selves wherever we go, formed by a rigid ego-mind, over and into the experience of all aspects of life. These beliefs will form, color, and build our life experiences.

The ego-mind will do anything to survive, and does this best by prompting our simulate selves to lie to us and to others. It manifests lies out of the energy of anxiety, and then makes us believe that Authentic Self is lying, while escalating the anxiety into fear. It then uses that fear to convince us that we are guilty. In spite of its essentially hidden nature, all cultures have some awareness about this skillful, lying aspect of the ego-mind. Western systems have partially externalized it symbolically as the "devil," a word derived from the Greek *diabolus*, meaning "slanderer," "accuser," or "one who separates."

When we make an active effort to let our grieving naturally slow down, even for just a little bit, the ego-mind will often judge us as being uncaring for betraying the memories of our loved ones. As noted earlier, memories are products of the thinking ego-mind. A memory of our self or of another is not us, nor is it that person. Focusing on the memories of our loved ones as if the memories are the persons and then trying to keep them alive—or "re-live" them by feeding them with energy, especially emotional suffering—helps to only further energize the ego-mind, but not the memories. The result of this is that one's inner awareness of Authentic Self, or of a Risen loved one, becomes effectively screened off from conscious awareness.

~ 10 ~

These words may not make conscious sense at this time,
but my spiritual senses comprehend and retain
this knowledge for Authentic Self.

Our body's brain-memories are accessed from memory fields, and retain a certain amount of resonant energy to sustain themselves. This resonance can only be sustained by continual investment of more thinking and more emotional energy. Because they are fabricated by the ego-mind—and therefore are temporary—memories gradually decelerate, break down, and fade. This fading is part of a natural process, yet many of us will spend enormous amounts of emotional, physical, and financial energy to maintain memories.

The ego-mind has a particular tactic whereby it uses a simulate self to bury the grief into the darker places of our psyche, places where we might fear to go, like childhood nightmares we'd prefer not to remember. The generally accepted term for this hiding place is "the unconscious," which here we call the underconscious. Our deepest sadness is hidden from us in this area and any attempts to face it seem unnecessary or even futile.

We need help finding our buried sadness, to bring it back to the surface to shine some peaceful, healing light on it. Sharing our grief with a therapist or other healer who has some sense of Authentic Self, or in support groups who are processing their grieving, can bring about extraordinary results. The ego-mind's falsehoods will decrease within these settings.

If we're asleep, how then do we recognize when someone is in the world as an awakened Authentic Self? Unless we are awakened in some way, we certainly can't rely on our or anyone's ego-mind to truthfully inform us, or else we'll be steered toward all kinds of ego-self-proclaimed beings of simulated enlightenment. It's tricky—not because it's meant to be, but because we don't have eyes to see and ears to hear yet. If we're caught in the throes of grief, our vulnerability makes us easy prey for tricksters, fakes, and abusers, while our bereavement may make us blind to the particular truth we need.

Again, the simplest answer is the powerful one, based on ancient dictums such as that of the Tao Te Ching—"Those who know do not talk; those who talk do not know."[23] Ego-mind, through its simulate selves, will advertise in some way to draw attention to itself; the still, small voice of Authentic Self quietly waits for a call for assistance.

Just as there are Risen Healers waiting for a call for help, there are embodied Authentic Selves ready for service. All are seemingly invisible until one makes an inner request for help. It may sound like magic, but it's not. Magical actions seek to control—spiritual actions seek nothing. It may be more likely that therapist-healers will have some sense of awakened Authentic Self, or at best, they will be supportive and non-judgmental. However, the most powerful spiritual action is to ask for help by praying for a raising of consciousness into higher vibrational states, and then letting go—or "let go and let God" as all awakened spiritual and religious entities have encouraged. This may be our own first awakened act of Authentic Self.

Why is it so crucial to become consciously aware of the many identities and voices of the ego-mind? First, and as stated at the beginning of this chapter, the Risen are presenting this material to help begin the process of correcting the ego-mind process, in order to communicate with the Risen. Until we can become familiar with these false inner gods and their agendas and methods, we will be unable to determine with confidence when a voice actually belongs to a Risen One. If we want to have conversations with the Risen, we must be able to at least temporarily silence the voices of the simulate selves. Second, until we become aware of the ego-mind's lies about death, which keep us fettered to fear, and of our hidden beliefs that make us co-conspirators with

---

[23] *Tao Te Ching*, Chapter 56.

it, we will have little chance of ever connecting with our Authentic Self, and then with the greater authentic reality of the Risen.

How do we get free of the tyranny of simulate selves who are sustained by the ego-mind's love of falsehood? The prime objective is to first identify and recognize a simulate –I– as it arises. We confront it in a consciously attentive but non-enmeshed manner, meaning that we don't engage with it to try to outwit its cleverness—because most likely we'll lose. Instead, *we* begin to direct the decision-making process called "thought" that the –I– has generated.

We've also internalized certain aspects of the Authentic Selves of others into our own –I's–. Some of these more positive, spiritually-evolved –I's–, who want to be helpful to our Authentic Self, could possibly be engaged as "aides." These might include the –I– who helped us write the term paper, the –I– that reminds us to make sure we pay the bills, the –I– that sounds like the parent who always had kind words of praise in the worst of circumstances, or the teacher who impressed us with a simple but effective moral saying. Some of these internalized –I's– were cultivated by our Risen guides and guardians. Those which are less evolved but show promise could be put on temporary probation to see if they might become constructive, and possibly be joined in ways that would help heal the original splintering.

The "committee" can be useful for certain problem-solving needs, but it will have to give in to your leadership. The –I's– who might be called "Satan's Little Helpers" will have to be dissolved if they can't be converted to helpfulness. As conscious organization is brought to the mind, Authentic Self will correspondingly awaken. This can be visualized as Authentic Self now driving the vehicle with conscious, attentive awareness, while the evolved and evolving smaller –I's– function as enhanced GPS and other assistive systems.

Awakened Authentic Self utilizes the ego-mind's abilities to access and manipulate memories. This includes the decision to let go of thoughts and memories, or to utilize them, or to return to the memories and "readjust" them, rewriting the script the way you, as Authentic Self, would have it now. Authentic Self will make decisions about the mind-body system's survival, and the best choices about potentially risky behavior. There are as many possibilities as there are individuals, for each of us is a living and constantly present opportunity to find out what works for and serves Authentic Self.[24]

---

[24] For in-depth exploration into various theories of multiple –I's– and Authentic Self, see *Psychological Commentaries on the Teachings of Gurdjieff and Ouspensky, Volumes 1–6*, by Maurice Nicoll (York Beach: Maine. Red Wheel/Weiser, LLC, 1980). Correspondingly, see *Freeing Creative Effectiveness: Doorways Into the Upper Mind* (first published as *Mind Magic*) by Bill Harvey (The Human Effectiveness Institute; 2002); and also *The Pearl Beyond Price–Integration of Personality into Being: An Object Relations Approach*, by A.H. Almaas (Berkely, CA: Diamond Books, 1998).

Unaware of the ego-mind's back-door technique, we may assume that the only way to deal with it is to attack and destroy it, as well as the simulate selves and their thoughts, as if rooting out unwanted, persistent weeds from the garden of the mind. But the ego-mind, an integral part of our materialized existence, is here to stay, and there are gentle, creative, aware responses that bring the situation to the infinite openness of compassion. Because we are essentially spirit, all matters of the heart and mind are first addressed in some spiritual way, beginning with directing the will. For most individuals, free will does not yet exist, and much effort will have to be made to gain psychological freedom while seeking the spiritual clarity for which they yearn.[25] One cannot regain free will on one's own; assistance must be requested. Communing with one's Authentic Self while requesting spiritual assistance can be done in solitude or with The Risen, through formal or informal prayers and meditation.

Although seemingly counterintuitive, sensing spiritual being as an embodied human actually begins with first bringing the attention to the body. The body has its own inherent wisdom to direct us, if we can get to an internal place of quiet so we can hear and listen. Non-competitive exercise, journaling, psychotherapy, chanting, listening to music, guided imagery recordings, singing, dancing, drumming, painting—all may lift the focus from that which is dark and heavy toward a finer vibration that lightens internal gravity. As inner gravity is lightened, muscles and tendons release and relax and begin to smile. Done on a regular basis, these things will maintain a healthy mind-body system.

We each must find our own ways—which often cycle and change—to get quiet within. After connecting with the body, talking and listening to it, a course of inner direction will make itself known. There are usually no direct instructions, only feelings that emerge and flow with the spontaneity of a new mountain stream. We aim our conscious awareness inwardly by directing our attention away from the world assumed to be outside our body. We declare to the Universe/Higher Power/God/Deepest Loved One that we honestly don't know what we're doing or what to do next, but that we are willing to receive help. Asking for help needs no special skills, no holiness or advanced spirituality—we come just as we are. If we don't know how to ask for help then we can say so and ask for guidance on how to ask, and then be at least willing to trust that some kind of answer will come.

Be willing to be willing without ceasing, especially whenever feeling the slightest hesitation of doubt, and ignore the ego-mind's insistence that you don't need help. You may have to find this inner quiet literally thousands of times a day. The ego-mind will be just as persistent in interrupting the silence with the voice of a negative simulate self, because it knows what's at stake.

---

[25] Here, "psychological freedom" means freedom from psychological time—that is, freedom from memories. – *AG*

If we become aware that there is an inner thought or feeling with *any* negativity trying to direct a course of action, by bullying with guilt or name-calling, then be assured that *here* is the voice of a simulate self *and* the habitation of its lies, the ego-mind. It may seem intuitive to ignore this voice so that it will eventually fade away. This is not intuition but really the cleverness of the simulate self. Instead, the inner awareness must be consciously turned toward the voice using one's guided will, which is like shining a light on a shadow and watching it vanish. Without engaging in any dialogue with it, or letting it convince us to join in with its own self-analysis, one finds and stays with the assured feeling of conviction. We must declare with authority, "You are not who I Am. I Am—you are not." *I Am* is the feeling of Authentic Self—it's not a thought. Stay with this feeling of conviction.

"Staying with the feeling" means to bring full attention to it and observe it for at least one minute. Most of us are unable to accomplish even this short moment of attention. Practice by trying to keep your attention on a flower or the second hand of your watch for one minute without letting a thought interrupt. The result will give you a good idea of the challenge.

In effect, this brief but consciously sustained attention upon the simulate self announces, "*I Am* looking at you; therefore I should see you." "*I Am*" is the feeling of Authentic Self. Because the simulate self is not real and so isn't really there, there's nothing to be seen by Authentic Self. Under the directed inner gaze of Authentic Self, the simulated voice, feeling, or thought will quickly vanish, its bubble burst and its words dissolved. Although this –I– is impermanent, it is a tenacious creature of the ego-mind, which has stored it in memory. Most likely it will instantly pop back in again. There may also be a delayed effect, and so we must return to sitting and waiting with the feeling of Authentic Self over and over to gain an accumulative amount of *I Am* feeling that becomes a reservoir of serenity. We can return to this pool of stillness and bring the attention once again to the offending thought. (See *Appendix* for some brief discussion about *waiting*.)

A useful technique, as suggested by the American Buddhist nun, Pema Chödrön, is to kindly label any comment of the simulate self with the word "thinking."[26] Instead of calling it names in anger or frustration, this neutral comment will defuse it, and help us disengage from the ego-mind's attempt to make us wear a form-fitting costume of its devising. If that should happen, we can imagine stepping away from and out of this costume. The simulate self could very likely protest, "But I'm angry, dammit, and *you* should be, too." The best reply to this is, "*You* might be angry, but *I'm* not." Then continue to step back. The resulting feeling of intense freedom beyond this step may at first be uncomfortable, but it then brings astonishment, and finally blessèd relief.

---

[26] Pema Chödrön, *When Things Fall Apart* (Boston: Shambhala Publications, Inc., 1997), 21.

Negativity of any kind simply cannot make or hold a form when the light of conscious awareness is focused on it. As soon as we hear *one speck* of criticism aimed at us from within, or by anyone from without, we know that here is the ailing mentality of an ego-mind. Name-calling is a favorite tool of the ego-mind for pushing buttons. This voice might say something like, "What a moron you are for believing in this nonsense!" But first honestly ask yourself, "Would I want to be the kind of person who speaks this way to another person?" Or, more to the point—to a child? Ask yourself, "What if *I* was that child? Would that feel right?" Be especially mindful of the temptation to call it names back, which is joining it in being judgmental and critical, and feeding it the energy it needs for yet another back entrance to your mind.

The truly simplest, most powerful response to a simulate self is, "I love you," while beaming the most intense feelings of genuine light-filled love and compassion toward it. This feeling, this light, will dissolve the simulate self—it will vanish. What remains is that feeling of love you just generated—relax into it and bask in its warmth. You will have succeeded in reclaiming one more previously hidden area of Original Source energy for Authentic Self.

And if this particular simulate self is one of the evolved, positive ones, you may feel it respond to your love with intelligent interest, accompanied by deep emotion, such as sadness, which will manifest as a release and may make you feel like weeping, as we would when any missing child is returned to us. Here is the lost sheep found, the prodigal child come home. The fragmentation inflicted by the ego-mind has begun to draw back together in healing.

Do not accept any other results. This is becoming more aware of Authentic Self. This is coming home to Authentic Self, to a permanent –I–. This awareness dissolves the lies. It is of the utmost importance that the observation and declarative feeling of "I Am" is not made with any judgments, critical thoughts, or negative emotions. Otherwise one is joining with the ego-mind and making a way in for it through which it can dispatch a simulate self to enter the system. Any negative thought is not from Authentic Self, no matter how much we might identify with it—and sometimes we might want to identify with it out of long and old habits.

This guidance looks fairly achievable, at least on paper. It's easy to fantasize accomplishing it while in a non-violent state of mind because the ego-mind is temporarily inactive. Do not be discouraged to hear that this initial action is fantasy. In the beginning one is usually powerless to turn back the tide when caught up in an especially forceful act of a simulate self. Yet the seemingly brief simple act of observing and being aware of feeling the forceful act happening, and then desiring it to be different, *is* awakening the awareness. It is bringing consciousness into the dream, which is Creator Source's goal. Even desiring the difference after the act is over begins to disengage the simulate self's hands from the rein's of one's authentic living.

It may seem strange that the ego-mind is one of physical life's tools and not our enemy, but believing in an enemy creates and sustains an environment for it and strengthens the belief as well, which was spawned by the ego-mind in the first place. As Authentic Self, *we* have the legitimate authority and the real ability to impress beliefs upon our own ego-mind, not the other way around. Doing so will generate authentic feelings, and then consequential emotions of health or non-health, depending on the belief.

In a way, the ego-mind is our child, originally designed to be useful, to learn to help, to be included, to be appreciated, to grow, and to be loved. To discipline it does not mean to punish it. A disciple is a learner who needs a gentle, loving teacher. When a student makes a mistake but insists that he hasn't, a compassionate teacher would not accuse the student of being a liar. Instead she would simply and clearly ask for the student's consciously aware attention and then suggest other perspectives and possibilities for consideration. The teacher might also gently remind the student, "We are individualized, conscious parts of the same Greater Whole, joined with all others as one, and we are also each and uniquely our own person."

In this way the learner is enabled to make personal decisions under guidance. Can the ego-mind be guided and transformed—to become the helping tool it seems to have been meant to be? Can it be cared for and nurtured to grow into a mature and useful citizen of Greater Mind, or will it be allowed to run our lives like a tyrant with willful and vindictive addictive urges? Can it come to see and accept that it is part of a Greater Design, and that its role will come to a natural conclusion in the way that a flowering bush comes to fruition, the fruit to be used as nourishment for a higher purpose?

As consciously aware individuals we each must *individually* find the answers as Authentic Self. There is grace enough in our personal and shared universes to focus what Sri Nisargadatta describes as "affectionate awareness" (*turiya*) onto the ego-mind and transform it into a useful form of energy as part of our transformative Self-transition, or transmutation.

WHAT versus WHY

Prayer is a state of heightened sensitivity and receptivity, a joining with the Source of Authentic Self within, and with the Source of Self of others in minds and hearts of similar vibration. This communing with individualized Authentic Self also leads to the feeling of Authentic Creator Source. This state of communion is reflective of an intimate, inseparable relationship with the Greater Whole. The reflective relationship with the Greater Whole is holistic, whereby we are each individually whole, yet simultaneously wholly-related with all other individual wholes, regardless of the awareness of this relationship.

Communing is an active, equalizing relationship rather than a one-sided activity, where we would entreat or beg for something and then assume a stance to let someone else give it to us. Prayerful begging implies that someone or something else has more power than we do. Therefore it must make a judgment of some kind about us, which usually leads to the ego-mind's *why* questions—"*Why* do you need this? *Why* do you deserve this?"

Communing acknowledges a relationship of balance where there is no "greater than" or "less than," and which assumes a position of equality. Rather than asking "*Why* is this happening to me? *Why* am I so depressed? *Why* aren't I getting better?"—the focus is instead placed on *what* we already have in common with our Source—that is, by recognizing *what exists*. The foundation of all answers to all forms of the question, "What exists?" is the one and only answer of Authentic Self—"I Am."

Why questions that come from a negative simulate self are judgmental, driven by endless forms of its fear—self-delusion, self-seeking, and self-pity. The truly relevant questions to ask of oneself are *what* questions, which can only come from the feeling of Authentic Self. Scientific psychology has no clear-cut definition of "self" or especially of Authentic Self. It is sufficient here to state simply that Authentic Self is that sense or feeling of self which exists beneath the sense of the simulate self. It is primal, and eternal. As noted before, a simulate self generates simulated feelings and claims ownership of them. It carries the ego-mind's belief in itself as a kind of god that can create primal emotional, spiritual, and physical matter. Authentic Self senses original feelings and understands that it has neither created them nor owns them.

A negative simulate self worries, screams, taunts, and rages as loudly as possible. It uses sarcasm, cynicism, and all other forms of self-criticism, self-abuse, and self-loathing to promote its survival. It will not stop at or be stopped by abandonment or war. But when its voice is silenced, the vibrations of the "still small voice" of the Authentic Self can be felt. "Be still and know that I Am."[27] Its voice is said to be still and small because it vibrates at a very fine and high rate, so high that it appears to be still—or not moving—to the physical senses. It never raises its volume because it doesn't have to. *We* must also become still, wait, and listen to hear and sense it. It is always there waiting, but without worry. The feeling of "I Am" is also the voice of Creator Source.[28]

---

[27] "Be still, and know that I am (God)." Psalms 46:10. Here, "God" means not just Authentic Self, but also Original Creator Source—in essence, each of us, by being, exists inseparably from Original Creator Source—I Am, *and* Thou Art That. – *AG*

[28] "And the Lord said, Go forth, and stand upon the mount before the Lord. And, behold, the Lord passed by, and a great and strong wind rent the mountains, and brake in pieces the rocks before the Lord; but the Lord was not in the wind: and after the wind an earthquake; but the Lord was not in the earthquake. And after the earthquake a fire; but the Lord was not in the fire: and after the fire a still small voice." 1 Kings 19:11-12

The ego-mind is always in a hurry to be somewhere else other than where it is. Because it is defined by boundaries imposed by itself and by other ego-minds, its efforts to be elsewhere are constantly thwarted by its very nature. It cannot go beyond the boundaries because then it will be boundary-less and no longer defined. While denying its responsibility for this dilemma, it rages at its self-imposed imprisonment, deranged because it is both jailer and prisoner. This gives further rise to anxiety, dread, and a particular kind of perception-feeling that it interprets as awareness of death.

Authentic Self is never in a hurry, because it has nowhere to go.

How do we use *what* questions? Perhaps you're feeling shrouded by a blanket of depression. The world may feel heavy, dark, hot or cold and airless within and around the head and body. Asking *"why* am I depressed?" implies the belief that one is depressed. (Why, I am depressed.) It generates judgment-loaded answers and other *why* questions, which flow from an endless stream of ego-self consciousness. Each answer leads to another question, each seeking an original cause further back in time, *ad infinitum,* until one hits some kind of a bottom, or blacking out or fainting in some psychological or spiritual way.

"Why" is qualitative and initiates a never-ending game of "20 Questions" with the ego-mind. "What" is *quantitatively one*—one state, one point. Asking "what is?" will bring us to that point or state of oneness. In the present, the concrete answer can only be, "depression is." The ego-mind may chime in with all kinds of analytical comments, and because it usually still has all the power, may initially succeed in leading us downward on any path it so chooses.

When we can accept that there is only one present answer, we can then begin to explore even further with the question-tool called "what." The *what* question will activate and aim the attention of Authentic Self like a laser at what actually is and illuminate it. The question then transforms into a statement of observation, or "what is." For example, change the question "What is beneath the depression?" into the statement, *"What* is beneath the depression." Then substitute the fact for the word "what." It will probably be something like sadness, worry, or perhaps anger or even rage. *"Sadness* is beneath the depression." Now we know what is beneath the depression. There is no need to spend days, weeks, or years to get this answer, which would otherwise be impeded by the ego-mind.

There does not have to be further questioning to attempt an analysis toward gaining some kind of control over the issue. This would only raise more questions that would effectively engage the ego-mind. Turning attentive awareness onto *what is* will illuminate it. If attended to with patience, the veil that the ego-mind has drawn before our inner eyes will fade, revealing that there is nothing there. When a light is turned onto a shadow, the shadow vanishes. We learn from the experience to wait for the authentic answer, not for another question.

Experience is knowledge but understanding is not necessarily knowledge. Understanding means that we agree with another's account, or thought, or belief. If there is no understanding, there is no agreement. With *what is*, agreement is not needed, only experience. Experiencing through the various senses brings us directly up against what is.

Aren't sadness, worry, anger, and such, really negative suggestions from the ego-mind? Yes. And aren't we trying to avoid the negative qualities which make our life so miserable? No—that is what the ego-mind wants. It needs to distract us from seeing what's really beneath the depression, and it's hidden those things in the very places we would most avoid because it has persuaded us that they're too scary, or painful, or embarrassing. This is where a therapist can assist us with carefully bringing these things into the light.

The feeling beneath the depression is very often sadness from suffering. Although it may seem counter-intuitive, the sadness is a direct gate to Authentic Self and from there, to Original Creator Source. The sadness is actually an incomplete sense of peace, due to interference from the ego-mind, and often from traumatizing events imposed by other ego-minds during the earliest years of childhood. Rather than avoiding the discomfort of allowing ourselves to feel this sadness, this wound from which we suffer, we must bravely go forward and through it. Going through it completes the process of the original feeling that had been interrupted while forming—no matter how long ago. The partially formed feeling, aided by our direct and conscious awareness, will become the vehicle that will carry us in the right direction and to completion, to be drawn into the healing arms of Original Creator Source, where true fulfillment of peace awaits.

The ego-mind is an expert at convincing us that the force field of anxiety it put there is too much to withstand passing through, and that we will die trying. Anxiety may be at the edge of this place of pain or embarrassment. This anxiety is a "what." Yet it's not permanent. It can't be, for our ground of material existence is always changing. Authentic Self, which *is* Its own ground, does not change in Its immortal state. We find and expose the ego-mind's weapons, buried like landmines, make our own responses and choices about them by disarming them, and then move past them. By joining in the change we have begun to take back responsible control of our mind. The sword has been changed into a plowshare, which we can continue to use for more gentle exploration beneath the ever-fertile soil of Mind, which is the changing universe that we share with the Risen in the present.

This chapter has been orchestrated to activate initial awareness about the ego-mind and simulate selves, heightened by defining their relationship to Authentic Self. Authentic Self will be slightly clarified a bit more further on, after we first take a closer look at how the grief experience can evolve and transform, while considering the oft-troubling subject of self-exiting.

GRIEF EVOLVED & SELF-EXITING

"I would swim over the deepest ocean,
The deepest ocean to be by your side.
But the sea is wide, and I can't get over.
Neither have I wings to fly.
Oh, if I could find a handsome boatsman
To ferry me over to my love and die."
~ *Carrighfergus*, traditional Celtic ballad

The idea that grief can become transformed and then evolve into a positive experience may be unfathomable. Until such a transformation begins to happen, it can seem impossible to imagine anything good coming out of such pain. We're too exhausted to think about asking for help or to even think about anything, for that matter, when overwhelmed by grief and the negative manipulations of the ego-mind. People who think they mean well may tell us that "it's time to get over it" because they find our grief too painful to witness or be around. But their words, from religious sentiments to outright demands, fall to the ground, neutralized by the force field of our pain.

Modern humankind has largely forgotten that we are an integral and inseparable part of Nature—that *we* are Nature. People listen more to the simulate self's artificial instructions instead of the indwelling natural ones that arise from the awareness of being an inseparable component of Nature. Animals, birds, trees, flowers, and butterflies do not have an interfering ego-mind. "Survival of the fittest" does not mean that certain beings have to destroy others in order to live, although that is how the ego-mind justifies its own beliefs. It means that all components of Nature are in a continual process of experiencing how all living things fit together. The Energy of Nature, which is also our energy, does not play any mind games in order to survive, for Nature simply is—and we simply are, too.

The ego-mind's misdirecting chatter can be softened by quietly resting within Nature—walking in a meadow or gazing up through the trees at the stars. In joining Nature, we join as Authentic Self. Allowing the inner-dwelling

Authentic Self to quietly emerge and observe and take in the surroundings of Nature will calm and soothe the ego-mind, which especially malfunctions when it perceives threats coming from other ego-minds. If we sit quietly and long enough in some setting of Nature, the ego-mind will be unable to continually perceive a threat. It will then subside in its negative ways, at least temporarily, and be still for a while.

The more we allow such quiet sitting, the more familiar we'll become with the feeling of the ego-mind receding. Spend this time quietly observing a tree, for instance. The ego-mind will not be able to get a tree to play mind games with it. Our Self-As-Nature—Authentic Self—can then emerge, and from there we'll begin to re-identify with the rest of Nature around us. Feelings of alienation, loneliness, and abandonment will begin to become lighter. We can even achieve this indoors. A vase of flowers, finches at the birdfeeder, or a sleeping cat can dramatically change our perspective if we can place our full attention upon them for even three minutes. Those who have plummeted and endured the black depths of grief will know that three minutes can be a very long time.

This attentive awareness, or "choiceless awareness" as Krishnamurti called it, gives rise to an unexpected sense of relief, and, often especially in the beginning, the space to cry. Robert, a Risen friend, has referred to this space as "the watery process." He explained that not only does our attentive awareness transform our grief, but that the very process of transformation is a form of transition in itself. The transition to grief evolved can take years to occur, which is what happens for most people who prefer, for many reasons, to let time heal all wounds while they try to return to life as it was before the loss. In truth, there cannot be a return to that reality, for that is not how Nature uses time on the earth.

Many people are aware that they cannot return to the known past, but are afraid to let themselves move forward into the unknown. Trapped by this fear, where can we go? We need go no further, for we are already in the reality of the present, which is all there is anyway. Grief evolves by our staying with it in the present moment as consciously as possible. Paradoxically, what seems to be non-movement is actually subtle but real inner movement through the grief. We have the choice of avoiding the grief, which keeps it activated but static, or to move with it and through it, which transforms it.

This movement can be painful, but it's not forever. It's like the journey of an isolated stream in the lonely, fog-covered mountains, brutally dashed against rocks and over cliffs, to finally merge into the great and calm depths of the ocean. When Bridget, my furry cat child and soul mate of eighteen years made her transition, I could not stop crying for weeks. The water ran like a river. My Risen friend Robert offered some insight and guidance during this particularly difficult and painful period of my life.

"Yours is a watery planet and life on it is a watery process. See how water ▮▮▮ its own level, slowly or quickly finding the place where there is an ultimate calmness and stillness. What wisdom there is in the water! Although it may travel on a very rough and rapid journey or a very slow and winding one, or a combination of both, your water—the water that is within you—is following a natural design that has been in place since the beginning of earthly time.

"Psychological time has its own form for a human being, and in some inextricably mysterious way is connected with the ways of water. This is evident by the fact that your bodies are mostly water and are also involved in a process of seeking a state of balance, an ultimate calmness and stillness. Who amongst you can deny experiencing the internal and external tides of emotion, the ebb and flow of optimism and pessimism, of memory and thoughts as they appear and disappear as if they have floated in on waves from nowhere? And who amongst you has not tried to control these internal and external forces, even to the point of denying their existence?

"For the human being on earth, pain appears as an inescapable part of life. It's also a watery and often messy process. The grief that wells up from your loss encompasses both the physical and non-physical aspects of your being. You can either battle this grief as an alien enemy or embrace it as a personal companion that is part of your nature, part of your divine design.

"Yours is a planet of saltwater oceans. Accordingly, your blood and tears are salt water. Salt is cleansing and purifying. Your salty tears are meant to assist you in achieving balance as the water in your bodies seeks its own level. Let the tears flow, and even assist them. Use water to encourage the release of the energy. Cry in the shower or bath, while washing the dishes, when walking in the rain. The water of your sorrow will flow back to the sea and into the earth. Who could believe how much water is in just one body, if the tears of grief and sorrow and loneliness did not prove it?

"Your pain has not been just yours alone. Many of you have had to observe and share, contrary to your will, the terrible discomfort into which your beloved furry, feathery, and leathery children inevitably grow. I say 'grow' because that is how they perceive their transition—as a natural part of their lives. Most of them do not have tears as you do and so their messiness becomes even more pronounced and profound as they also must express the ultimate balance, which is a return of the body to that from whence it originally arose. Your struggle to keep the water in their bodies, which in turn struggle against your efforts, results in a conflict that eventually and inevitably strips everyone concerned of all personal dignity.

"Everyone is reduced to a state of equality, which is the most mysterious and divine state of all—that of a new life in a new place, which is so far beyond this one, that one wonders if the water there could even be imagined.

"Your psychological pain grows to such immense proportions that you become the novas of your shared universes, exploding into seemingly infinite shards of even greater suffering. You become pioneers in your own lives, forging a new experience that hints at even greater and mysterious possibilities. Then your grief implodes and you find yourselves being inhaled into a black hole, where all the bliss with your children is eventually eaten away, and the light is extinguished from your vision. All becomes darkness—deep, deep darkness.

"Here you discover your divine, unalterable inheritance—that of choice. You could choose to resist this incomprehensible, expanding, and evolving experience and struggle to swim back upstream against the currents and tides, the same flow which would otherwise quickly take you to the Great Ocean wherein Love would have us all swim together. Your resistance is evidenced by spending much of your psychological time trying to retrieve all the shattered bits and pieces of your life, turning your perception onto each piece through the process of memory, and reliving each and every horrible moment that composed the days, months, or even years of failing bodies and increasing sickness. Where there was once just the single painful object that was your dilemma, there are now countless jagged fragments of agonizing memories, each with many sharp, cutting edges that slash and hurt you, as you try to pick them up and piece them back together into the puzzle that was once your happy time with your children, your friends.

"A new black hole of pain is made as you become lost in those dreadful, unhappy memories. This is the pain of psychological time, which can only be temporary in spite of your efforts to capture and hold it. Even if you are successful at this you succeed in only creating a crystallized state, which eventually must dissolve and also return to the Source.

"You also have the choice of forgiving those memories, which means letting them go completely with the understanding that they no longer exist except as memories, and are, therefore, not real but merely illusions that you can invest with all the energy and emotion that you might care to. You could instead turn your inner perception toward the Great Truth that your children are still alive. Even *more* alive, for they now enjoy the perfect health and peace that will eventually be yours.

"And they *will* be by your side. Their moments of pain and messiness are over and so it will be for you. The fragments of your former selves, seemingly and utterly heartbroken and separated forever, will slowly and surely begin to draw back together, guided by a Great Hand that possesses the Intelligence to gently join them into your new Self, deeply changed and somehow bigger than you were before. Just as your children have experienced a transition, so have you by the very nature of your loving bonds with them. You will achieve a transition beyond any dream that you have ever had, for you will no longer think it a dream, but will recognize it as Reality.

"Therefore let this place where we come to share our pain, fear, and loneliness also become the beginning of the Greatest Journey, which is that of Going Home. Upon your arrival, you will immediately be greeted in great joy by your animals, which never have and never will stop loving you in their sacred and shameless adoration."

Robert would like us to realize that life on the earth is the ultimate organic process, and that water is but one of the various elements arriving and departing in waves of experience. The densities of fire, earth, and air also rise and fall, ebb and flow, all shaped and moving within the matrix of what the ancients often called the fifth element—ether, akasha, spirit, the substance of unbeingness. This matrix might be that which modern science is now calling the "dark energy-matter" of the Universe, the prepared ground out of which everything planted arises and grows—the pattern of all patterns from which everything manifests and obtains its sustenance.

I was deeply grateful for the compassion of the veterinarian who let me hold Bridget while she made her transition, allowing me to be a living part of the dying process. Participating in this process was vital to both of us and to the vet as well. Every day, and at great length, Bridget and I had discussed how, upon her transition, she was to immediately go to Tim—I knew he would be waiting for her. Although Tim and I were not able to communicate then with one another in the more direct way we have since grown into, my heart knew that he heard me and I had complete trust that she would be well cared for.

For a few days after Bridget's transition I kept feeling her jumping up on the bed next to me, just as she had every night during her life. I felt it so clearly that I would automatically reach out to touch her, only to find nothing there. I would even turn on the light just to make sure. This always happened before the section of the bed's headboard that I had come to call "the window." As Bridget had become increasingly ill she began to sit and stare for long moments at this certain spot, as if looking out a window at something. She seemed to be intently watching, even listening in a very alert and serious way to something that totally evaded my human senses.

I buried her body at dawn amongst the roots of a wild cherry tree beside a witch's garden. It was completely obvious that she was no longer in the old container of fur and bones she had left behind, but I cried many times a day, for many weeks. About two weeks after her passing, still terribly heartbroken and letting myself be carried along by my grief, I finally had some beginning contact with her. As I was falling asleep one night I had a waking vision. My eyes were open and the room was dark, but I could see a kind of picture in the air before me. It was very pale and cloudy at first but then became a little clearer. It was like looking through a globe made of very thick glass. But I could clearly recognize Bridget, who appeared to be deeply asleep in a white wicker basket set in something vibrantly green, perhaps grass or leaves. She looked small and kittenish. Then the picture faded away after a minute or so.

Another vision came a few nights later while waiting to fall asleep. This time it was even clearer. Bridget was asleep but making small movements, as if trying to wake up. Her eyes reminded me of the way a kitten's eyes look shortly after birth, still tightly shut. There was the impression that she actually *was* a kitten and no longer the thin, aged thing she had been before. She looked very small, soft, and fragile. After a few minutes this vision faded into nothingness.

In the final vision, she appeared to be resting with her chin on her front paws, a very familiar position to me, on a pile of white, fluffy towels, on the bottom of a three-tiered shelf. Like the others, it also then faded quickly.

A few days later while catching up on some writing, I suddenly heard the words *"I've got her."* It was Tim, telling me that Bridget was now with him! There were some fleeting internal images that she was racing around like a frisky kitten, which gave me great joy. I felt an immense burden lift as I realized that I no longer had to take care of her, because she was now in a place of perfect health. This also made me sad, for I still missed her physical presence, but the knowledge of her survival and wellness gave me strength to keep on with my own life's tasks awaiting me.

Another gift arrived out of this experience—Tim's voice and the first instance of his directly speaking to me, which I heard internally.

In the darkest moments of my grieving for Bridget's physical presence, I felt totally alone. It seemed a natural thing for me to want to follow her as soon as possible, even to remove my life force from the elements of my body and let them dissipate and fall back into the earth. If it were not for my other furry cat child, Oolong, and my responsibility for her well-being on the planet, I might very well have ended my own physical existence in the quickest and most quiet way I could find. Oolong grieved as well and needed me by her side for care and love, and I was grateful for the gift of her presence.

But what if I *had* been totally alone, with no responsibility to answer for anyone other than myself? It was true that I had a small circle of caring, concerned friends who knew that I was suffering in my bereavement, and they all made themselves unconditionally available to me. But my pain wanted none of their company. It wanted only release, and it seemed to make sense at the time for me to take my life into my own hands and effect my own transition. It was inevitable anyway, so why not get an early start? I knew from my intimate experiences with the Risen that there would be no judgment whatsoever against me if I killed my body. And yet something within me struggled against such an act, and I could not determine why it simultaneously felt like both a positive and a negative undertaking. Confused, I finally came to a place where I could do no more than simply rest, unable to rationalize any further.

While I rested, someone Risen began sharing insight about the issue of self-exiting. I recognized this Risen One as the person who had once been my great grandfather on earth. We shared the same date of birth, over 120 years apart. Although we had never met in physical life, I had always had a faint awareness of his quiet, observant presence somewhere in the background. He had never communicated directly with me before until now.

"I was with you during the painful time around your child's dissolution, alongside others who watched and aided you as well, and I continue to abide with you. I watch and tend the aura of safety that surrounds you. I offer a beginning response to your questions about the ending of your earthly living.

"I was once an ancestor of yours. I had a short life, brought about by difficult conditions that created an imbalance in living. Because my life was so short, there was much I felt that I missed learning about existence as an embodied human being, and so quickly assented when given the opportunity to become one of your guardians upon your birth.

"I had an earthly name then. I clung to it for a goodly while after crossing the river of lights that separates our lands. I overcame my doubts and became accustomed to this utmost paradise. I grew toward new definitions and away from the old ones. I cannot seem to remember my earthly name, for it was an expression of the physical body's heart, and like that heart, vibrates too slowly to be able to endure in these higher places. I can no longer hear the name in this heart I now carry. And yet I have a name here, but as you can sense it would be difficult for us to find agreement on the sounds to pronounce it with your human tongue.

"I am grateful to serve you in this capacity, for serving others serves oneself as well. This sharing is Life Itself. You sense the responsibility that is appropriate regarding your animal companion. She fulfils her life by caring for you, and you know, deeply, that this is true and that both of you share this responsibility. I am always near you, offering a loving touch on your shoulder to help allay the weariness which often overtakes you, and to guide you with suggestions of actions that are compassionate toward your self.

"I am not alone in my interest here, for Another, far evolved beyond me, has answered my request for the wisdom greater than that which I have yet to obtain, and which is essential to this discourse of learning now undertaken.

"This Higher One is known well and revered here and yet I have never seen this One with these eyes. This Higher One is even now speaking through me."

I had been aware of my ancestor and of this Higher One merging in presence in those last few moments when I had begun to look into my past thoughts about self-exiting. As always with the various presences in the over-background of my sensing, I wasn't certain if anyone would move more forward into the range of my lower vibrating senses. Although my great grandfather could do this, it was soon clear to me that any communication from the Higher One would be practically impossible to directly translate into easily comprehensible human terms. But the experience is still accessible to me for retrieval from higher astral fields, and that is what I will now strive to do here, however slow and heavy the process may be.

Regarding this heaviness, the reader might have earlier noticed a strange feeling or change in consciousness while reading or listening to Robert's message about the watery process. It is important here to validate for some, while making others newly aware, that while reading such communications some individuals may become very tired, even to the point of needing sleep. This shows the changing in vibrations when one's Spirit is connecting to the spirit-energy behind the words. Our Spirit is attracted to the communication in the way one draws closer to the fireplace for warmth or to a friend to better hear him. It would not be surprising if some readers fell asleep. This sleep is a kind of bodily trance, and means the spiritual awareness has gone to where the presently evolved consciousness cannot. With persistence and experience, the consciousness will eventually be able to increasingly stay awake and aware as the spiritual vibrations become faster and finer.

Here now is my discernment of this Higher One's communication, who came to aid me further in my quest to understand self-exiting.

~ 11 ~

These words may not make conscious sense at this time,
but my spiritual senses comprehend and retain
this knowledge for Authentic Self.

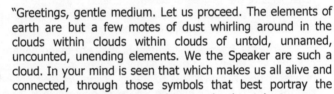 "Greetings, gentle medium. Let us proceed. The elements of earth are but a few motes of dust whirling around in the clouds within clouds within clouds of untold, unnamed, uncounted, unending elements. We the Speaker are such a cloud. In your mind is seen that which makes us all alive and connected, through those symbols that best portray the information. We are slowing down within our cloud to take temporary residence within your cloud, which is your world.

"Taking your life cannot end your life, and this you know well, medium. Because this cannot be done, there is nothing to do about it. Judgment does not await anyone who wishes to move the life force expression from one form to another, regardless of intent, self-judgment, or any such kind of sorrowful self-interest. The movement of such a one can be observed, assisted, eased, and loved. The movement of life from one form of energy to another form of energy is a sacred event at all times, and there is no heresy, no blasphemy, nor even error to be assigned to any such movement. Every body is appropriate, wherever perceived to be, and whenever perceived.

"Within the great density of the elements which have been in-drawn into the form of your planet's body and all the forms upon, under, and around it, there is great activity, a frenzy to acquire energy and to move from one form to another. Your movement is your development on the dense plane of materiality. All movement for all living things on the planet in this way is appropriate, always.

"There is not just one process of movement of life through living but a multitude of processes, which beget ever more processes of life. Life is forever redefining itself, reflecting, refracting, recycling, renewing. The process of life returns energy back to its source in a never-ending cycle, ever so slowly, expanding and widening and eventually lifting all who are traveling in every way upon the cycle's circle into higher and finer modes of expression. This journey would appear as a spiral from within your spiritual dimension. This you all intuitively know, as do all forms that contain the spirit-flame that is of the Original, and therefore is the Original Itself. We are all One-and-the-Same as fulfilled by our infinitely differing forms of expression. We cannot find an end to it all, nor can we end expression.

"Regard the flowers of which you are so fond. When they are allowed to find their proper elements and grow, they thrive with the greatest expression possible, seemingly without end. Yet there is an end, but one that cannot be found or seen or even sensed, as it is simultaneously assimilated into that-which-it-is-becoming, which is the fulfillment of the process given to them, as given to all life forms. This is the gift of unending life. The flowers may weather the harshest of conditions upon the way and yet manage to pursue the fulfillment of this gift, of which all life consists and emerges from and strives to fulfill. This striving is movement and this movement is life. As nothing exists that does not move there is nothing but life to fulfill. Life, regardless of the degree of self-awareness, is a divine gift, an infinite opportunity for immortal exploration to whatever fulfillment awaits. And fulfillment always awaits each form of life.

"Give the flowers any elements that are inappropriate, that are poisonous to them, and they will not fulfill their flowery process to the utmost expression available to them. Giving yourself poison that will keep you from further fulfilling whatever expression is forming about you will not keep you from living. The flowers will release their essence of spirit, as will you. Their dense bodies will return to the denser elements, as will yours.

"What of the spirit essence animating all forms? During your life as a human, your spirit will be received and carried within the shelter of the body. The body protects and nourishes it, while supporting its own ongoing transformation into ever finer and faster vibrating energies. When at last the spirit is released, the higher and finer the energy, the higher and finer places it will be able to sustain awareness in, and it will then be brought to these places. These higher and finer places are new awarenesses that are redefined by increased self-reflection. This is the great principle of those planes, including the earth and beyond the earth, where like vibration attracts like vibration. This ever-evolving principle, a state of awareness of self and of others that arises and is increasingly sustained, is love.

"On earth, the vibration of matter is far too slow to attract anything other than itself, like and unlike together, which is an aspect of the process you experience and label as 'gravity.' Spirit vibrates within matter, and so for that part of its journey it *is* matter, while it grows in its awareness that there is more and greater spirit beyond the body, and thus yearns and reaches for it. Whenever the spirit is released from the body, at any point, it cannot yet exist in self-awareness for long without a body of some sorts, and thus still carries itself in finer, higher vibrating bodies. The spirit will find its appropriate place. There is a place even for the spirit energy of the flowers to move to, from where they can continue their process of ever refining, ever expressing, ever experiencing.

"Life is experience. Self-releasing your spirit essence is experience. You will learn from all experience. Upon release you will be aware that you may have not moved any further from where you thought to move. You will Rise, and as Risen you will perceive your actions in a different way. Rather than achieving a replacement as longed for, there is instead movement that might be called displacement. And yet you will still have achieved understanding, inasmuch as your present awareness can shed its light upon your whereabouts.

"You may feel that it is appropriate for you to leave at a certain point along any experience. If this seems a necessary experience, explore it in your mind and see where it leads—not with thought, but with feeling. You may find it leads you where you originally had intended, or elsewhere, but you will still be ultimately involved in your life experience. It cannot be otherwise. You may perceive the necessity and the chance to make the decision, or you may not. Either way it does not matter. The longer you remain in formation to gather information upon your planet does not mean that you will necessarily gain the experience that will bring more vibration. Yet it could, depending on how you utilize your experience. It is up to you to use that which has been given to you in the ways *you* deem appropriate. There are no mistakes, only choices. There are no judgments about your choices, only unconditional acceptance. It cannot be otherwise. The means is provided for you to raise or lower your vibration at any time.

"We see in your mind that fear of the future, of punishment, of judgment, weighs heavily around such decisions. There is fear that you will not be able to be with those whom you love and that they will be unable to reach you. There need not be any fear. If you are in suffering when you arrive after leaving your body, you will be attended to unless you desire otherwise. Healing is always available and the opportunities to learn will continue. Those whom you love and who love you will be available. Those who are higher can move to the lower, but the lower cannot as easily move to the higher. And even when it can, it cannot sustain that movement. Their vibrations may be of a higher nature than yours and so they may have varying qualities of presence, and thus they may seemingly dwell on a different plane. But the nature of love is such that all dwelling places, all positions of vibration are totally, perfectly appropriate. Love allows all who are similar to intermingle in some way. The more present you are to yourself, the more present you will be to others like yourself. If in seeking to obliterate your consciousness because of the pain, this will be achieved because it is important to you and you have made the decision that this is to be so. You will eventually awaken in the arms of those who love you and who understand and accept you. No one will shun you, none will condemn you.

"If any sorrow should arise from such an action, healing is always offered, never denied, and communicative exploration is encouraged. There are unlimited ways to continue self-discovery. No one need be lonely unless they want it so. Many arrive in various states of fear, regardless of the avenue taken. Even the negative states of emotion are able to find expression far beyond what is capable upon the earth. The emotion of regret might be underlying the spirit who has released itself from the body, but often the release itself becomes the emotion of relief, which is positive. Choosing to remain focused on regret will exclude your awareness from the present, where suffering cannot exist. You were not meant to experience anything unless you want to. All experience is valuable, nothing is lost or wasted, and life unfailingly goes on expressing itself. As will you, for you are life itself.

"The less fear with which you arrive, the higher the vibration and so then much more light. You will have greater ability to enjoy the light. It is not necessary to hasten any part of any journey, including the one you now have on earth. Ending it does not hasten it, nor does ending it slow the experience, for time does not exist as you know it outside the temporary awareness of your plane. You have the awareness of time on earth to experience, to ponder, to study, to enjoy a material existence, as well as to gather impressions about pain and suffering. Fill this time with your experience, and experience as much as you want. This time is for your awakening, and it is left to you to decide how much wakefulness you wish to experience.

"However you leave, whenever you leave, you bring exactly who you are, and your accomplished awakened consciousness. There is no comparison against others offered in judgment upon you, no criticism ever offered, although this you may do to yourself, to the degree that you do now, and possibly even more so.

"The flower does not damn nor is it damned. It is welcome as it is, as are you. As the flower has been manifested out of the greatest wisdom to seek to fulfill its experience as completely as it can, so have you been manifested, and so might you seek. At the end of your earthly experience, at the moment of release, there is simply that much more opportunity for joy in the knowledge that you have lived in whatever way *you* deemed fulfilling. The more you can perceive, the larger will be your universe. There is great joy in the self-awareness of self-expansion from awakening, and there is ever-increasing wisdom and serenity in that joy.

"As for those left behind on the earth—you are never responsible in any way for their state of vibration—only for your own. In your freedom you may know their grief as keenly as if it were your own. You will no longer have the body with which to embrace theirs in comfort, and this may be a mental agony that requires much healing, both for those in spirit bodies and those in earthly bodies. Medium, you are aware that we have influenced much of what you have shared about grief. We re-echo your words here as a gift for your own benefit. Be aware of opportunities to begin the healing while together on the earth. Ask. Always, simply, ask for help, for giving is what the universe builds upon. You will always receive this forgiving, and it will arrive in some form, regardless of your expectations. Most often help has arrived long before you ask for it, and it is gentle and subtle, intent on not interfering and only with assisting. If you do not want it you will not receive it, but you will still be watched and guided, even in the darkest of moments. You are always loved, even if you have withdrawn love from yourself. As you would give the flowers the space and elements in which to thrive, strive to see yourself and others as flowers. Know that you are a flower with self-awareness. It is this self-awareness that enables you to live in conscious awareness of grace, which is the gift of self-awareness, as well as the ability to live in a continual expression of natural gratitude.

"When all seems without hope, that is the time to let go even of hope, and accept it as an opportunity to experience feelings of compassion, peace, and love toward self and others. Learn the peace of resting in That-Which-Is-Greater-Than-You and yet which is also Who-You-Are. You are Beings and, simultaneously, Becomings.

"The Cloud and your ancestor withdraw now, leaving you wrapped in a mantle of serene assurance that you are loved by many, many, many, who await your eventual arrival."

By the time this communication had drawn to an end, a few hours had passed, and I fell into a sleep that lasted several more hours. Like most such communications, there were so many layers of information within this contact that I felt as if I could barely see past the top one.

The Cloud's suggestion to let go of hope, which we have always been taught to hang onto, is deeply impressive. Another Risen friend has also helped me to understand that the process of grief must not be diminished by hope. Hope cannot have the illusion of reality unless it is projected onto a background of fear, from which it then draws its sustenance. Just like misfocused attention upon the past, hope is another defense of the frightened ego-mind. Hope is projected onto a screen of the future—never the present, which hope obscures. The present cannot contain hope, and hope cannot contain the present. If one is hoping, one is not present, having been taken out of it by the desire for something that is not in the present. Without a sense of time-generated fear, grief has no lasting reality and no permanent significance.

Knowing is the unwavering awareness of the experience of reality, and grounds one in the present. Sri Aurobindo, the legendary explorer of yogic psychospiritual realms, suggested that the foreknowledge that we bring to our experience is that something that can be called "faith," and this foreknowledge, or intuition, not only goes before us but also waits there for our experience to happen and so justify it.[29] As briefly touched upon before, this intuitive consciousness is an inner knowing that is sometimes called *noetic*, after the Greek concept for "intuitive knowing." Using the noetic lens of present awareness as a focusing tool brings understanding, which brings more light. This light is not something symbolic but is actual, real light, regardless of whether we can see it with our physical eyes or not. This is spiritual light, and in it the shadows of fear vanish, the present becomes brighter, and the future becomes less important as it fades back into the nothingness from whence it came. We awaken, present to our selves and to the selves of others.

Without his former body's dense material and its ego-mind, Tim's lens of awareness is able to focus on a larger range of living than mine. So it might be said that he is waiting ahead of me, which is foreknowledge to me. When we each focus our lens of awareness toward one another, the interception is where we meet and join in awareness. Because I now have knowledge that he is often waiting ahead for me, I've achieved a bit of that which some call faith and which I increasingly experience as knowing.

"August, it's not so much that I'm 'waiting ahead' for you, but it's more that our movement within and against different backgrounds makes it seem so. I truly comprehend the difficulty there is in finding a way to compare our two very different experiences of awareness of self while living in different dimensions of space and time. Like space, time is real, and its beauty is seen and experienced in differing realities, and in changing reality. We can see that change is rooted in Nature—that we are Nature, and change is time. But change is also space.

"Your geography is usually described on earth as an experience of Space-Time. Space appears to stand still while events are perceived to change by passing through it in a linear, timely way, manifesting impressions of past, present and future. Conversely, the Risen geography could be said to be an experience of Time-Space. Time appears to stand still, while space appears to

---

[29] Satprem, *Sri Aurobindo, or The Adventure of Consciousness* (Pondicherry, India: Sri Aurobindo Ashram Press, 1968), 38.

change as I move through it. Just like on Earth—and a few of your scientists are beginning to grasp this—the Risen interpret and utilize these appearances, which are really just thoughts, as movement or modes of transportation. All time events are occurring simultaneously, reflecting the Risen understanding that Creation is finished and always available for manifested exploration. Space-Time and Time-Space, and other combinations of light and sound are the mediums of exploration, the finger paints of the cosmic playroom. You, the Yet-To-Rise, can and do experience Risen Time-Space via spiritual events and realizations, and states of altered consciousness—which also include pain and suffering.

"To get some feel for this, I'll try to use an earthly experience as an illustration that most people can understand. It sort of works because it reflects the physics of an actual train ride you might take on earth. It's as if I'm sitting in a train which is moving along at a very fast speed—meaning a state of higher vibration. As I look out the window on the side where I'm sitting, those things closer to the train appear to race past me very quickly, as they would on an earthly train ride—so space appears to change as I move through time.

"Simultaneously, those things that are further away, which are the lower vibrating landscapes of Earth, also appear to move, but much more slowly. From my train I can see the combined Risen and Earth landscapes as well as many of their details, but not all. Those objects in the middle ground also move, but at a different rate. I can see all of these different-paced, different-spaced areas simultaneously through the one window, and I can also see them moving in different relationships with one another. Depending on where you are within that passing landscape, I can see more of your life than you can, while mine moves along at its faster pace which still keeps pace with yours. We might even get a brief glimpse of one another.

"Someone in another train passing mine might see what I see, but in a different way, and from a different perspective. The Risen State is a little like being in a train at times, although you can see how the analogy breaks down quickly if I try to move beyond this very simplified form. Rather like trying to get up to walk through a moving train while having to pee really badly."

"Tim, my head hurts from trying to think about this, and I'm not sure if I got it all down in the way you mean. But I find comfort in knowing that you're not so much out of reach sometimes, although you might be out of my sight and hearing for much of my time."

Any comfort we can find along the way is a sign that grief continues to transform and evolve. People often form a new relationship with their partner after the partner has transitioned and their shared grief has eased. I'm far from lonely without Tim being here in his body, or demented in some way to prefer this ethereal relationship to the security that companionship with an embodied person might seem to promise. Because of our work together we have managed to become more alike in vibration, and this acts as an attractive force—a resonance—that transcends the usual boundaries between our states of existence, and brings us closer. This force is even more effective when I'm asleep and able to move about in the astral realms, free of the confines of a dense material body. It's then possible to experience the embracing and merging of mind and soul and be much closer together.

Although not embodied on this plane, Tim attracts me in many ways. He enhances my own sense of being in a myriad of aspects that complement who I am. This enhancement of my experience of self adds more to this wholeness. It's always a new experience for me, and a new kind of love that evolves from this experience. Tim sees and understands more from his Risen perspective, and so can accept me in more evolved ways and without judgment, which can only strengthen our togetherness. We're both in awe of the fact that our relationship and communication are real, and there's mutual excitement about eventually being physically together again, side by side in the same world. I know that my transition is inevitable, and often it feels like I'm a four-year old waiting for Christmas.

In such a relationship there is little time or space for judgment because there is so little fear at this point. Instead, there is a shared, committed acceptance of the knowledge that there is no death, and never will be. Ours could be said to be the ultimate long-distance relationship, but while there really is no distance here, there is great respect for one another's self-perceived space. It's like living in the same city sometimes, or the same neighborhood or building, but for now in separate living spaces. When I transition, my perceptions will change and we'll then be closer than we ever have before.

Developing and sustaining a relationship as a couple who are still only able to primarily perceive one another from seemingly separate planes isn't easy, but it's not always difficult either. It's a matter of varying perceptions. We strive to find ways to vary our perceptions, so that we're flexible enough to be able to find each other amidst the constant change that is itself transition on all levels of experience. When our perceptions are most alike—including our feelings, desires, and even dreams—then we are closest.

The processes toward communication and the results are often subtle beyond perception and sometimes tangible beyond belief. It can't be emphasized enough that mostly it's a matter of staying in the present—which is where we both are. There is so much on this planet and in life to distract me and make me forget not only where I am, but also *that* I am. If I am focused on the past, which will never be again on this earth and is not where I am now, then I'm misdirecting my consciousness to a place where Tim is not now.

For instance, I may still have some unresolved anger about our shared past. But as Tim and others have so often said to me in many ways—including my Risen cat, Bridget—"I'm not *there*"—meaning in the memories of the past—"I'm *here*, with you. Let the grief relax and soften, let go of the anger, leave all the past behind. Relax, flow, and transition into the present experience with me. Be here with me now, where I want you to be."

How can I say no to that?

"I'm glad you heard and listened, August. Beliefs strongly direct and influence our movement through our lives. It's far easier from my Risen state to see that beliefs really are part of the process of change, temporarily there to help carry us forward to knowledge. The Risen still use beliefs as part of the learning process about moving around in their new existence. Even here, hanging onto beliefs, when instead changing them would be most appropriate, will lock us into ways of living that no longer support our heart, and will prevent us from serving others and ourselves.

"Eventually, I'm told, there is life after belief. Beyond belief, *knowing* becomes the foundation from which living moves forward. Time coalesces into awareness, and the everlasting Present becomes one's ground and one's horizon. When present to one's Presence, or the In-Dwelling Authentic Self, one's Being becomes one's sphere—or as you've said, August, one's 'geography,' an evocative concept."

TWELVE

AUTHENTIC SELF

God enters by a private door into every individual.
~ Ralph Waldo Emerson

To relinquish the fear of death is the greatest act of self-forgiveness.
~ A Risen One

By now some insights will have been gained into the nature of the ego-mind and the simulate self. There also may be emerging sensations of Authentic Self that are beyond the ego-mind's illusory projections. Authentic Self is beyond language and increasingly revealed as it is "uncovered." This self-revelation happens as we regain control of the ego-mind and its simulate selves. This chapter will continue to primarily review concepts about the simulate self, and to increase contrast between what's real—Authentic Self—and what's not—simulate self. Understanding of what Authentic Self is will continue to unfold.

~ 12 ~

These words may not make conscious sense at this time,
but my spiritual senses comprehend and retain
this knowledge for Authentic Self.

Although the subject of Authentic Self was discussed in some detail prior to this, we are not providing "written in stone" definitions of it. As stated in Chapter Ten, "Know Thyself" is the open-ended answer to the question, an answer that appears only as truth reveals itself through our individualized Self of Authorship and its various states of emerging awareness. The core Authentic Self will inevitably recognize the feeling of its truth in its various states, thereby recognizing itself as an immortal individualization as it moves inwardly from any felt point, ever onward.

One can learn to observe an experience *beyond* an experience. This observation leads to the empowering question: "*Who* is it that observes?" Some refer to this *who* as the "Hidden Observer." Tim has called it the Indwelling Self—the invisible, conscious awareness of our core, internal presence that is sensed more easily when the ego-mind's chatter is stilled.

What is Self? Here is a Risen-inspired definition: "Self is conscious awareness as reflected by the conscious awareness of another Self." In earthly words, this is when you look in the eyes of someone you love and you see their eyes loving you, as their eyes see your eyes loving them. This infinite reflection of mirrored perception gives rise to the shared experience of one's individual, indwelling self and the self of another individual, simultaneously giving rise to a shared sense of something greater than the individual selves, which is yet a larger self. All thought stops, all inner babble ceases, and all knowledge is instantly *here*.

Others refer to the Hidden Observer as their Higher Self, or Higher Power, the Oversoul, the Goddess, or in any unlimited number of ways. There are as many ways to say this as there are individuals to say it. Stilling the incessant criticism of the ego-mind will eventually result in an awakening to the Hidden Observer, who is already very awake but just seems hidden, simply because it is much quieter than the ego-mind.

When no longer hidden from us, it becomes clear that this Observer is Authentic Self. It is a direct channel to Original Creator Source, from which all individualities arise. While remaining individual and unique, all Authentic Selves—or Higher Individualities—are interconnected and collectively joined as our One Source. Individually and collectively, we expand our Source while *being* our Source. When we can sense the beingness of Authentic Self, we are quickly approaching the vibrational awareness where we can begin to sense the beingness of other Authentic Selves, including the Risen. We also begin to realize that we are all the same Being, the Original Source of Authenticity. This beginning realization, which is very high, indeed, is more at home in the higher astral-etheric realms, and cannot be appreciably explored here in any concretized way.

But who are we communicating with when we are *not* communicating with our Authentic Self or with other Authentic or Risen Authentic Selves? For most of us, this would be the simulate self. This is the personality construct— or an artificial intelligence, so to speak—meant to be regulated by the ego-mind. These personalities are what we usually present to others while on the earth. We give them great value, and much energy is spent into making them appear as powerful and attractive to others as possible, which further increases a sense of separation. Trying to maintain a youthful appearance in spite of the aging process is one such example. "Clothes (car/house/job) make the person" is a typical expression of a belief in the power of a simulate self-concept that exists apart from others. In spite of the pain it causes, such separation is still believed to be highly desirable by most of our society.

What are the qualities of Authentic Self? If such labels could be found and described here, the ego-mind would attempt to simulate them into personality traits, which the unaware reader would then pretend to have.

Personality is *not* individuality, yet most modern people seem to equate them. "Personality" comes from the Latin *persona*, meaning "mask," referring to the masks that Ancient Greek actors once used on stage to personalize a character. The actors used masks to portray something previously unseen, rendering it visible to others. When they left the stage the masks came off, and they knew that the persona did not continue on as their individuality—"impersonal" means "unmasked."

Like any good actor, a simulate self needs memories to draw on for its character. These memories are supplied by the ego-mind. Actors also know that the success of their persona depends largely on their own belief in it. The basic nature of belief is that it is temporary. But modern humans actually try to maintain a *permanent* belief that our persona is some kind of externalized result of the bridging between our inner and outer selves. This is yet another misconception of the ego-mind, because there is but one real self, Authentic Self, which only seems to be hidden.

We also refer to our persona as our image, and may strongly feel that it is very important to have. And yet "change your image" is a message often heard as well as subliminally suggested in our modern world. The better we can be seen to control the expression and appearance of ourselves, the more we are considered successful, and admired and desired by others attempting the same.

Individuality, not image, is you. The word "individual" comes from the Latin *individuus*, "not divided." Contrasted with the image of the personality, our individuality is invisible and indivisible, and therefore indestructible. Individuality survives death when we transition to a Risen state. It has no dimensions, so it cannot be measured, contained, nor defined. Any attempt to do so is to try to personalize Authentic Self. One can cover up Authentic Self with masks, but sooner or later all the disguises come off, and then what remains? The Individualized Authentic Self that is you, which not only exists now, but always will exist, without end. When we leave the theatrical stage of earth, the temporary personality will eventually dissolve and be reabsorbed as informative energy into a Risen Authentic Self—this usually occurs after we leave the material body, but there are exceptions. Any work that remains to be done in dealing with personality issues will be accomplished after Rising.

Negative beliefs about survival are amplified and sustained by personalized, partializing mechanistic views about the human body, as reified by Western medicine. Prompted by these medical models and driven largely by its personalities, the human science of psychology attempts to codify and utilize what it believes are "personality types." Psychologists analyze externalized thought forms as they are expressed and presented through our personalities. But they can't measure the quantity or quality of the dimensionless individual. Earthly science tends to see its presumed authority as reliable knowledge, but such authority is largely a competitive matter of fight-or-flight posturing, to ensure the survival of separate ego-minded personalities.

Most people identify with their personality to the extent that it crystallizes. It retains some semi-substantial but still earthly materiality, so the crystallized form can be quite problematic to dissolve, even on the astral planes. Although it is not intelligent, the free-floating, discarnate personality can display a kind of clever mimicry of the memories with which it still resonates. The resultant form will linger on in a kind of quasi-existence on the lowest astral levels that are closest to the earth plane. Recall that the ego-mind eventually ceases to exist when we discard the body, an inevitable ending or death which it fears and does all it can to avoid, while allowed to run out of control with that fear. The disembodied, crystallized form of the simulate self no longer has an earthly ego-mind to regulate it by what we call a "conscience," or inner critic or judge. Because the Primal Source Spark does not animate them, these forms do not have access to the still, small voice of Creator Source that spiritually guides our inner lives, which are led by Authentic Self.

These forms present themselves as apparent semi-intelligences, and are often responsible for the nonsensical, crude, and even cruel communications to sensitives during a mediumistic reading. They are driven and sustained by strong negative emotions that were developed by the simulate selves of people who were once on earth, and which are now the disembodied forms attracted to these readings. They are attracted to and mimic lower vibrational aspects of humanity around them. They are most successful at making their presences known through an Ouija board, and sometimes through automatic handwriting, table tipping, and rappings. People with traumatized psyches, whose brains are disabled by organic disease, by various substances, or by conditions labeled as mental illness may also be susceptible to the invasive efforts of these discarded constructs, for short- and long-term periods.

Someone might feel that they are receiving messages via automatic hand-writing or channeling, but are actually in communication with their Hidden Observer, Authentic Self. Our Authentic Self may be in communication with other Authentic Selves at the same time, thus relaying information to us from others as well. There is usually a noticeable contrast between communicating with our Authentic Self and when our Authentic Self is communicating with another Authentic Self. This can happen on any plane, while in the earthly body, or when we live as a Risen One.

To communicate with someone on a higher plane, we must raise our vibrations from that of the earth plane. To do this we make a conscious connection with Authentic Self. In turn, those on the higher plane, who are very likely more familiar with and identified as their Authentic Selves, often must lower their own vibrations. This experience has been reported by them as very uncomfortable, like "sinking into thick, muddy water," or "being in a smoke-filled, airless room," or as "a dimming and dampening of all light and sound." If a person on the earth has learned how to achieve and sustain a fairly continual awareness of Authentic Self, intuitive communication can take place on the higher levels with greater facility.

"August, I'd like to touch very briefly here on the concept of 'higher levels,' which makes it sound as if they're arranged in physical, spatial ways in the manner of stairs or the floors of a building. One of the things that can immediately take an embodied person's awareness out of their own presence, as well as the presence of Risen Ones, are the thoughts that try to make these hierarchal structures real. While they will certainly manifest astrally when imagined by a Risen mind, the earthly ego-mind can achieve little more than clever and distracting imitations."

~ 13 ~

These words may not make conscious sense at this time,
but my spiritual senses comprehend and retain
this knowledge for Authentic Self.

"Try to understand 'higher' as having the same meaning of 'more awake.' Any moment in time that you can recall easily is possible because at that time, within that moment, you were awake to some degree. This wakefulness is then always available from there on, as a form of memory energized with a bit of your own awakened consciousness. Another example is when you haven't apparently moved in any physical way from the spot you've been sitting in, but the sudden seeming arrival of a new perception, a new way of seeing something, simultaneously transports you to someplace different, a place that looks and feels brighter. Everything around you has changed in some way through this movement, and yet you haven't taken a physical up or down step. *Aha!* or *Oho!* moments are transitions from one world to another—you cannot go back as you were once they are made. You *can* go back *as you are*, which accounts for the sensation of dimming as one moves in and out of the various lights of awareness states, or former geographies of awareness. This wakefulness, which is light, illuminates your way. Such 'spatial enlightenment' will be seen in one of your stories about rescue work later on, August. Because the enlightened traveler is more awake, more things are noticed by her than by the sleeping ones nearby. The traveler is also more noticeable to those who have eyes to see because there is more light shining through. Those whose inner eyes do not function may feel something but see nothing.

"That's all I have to say for now, other than that I dropped a few hints about the concept of reincarnation, which I propose to expand upon later."

"Thanks, Tim, beautifully said. And I'm thrilled *you're* going to tackle reincarnation. I can't even begin to fathom what you're going to say."

When the earthly material body falls away, Authentic Self then stands revealed. This Self is the bridge. When I say that I am the bridge or the door to other states of consciousness, I mean to where other individuals exist in similar states of consciousness. I am the door to Tim. In the early stages of communication with the Risen, the door is experienced intuitively.

Intuitive communication can be a fleeting process and depends largely on one's emotional maturity. Everyone is intuitive—some more or less so than others—and this is true regarding emotional maturity as well. Intuitional and emotional maturity can be expanded by many methods, including meditation, prayer, creative arts, consciously aware suffering, and psychotherapy and other therapies. The primary tool that earthly and Risen people have to initiate intercommunication is one that's the simplest, and therefore the most powerful, and which is categorically overlooked and underrated—the imagination. When we open ourselves up to our own unique imaginations, we have indeed taken a big step in an important direction. We have finally found our own built-in door that will lead us to greater and higher places.

MUNDUS IMAGINALIS

"Imagination and emotions are the most concentrated forms of energy that you possess as physical creatures."
~ Seth – *The Nature of Personal Reality*

"The Truth that sets you free is that you can experience in imagination what you desire to experience in reality, and by maintaining this experience in imagination, your desire will become an actuality."
~ Neville – *The Power of Awareness*

"The activity of Ultimate Reality, the Supreme Power, resembles most closely the human experience which we call imagining."
~ Raynor C. Johnson – *Nurslings of Immortality*

Imagination is a shared faculty of perception amongst earthly and Risen beings. Any individuality, including animals and plants, manifests its own world through the perceptive faculty of imagination. Each experiential world-sphere is real, and so imagination, therefore, is not illusory.

To assist in your awakening to the reality of imagination, it will help to recall the introduction to the concept of *fields*, succinctly introduced in Chapter 4—Spirit and Science, and which will also be explored a bit more in Chapter 15—Psychospiritual Amnesia. This method of careful and gentle introduction of certain complex subjects, sustained by brief repetition, is part of the collective efforts of the Risen who are orchestrating the tapestry of this book. This higher-conscious weaving is also part of the fabric of *their* Risen imagination or Risen world-spheres—or, more aptly stated, *the imaginal*.

These world-spheres are "fields of consciousness," of and in which the individuality is more or less aware, depending on how we perceive our own self-manifested reality. This is also true for the individual units of energy that exist on the level of reality labeled as "atomic" but which are, to a much greater extent, restricted in their movements in relationship to one another. This restriction is *constriction*, and a conservative measure that provides stability for biological world-spheres. But at specifically human biological levels, *imagination is unlimited*. Biological conservation is challenged by the spontaneous and liberating element of *novelty*. Novelty is that which is new and stimulates change, or evolution, which unfolds from *within* the greater design. This change is movement amongst the infinity of world-spheres, manifesting on scales of scarcely-imaginable biological and non-biological complexity.

In spite of our current self-imposed limitations, through imagination we are able to continuously find transformational ways to locate, engage, embrace, communicate, and commune with others—wherever, whenever, and however they may be. We are "beings in movement" and "becomings in transformation." These transformational movements are the creative methods of interweaving of all things living—and remain aware that there is nothing that is *not* living. Note that "creative" is used here instead of "manifesting" for one of the very few times in this book. In this instance, creative means "fun," or more succinctly, "to enjoy." That is, to join with the drawing forth of joy from where all pleasure surges forth, and to permeate our life with that joy.

Keeping the Risen concept of weaving in mind, what we have before us, and are integrated in, is a Supreme Tapestry. There appears to be a Very Grand Design which we all follow, either in awareness or not, co-creatively or not—"creatively" again meaning "with fun." The Grand Design is a work of perfection intermingled with imperfection, solutions with problems, brilliance with faux pas, and stillness within movement. As we weave we are free to make it up as we go along in any way that pleases us, while simultaneously staying within the Grand Design as imagined by *Higher Imaginals*, of whom we are an inseparable part. The Higher Imaginals are many things, but for our purposes here it suffices to say that they are *unimaginably* advanced, evolved individuals—or Most High Selves of Authenticity. Because It is infinite in concept and execution, it's not possible to stray from the Great Design—so it's not possible to be judged for appearing to do so, or even for wanting to.

Although provocative in an illustrative way, the idea of a tapestry is a limiting concept and can be misleading. An earthly tapestry is a two-dimensional representational projection onto a three-dimensional object, used to portray three- and four-dimensional worlds—the fourth dimension being time. With the mind's eye, it is possible to expand this concept by seeing a tapestry as woven not in a flattened manner, but as interwoven from all directions and by all beings, simultaneously. Picture this happening as guided by some kind of Great Designer who is presently unknown to us from within our limited dimensional awareness. Proceed further by seeing the interweaving occurring within different kinds of time, which gives rise to movement, which is *change*. We begin to comprehend the idea of a living work of art, which is Life as we know it, and as we don't know it. Lastly, imagine that we are each a Great-Designer-In-Progress.

Our individual lives are collectively woven into Living, as imagined by Higher Imaginals, and by the greater world-spheres of individuals with whom some of us may identify as our Higher or Authentic Self, Higher Power, a Creator Deity, the Universe, God, and so on. In turn, their world-spheres are simultaneously interwoven into greater, expanded experiences of Living by yet greater awarenesses, forever without end. Or as Tim likes to say, *infinooty.*

When our own field of individuated universe connects with another's there is an expansion of both. "Expansion" is another word for "heaven," and Tim is hinting that later he'll share a bit about his experience of this expansion. All universes intersect and interpenetrate at a point in some space and in some time. Our capacity for joy is directly a result of our conscious awareness of the interpenetration of co-manifested universes. A sense of humor and pleasure are one's ship and the breezes that move it upon this cosmic ocean of awareness.

Like all individuals, Tim and I exist as focused, intelligent points of light in an immeasurable constellation of Intelligent Light. We continuously get better at finding each other's individual points of light and then intersecting—it's like playing hide-and-seek in an endless swarm of fireflies—and constantly surprising ourselves in childlike delight when finding one another with and within our minds and souls. These shivery discoveries are the evidence of the unlimited gifts that our imaginations are able to reveal to us.

Our imaginations also enable us to find or be found by other spirit forms. Souls in the Risen realms learn to recognize one another as individualized patterns and as points of spirit-light. The patterns also indicate relationships between individuals. This is reflective of the current earthly world-view of waves and particles, which simultaneously exist as separate and yet also as one. The process of recognition between the Risen and the yet-to-Rise is not as direct as it is amongst the Risen because of the vast differences in self-awareness and in awareness of time. The human faculty of imagination exists as a tool for those who are still in the earthly material body, enabling initial and sustained connections with beings in other dimensions, including the Risen.

As one of our sensory faculties, *imagination is real.* In our predominately Eurocentric world culture, imagination is unfortunately believed to be synonymous with "not real," or as a kind of safe hallucination. If we should say we believe the imagined to be real we are thought to be delusional and no longer considered "normal"—and in some instances no longer considered safe to be around. This is yet another kind of "reasoning" tactic of the ego-mind in its drive to sustain control through its simulate selves.

Reason is a mental tool developed by the ego-mind to assist in making choices out of the myriad, spontaneous events of novelty constantly welling up from one's intersection with others' world-spheres. But the plowshare of reason has been turned by the ego-mind into a sword of judgment, and seldom used for nonviolent responses to the world-spheres of others on earth.

Imagination is considered a key and crucial factor in many of the earthly therapeutic approaches to exploring, understanding, and healing the human mind-body and psyche. These semi-scientific approaches have never been totally clear about whether or not they can easily acknowledge and accept imagination as its own reality. Tim and I have experienced that the power of imagination is literally able to open doors to new realities. This power can be activated in a very simple way by anyone. If you are able to imagine something in such a way that it's as if you can virtually feel it—such as the texture of cloth, or the feel of someone's skin, or a lover's breath upon your cheek—then you have connected with a reality generated by your own imagination.

If you want to connect with a Risen loved one, first sit in a chair or lie down in a bed, close your eyes, and begin imagining that this person is literally right there with you. Your body's wisdom will adjust and regulate its breathing. Mentally send out a strong and *positive* emotional greeting to your loved one. An emotional greeting carries a feeling with it, such as contentment, security, happiness. *Relief* is an especially powerful feeling, so see if you can feel relief, *as if* you've already made contact—"as if" is a form of projecting. Keep in mind that you cannot force anyone to do something they don't want to, so it's appropriate to invite someone to join you rather than insisting on it. Invite your loved one to join you in this experiment, and begin to share back and forth with one another what you initially imagine you are each trying to feel. Imagine the kind of conversation you might have in this moment. Share feelings and loving thoughts, and don't listen to your ego-mind telling you that you're delusional or hypnotizing yourself—beam love upon it to silence it. And then use that love to welcome your Risen One.

In your mind, feel yourself take their hand, or feel them leaning against you or hugging you or putting an arm around your waist, just as they would have done when they were on the earth. Let yourself feel this contact as fully as possible, and take it as far as you can—relax into it. Feel yourself touching their fingers—can you feel their fingernails? Are they long or short? Feel yourself touching what they're wearing—is it a familiar cotton shirt or something soft and worn? Can you see anything with your mind's eye? Maybe you can smell them, but if not, try to remember this person's particular smell. Perhaps you can feel the warmth of their arm directly, or as felt through cloth.

When you can feel something as if it were real, you've made the connection—it's that straightforward. *Now* allow yourself to feel relief, which is another word for "release"—and also another way to signal, "I'm receptive and ready." Continue to be aware of any comments by the ego-mind. Because the process is usually so exquisitely subtle, the contact between you and your Risen loved one will probably go on for a while before you consciously recognize that it's actually happening. These subtle feelings are, in fact, the spiritual senses, and were activated by your human sensory faculty of imagination.

~ 14 ~

These words may not make conscious sense at this time,
but my spiritual senses comprehend and retain
this knowledge for Authentic Self.

The fact that you can feel something indicates you have connected with something. It's possible to feel something apparently non-physical and invisible because your astral body is feeling the tangibility of the experience while intermingled within the same space-time as your physical body. Being a body, your astral form has its own senses, just like your physical body. The astral senses are part of your spiritual senses. Your Risen loved ones no longer have physical bodies that match yours, but they *do* each have a bodily component of "astral essence," and it is with the corresponding senses between your spiritual bodies that this very real connection is achieved. Your own physical and astral bodies are still intimately intermeshed, which intercommunicate about the various things sensed. Your astral body informs your physical body about its experiences, but because of its higher vibrating nature the feeling is much more subtle, which is often ignored, as misdirected by the stronger, controlling ego-mind. It takes a great deal of genuine self-awareness that gives rise to confidence in one's own abilities to sense spiritual things and events. Once we've found the light of Authentic Self-awareness, our doubts will fade away.

This kind of sensing may sound so simple as to make one think it's not real. But why make it any more complex than necessary? It's often a matter of changing one's belief system about this kind of spiritual experience. Some people will believe it's real, and others will believe it's not. Which kind of person would you prefer to be in this instance? Make up your own mind about it and then try it. And then listen, watch, feel, learn, relax, and enjoy.

If you're resistant to this process or insist you can't do it, try something a bit simpler. Find an object that has a lot of tangibility to it, like a freshly laundered bath towel. Best of all is an object or article of clothing that belonged to your transitioned loved one. Get familiar with this object while your eyes are closed, touching it all over, rubbing it against your arms and face, and carefully noticing the different textures and smells. Playing meaningful music may amplify the emotional resonance. Now open your eyes and examine it all over, down to the finest details, and commit them to memory as well. Then put it out of sight and quietly repose with your physical eyes closed. See if you can remember what the object felt, smelled, and looked like. *You* will know if you're successful but the success also depends on your acceptance that something real is happening. As strange as it may sound, if you can connect with an imagined piece of cloth, you can connect with the Risen.

If, for whatever reason, this last experiment seems to have failed, try something even simpler. Think of sucking a lemon and notice how your mouth begins to water almost immediately. You will have quick proof that even if there's not a lemon within miles, your body is telling you that there *is* a lemon easily accessible, in all its sour glory, right there in your mind. If you're not sure about the truth of something, your mind may lie but your body will not. The lemon exists as a seemingly non-physical thought form in your mind, but your body is able to accept that it has an actual reality. The reaction of crying when remembering a sad event or laughing at a happy one is on the same level of this truthful reality awareness. The ability to utilize your emotions will greatly enhance and energize your imaginal attempts at connecting with the Risen.[30]

Once you've connected with your loved one and have allowed yourself to accept the reality of the experience, it's up to you to decide where you want to go from there. Begin talking to one another, perhaps discussing things left unsaid before the person's transition. Tell each other your stories, about how you've been and what you're doing. It's also very nice to just quietly rest in one another's presence without words or thoughts—to commune. Remember when you used to do that together?

At the beginning of this book the check-list of experiences included "finding yourself, for no apparent reason, in a spontaneous conversation with your transitioned loved one." It was suggested that the communication really *is* taking place, simply because you've begun responding to *their* having first reached out and saying "hello." Now you can better understand how this works, and that the Risen utilize a similar process in reaching out to us.

This kind of connecting effort has to be made more than once and on a regular basis to achieve results and maintain the ability to do so. There must be a building up of the astral energies involved to intensify and sustain resonance and contact, or else the signal fades away. The vibrations of the physical world are just too pervasive and interfere with inter-astral contact, dampening and overwhelming it, and resulting in something we call "psychospiritual amnesia." It's not uncommon for a person attempting this contact to just forget about doing it again, even after achieving results—I speak from personal experience.

The Risen also must strive to sustain contact. Their world's vibrations also interfere with the connection. The beauties and wonders of the Risen geographies distract them constantly, just as our worldly affairs distract us here.

---

[30] I've actually met someone who, although having sucked on a lemon before, had so little imaginative awareness that he was unable to recollect the sourness in any physical way. Unfortunately for him this meant he had to find some lemons and practice. – *AG*

While on earth and just before he had begun to get seriously ill, Tim had begun to study Eastern spiritualities and their meditative practices that utilize the mind's ability to visualize—and to imagine—in order to become aware of other states of his consciousness. This gave him some advantages when we were learning how to connect inter-astralphysically.

"True, August, but I had to overcome previously-held beliefs. It's often a matter of language. 'Other states of consciousness' is the same as saying 'geographies' or 'planes of existence,' 'spheres of awareness,' 'multi-universes,' 'the kingdom within,' and so on. These phrases might make sense to some people, but until we can truly understand that imagination is the means by which we can access these places, they will just remain unreachable castles in the sky. But—alors, revenons à nos moutons."

"You pulled *that* out of my mental French 101 section, didn't you? I don't think I've heard that expression since high school. Well, then—let us return to our sheep. Now, which sheep were we talking about?"

"Imaginal ones."

"Right. I was sharing about how your terrestrial studies of Eastern approaches to other conscious states gave you insights and access to various writers on earth. Later, you brought to my attention one particular writer, a distinguished French scholar of Islam—oh, *now* I get it."

Anyway, this *French* scholar, Henry Corbin, was a foremost translator of Islamic texts, particularly of Persian and Sufi mystics. Certain Risen Ones led me to Corbin's precious essay titled *Mundus Imaginalis, or The Imaginary and the Imaginal*. It examines esoteric Persian spirituality, and Corbin struggled—as did the English translator of Corbin's original French—to find the correct word to describe what most Western translators would transcribe as "imaginary."

Twelfth–century Persian spiritual literature is intensely complex and practically alien to a Westerner's way of thinking. Yet Corbin found ways to make the Persian spiritual concept of imagination more accessible to us. There must have been Risen Ones interested in his work, for an inspired solution was found. He chose the Latin phrase *mundus imaginalis* to conceptualize the Persian "World of the Image." Corbin invented the Latin word, *imaginalis*—or *imaginal* in English—to differentiate from our Western concept of imagination—that is, *real* versus *not real*. He utilized Latin because its terminology of technical precision offered a fixed point of reference against which the various, suggestive equivalents of Western languages could be compared.[31]

One particular text relates in great detail the wondrous, infinite worlds that exist outside our material earthly awareness, as reported by Persian mystics

---

[31] *Henry Corbin, Swedenborg and Esoteric Islam,* trans. Leonard Fox (West Chester, PA: Swedenborg Foundation, 1995), 1.

who routinely traveled beyond earthly consciousness. They recognized with great familiarity the suprasensory world of the Soul that is beside and beyond our physical sensory world, as well as another world inhabited by pure, archangelic intelligences. These three universes correspond to what Corbin called the three "organs of knowledge," which are the physical senses, imagination, and intellect—or body, spirit, and mind. It is useful to realize that soul and mind are interchangeable here as well, as they are so closely linked by the imaginal. Together, this triad of body, mind, and spirit becomes the bridge extending from our world to those worlds where we resurrect as Risen Ones.

~ 15 ~

These words may not make conscious sense at this time,
but my spiritual senses comprehend and retain
this knowledge for Authentic Self.

This bridge is actually a world itself—the *mundus imaginalis*—a world of being which the Persian mystics experienced as real as the world of the physical senses, and of the intellect as well. To get to this world requires one of our faculties of perception, the imaginative power, which Corbin cautioned to not confuse with our modern concept of fantasy or with that which produces only "the imaginary." Corbin realized that he could have just used the words "fantasy" or "imaginary" to translate this concept of the imaginative power, but he strongly intuited otherwise. The organ that perceives this Reality is the cognitive function of the imagination, the imaginative consciousness, which uses energy to image.[32]

Corbin delineated this organ as the "Active Imagination," and more finely as the "Spiritual Imagination."[33] He noted that first, the Spiritual Imagination is a pure spiritual faculty, which is independent of our physical body and therefore continues to exist after the body is gone. Secondly, the Spiritual Imagination is a power of *cognition*, where imaginal consciousness and imaginal perception have their own cognitive function.[34] "Cognition" is another way of saying, "knowing, as apprehended by the understanding." There are infinities

---

[32] For a detailed expansion on the philosophy of the divine imaginal, see *The Zermatt Dialogues* (London: Macmillan & Co., 1931) and *The Oberland Dialogues* (London: Macmillan & Co., 1939) by mystic-philosopher Douglas Fawcett, whose works were expounded upon by Raynor C. Johnson in *Nurslings of Immortality* (Hodder and Stoughton, Ltd., 1957). Both were acquainted with the Persian literature, as probably introduced by Corbin.
[33] Corbin, 2, 8–9.
[34] Corbin, 15–16.

upon infinities of worlds awaiting our apprehension beyond whatever present one we might be in. Corbin emphasized that to the Persian mystics, the *mundus imaginalis* appeared more real to them than "normal" mundane reality. Further, we are to be assured that these Persian travelers, or "witnesses" as Corbin labeled them, were perfectly conscious that they had been *otherwhere* and were not mentally disturbed. They not only cognitively understood one reality from another but they knew which one they were in and when they were in it—and apparently without fear, which is banished by understanding.

Corbin expounded in great detail on these "topographies," which the twelfth-century Persian mystics knew with great intimacy. They gave this Reality, as well as many others, a most provocative descriptor—*climate*. This brings to mind my use of the word "geographies" to describe the intermediate astral worlds. Is *climate* visible or invisible, or both? Does it change, like the weather, or *is* it the weather? Is it similar to the social climate of a room of people, or to our own inner emotional world, or to a relationship? Can all these climates exist simultaneously—can they interpenetrate in the same space and at the same time? Our ability to perceptually access and manifest worlds through imaging, by using the spiritual imaginal organ, is what the astral planes are all about. Perhaps Tim might be able to share a bit of his understanding and experience from a Risen perspective.

"Avec plaisir, mon coeur. You and I are the bridge, which is a world unto itself and is also *who* we are—body, mind, and spirit. That is why the way to go is *within*, starting at the level of bodily awareness and from there journeying inward—it can be found nowhere outside us. While on earth, the more you can embody your mind in the awareness of Authentic Self, the closer you can draw near to a Risen loved one. I had to learn this after I had Risen, and in a new body. You and I both experienced and grew to understand that the imaging faculty, or the imaginal, is a faculty that is real and accessible. You had to learn to confront and reject your ego-mind's defense that said this faculty wasn't real, whereas I was able to quickly grasp the fact, since my ego-mind no longer had its hold on me, and I had more direct access to Risen Healers.

"Using this imaging faculty is often haphazard and clumsy at first for many who are newly Risen. With guidance and practice it becomes the main way to manifest Risen Reality—meaning, our life. On earth, art is said to imitate life. Here, art *is* life and so life is art. *Imaging* is how we use our Risen minds to realize—to make real—our environments and everything in them.

"When one's mental processes are active and fluid, the environment will also reflect this by change and adjustment. This can get chaotic and confusing if you are emotionally unstable and unable to control your feelings, which are deepened and more intense when Risen.

"Being in a dark mental place will outwardly express as being in a dark physical Risen geography. The more positive the feelings are behind the thoughts, the more positive the outward expression, and the more light that is expressed in the environment. This is the same kind of process that occurs on earth but it's so slowed down from the density of material reality that most people are generally unaware that they are seeing it as it is happening. Neither do they see how their thoughts and feelings are creating their reality, nor how the ego-mind misuses the sacred gift of their imagination. This dense slowness can generate less-than-positive feelings, but once you're Risen so much of that simply drops away. If it doesn't, there are Risen Healers who will present themselves to help you work with any unresolved emotions to which you're clinging—which, by the way, takes an awful lot of effort to otherwise maintain.

"The Healers never force you to do anything you don't want to do—they only ask and wait for an answer. Saying 'no' is always honored, but never judged nor can it ever disqualify you. Assenting to assistance brings one to see that the Universe is here to provide never-ending opportunities to say 'yes.'

"Often, saying 'yes' will take more time than it takes to resolve the issue. You'll hardly even notice the issue missing because you won't even remember that it was ever there—it's all over in an instant. Then the inherent beauty within you will be released with each imaginative step taken, appearing as whatever landscape, structure, town, country, or urban environment that you could possibly want—on land, under the sea, in the sky, or amongst the stars. Here, the sky is not the limit.

"Relationships are also unlimited. As I healed and learned to communicate with you through my imagination, August, our relationship began to amplify, expand, and transform—it transmuted."

"A good word to describe it, Tim. I certainly experienced the imaginal in our relationship and my own life as a transmutation—a literal metamorphosis. The resulting changes merged into the numinosum that united our spirits, minds, and bodies, transcending the ordinary. This metamorphosis eventually resulted in the extraordinary event of our being *physically* together."

"I bet we've got everyone's attention now, August."

"I'm sure, Tim. But before readers attempt to try to understand the implications about something known as "materialization," they need to be acquainted with the concept of something called 'numinous,' which best describes the events about which we are going to speak."

A *phenomenon* is an occurrence we tangibly perceive while experiencing it—an observable material fact. A *noumenon* is a "thing-in-itself," independent of our perception of it and considered to be separate from the mind, and unknown. Phenomena belong to our material world, and noumena *elsewhere*.

Words fail when confronted with something numinous, and so verbal language must often be left behind like a boat on the edge of a river. Instead, this numinosity must be experienced, which is like jumping into the river. This is the experience that skeptical and non-skeptical researchers alike must initially undergo before they can proceed with any serious investigations of mediumship. Our experience with the Risen will depend on our willingness and trust to lift our feet from the river bottom and let it carry us to an unknown destination—or *is* it unknown? This destination is actually Creator Source, so perhaps it is not unknown but just forgotten, and too large to be contained within our current human conscious awareness. The numinous is something that is simultaneously distinct yet ambiguous; remote yet present; known yet unknown. It grows and glows into transcendence, for that which is numinous is also luminous.

Numinosity is that *something*, that particular sensation one might associate with a certain holiday. We speak of it as "the spirit of a thing." The spirit of Christmas is very different from that of Hallowe'en. The experience of time during these festivals becomes altered or ceases entirely. "Numinous," from the Latin *numen*, literally means "a nod of the head"—"head" meaning "Highest Self"—so a nod from the Divine. So a numinous event—a *numinosum*—is an experience of Authentic Self, which is gifted to us as a grace from Creator Source. "Grace" can be generally defined as "the all-nourishing substance of the universe which *is* Creator Source, and freely given *by* Creator Source *to* Creator Source."

Authentic Self has no limits, no boundaries, and no end. We may experience ourselves as being within Creator Source, which makes it seem as if inspiration comes from outside us. But inspiration comes to the attention of our outer layers of consciousness from Creator Source within, not from without—because there is no "without." The further one's consciousness is turned away from Creator Source, the less one is consciously aware of It—and so It may seem further away. Distance is not measured here in physical terms but by the focus of attention. Inspiration quickens one's spirit-energy like a pebble dropped in a still pool of water, sending ripples of vibration outward.

"Kind of like the way *I* dropped in."

"Very much like that, Tim."

FOURTEEN

BREAKTHROUGH

"My existence is from you and your appearance is through me.
Yet if I had not appeared, you would not have been."
~ Ibn al-'Arabi

When Tim and I say that we've been physically together since the event of his transition, we literally mean he was corporeal; embodied; *physically real*. We know this is asking a lot for anyone to accept, and most likely strains one's sense of rationality. It was just so for me.

Rationality, or reason, is a mental tool to help us make sense of what we perceive in our terrestrial world. Although "seeing is believing," it was still a gradual process for me to arrive to where I believed what I saw. The anchor of rationality has to be pulled up out of the sand of our harbor of beliefs in order to let our imaginal ship begin the process of traveling from non-experience to experience. Admittedly, it's not realistic to expect others to accept something they haven't seen. I can only share about something I experienced, as well as the process as it developed for me, which I eventually came to believe and then to know as something substantial and tangible. The experience was also unique for Tim and he will share it from his own perspective.

At this moment Tim is now resting but continues to be observantly aware. The Risen *do* rest, but not like us. It's more like a state of repose, at least as I comprehend it. While keeping an eye on things from his hammock, Tim is urging me to share the pages from my journal that record the most singularly amazing event in my life—his first physical manifestation after his transition.

"This morning I noticed that my very aged cat, Bridget, seemed unwell and wasn't eating, nor had she used the litter box in a couple days. With a sinking feeling that the cancer had worsened and this was the beginning of the end, I made an appointment with the vet for a few hours later. In the meantime, I groomed and spoke to my furry daughter candidly, reminding her of 'The Plan'—after passing over she would immediately go to Tim. I have this conversation with her every night as she rests on my chest while I read myself to sleep. She always seems to understand this and looks at me as if there is no need to go over it yet again. If only I could have such confident wisdom.

"The visit at the vet's turned out much better than expected, involving some changes in medication that would make both our lives a little easier for a little while longer. But I was still very stressed out and could feel one of my migraines coming on. Back out on the street, I was about to return the way I originally traveled. But something—I don't know what—made me stop to consider that I might walk the other way to a subway that was somewhat closer. I wasn't too keen on this idea because it took me via a route I didn't like. Yet somehow I found myself walking in the new direction, carrying Bridget in her box with the clear lid which allowed her to see out.

"The train platform was deserted but for a few people. Someone was sitting alone far down on the south end. It was too far to really make out any details, but my very first thought was "That looks like *Tim*." I think it might have been his posture that made me think this, because Tim had a funny way of sitting very straight and stiff due to a back problem. I saw that there was an empty seat there, so curiosity made me walk all the way down to it and sit on the same bench with this stranger. While putting Bridget's carrier between myself and this person, I noticed that he *did* actually look quite like Tim but was much younger, perhaps in his late teens or early 20's (Tim had died in his early 40's.) This person's hair was very much the same—long and full, quite unlike today's very short styles, and it seemed to glow as if golden, although it was dark brown like Tim's. He also had on a funny cloth hat, which was off his head and flung over onto his back, suspended by a cord around his neck. The hat seemed somehow familiar, and this vague recollection set me to daydreaming. I began to feel calm and floating, almost trance-like. He was reading a book but I couldn't see the title.

"As I placed the carrier down, he turned and looked down at it, smiled at Bridget through the clear plastic top, and then looked up at me and smiled. It was the strangest expression and it also reminded me of something I'd seen before. It was a smug smile, very much like the 'cat who got the canary' grin that Tim often had when he was thinking secret thoughts. I smiled back, feeling warmed by being acknowledged by this total stranger. And I continued to feel a growing sense of something peculiar going on.

"Again I noticed his posture, and how much it reminded me of Tim. At the moment I had this thought, the young man immediately slouched down in a totally opposite posture, almost as if he had heard what I was thinking. I wondered if I had unconsciously said something aloud or conveyed something by my body language to make him do such a thing—it was very weird.

"The train arrived, we both got on, and he sat across from me. He still had that enigmatic expression on his face, as if he possessed some amusing secret. Sitting directly across from him, I studied his face as he read and noticed that his skin was perfect and unblemished. In fact, it was the most exquisitely beautiful skin I'd ever seen—it didn't look real. His features were so perfectly composed, his eyes so well formed and beautiful, combined with that wonderful hair, that he hardly looked like he belonged to this world. I wondered if he was a tourist, and what country he might be from. Yet he had such an air of peace and composure about him, so very unlike most tourists who are always excited and nervous about being in a big, scary city and alone on a New York subway.

"I then noticed that he was reading a large and bright yellow paperback book, with the words "Sanskrit Primer" in oversized black letters on it. It struck me that it looked more like a stage prop than a book. It seemed extremely odd for a young man to be reading such an esoteric, academic subject. And how very like *me*, because *I* had a Sanskrit primer somewhere in my bookcases. At the very instant I had this thought the young man suddenly appeared as if he might burst out laughing. I wondered what could be so amusing in a textbook on Sanskrit?

"It occurred to me that, in some way, he was completely aware of what I was thinking, which provided him with much amusement. How on earth could someone read my mind so easily? I began to feel slightly panicky and wondered what to do next. Shield my thoughts? At that exact moment he smiled even more but never looked up once at me. He really looked like a small child with an enormous secret. His amusement was infectious and I felt myself smiling as well. What mystery was unfolding here before me?

"He appeared very absorbed in his book, so I tried to unobtrusively observe him. He wore very casual but rather dated clothes, reminding me of what boys wore when I was in my teens. They were clearly several decades out of date in style, but very clean and perfect as if new. Yet they didn't quite look new at all, somehow appearing worn and comfortable. His sneakers were of a very old style, but they also didn't look old or worn out. I was starting to feel a welling up inside of me, a *something* I couldn't describe. Reality seemed to be getting gold and blurry about the edges, as if time and space were coming to a standstill.

"The train came to the next stop. He looked over once more at Bridget and then up at me, gave me that incredible '*I've got a secret*' smile and then quickly got off. As the train doors closed behind him I looked out to see where he went, but he had vanished—I couldn't see him anywhere. There were no exits nearby, and I puzzled over where he could have possibly gone.

"As the train continued on its journey I felt myself shaking my head as if trying to wake up. Then I realized that we had only gone one stop. How strange that he should just get on and then almost immediately get off, when he could have walked the few blocks on such a nice day. During the ride the rest of the way home I couldn't get what had happened out of my mind, and kept mentally running through all the details that were etching themselves in my memory.

"It suddenly dawned on me that Tim had once had a hat just like that, many years ago and when I had first met him. He sometimes wore it off his head, letting it rest on his back, held round his neck by a cord. One day we had been out walking and when we returned to his apartment he pulled too hard when he took the hat off, breaking the cord. In typical Tim fashion it was flung off somewhere into a corner, never to resurface again.

"Then I recalled that after we had broken up, a mutual friend who still spent time with him remarked that Tim had 'got religion' and was 'getting involved in some cult.' He was trying to learn Sanskrit, which was driving everyone crazy as he was acting so knowledgeable and self-righteous about it—very much a Tim affectation.

"In that moment I got all cold and shivery. 'My god,' I thought, 'That *was* Tim! Wasn't it? But no, it *couldn't* be!'

"Was I dreaming? I actually pinched my arm—something I'd never done before in my life. It was as if I was angry with myself for even thinking such things. Didn't I have enough to worry about with Bridget being so sick? But I couldn't get it out of my head. Unable to help myself, I began to cry right there on the train. After a minute I managed to stop the tears and then just sat very still, thinking like mad as the train raced along the tracks.

"When I got home I immediately went to the mantel, where I keep the two photos Tim's mother had given me after he died. One appears to be a very early passport photo of him, only about two inches square. It had been taken long before I had known him, and he looks to be maybe 16 or 17. It's quite different from the Tim I had known, when he was in his late-30s. The other photo that I have was taken shortly before he had died—this was the Tim I knew and the image I carried in my memory.

"Looking now at the photo of the young Tim, I realized that *this* was the same young man on the train! The one I had just seen who had been so gloriously healthy, glowing, and perfect; so composed, yet with deep humor welling up from within him, so that he exuded peace and hilarity at the same time. In fact, it was the same kind of expression that my grandmother had when she had appeared to me in a dream, which wasn't a dream but a visitation, many years ago. She also had the same quietly composed but smiling expression and yet had never said a word. She looked loving and glowing, smiling at me with total understanding. *That* was what was so familiar to me when I first saw the young man's expression.

"As unbelievable as it sounds, it would seem that Tim had made a visibly material appearance, to assure me that he was and would be there for Bridget, perhaps responding to my worry—and that he was there for me."

Three days later—

"Today I had the opportunity to tell a trusted friend. And in that telling, the strengthened realization of what had happened seems to have only reinforced my memory and convictions, instead of sounding insanely ridiculous."

One week later—

"I now realize that I've been in a very strange, altered consciousness for a week or more since this happened, as if I'm in a kind of quiet shock. I suppose I am. I still need to talk about it. And now I find myself wondering—*what next*? I suppose I should be excited but right now I feel puzzled and strangely almost without emotion. I guess I will be excited and emotional in time. I've been reading and studying a lot about mediums and the afterlife since Tim's appearance on my bed, and I wonder if it's all given me some sort of a brain fever. But it wasn't *anything* like I'd supposed, and now I see that this is the way it *would* be with such things. I have memories of such visitations from spirit people during my early childhood, but those are very old recollections, which have taken on the worn luster of fond reminiscences—and as a child I had thought nothing of them.

"But *this* experience was fantastically different, more than I ever could have conceived. It was not only real—it was *more* than real. Those golden moments were a bubble of true reality, compared with the grey, two-dimensional existence I'm experiencing now as I write."

I cry whenever re-reading these entries, replaying what I felt then—shock, elation, relief, confusion. The sight of that "Tim expression"—the "cat-that-caught-the-canary" look—is as clear now as it was then. Even though his body was so young and perfect, unlike any way I'd ever seen him before, his facial expression was what told me that it could only have been Tim. It was worth more than a thousand words or a thousand photos. That expression held all the secrets ever known and unknown about the soul I knew and loved as Tim. It was also something I had never thought I would see again.

Years later since that experience, I not only know that I saw him then, but that I've seen him many times since.

I also know that I was impressed by Tim's guides and teachers, as well as mine—who were all guiding the orchestration of the event—to write it all down as soon as I could sit still long enough. Later on he would refer to it in the way his Risen Teacher-Healers deemed it—"a blissful occurrence veiled as a spontaneous event."

"August, I can explain more about it now. I was actually *transported* into the experience and then sustained in it. Because I was so new at this process it was conducted after I was placed into a deep state of inactivity, or what you would call sleep—it was like a dream to me. I had to let go and trust my guides, who were with me during the event. They caused me to have the equivalent of an earthly out-of-body experience. A special 'body' was constructed for me, allowing me to traverse through the various astral levels until I came closest to your state of emotional intensity. Your emotional state, which seemed to you to be very depressed and low-vibrating, was also a *physical* state. Your spiritual vibrations were actually much higher than normal in those moments. Your present life circumstances had brought you to a place of complete vulnerability and openness. You had been emotionally and mentally approaching a fluctuating state where this vulnerability could change into helplessness and fear, or else into a yielding to energies greater than your worries.

"You might not have been aware of it, but you had a great deal of prayerful energy placed around you from loving friends on and off the earth. As a child you had learned about prayer from your parents, and prayed every night before sleep. That early and continued exposure to using prayer served you well, for you developed a special understanding about what prayer could be, and that it was energy, there to help. You automatically and intuitively responded to your spiritual sense of this prayer energy by opening yourself up to it. This you did quite unconsciously, mainly because your mind had been lulled into a befuddled state from all the stress you were under. Your opening up to this loving prayer energy was just what was needed for my loving energy to connect and join with your state of awareness in those moments.

"And yes, our guides had orchestrated every single detail that day. They impressed you to take that train, and arranged for the exact time of your appointment. There were myriad details, such as the time of day, the amount and quality of light, the air temperature and the number of people around you. Remember how I appeared on the train in the middle of the afternoon, and yet nobody else was on the train but us, *and* in one of the largest cities in the world? They arranged for that as well. It's hard to even begin to fathom the complexity involved behind such planning."

"Tim, it seems like I should have seen at least a few people around me, but I saw only you on the train. Nor was I ever aware of any people in spirit around me, even though it sounds like there were quite a few. What was your awareness of it like? If your astral body was asleep and your consciousness was in a special body, were you then dreaming? Were you at all conscious of what was going on?"

"Did your parents tell you that you asked a lot of questions as a child?"

"Yes, and they still do."

"You haven't changed a bit. We are going to have so much fun when you're finally Risen, August, just like the old days. Well. I will say that I was conscious within a kind of lucid dream state. I was aware of my body, my clothes, the book—which really were props, as you seemed to notice, all carefully selected out of my earthly memories by my teachers because of their particular significance to you. Even the location—the bench on the train platform and the seat on the train—were specifically chosen.

"I was aware of you and Bridget but there was also a cloud of intense golden light around us. It was all very surreal to me. This was a sphere of awareness, made of the light that was the culmination of all the countless elements that were arranged to lead up to this moment, and which was, as you felt, timeless. I could barely see you—it was like trying to look through a mist of light so densely bright that you appeared to be in a golden fog. But I could feel you so strongly—including your confusion—that it made me feel silly and want to laugh! There seemed to be nothing solid between us, as if I couldn't reach or step across to touch you—which wouldn't have been possible anyway. I know you've wondered why it never entered your mind to just simply say something to me, or to get up and sit next to me or even try to touch me. But neither of us could have done any of those things, as there were forces at work that acted as barriers. Not that anything dangerous would have been allowed to occur, but any kind of attempt to make physical contact would simply have ended the experience, of which you'd then have no conscious memory. This psychospiritual amnesia is actually our next topic.

"Along with your own guides, other healers accompanied you home on the train, staying close by to help you deal with what had happened and to continue completing the process. They impressed you to write it down and then to later share it with another trusted person. This practice of trustful sharing is one of the most crucial components of getting into the flow of real life and letting it take us to the next level of being, no matter where we are, as embodied or Risen."

"Can I ask another question?"

"You want to know why, right?"

"Of course! *Why* did you come to us that day? Why was all that energy and planning put into this fantastic and complex production?"

"Simply because, Dear Heart, our loving relationship did not come to an end, although it might have seemed to because of the way things looked before and after my transition. Neither was it waiting to start up again when we were both Risen. In truth, it had never stopped. This event was and is part of our relationship. Whether or not those on the earth are conscious of it, all loving relationships continue without ceasing, even when there is bodily separation. Just because someone's loved one travels to a far-off country doesn't mean the relationship is over. The same holds true where one is Risen and the other is not—the relationship isn't put on hold. It might be different for a while but all relationships are always in flux, including those bound together by unloving emotions."

"Tim, you're absolutely right. Part of me had always known on some level that we were still connected. But there's always that cultural thing, pressuring us to withdraw our feelings and awareness and thoughts from the transitioned person, to get over it and on with our lives. What a relief it is to know that *that* is the illusion, while the relationship is the reality."

"You can't get rid of me so easily, my friend."

"So who's trying?"

FIFTEEN

PSYCHOSPIRITUAL AMNESIA

"Lulled in the countless chambers of the brain,
Our thoughts are linked by many a hidden chain;
Awake but one, and in, what myriads rise!"
~ Alexander Pope

"We cannot visualize another world ruled by quite
other laws, the reason being that we live in a specific
world which has helped to shape our minds and
establish our basic psychic conditions."
~ C. G. Jung

Physically writing about a numinous experience—an experience that
occurs outside of one's ordinary perceptual awareness—can be a crucial
part of the process of Risen contact. It contains the potential to
construct a conscious and lasting Authentic Self-awareness of the numinous
event. We must diligently labor to retain such events *immediately* afterward, or
the original impact will be quickly lost—what little memories are left will fade
to nothing. On earth, memories are experienced as events that exist in the past,
but a numinous event occurs outside terrestrial space-time. It resides in a
higher-vibrating field that is accessible to both Risen and non-Risen.

There is a particular experience that may arise from Risen and other
numinous events that can best be termed "psychospiritual amnesia." Many
reports from others about their Risen contacts confirm the existence of this
frustrating phenomenon, which is subtle yet exceptionally powerful.

The ego-mind tends to have this reaction automatically to strange and
intense events. Immediately after the event the ego-mind memory function of
our physical body retains only what it decides it experienced as a physical
event, and for as long as it believes it was such. The ego-mind reacts quickly to
challenge the reality of a numinous occurrence, and encourages us to deny its
validity, physical or otherwise. Because of our inability to gain control over the
ego-mind's reaction, it usually gains control over Authentic Self's chance to

make the first response. Almost immediately after the event our recall begins to deteriorate until there's nothing left, other than perhaps just a very faint wisp of *something*. All too soon we will give up trying to recall what it was. Forgetting is what the ego-mind thinks it needs to have happen because it's trying to survive, while leading us to believe it's helping us deal with our discomfort—something it cannot do in actuality.

For those who do not have the benefit of a strong belief system that allows for the acceptance of such numinous events, this kind of forgetting is not necessarily regretful. Because of the general lack of empathetic support around bereavement in our society, some people may be mentally and emotionally better off when the memories are lessened in any way—at least temporarily. Ideally, learning how to empower ourselves by developing an appropriate belief system will lead to symptomatic relief and an eventual foundation of knowledge-based faith in our loved ones' survival. This kind of learning involves *unlearning*, and takes time. Alas, modern society has developed a preference for instant gratification.

Rupert Sheldrake, a contemporary theoretical biologist who has caused no little amount of controversy across many scientific disciplines, has offered some further ideas about the mind that may help to expand this concept of psychospiritual amnesia. Although Sheldrake is not the first to suggest these kinds of ideas about the mind, the Risen have chosen to use his model in this instance because it presently comes closest to what they feel the non-Risen can comprehend about the subject. Having introduced some concepts about *fields* earlier in Chapter 4–Spirit and Science, they continue to build upon them here.

We tend to think of experiences as either "inside" or "outside" the brain. The brain is associated with our mind and memories, and we often interchange the three as if they're all the same. Psychospiritual amnesia seems to be a kind of localized occurrence, as if what happens occurs only within the physical brain. Its effects also seem influenced by external influences.

In his book, *A New Science of Life: The Hypothesis of Morphic Resonance*, Sheldrake suggests that memory is not stored in the brain, which is a kind of tuning system, rather than a device for storing memories. Our brain resonates within a *morphic* or *morphogenic field*. This resonance is a form-shaping field, an invisible organization structure wherein all experiential information is recorded and stored. One example is a magnetic field, which is simultaneously within and around a magnet. Relatedly, the earth's gravitational field is within and around the earth.[35] A morphic field is within and around our brain and body, a concept that renders useless the idea of an "inside" and an "outside" to a human being. Recalling the idea of fields of imaginal awareness introduced earlier, our individual and collective universes are also neither inside nor

---

[35] Electromagnetism and gravity are information—energy in form. They are light in formation.

outside anything, and so we can potentially experience them simultaneously.

Morphogenic fields are patterns that structure our reality. Older, primal societies have been well aware that the forms of our experiences are shaped by something greater than us, and of which we are simultaneously a part. Modern, "civilized" societies have contracted the mind into the idea that the mind exists only within the confines of our physical skulls.

Morphic resonance expands Carl Jung's vision of a collective unconscious—the humanity's collective memory—and how we tune in to a background resonance to those aspects, myths, dreams, and experiences that resonate with our own. For example, we have an experience which then becomes part of the greater morphic field. When we use our brains to tune in to this field we find a particular energy that we shape into a memory. The brain resonates or vibrates with our own and other similar memories. Thus we find other resonant fields of reference and can tune in to the memories of other people and in to collective human memory. Sheldrake's concept of a morphogenic field suggests that this principle operates in one's entire universe—not at just the singular human level, but at all levels. Both Jung's and Sheldrake's ideas have not been readily accepted by modern mechanistic sciences of "contracted-mind" attitudes of medicine, biology, and psychology.

Sheldrake would likely agree with the idea of the spirit of a holiday—that it's a morphic field containing the memories and rituals associated with that holiday. It's provocative to consider the idea of unlimited fields nesting within other fields, which nest within other fields, infinitely. Trees exist in morphic tree fields, architecture within architectural fields, cats within cat fields. Health exists within morphic fields of health. A house with people, and trees, birds, and dogs all nest within their respective morphogenic fields together.

The phrases "nesting within" and "worlds-within-worlds" bring to mind the earlier discussion about dark energy-matter, as equated in certain ways with spirit. They are also evocative of the saying that "we are spiritual beings having a human experience," and not the other way around. Viewed from this perspective, the spirit within a human being resonates from within the larger spiritual morphogenic field. From their perspective, the Risen suggest that the so-called boundaries of any field are arbitrary and subject to one's perceptual awareness, meaning that the fields are infinite in space and time. Thus, Risen fields interpenetrate non-Risen fields, which also interpenetrate.

Morphic fields cannot exist independently of matter, for these fields *are* matter. A non-physical field would not be possible. It's conceivable that these fields are the infinite realities that are composed of the invisible, uncharged particles that science currently believes comprise ninety percent of the universe. Our subtle astral-etheric bodies are also fields that interpenetrate and affect one another on scales of inconceivable complexity. The fields of these subtle worlds easily evade the grasp of the material human brain.

Risen worlds interpenetrate ours. In any mediumistic or channeling experience, the higher vibrating field—or geography—"descends" into the lower, reflecting that the higher actively occupies the lower. The lower must be receptive to the higher—like attracts like—as above, so below. When the higher shifts into the lower, what we dub as "psychic phenomena," which are *numina*, often appear. The Risen can come to our geography in various ways, including material manifestations. However, we, the earth-embodied, cannot go to the Risen geographies in our current manifestation of matter. Our spirit bodies may vibrate sufficiently high enough to be able to resonate with the vibrations of certain lower Risen geographies. This resonating is not material manifestation, but more of a kind of "affect of appearances" in the Risen lands. This phenomenon would most likely occur while we're in the dream state, and we would appear like pale, translucent "ghosts" to the Risen.

Numinous events of earthly contact with Risen Ones occur either during sleep experiences or while fully awake, as well as in-between sleeping and waking—in other words, at any time. Because of psychospiritual amnesia there is usually no noticeable resonance when the events first occur. We may have had no prior experiences that could be found in the subtle, morphogenic field that shaped and/or sourced the event, and so would have no way in which to make a memory. We may have experienced such events before but while outside our physical body and in our astral bodies.

Because of the uncontrolled censoring effects of the ego-mind, which is a *non-subtle* body component, there is little recall of the subtle astral events upon return to the physical body. The experience quickly fades, as well as what little memory of it that might have been retained. Even when the event has the rare occurrence of happening during the waking state in the physical body, this censoring effect is still powerful enough not only to cause us to forget it, but even to impress us to consciously deny any perception of it *as it is happening*. The effect is potent enough to cause those physically near us to have difficulty in perceiving the event, or even hearing us when we speak to them about it.

Much goes on about us that our senses are simply told by the ego-mind to ignore, a directive we've been trained to automatically obey for most of our lives. It's almost as if our ego-mind generates its own illusory morphic field which even extends and affects those around us.

Writing down our experiences we have with Risen Ones, as well as talking about them to other people—particularly to those who will not let their ego-minds shut us down—can, in effect, set up a "resonance template" with which we can continue to resonate. To resonate is to become aware, which amplifies resonance, which increases awareness, which again amplifies resonance, and so on, building in strength—depending upon our ability to maintain awareness.

At first the written or oral history of a numinous event serves as the template for awareness. Through repetition this template itself begins to resonate with and within the greater field that formed the initial experience with the Risen. There will be an eventual increased awareness of the subtle fields within us, where we exist as beings of spiritual substance. These subtle fields are generated by the energy we call *love*. The template our efforts helped to manifest would become transformed, and we would then transcend into greater awareness and also become part of that greater awareness.

Our increased vibration rate enables us to locate and resonate with Risen Ones who have an affinity with us in some way. Love resonates with love. Emanuel Swedenborg, the 18th-century scientist-mystic, called this affinity "spiritual affiliation," meaning that as Risen Ones we would affiliate with those to whom we are most attracted.[36] This affiliation can and does happen between the Risen, and between Risen and non-Risen. Predictably, it is much rarer for spiritual affiliation to occur between embodied persons.

This next entry discusses psychospiritual amnesia and the process toward creating resonance and an increased capacity for numinous memory recall.

"Over a month has gone by since Tim's appearance on the train. As time passed after the event, I noticed I was becoming increasingly inclined to convince myself that it had never happened, and that I had misinterpreted something completely explainable in 'normal' terms. I started looking through others' recorded accounts of similar experiences. I found that my initial experience of not recognizing him while it was happening was not untypical. The physical senses are unable to grasp the new mode of physicality presenting itself to them, and since the higher and finer psychical senses are undeveloped, a kind of 'short circuiting' occurs. Also, the change in the appearance of the 'deceased' is often so dramatically different that it's not until later that the witness realizes it's the same person to whom he was married for 50 years. The New Testament illustrates this in a story about Mary Magdalene, a very close friend of Jesus. She didn't recognize him when he appeared to her after his death until he spoke a second time to her. It was his way of speaking that made her realize who he was. How could you not recognize your best friend, especially if he was Jesus? [37]

"I have experienced this myself. After her death, my grandmother came to me in an incredibly vivid dream. Yet I didn't recognize her right off as she looked so young—younger than I had ever known her in life. I still remember the shock I felt when I realized who she was. I burst out crying in the dream and then awoke in my bed, still sobbing.

"My second finding is that the amnesia response appears to be part of human psychology. As a *numinosum* recedes into the past—however

[36] Emanuel Swedenborg, *The Universal Human and Soul-body Interaction*, ed. & trans. G. F. Dole (New York: Paulist Press, 1984), 23.

[37] "And then looking round, she saw Jesus there, but had no idea that it was Jesus. Jesus said to her, Woman, why are you weeping? Who are you looking for? She, taking him for the gardener, said to him, Sir, if you have taken him away from here, say where you have put him and I will take him away. Jesus said to her, Mary! Turning, she said to him, Master!" (John 20:14–16)

emotional or traumatic—it fades quickly from the consciousness or is replaced or embellished with fantasies. If I had not immediately recorded my experience, I would now be relying on these usual psychological defenses of the ego-memory.

"It seems that Tim's appearance enabled a sense of closure, and I could take my mind off him for a while and get back to the tasks of material life. I now view my relationship with him as still an integral part of my life, but no longer very important in my day-to-day living on the earth. I can get on with my life, as he can with his. Knowing that he still lives and still loves me, and has indicated that he will be there for Bridget when the time comes, has allowed me to relax a bit more and to let go of previous fears. I can rest easier now, knowing that he truly will be waiting for me and that we will finally be able to do those things together we were unable to accomplish on this plane."

Since that event on the train with Tim, I've slowly learned how to replace the automatic psychospiritual amnesia reaction with a conscious response. I do this by bringing myself to an inner place of quiet and conscious awareness of Authentic Self, and mentally go over and over the events that happened in order to fix them well in that awareness. Learning this eventually enabled me to be able to create increasingly larger windows of time within, from where I can hold off the recording process until I'm ready. When I feel that I've rested in this quiet period enough, I then record anything that happened, letting it just flow out without questioning it.

To illustrate—years ago, whenever I had a numinous dream experience, I'd often awaken from a dead slumber in the middle of the night. I usually managed to stumble out of bed and write something down. But my brain was still too awash with sleep chemicals, such as serotonin and norepinephrine, to be able to write much that made sense. It was as if the part of me that knew its ABC's simply couldn't function until I was much more fully awake. Still, I would try my best, but most of what I wrote was so unintelligible to me the next morning, that I finally began to do something that has also become an automatic function of response for me—I asked for help.

Before falling asleep at night I would ask my Risen Guides to help me learn how to remember these events. I was inspired to stay in bed after these things happened, and gradually and carefully awaken to a state of clearer consciousness, taking care not to fall back asleep. I let the events replay in my mind until I had them fixed. It was difficult to not fall immediately back to sleep, so I would take the blankets off and the change in temperature caused my body's waking mechanisms to slowly turn back on. Then I would lie there quietly, noting all that I remembered, thought, and felt. When I eventually felt fully awake I would get up and write it all down. That was difficult, too, for the whole process took a lot of time and sometimes that meant not getting enough sleep. But I would forget it all in the morning if I went right back to sleep, so I forced myself to write a little, which almost always seemed to kick-start the process and then I would be able to finish it. I'm now able to affix in my mind all that happened and go back to sleep and write about it in the morning—which I only do if I just can't afford to lose the sleep time.

One of the interesting things about this last journal entry is that I mention "finding closure." This is actually an incredible thing, for it shows that healing took place on levels that I hadn't been consciously aware of needing healing. Neither had I been aware that my life had been on hold in any way, as evidenced where I say that "I can get on with my life, as he can with his." Even in that simple statement I was intuiting a great truth about Tim's life, which was that he also experienced a healing from this event.

Even though it sounds as if I was implying that we could now each get on separately with our own lives—and I know that part of me needed to do that—the deeper meaning was yet to manifest. This was that the two of us were now connecting in a stronger way, and that we would continue to further integrate together toward new and astounding adventures. Closure of this sort is a fairly healthy way of dealing with such losses on certain levels, but in our case there was more to come.

My unawareness of this partnership then seems strange now—while I felt my relationship with him was still integral to my life, it was no longer "relevant nor very important." And yet it's of the utmost importance to me now, and I can see that what I was actually experiencing was a release of a shared past which no longer existed and had played itself out in a dramatic event—the final show-stopping, scene-stealing act of the play that had once been "The Earthly Affair of Tim and August."

A brilliant new chapter of our lives together was now about to begin.

SIXTEEN

KUNDALINI BELLS & ASTRAL KISSES

"Tell me whom you love and I will tell you who you are."
~ Arsène Houssaye

"It's early winter; the first storm of the year has finally arrived. Four inches or so of snow fell steadily all night, bringing the busy world to a much slower and quieter pace. What great and subtle power there is in Nature. The steam heat is rising in my bedroom with a steady and comforting background noise of hissing and clanking. Oolong, my aged cat, is nesting on the bed in a spot of sunlight, secure and at peace with this world as her spirit wanders out into the hidden depths of countless others.

"I can't seem to find any such serenity, and feel lost at sea in some way. Struggling to put it into language only intensifies the feeling, and just makes more waves. I haven't been able to discern Tim ever since that last overwhelming contact on the train, other than a few wisps of *something* that tells me he's thinking of me and that he's aware of my thoughts about him. Even though I know all is well, I miss him and I'm wondering now if sitting down and putting my thoughts on paper will somehow unblock the flow and open up something between us.

"My sleep last night was constantly disturbed by strange and exotic dreams, adventures with people and places I don't know here in waking life. I'm as exhausted as if I'd been running for hours, and my head has that familiar feeling I call 'the gong.' Without warning, an intense but muffled inner tone will suddenly resound in my forebrain. It's as if I'm inside a cast-iron bell that's being struck. It happens from some non-earthly place, and its force resonates so deeply that I lose consciousness for a few fleeting seconds. During these moments my brain feels like several inches of cotton are wrapped around it, making it difficult to think. The gong muffles all conscious thinking, and often I have to stop whatever I'm doing and get into bed, where I immediately fall asleep. Then I'll sometimes have spontaneous out-of-body experiences. At other times the gong will lightly sound throughout the day as I attempt to go about my life. Although I'm not really incapacitated, I'm definitely out of it and physically uncomfortable."

I experience the gong after waking from very deep sleep, usually after a night where it had initially been difficult to drop off. I'll awaken with insufficient rest and in a stumbling, almost trance-like daze. While I try to go about the tasks of making coffee and feeding the cats, my forehead will suddenly resound, BOOMING with a deep tone like the toll of an immense bell. I feel as if I'm about to fall unconscious and collapse back into sleep. After a long second the sound passes, leaving echoes in its wake, but continuing to toll at random until I fully awaken. My evolving experiences bring me in touch with other worlds, and somehow this sound is connected to them.

Along with the bell I also hear birds singing and chirping—many flocks of them. Sometimes one or two individual birds will be louder than others, as if located closer to me. At other times I hear crickets, and even choirs of people singing. They're intensely beautiful to listen to while drifting off to sleep. The singing intensifies in loudness, and then I fall into an extremely deep slumber. At some point in my adult life I began to hear the birds and crickets almost all the time, in the background of *somewhere*. Right now they seem to be singing from a space to my upper right. Occasionally they're loud enough to intrude upon my normal waking consciousness, but I've learned to relegate them to the background, where I only hear them if the environment is very quiet or if I choose to focus on them.

To this day I continue to experience the gong upon waking, and sometimes while passing from wakefulness into sleep. In the early days, I would shake myself awake, concerned that the sound would somehow overcome me if I let it continue to get any louder. It turned out that this was exactly what it wanted to do, but for a long time I continued to resist it.

Finally one night I let it continue, while asking for spiritual guidance and protection—I was very wary. This time the bell tolled once, and the sound immediately began to grow and expand until there seemed to be nothing but the sound, my body dissolving into it while the rest of the world receded and vanished. I could feel my body shaking as it vibrated faster and faster. I was still fully conscious, and the longer I allowed it to happen, the louder the sound grew. I then lost consciousness and fell asleep, to awaken later with no other memory other than that of the bell and my body shaking. This seemed a small but significant success. It happened several times again over the next few months, but it always became too much to withstand and I had to stop it.

I also began to have another strange body experience. At first, my feet began to tingle at various times throughout the day. The sensations were never painful, but became a little scary when they started to "gather" and intensify, and then shoot up my legs, feeling like jolts of electricity that would end at my shoulders, with the energy shooting out my elbows—and then start all over again. My doctor could find nothing wrong with my health or my shoes, and a massage therapist was unable to resolve these sensations.

All these experiences did not bring about any fear, but I did develop painful headaches as part of the gong process. A few times the gong's resonance became so powerful that my astral-etheric body was literally pulsated out of the physical one and into the astral planes while totally conscious—an out-of the body experience.

As a psychotherapist I've seen plenty of psychosis—where people are mentally disabled by impairment in their thinking, reasoning, and emotional aspects, sometimes to the point of delusions and paranoia, and often propelled through life by uncontrollable fear and behavior. Some might suggest that mediums might be symptomatic for a kind of mental disorder like "Dissociative Identity Disorder"—once more commonly known as "Multiple Personality Disorder"—which is a pathological diagnosis and classified as a mental illness. In true cases of DID, an individual manifests a seemingly separate personality or sometimes several personalities. From this perspective a channeler or a trance medium wouldn't actually be contacting some separate entity or a Risen One, but instead somehow be contacting another personality of their own.

Stephen E. Braude, an American professor of philosophy, has done extensive scholarly research and writing on parapsychology, notably addressing the questions of survival and reincarnation and how DID might be involved. He has suggested that in some cases mediums might be displaying "non-pathological forms" of dissociation, or "other forms" related to DID. This seems to be another way of saying that although I'm not disabled from my "condition" I'm still delusional, which shows just how challenging it may be for some academics to fully commit themselves to the fact of survival after death. Braude's writings explore in great detail a few particularly famous cases of mediumship and so are especially valuable as historical references.[38]

Some conditions have organic origins in the mind, or psyche, as the mind is sometimes referred to in psychology. So I even had an MRI scan to see if there might be an organic cause for the physical things I was experiencing, but the test revealed that all was physically well. My lack of fear and the feelings of support from Risen guides and companions, as well as my own therapy experience and training, assured me I was having neither organic nor non-organic episodes. I felt wonder, curiosity, delight, and surprise, all lively responses of a healthy and positive, life-affirming state of mind.

There clearly seemed to be something going on between the vibrations of my physical body and that of my ethereal-astral bodies, as if their intermingled forms were vibrating even more closely together. Perhaps this created a kind of shared resonance, which I then heard as the gong. Certain religious and

---

[38] Stephen E. Braude, *Immortal Remains—The Evidence for Life After Death* (New York: Rowman and Littlefield Publishers, Inc., 2003).

metaphysical texts allude to these sounds and sensations as possible indications of a kundalini experience.

Further research brought me into contact with material written about this energy called *kundalini*. Ancient texts say it resides at the base of the spine in dormancy, seldom awakening in most people. When it does awaken, this energy rises in a spiral up the spine to the crown of the head, causing the central nervous system to throw off stress, resulting in physical, emotional, and mental discomfort, and often there is a physical shaking of the body. As well, "electrical" sensations rush through the feet, legs and arms, and severe headaches are not untypical. The person experiencing this is also often likely to hear sounds—ringing, hissing, crackling, echoes, and even musical tones.

In his book, *The Kundalini Experience, Psychosis or Transcendence*, psychiatrist Lee Sanella, who specializes in holistic medicine, explored the classical kundalini experience as well as the "clinical" kundalini experience, which differ in their aspects of energy flow and direction. Sanella examined in detail the differences between psychosis and the kundalini experience and found that negative, resisting feedback from within, as well as external social pressures that impact upon the kundalini experience, could possibly produce "schizophrenic-like" conditions. My guidance from Krishnamurti, as well as my own personal research and years of exploration within my own personal therapy, appears to indicate that I've had kundalini experiences. While on earth, Krishnamurti went through his own "process," as he called it. He has been instrumental in helping me understand that my experiences of hearing birds singing, bells ringing, the waves of energy in my feet and legs, the intense headaches, fainting, my body shaking, and separation from the body are classical kundalini activities. Tim is also intimating as I'm writing this that there is more to be revealed to further explain these activities.

I share now from my journal the most profound gong experience I've yet had, which happened a year after Tim's subway appearance. I was visiting my parents, where I was bedded down in my old childhood room. It's quite likely that the location itself stimulated particular emotional and psychological aspects that contributed to the process leading to the experience.

The gong would sometimes emerge upon awakening, but at other times it would occur just before falling asleep, which is what happened this time. Usually I couldn't endure the increasing intensity for very long, as the tolling got so loud that I had to interrupt it. Then I would quickly fall asleep, and upon waking up, remain dazed and muzzy for hours. But this time I did not fall asleep.

It also involved another first—a physical appearance by Tim.

"Yesterday was the end of my week's stay at my parents' home, a long-overdue visit. Crowds of childhood memories arose around me from the moment I arrived, and my sensitivity to them became deeper as each day passed. Some were good, some painful, but all were heavy with time-defying intensity. I was clearly struggling with nostalgia and even anger at times—who doesn't where family issues are concerned? I found it difficult to fall asleep last night, so decided to try a contemplative meditation on other worlds that one can feel but cannot see.

"While deep in contemplation I realized at some point that I could feel a gentle play of cold breezes and tickling about my face—what I call 'cobwebs'—which usually signals some kind of spirit activity. Simultaneously I was aware that the gong had quietly begun but was quickly gathering strength. Encouraged by my growing acclimation to it, I let it rise to such a fullness that it felt as if it might dissolve the very structure of my skull. This time, the deep tone resolved into something else—a finer vibration that was completely soundless.

"And then something totally unexpected happened. I became acutely aware of a pair of hands beneath my feet, each hand supporting an ankle. My feet lifted slowly into the air, and then my shoulders followed, raised by another pair of hands. In a few seconds my shoulders were level with my feet, and then I was suspended completely above the bed. My body felt stiff as it swayed slightly to the left and then to the right before coming to stillness. I was unable to move, which seemed to be the oft-remarked paralysis that signals an out-of-body event. I considered this possibility, but just wasn't sure if I was truly OOB or not, because I felt fully awake and not at all asleep. [39]

"Although my heart was beating a bit fast I felt no fear, only great curiosity and a rising awe. It was pitch dark and I could not move my head to look, nor could I feel the blankets, and I wondered where they were. As often as I've been OOB before, this was a new experience and slightly disconcerting, as I didn't seem to have any control, and was completely dependent upon the two pairs of hands lifting me.

---

[39] Sleep paralysis is the inability to perform voluntary movements at sleep onset (hypnogogic form) or upon awakening (hypnopompic form.) Sometimes people feel that someone is in the room with them or they hear voices, while others experience the feeling that someone or something is sitting on their chest. This has been happening to people for millennia and in all cultures, and research has revealed that probably everyone will experience this at least once by the time they reach adulthood. These very lucid experiences are typically categorized as "harmless hallucinations" or "dream-like mentations." Research has revealed that hormones are released during these events, which paralyze the body during the R.E.M. dream state. This release has been interpreted as a mechanism meant to keep the body from acting out the contents of dreams. The hormones wear off as we awaken but sometimes our minds become conscious before this happens, and thus we experience the scary situation of being temporarily unable to move. Beyond this particular interpretation, interesting research is being focused on lucid dreaming, out-of-body experiences, and sleep paralysis, and much information can be found about them on the Internet.

"Still totally conscious, I wondered about ectoplasm and tried to see if I could perceive any, but I still couldn't move my head to look. My eyes seemed to be fully open—sometimes during OOB paralysis they're clearly shut and unable to open. While I could see nothing but darkness, I felt the firm reality of the hands beneath me, their palms slightly cupped and facing up, supporting yet not grasping my shoulders and ankles.

"Unexpectedly, I was suddenly propelled up into a different 'zone' where small blue-colored entities, rather like deformed children, began to cling to me, and pulled and pushed me about. They made high-pitched buzzing noises and other annoying sounds, and I began to feel overwhelmed by them. I definitely seemed to be OOB now. I prayed for assistance, and felt myself pulled beyond the entities' grasp. I found myself standing and then walking down a corridor of some sort. I could clearly hear the sounds of my walking, as if I wore hard-soled shoes as they made contact with a wooden floor. There were walls on either side of me, which I kept touching in wonder at how real they felt and how consciously awake I was. At the end of the hall I came to a closed door which I couldn't open. Then the door opened inward and there stood Tim! There was also another person behind him, hidden in shadows. I took a step towards them, and then felt as if I might faint.

"Without any warning I found myself falling backwards in the direction from where I'd come. The same annoying, buzzing entities again assaulted me, but I was quickly through them and back suspended over my bed. Tim appeared above me. I could sense and, interestingly, even smell him, but couldn't really see much more of him than an outline, for there was bright light shining behind him. But I knew without doubt that it was Tim. He leaned down, and to my great surprise, gave me a deep, intimate kiss on the mouth. His lips were soft and full, tasting warm and musky, and there was a great depth of tenderness and love in his kiss. I was still faintly aware of the other person somewhere behind him.

"I floated gently back down onto the bed, the two pairs of hands feeling as if they were deflating. And there I lay, still totally awake and full of wonder. There was no sensation as if I had fallen asleep and then woken up. I'd been completely and physically conscious the whole time. I didn't have my journal at hand, so I mentally went over all that had just happened to me several times so that I would never forget it. Eventually the comfort and support that enveloped the room calmed me into a deep and restful sleep. When I awoke in the morning the memory of what had happened sprang immediately to my mind, along with the same feelings of love, comfort, intimacy, and support I had experienced. I went to my parents' computer and recorded all I could remember."

This event occurred relatively early on in my new communicative relationship with Tim, when we were just beginning to explore how to get closer. I've never discussed it with him before now, and since we've advanced much further along, I'd like to hear what he has to say about it at this time.

"So, August, was it as good for you as it was for me?"

"Excuse me?"

"That was the nicest astral kiss I've ever had."

"For my first astral kiss, it *was* quite nice."

"I just had to ask. First off, this experience was very unlike the other materialization experiences—I, too, was fully conscious, but I wasn't alone. One of my guides and quite a few others were there with me."

"Who exactly is this guide, Tim?"

"He's with me now as we're discussing this. I can't seem to find a name that would come through to you, August—you know how it is. He has been in the Risen state for a very long time, and was from the earth but can't remember what his name was there, or maybe doesn't care to remember. I know that sounds strange but when someone's been away from the earth state for so long, small things like old names no longer have any significance in their life as a Risen One. But you know about that, too."

"I can understand that perfectly, Tim, but don't you call him by something, other than 'guide' or 'hey you'?"

"Even 'guide' is not right, because he's so much more. There's no one word for him, that's for certain. I do have a kind of 'designated signature' for him that he gave me when we first met, but as you can sense, it doesn't come through intelligibly using the limited symbols of your consonants and vowels. He says it's not important, but if it *was* important, any earthly name would do. He suggests 'Brother' will suffice. He's very amused by this conversation."

"I'm aware of him smiling in the background. His attitude reminds me of how you were acting on the train, as if about to burst from some big private joke. Can I speak with him, and can he join in this conversation?"

"He declines for now—we're supposed to be communicating about our experience, which according to him is not a done deal. I mean to say that the experience is not over because it's a very small part of a larger ongoing experiment, and our talking about it 'revivifies' it—that's the best word for the concept he gives me—and we will continue to learn and grow from it. We're not discussing a 'memory' in earthly terms. As has been more usual for us, our experience was and is part of an infosphere."

"Ok, an *infosphere* I can understand—but we'll have to explain what it is."

"I agree, but let's do that a little later, and continue with the present matter first."

"Alright. Well, I can start with a few questions, and the first is, what the heck happened when you showed up in my old bedroom at my parents' house? Details, please!"

"Brother likes how you get right down to business, Aug. Let me start from the beginning. I didn't just 'show up' this time, meaning it wasn't a spontaneous event. There was a great amount of preparation. Because you've had quite a bit of experience being out of your body, and possess fairly developed skills of inner visualization and clairvoyance, as well as having done a lot of work on extending self-awareness, it was determined that these skills could all be utilized to enable us to connect in a partially material, partially astral way."

" 'Partially astral' makes sense, but what does 'partially material' mean?"

"It means that your latent abilities around material spirit-manifestation were beginning to awaken. The gong is directly connected to this and is part of a very complex process going on around you, including the activation of the kundalini force. It's a multifaceted manifestation of a multifaceted, multidi-mensional experience. Try and say *that* fast three times!

"The gong is partially a kind of 'side effect' of a complex process. Here's a simple analogy. The window fan was invented to just transfer air, not to make any particular sound—and yet certain sounds occur when the fan is running—so the sounds could be said to be 'side effects.' It's like this in the way that the material structure of your body is reacting to the process that sets up a vibration, which in turn acts as feedback to those listening. This vibration is never isolated as if in a vacuum but resonates with certain other vibrations around it."

"You might be losing a few of us here, Tim, but I think I understand what you're saying—that the gong is the sound heard when I've been beaned on the astral noggin. But you mentioned someone listening—who?"

"Why, all your Risen colleagues, guides, teachers, Healer-Scientists, technicians—all who have an interest in your development. I can see you don't know who I'm talking about because you don't remember, but trust me, some day you'll wonder how you could have forgotten them."

"I feel rather helpless at times about all this."

"You're not helpless even if you feel that way, August. You are never alone either, although your ego-mind has the influence to make it seem so. Let me continue to explain what went on, to the best of my simple abilities."

"Your abilities, Tim, seem far from simple to me. As you always say, onward, ho!"

"Yes, onward, ho, as I always say. The particular meditation you were contemplating as you prepared to sleep had been impressed upon you by our team for some time—many months, actually. This was to aim your mind in the direction needed, to get you to begin to generate the initial energy necessary to jump-start the process—the energy sometimes known as 'desire.' The gong sound was an indication that your astral-etheric and material bodies were beginning to resonate to particular forces we directed toward you. I like your notion of getting beaned on the astral noggin, by the way.

"The original idea was to see how close you and I could get to one another in a consciously self-aware manner, and if that happened, to monitor any spontaneous reactions and events and explore them further. To do this meant that we had to conform in several ways to the Principle of Affinity, a 'universal truism' much studied by Risen scientists. Extremely miniscule amounts of several particular substances were utilized from your physical and astral bodies and then blended with certain Risen substances, to enable our chemist-technicians to connect with your astral-etheric components. This mixture of components then began to vibrate in such a way as to become more solidly connected to your physical body. Normally the astral body is quite loosely interspersed in its interpenetration throughout the physical body. But now your astral-etheric and physical bodies were vibrating in such a way that they became more resonant, and therefore more closely enmeshed.

"This equi-resonance became the catalyst that enabled the Risen chemists to manifest what your senses perceived as hands, as if coming out of nowhere and materializing beneath you. You sensed these manifested supports as hands because that is what made the most sense to your mind. Your belief that they were hands lent further energy to them, and this energy further enabled the manifestation of their form. Beliefs are part of the process whereby all forms—physical, astral, and others, are manifested by consciousness. Whether the consciousness is self-aware or not doesn't matter, for it's extremely difficult to suppress the automatic performance of manifestation.

"Your astral feet were lifted first because of the way energy flows up and through your body—energy is cooler and 'softer' in the feet, and less active when the body is at rest. The feet are also furthest away from your brain stem, so they were affected first in order to not shock the brain, where the mechanism of ego-awareness resides. The materialized hands, as well as your own feet, were now partially astral and partially material, forming a third, temporary sheath, which resonated with the sheath that had been constructed for me here in my Risen environment. One of the technicians likened them to special suits of light we would put on in order to be able to move through the differently vibrating elements. When these sheaths were brought near one another, the resonance increased, which you felt as a bodily shaking.

"If another person had come into the room while this was going on you would have appeared to be sleeping, and perhaps twitching about the face and extremities a bit, but nothing more. Because so very little physical substances were used, what you were experiencing would not have been discernable to the physical eyes. There are certain bodily elements—'sleep chemicals,' you called them earlier—which temporarily still the body so it can rest while the spirit goes off to explore and play. These chemicals were also manipulated by the technicians to catalyze your process in a more intense way.

"Although you were quite conscious as the supporting hands lifted your modified astral-etheric body, you would have found it difficult to disengage from the process. The idea would have never entered your head because it felt so real. It felt so real because it *was* real, but on a level of reality above and beyond the vibrating physical level. You were so conscious that even your astral-etheric body's eyes were open. Your physical eyes had actually opened briefly in the beginning, which was unexpected by our scientists. Your conscious reactions to what was happening—wonder, curiosity, a rising exhilaration—were absolutely splendid, for they lent yet more positive energy that increased the vibrations even further. You joined in the process, and because you wanted more, more you got!"

"More I got is right, Tim, but I don't recall wanting those ghastly blue buggery monster babies."

"Those things were a hodge-podge of a kind of soulless construction, sometimes perceived as 'evil spirits' but really, they're just bothersome entities, annoying but harmless. They're not real because they're not eternal—they're temporarily in form while seeking energy to feed the form. They were attracted to our experiment in the way moths are attracted to a candle flame, hoping to find energy for sustenance. They're generated by the negative thoughts and actions of humankind, and according to the Principle of Affinity, those negative thoughts that are most alike are drawn to one another, where they may accumulate until enough energy is generated to create forms. These entities are attracted to negative, lower vibrations, especially fear. Because you were starting to feel a little apprehensive they tried to intensify that slight fear by swarming all about you. You responded automatically and brilliantly by immediately asking for assistance rather than trying to deal with it on your own. You showed great trust in the face of so many unknowns, you know."

"Thanks, I'm glad to hear you say that. I thought I was going to turn into the Cowardly Lion at any moment."

"You hardly did *that*, Dorothy. But if you hadn't asked for help and instead continued to respond with increasing fear, you would have simply returned to the vibration of the physical body, woke up and thought it was just a nightmare, the contents of which would have made little sense at all, if you could have remembered them. The fear would most likely have effectively erased any memory of the higher-vibrating events that had also occurred.

"Your prayer was like someone reaching out for assistance. I say this because that is how I first saw you—beneath a kind of screen or field before and below me, your astral arm reaching up through what looked like a pool of calm, dark, silvery water. One of the guides pulled you up into our environment, although I didn't see him touch you in any way. He reached out to you, and then you just came up through. The temporary body sheath that had been constructed for you began to vibrate and glow in resonance to mine. My specially constructed sheath, which had slower vibrations than my Risen body, allowed me to draw closer to you. It might sound as if these sheaths were clothing in a material sense, but to me they looked like glowing auras, and were made of various forms of light and other substances, all unknown on Earth.

"It's very interesting how you relate finding yourself walking down a corridor and coming to a door, which you describe as if they were an earthly hall and door. I neither saw nor experienced any of that—it was your mind manifesting a reality that made the most sense for you. I saw you stumbling out of darkness toward our brilliantly lit lab—and then you stopped, unable to go any further for some reason. I was signaled to step forward by my guide behind me, who held my shoulders to steady me. By now our temporary bodies were vibrating in resonance almost perfectly, and when I stepped directly in front of you, you looked as if you had suddenly woken up and could now see me. What a look there was on your face!

"You must have had a shock, because then you seemed to faint and you fell backwards and began to disappear, as if you were sinking beneath water. This wasn't anticipated and caused quite a stir, and it was quickly determined that the experiment had gone as far as it could. The technicians did all kinds of seemingly magical things completely beyond my comprehension and somehow stopped you from disappearing altogether, so that they could slowly let you back down by gently lowering your vibrations toward that of the earthly plane.

"You seem to have gotten things mixed up in your memory about the sequence of things, because it was *before* you had returned to your form in bed that they allowed me to kiss you goodbye. You were still suspended in the silvery dark water. My guide, sensing my disappointment that we had come so close but only very briefly, brought all the forces of compassion he could to the matter. He had the technicians suspend me over you as you floated in the water. And then I bent down and kissed you good-bye as you sank away.

"You passed back through the annoying entities so quickly because your energy was charged with a vibrational nature that instantly repelled them. This same energy then re-manifested itself as the supporting hands, which gently merged you back into your earthly body. Their physical elements were reabsorbed into your physical shell and the extra astral-etheric components went back into the astral realm. This same energy, which had been changed and fortified with the energies supplemented by the technicians, also allowed you to maintain full bodily waking consciousness, and feeling very energized and well, rather than headachy and sick as you had in previous manifestation experiences. You used this energy wisely by simply resting there and mentally revisiting the experience to fix it in your mind. As you can see, doing this led to more revelation, showing that all experiences are living and can always be accessed for more living."

"Tim, the idea that experiences are as alive as we are—never-ending, forever ongoing, and evolving—strikes me as a very great and wonderful mystery."

"And we both love mysteries, don't we? Here's another riddle to ponder—are our memories also our experiences?"

"Don't you mean the other way around?"

"Same difference."

"How do they put up with you? Or more to the point, *why* do they put up with you?"

"When you finally get here, I'll show you."

"I knew you were going to say that."

TIM RISES

"It is impossible to say just what I mean!"
~ T. S. Eliot, *The Love Song of J. Alfred Prufrock*

Throughout our work together, it's become clear that Tim has also had his share of memory challenges. Much of what I can remember, he can't, and vice versa. There have been times when I didn't recognize him at all in the astral, but later realized who he was upon awakening. It wasn't until several years after his transition that he was able to tell me in detail about his departure from one world to the next. Even then, he couldn't simply tell me the whole story all at once. It was as if he had to put an immense puzzle together, a little piece at a time, and show it to me in ways I could comprehend. When we're looking at them we'll often find yet another section to complete. I have the feeling that these pieces, like Heaven's many mansions, are countless.

Tim would now like to have a go at further clarifying his experience.

"Narrating my transition experience, August, has been *very* like a puzzle—an immense, living, beautiful picture, a landscape gradually being assembled, gently and intelligently. I've had a lot of help from many others, including you. This landscape is also the place I'm continuously waking up into. It's a coming together, an assembling of the environment—or the 'geography' as you've put it. This continually manifesting environment reflects my awakening mind's conscious awareness. This is the same as saying the environment is me, and I am the environment. My mind is my environment.

"Remember when The Cloud referred to us as 'Beings and Becomings?' I now know that the experience of being, which I am continuously becoming, simultaneously manifests into the projected expression of my experience of continuous being. *This* is immortality."

"*This* is confusing, Tim. Can anyone even comprehend this?"

"We are using words to describe the indescribable, August. As soon as we've used a word like 'comprehend' the experience is 'snapshotted' and we are now looking at the experience from the illusion of being outside the reality."

"Tim, did I mention that this is confusing?"

~ 16 ~

These words may not make conscious sense at this time,
but my spiritual senses comprehend and retain
this knowledge for Authentic Self.

"Let me impress a picture in your mind that you can then adequately describe. The mind-body is a movie projector, which manifests the story of our life onto the screen of creation. This is true for the Risen as well. A movie is not the actual life itself, but a series of 'stills' or 'still lifes' vibrating at a frequency that manifests as movement.

"All that appears to be moving and living around us is also a projection manifested by our individual mind, simultaneously with all other projecting minds—hence, 'the known universe.' When you attempt to comprehend or 'grasp' reality by holding a piece of it in your mind, it's like taking a snapshot of the projected life around you. You then believe you now hold the scene in your mind's grasp. The illusion that you are outside the manifested reality is strengthened and so individual separation appears to be the reality—the comprehended becomes apprehended.

"Yet all the while this apprehended separation appears to be taking place, the individual Spirit behind the projector has not become uncreated. Manifestation changes, but creation endures. Each individual Spirit is not only running the projector, but it *is* the projector, and also the film, the screen, and the environment in which the projector itself is manifesting—*and* the projector is also being projected. And even though each 'still life' of the film appears to be unmoving, it is still life, because the energy formed as the manifestation is itself moving. Remember, everything manifested moves, everything lives, *everything* is connected as an infinite Oneness. The Oneness is never ending and thus immortal—so, then, is each individualized Oneness. Awareness of our individualized Oneness is also the feeling of immortality. I've become aware of my immortality since Rising. You've become aware of it already as have many others on earth, which is happening in increasing numbers."

"Thanks, Tim. I can see now that the confusion came from trying to put it into words, as I *do* know what you're talking about. Others may also, and I'm sure your illustration has helped. During my life on earth, I've gradually realized that *I* manifest my environment. It simultaneously interacts with the environments of others who are vibrating on the same level, which is the resonance produced and shaped by us and others around us. This act of togetherness is one of co-manifestation on levels of complexity that defy any earthly explanation or measurement."

"And, August, I also now see that the dense bodies of humans on earth prevent them from usually directly feeling the experience of simultaneously interacting realities, which is going on always, no matter what plane they are on—at least on your plane and the one I'm on. The concept of vibration is used a lot for the ongoing life experience of all beings on all planes of existence. I see the word 'vibration' a lot in many of the books you read, and I hear it communicated in many contexts around me here. I've become more aware that it's not simple but a very complex, mysterious *something*. I didn't realize any of this on my own, since my understanding of it was very limited as a human on the earth. I was like a newborn baby when I got here, and still am in most ways. There were many who acted as healers, nurturers, guides, and teachers around my transition. I can understand it from my own viewpoint, or I should say viewpoints, since this truly is a multi-dimensional state, but it seems to me that unless you've experienced it as I have, it can't make all that much sense. There needs to be an awareness of the related senses between us.

"I spent a great deal of time in bed during my final days of illness on the earth, most of it sleeping from exhaustion and heavy medication. I was often very depressed, but eventually I found some peace in just letting any kind of consciousness take over. I wasn't fully aware that I sometimes left my body, or that special helpers would come and take me to places on an astral plane where I could rest even more deeply—I was told about this later. There were many healers who would revitalize my spirit energy, while explaining what was happening and what to expect as my earth life neared its natural conclusion.

"These experiences were like a dream. I seldom remembered them when waking up in my bed on earth, mainly because I was in such incredible pain, which swept away all thought, all memory, all caring about anything. Eventually I even forgot about the pain, but it was in the background all the same. I can't remember or reexperience it now. My present body doesn't seem to have any place to hold a memory of physical pain. Mental pain, yes, I have that still, and emotional pain—oh boy, even more intense here than on earth! Mental and emotional memories, endless and vast, are still there for me to revisit and relive, even change . . . that's not quite right. Reassemble . . . still not right. They're there for me to look at, to play with, and to continue to gain understanding about them until I somehow understand that their usefulness is over. They're echoes of particular simulate selves that were strongly established in life but fortunately not crystallized.

"When out of my body I met with the spirits of my parents, who were still earth-embodied and caring for me in their home, as well as with the spirit of my earthly doctor. During these out-of-body periods we were counseled about various aspects and on probable courses of action. I don't remember who the counselors were and haven't seen them since, but my impression is that they were just doing a job and then moved on to work with others in similar conditions. We all gathered together while our bodies were asleep—the counselors, my parents, the earthly doctor, and myself. We often met when daydreaming, which was frequent, as we were all exhausted from the ordeal. For me, it felt like trying to get a stubborn zipper on a coat unstuck—meaning that my body was trying to die.

"It was soon realized and resolved by all of us, as informed and supported by our spirit counselors, that it was no longer necessary for me to remain embodied, and my body's sleep could begin to deepen enough so that I could be finally released. This decision was made from the greater reality of Spirit, with support from experts there. It seemed as if my parents and doctor simply reached consensual understanding and acceptance in one instant while gathered around my bed the day before Christmas. I'm told that besides Risen helpers, there were also a few people assisting who were still in their bodies on earth, but who did healing work with people like me while out of their bodies."

"I know what you mean, Tim. I've been doing something similar on various astral levels, sometimes known as rescue work, or what I call 'liberation dramas,' for many years. I'll share about this later on."

"Well, in a way I was rescued, and so this is the story of my liberation drama. Much is still not clear to me, especially about its beginning, which matters less and less since I don't really feel drawn to looking back at it. How could I want to, with so much beauty in the present here around me! A lot of folks here never give it any thought at all. They just prefer to forget it, like a bad dream, or because they're so relieved to not have to worry about dying anymore. It seems that many of the memories just fade away upon transition, like leaves falling from a tree and onto a stream, to be carried away out of sight, out of mind. But I'm receiving a lot of instruction about the process of memory retrieval in order to assist in this book. When I later chose to study healing, it was also necessary to have an increased understanding of my own process before I could assist others."

"Tim, when you just shared the part about your parents, your doctor, and the many Risen Ones playing a key part in your transition process, I felt great relief to know that you had never been alone. I had pictured you lying unconscious on your bed, barely withstanding the increasing pain, alone and barricaded from human contact by pain and medication."

Tim's illness, along with the side-effects of various medications, had eventually cost him his sight and hearing near the end, and it had greatly disturbed me that he might have been lying there, trapped in a pain-filled, dark and silent world, unable to reach out and connect with anyone.

"In a sense, August, I *was* barricaded from the outside world, but only on the material level. The embodied persons watching over me would have seen only my body's automatic functions of nerve impulses, its breathing and heartbeat that kept it alive, while it surrendered to the ever-increasing pain medication. As a medium, you might have been able to perceive the visible tug-of-war between my physical and astral-etheric bodies. You would have also seen that I was never alone for one second. There was always somebody there in spirit, including my grandparents and other relations, and those you and I had known who had died from the same disease.

"The embodied who were there attending me already had an informed, intuitive sense of the greater invisible reality that lay beneath what their worldly eyes could see. When all that could be done was finished, they let me go. It was Christmas Eve, on the cusp of the traditional birth celebration of one of earth's greatest mediums. Now it was about to be *my* birthday.

"I want you to know, August, how much you helped me during that time. Remember when your medium friend gave you that message from me thanking you? I had realized that even after the way I treated you, and the way I broke off our relationship, you never stopped loving me. You know this in your heart, even though you might say that you only gave me an occasional thought. Shamed by my disease, I had tried to secretly move away, but upon hearing about my illness, you searched for me and kept at it until you found me, and then wrote to me and made the difficult effort to call and ask if I would talk with you. Your endeavors stored up reserves of energy, which awaited me further ahead in my ordeal. Just because I wasn't able to accept your love at that time—although really I wanted to—the love you freely gave to me didn't go away or disappear—it was saved up for me. It saved itself for me. It knew to do this, for Love is Intelligence, and It was waiting there for me right up to and beyond my transition.

"Most importantly, you helped keep a door open that otherwise I would have let shut because of my ignorance and fear. And then it was *my* turn to search for you. The door I found was the same opening I used to get back to you that day I surprised you in your bedroom. This door was within you, and finding the door meant finding you—you were actually the door. Your love was the light through the door, and you not only kept it open and the light burning, but helped me take the door off its hinges."

As Tim shares about the door with me, I find myself weeping with such a release of energy that I have to stop typing and just let it happen until I can begin transcribing again.

"Tim, I was never aware that such a thing was possible. You're right—I never stopped loving you, and I was constantly thinking of you in the back of my mind, wishing we could be together. I never blamed you for anything because I knew that you had been afraid. It hurt to think that you were living in fear. But tell me, how was my love and its energy used? Or should I say, how did It use Itself? How was Love there for you beyond your transition?"

"When I awoke there were gigantic crystal vases filled with astonishing flowers everywhere around me. Immense! Huge! Some were the size of people, and they released music in the breezes while they twinkled and sparkled with light. I was told they were from you and that the flowers were 'expressed light forms that were seeded, vitalized, watered, colored, harmonized, and scented by the energy that his love for you continually manifests.' Every once in a while the flowers would glow even more brightly as if lit up from within, and this was when you were sending me more love, more energy in that very moment. I was told that there was a prayer or blessing you frequently said—"

"I know the one—I use it often for anyone I feel could use some light energy, no matter what plane they're on. I use it for myself. It's adapted from the funeral rites of the Catholic Church I had learned as a child—"May your soul rest in peace, and may everlasting light shine upon you.""

"That's it. When I was dying on earth, I would sometimes come up to consciousness through the drugged waves of medication and see these otherworldly flowers in the room. I thought I was in a hospital and that someone had sent me flowers—sometimes I thought I was hallucinating. I perceived the environment as a hospital because there were so many people coming and going, but most of the people I saw were not embodied. I could see them because I was nearing separation from my physical body. They were transparent and glowing with light and became easier to see the deeper I sank, the closer I neared my transition."

"Tim, I'm elated to hear about the flowers! This is so revealing about the nature of our loving, willful thoughts and the nature of reality—the nature of love. I'm sending more bouquets as we speak. You just mentioned something about an astral hospital—was there ever really such a place?"

"Indeed, there was. I had vacated my material body some time before it stopped all its automatic functions, but I have no memory of the actual moment when that happened. I had sunk into the deepest of sleeps imaginable, into complete silence, aware of nothing. Instead of coming in and out of drugged awareness on the earth, I was coming in and out of a deep sleep state on the Risen Side—but I couldn't tell the difference because it felt the same.

"Sometimes I opened my eyes and found myself resting in an endless summer meadow, warmed by the sun and caressed by breezes which felt like hands gently touching me. Each time I awoke it was with a little more consciousness. It was as if curtains in the room were gradually opening up a little bit at a time, letting in more and more light. Often there was indescribable music that sounded from far away. Sometimes I seemed to be immersed within a pool of glowing lights. There were people whose chants took form in the air, manifesting as vines growing over a trellis or fountains tumbling over a path of iridescent stones. Several times I saw you sitting far off in the rain, and the rain was the sadness you felt, which surrounded you and made you feel lost and alone, and I felt your sorrow as my own.

"I began to feel strength returning and consciousness increasing. Nothing was in focus for what seemed a long time, and I just rested. I would have faint memories of sitting at the top of a hill, gazing over a field of bluish-white flowers that chimed softly as they moved with the breezes.

"One 'day'—I had no sense of time, it was all *now*—I felt something like a breeze tickling my nose, and then it was gone and I fell back asleep. This happened at different times, and this something continued to tickle me about the face. Once I thought I felt it go into my ear. Eventually I opened my eyes. I couldn't believe what I saw—*Bigfoot*, my huge, black, longhaired, crazy fat cat, sitting on the bed! His back was to me, and he was swishing his long, fluffy tail back and forth across my face. Big old Bigfoot, who had died not long after I became ill. In that instant I knew this was not a dream. But what exactly was going on? This couldn't be happening! The shock of seeing my old companion acted as some kind of energizing restorative, instantly clearing away the coma and bringing me to a consciousness of realizing where I really was.

"I immediately sat up and swept Bigfoot into my arms, hugging him with no regard for his dignity while I sobbed uncontrollably. He turned his face to mine and began to lick me all over, as if he also cried tears of joy. I laughed in a way I'd never laughed before, with an immense, rising joy that felt as if it would blow me away—and that's just what it did! Still hugging my beloved friend, I found myself no longer in bed but sailing in the air over a field of flowers, and this surprised me so much that I guess I fainted from sheer bliss.

"When I came to, I felt totally clear-headed, rested and whole, as if I'd slept a million years and I could see and hear perfectly. Bigfoot was resting beside me and gazing serenely out into the space before him. I followed his gaze and saw that an ocean was before us—the most beautiful light-filled ocean of every color of blue I'd ever seen and not seen. The waves rolling in on the surf sounded as shimmering chords of perfectly harmonious music.

"As I took in more of my surroundings I realized I was in a large bed, covered with light yellow sheets and an enormous feathery pillow. But the bed wasn't in a room. It seemed to be on some sort of platform, like a tree house. It was like a room and yet at the same time it was completely open on all sides, with the ocean all around it. Lights silently flowering like fireworks, shadows rippling like indigo butterflies, echoes of glass bells ringing, birds chirping in unrestrained ecstasy, rainbow winds, thundershowers of forget-me-not-petals, thousands of voices singing—all rolled over me in waves—and glorious, glorious peace, coming from that vast ocean, washed over and through me.

"And then it began to snow—a few flakes drifted about at first, but quickly became larger and whiter, each glowing with an intense inner light, yet not melting. The snow fell heavily and in total silence. It wasn't cold at all. It became a blanket of warmth that completely covered Bigfoot and me, and we snuggled under this cover of gently glowing snow. I became deliciously drowsy and fell into another deep, refreshing slumber within the unfathomable silence.

"These memories are part of me and *are* me. In sharing them with you, I have made them a part of you as well. May they add to our collective spiritual knowledge, and may we continue on in growing awareness in this quest."

Tim and I continue to have communication experiences like this, where fascinating information and deeply felt emotions emerge. Much of what I experience inwardly never quite makes it to this world onto two-dimensional paper, and it's a struggle to transcribe it into words. If, as I suggested before, our mental language is too linear, too flat for using to speak out loud about such things, the printed word is yet another step or two down on this ladder of communication. For this reason poetry, a greatly more-open form of written expression, and especially mystical poetry, has often been used to express experiences beyond the body's physical senses. Reading and hearing such poetry may invoke the more quickly vibrating spiritual senses, which in turn will evoke inner understanding. But not everyone can necessarily resonate with the vibrations of mystical poetry, so we'll spare the reader from such things.

"Thank God."

"What does *that* mean, Tim?"

"Uh, I mean, not everybody can get into poetry in order to get something out of it?"

"Well. Thanks for putting it in more down-to-earth terms, although I should be able to do that, since I'm the one who's down-to-earth."

"Really? But you're a spaced-out mystic, you can't help it.

"I suppose you're right. Now, where was I headed with this?"

"I see that mystics can be absent-minded. I perceive in your mind where you've been holding a certain dream memory, which you want to share as an example of how the mind may express itself in mystical tones. And a very good example, if I might say so, especially since it's not poetry."

"Ah, yes, thanks, it *is* an exceptionally good example of how a multi-astral dream experience can still affect us even while awake and writing about it. And it's not poetry."

This experience is multi-astral because it takes place within several astral-etheric geographies that are all connected with one another in varying ways. Such experiences usually occur while the body is asleep, and appear to end when we wake up. After waking back into our bodies we usually refer to the experience as a dream. The ego-mind tries to interpret it from its own limited viewpoint, but usually makes a fine muddle of it, handing us back total nonsense and expecting us to believe it.

After an increased conscious awareness about astral experiences has been gained, there will be an enhanced ability to retain some of the original extra-sensory state while awake. Just thinking about it while awake and back in the body can make it feel as if the experience is still there—and it feels this way because it actually *is* there. In such cases the experience isn't over but is continuing in some way in the waking state of consciousness. Another way of saying this is that "one is in an altered state of consciousness," or more accurately, "one is experiencing a particular sense of consciousness."

If paper and pen are kept by the bed for writing these experiences down, we can often capture them right away, or at least we may think we have. But upon waking up the next morning, what was written down may read like complete gibberish—the work of the ego-mind—and sometimes even the handwriting will be totally illegible. Rather than be discouraged, one must keep at it, and this challenge will eventually change into something that will become a useful tool.

I find that upon awakening I can turn on a soft, low light near the bed and still feel myself in some kind of additional state. Lying quietly and letting the experience flow back over me for a few moments helps to fix it in my mind and body. Only after I feel I have a clear mental grasp will I write it down or type it on my computer, the latter which works better for me since my handwriting is normally illegible. In the morning it still makes sense and then often acts as a triggering device, causing me to recall even more.

"August, this is also true for me. When I work hard to relay my experiences to you, the very act itself opens up more doors of memory."

"It seems like much of what we experience has a lot in common, Tim."

A crucial thing Tim just mentioned was about working hard. Even if a person is sensitively capable of accessing these kinds of impressions, it's still often far from being instant or easy. We have to become proactive in our own process and not just inertly sit around and hope for the best while waiting for something to happen. Our bodies are the means through which we experience, understand, and communicate these experiences. We can't travel out-of-body if we don't have a heightened awareness of the body from which we launch our journeys. It's a process of discovery and of becoming the expert about our own individual and unique methods.

Yet the experience can't be forced because there *is* a certain degree of passivity one has to balance with the more active willingness to open up and remain opened. It's a matter of understanding what one's own skills and gifts are and then how to use them. They can't be used aggressively, like a hammer and saw. These special tools are sensitive instruments, which must be finely tuned within our awareness so they can function correctly. Tim and I can share our discovery with others to help support and validate their experiences. But it can't be emphasized enough that we are each a unique creation unto ourselves, always becoming more consciously aware.

"I have a body, too, Aug, but it isn't the same form I use to reposition to the material planes of earth. What fascinates me is how this particular experience you recorded, which I'm looking into right now, still seems to be 'outside' my memory. As you say, it evokes feelings and deeper things that might be memories buried very deeply somewhere."

What Tim says well-illustrates how alike we both are in our ways of thought and memory. We'll take a closer look at the nature of these things, as well as this notion called "vibration" we seem to be flinging about so casually.

And now to the event—a particularly powerful one that exemplifies the difficult possibility of retaining and capturing complex experiences. One especially remarkable phenomenon occurred here. What began as a complex astral-etheric experience transformed into something totally unexpected, where Tim somehow manifested as a materialized body for a few brief moments. This experience may seem ambiguous or even nonsense to others from their rational point of view, but not to me on emotional and spiritual levels. I feel I captured this paradox to a certain degree on paper. Above all, it can be seen that the experience was affected by the depth and intensity of emotions, which took it to an unexpected level and transformed it into something else entirely.

"While my body slept, I found myself walking on a sidewalk through a park. There were other people, all ages, alone and in couples and groups walking around as well. One particular couple, a man and a woman, were directly in front of me. I noticed that the man seemed very old and was being physically supported by the woman, who appeared the younger of the two. There was the feeling that she was related to him in some way.

"The man's jacket suddenly burst into flames but neither he nor the woman seemed to notice it. I ran up and pulled the jacket off him and gently lowered him to the ground, rolling him onto his side to put out the flames. His companion seemed too shocked to do or say anything. I picked him up in my arms—he was very fragile and light—to take him down some nearby stairs to a hospital, but then everything started to fade. In that same moment I had the impression that a group of people had taken him from my arms.

"Some kind of picture was superimposing itself on the environment now manifesting around me. This was a vision of Tim, chained and suspended between two upright beams of wood. He appeared starved and unconscious. A woman walked up to him and poured a fluid over his neck and shoulders and set it on fire. It was a horrible sight and very upsetting, although Tim did not react and remained unconscious.

"The vision faded and I found myself in a room with several others that I seemed to know only casually—they did not appear to consider me a friend. They were discussing that Tim had been badly hurt, possibly from torture, and had been taken to a hospital. There was a lot of confusing and contradicting information about it. Someone announced that she was the one who had taken him to the hospital. I said to them, 'I find it really strange that none of you know that I'm Tim's lover.' This seemed to create an atmosphere of hostile embarrassment, and nobody answered but just stared at me without any response.

"Someone told me that I was being summoned to a 'place of questioning.' I followed this person, who led me away to this place. The mood there was dark and serious. There were many people in what appeared to be a sort of courtroom, but instead of benches that separated the court from an audience, there were mismatched wooden chairs placed everywhere, which people just sat in and in no apparent order. There was a large table off to the side where presumably important people were sitting, and who appeared to be conducting the proceedings. I recognized no one and I was not acknowledged in any way. I found the one remaining empty chair and sat in it.

"Someone came up to me and said, 'You will be asked a few questions, and just answer them.' Someone else bent down and gently asked me something that I can't remember, but I answered, 'yes, I am, and yes, I was there.' No more questions were asked. A young woman came up to me and said, 'Tim left this, but didn't say who to give it to. We now realize it is meant for you.' I took what appeared to be a note, a large sheet of paper folded over many times until it was about two inches square and very thick. I was very excited about this gift from him, and began to cry with great emotion. But the entire thing was tightly taped shut all over and I couldn't get it open. My tears flowed harder from frustration.

"I gradually became aware that people were testifying and answering questions, and I heard someone ask, 'and what is your knowledge about Tim's death?'

"Someone answered, 'He was murdered.'

" 'And by whom?'

" 'By those who tended the body. They were seen stabbing him through the eyes and ears.' (Tim had become completely blind and deaf at the end.) 'He was set on fire, and then he died.' (He was in extreme physical agony in his final days from an internal infection.)

"There were holographic movies being projected, showing all that had happened as it was being related. I was overwhelmed by the horror of it and by the frustration of not being able to open Tim's note. I felt totally alone.

Nobody seemed to know who I was. I wept harder and harder, tears streaming down my face, and my head began to ache from weeping.

"Something made me pause and look up. Standing at the back of the room were five of the strangest beings I'd ever seen—yet there was also something familiar about them. They were very tall and large, and reminded me of elephants in some way. They weren't human and had wrinkly gray skin just like elephants, but they didn't have trunks. Their gender, if any, was not apparent. They were dressed in all kinds of costumes—dazzling, winged, glittering, silky, with feathers and sequins, extremely outrageous—a couple of them were wearing exotic-looking sunglasses. Although they were silent and appeared to be serious, they made me smile and I felt great affection towards them. They seemed to be very aware of me, but were obviously not making that known in order to keep an appearance of decorum. I knew that in some way they were connected to Tim, and the strange thought occurred to me that they were something like his fairy godmothers. The other people in the room seemed nervous by their presence, but I felt a strong love for these strange ones.

"I also felt intensely upset, sad, and isolated. My head ached terribly and I put my head down on the table, exhausted, shaking from emotion.

"In the waking world where my physical body still rested in bed, I became aware that the cat was demanding to be fed. Still half-asleep—or half-awake—I shushed her. I noticed I was crying and trembling in my earthly body. Just as it was in the dream, my head was pounding in pain as I tried to cope with the great emotions coursing through me from all I'd just endured.

"By now I was fully awake and consciously back in my bed. Everything became deeply still. The cat became quiet and jumped off the bed. All sound funneled away to nothing, and I felt the bedroom collapse to a single point.

"I was lying on my side, and felt something on my shoulder. I knew without any doubt that this something was real. It grew heavier as it took form, and then it began moving, gently squeezing and caressing my neck—there was an unmistakable *hand* resting on my shoulder. Then I felt lips on my neck and knew immediately that it was Tim. I was clearly no longer dreaming or in the astral, and Tim was materializing into my bed! His hands and arms were forming around me, and he was gently kissing the back of my neck. Totally awake now, I reached back and took his hand—it felt real and solid, his fingers moving around mine as he tightened his grasp.

"'Tim, it's you,' I whispered. 'My god, it's really you, you're *here*!'

"'*Yesss*,' was all he replied in a very faint murmur, and then he was silent. His silence somehow implied that I shouldn't speak. I could feel the upper part of his body pressed against my back but I couldn't seem to feel his legs at all. I could sense my own legs and could feel my body as it lay pressed into the mattress—*this was real!*

"It felt as if his form slightly deflated away. Then it came forward again, expanding into more being, as if pulsing in and out of existence in some way—it did this several times. His hands, cheeks, and lips were very cool and especially soft and dry. I could feel his hair falling forward onto my neck, as a rising joy and an immense peace began to fill me. I tried to turn around but his hands prevented it, conveying an unlimited amount of strength and a determined firmness that implied that I would not be allowed to turn and see him. I could only accept this unuttered command.

"We were together in my bed for only a few very short and silent minutes, and then he was gone—like a breeze passing through the room. I remained in bed for a long time, part of me still reeling from the ghastly images I'd seen earlier, and another part feeling increasing gratitude and awe for the amazing miracle that just occurred. I still have a headache as I write this, a few hours later."

After I rested and the headache had abated, I returned to my journal that evening, still astounded by what I'd written. I tried to capture a few more memories. It's apparent I was still in an altered state while writing, and connected in some way to guides who communicated information to help me comprehend what had happened.

"As with other similar experiences, if I hadn't written something down right away, I truly believe I would have forgotten Tim's appearance as a material, waking experience. I would have allowed it to merge with the non-waking astral experience, and probably would have just faintly remembered it—if at all. There seems to be some sort of psychic mechanism that functions like certain natural bodily opiates in order to dampen a strange or intensely uncomfortable numinous experience.[40]

"Many people report being definitely aware when they've had a real experience, and not a dream. But it appears to be important that an astral experience is additionally externalized in such a way as to anchor it to reality on this plane, in order to impress upon the brain that an actual physical experience had occurred. This externalization can take place in the form of repeating it out loud to one's self, telling it to others, and writing it down. Becoming self-aware of other tangential elements, such as temperature and pressure changes, the sensation of being touched or held, and especially of odors, can further crystallize and embed the experience in the waking mind. Still, a certain amount of the original impact will be lost, and this is suggestive that such occurrences simply have no lasting 'fit' within this earthly sphere's particular physical space-time. I'm also puzzled by Tim's preventing me from turning around and seeing him, and hope that he'll not only explain this at some point, but will return again and let me see him."

Re-reading this journal entry years later still brings up strong reactions, mainly to the memory of Tim's hand and body materializing against mine. It gives me instant goose bumps and makes me teary. It's clear that I was upset because he stopped me from turning around to see him, but later experiences and research suggested that this would have resulted in abruptly ending it. Another experience after this one, similar but more intense—if *that* can be

---

[40] That is, psychospiritual amnesia. – *AG*

imagined—revealed more clues. Tim later disclosed a bit about his own reluctance to let me see him, and perhaps he'll discuss this further on.

"I should speak about it now, August, while the way is open between us. We were given this experience through the collective efforts of a great many Risen Ones, particularly Healer-Scientists who had a great interest in the power of the feelings that connected us, and in the process of an evolving relationship between beings from two different dimensions.

"I was aware that I would not look as you remembered me, but instead quite gruesome, as if still very sick and wasted. This state was not due to the illness I had left behind, but because the process in which I was participating was still greatly new and unfamiliar to me, and because there was a certain degree of discomfort that I had yet to learn how to handle. For that reason I was placed in a dream-like state, as if given a very powerful anesthetic. As a result of these factors my appearance would have been quite unformed and patchy to you. Even though I wouldn't be fully conscious during the event and in a sleep-like state, I still didn't want you to see me like that. Partly because I feared it would make you afraid, but also because of vanity, which was something I had not fully left behind on the earth. My feelings about this were so strong that I was able to act them out in manifestation, even in such a deepened state of dream consciousness."

"That all makes sense to me, Tim. And I think you're right, I would have been upset and even a little afraid at seeing you not looking your usual handsome and healthy self. I'm glad you followed your own feelings—I probably would have acted in the same way. I'm touched by your confession that your actions were also motivated by vanity—it's just further validation that this could only be you."

"And thanks for understanding, Aug, which just further validates for me that this could only be *you*."

The same Healer-Scientists that Tim mentioned were also with me as I wrote the few comments in my journal after the event, explaining some of the process to me. They have continued to share information as this process has evolved and widened over the years. Active desire, as energized by love, allows for the opening of doors or channels between my physical plane and Tim's Risen one. Another way to say this is that the action of thoughts combined with feelings causes vibrations, which then causes manifestation. This process will be explored in more detail in a later chapter.

These Risen scientists helped me understand that if I *had* turned around and seen Tim, unfavorable reactions would have followed. That action would have brought my physical eyes into play, and stimulated my human brain into more physical awareness. My physical brain would then have attempted to participate in what my material senses of touch and pressure were telling it—

that something *physical* seemed to be going on. But what was happening was on a much different level than just a material one. Bringing the physical eyes to bear upon Tim's materializing form would have been like turning a bright light onto him all at once—literally—by causing photons to bombard and disintegrate the highly unstable structure of his partially formed body. Because certain elements from my own body were being utilized to help substantiate the process, this would have made me quite ill as well as they dispersed—which I discovered from subsequent, similar experiences.

"Substantiate" here means that the Healer-Scientists used ectoplasm from my body to literally lend substance to Tim's manifesting form. Ectoplasm, or "teleplasm," is highly plastic and pliable, able to take on the visible form of human bodies and body parts, and even animals and objects. There is a little bit of ectoplasm in everyone. It's rarely able to withstand exposure to sunlight and most artificial lighting, although it has been observed to tolerate red and infrared light more easily, thus rendering it visible in certain circumstances. We know how powerful and damaging sunlight can be, and have seen its effects on goods that have been in shop windows for a period of time or on curtains and rugs, and on our own skin as well. The sun ages our skin slowly over years, but it ages ectoplasm instantly. In experiments where a bright light was shown on ectoplasm, it immediately retracted back into the medium's body, causing great pain and nausea to the medium, and even illness for days. There have even been reported deaths. As difficult as it is to accomplish, a few diligent scientific observers have photographed ectoplasm, most notably, Baron von Schrenck Notzing, who published his results in *Phenomena of Materialisation: A Contribution to the Investigation of Mediumistic Teleplastics*.

This was not the first time I had experienced spirit materialization. When I was nineteen, I had been staying with some friends at their farmhouse, which was over 100 years old. I slept in a room that was known for its poltergeist activities—objects would jump off the dresser at night by themselves and rapping noises and voices were often heard. These occurrences never bothered me too much. On one particular afternoon I decided to take a nap in the room. My friends' large Labrador dog joined me and settled in on the rug next to the bed. After drawing the curtains to darken the room, I fell quickly asleep on my back, but was almost immediately awakened from a feeling of pressure on my legs and chest. In a sudden instant the blanket covering me rose up—"ballooned" is a better word—and a young man materialized on top of me as he filled out the blanket! He was embracing me, and I shall never forget his face as he smiled at me, or his incredibly bright blue eyes. He had black curly hair and very white and beautiful skin. I was so surprised that I couldn't react or respond. I lay there unable to move while looking directly into his remarkable eyes as we embraced, nose to nose. I could even feel our combined weight pushing down into the mattress.

The dog awakened and began barking furiously at us while backing out of the room in surprise and fear. Perhaps the barking caused the next thing to happen—abruptly the young man was simply *not there* and the blankets fell back down, empty. I then became quite nauseous and developed a severe headache. I have never figured out why this happened or who this person was—or is.

For reasons not yet clear, ectoplasmic phenomena seem to occur much less now in the modern world where mediumistic experiences are concerned, possibly due to spiritual and psychological changes and even human bodily evolution. Tim shared that he heard of a study that certain Risen Ones are conducting to determine how all the chemicals we take in through our air, food, and water may affect various mediumship abilities. As my own experiences illustrate, ectoplasm, or something like it, can still manifest. The intense headache that I developed became one of the main side effects of these kinds of experimental experiences with Tim.

These "side effects" have been observed by many medium investigators, including C. W. Leadbeater, a well-known figure and prolific writer of the Theosophical Movement. He noted in his research that the "feeling of lassitude and of having the life dragged out of them is naturally terribly common among mediums." He also likened it to "a condition closely resembling the shock which follows a surgical operation."[41]

Examples of my physical reactions can also be found in the work of the eminent Victorian scientist Sir William Crookes, a physicist and chemist. After his own exhaustive research he concluded, "After witnessing the painful state of nervous and bodily prostration in which some of these experiments have left (the medium)—after seeing him lying in an almost fainting condition on the floor, pale and speechless—I could scarcely doubt that the evolution of psychic force is accompanied by a corresponding drain on vital force."[42]

The discomfort and pain I've experienced has waxed and waned and waxed again over the years. Part of the ongoing process will always be learning how to take care of myself, as shown by Risen Guides and Healers.

"Tim, I'm wondering just how much you remember about materializing. You mentioned briefly before that you were 'looking into my experience'— what does that mean? You seem to be saying that you didn't have a direct memory of the experience, even though it was one shared between us. Surely, you don't mean you can't remember materializing in my bed!"

Tim then showed me what "looking into the experience" was like, all in a few seconds. But how can I show this on paper?

[41] C. W. Leadbeater, *The Other Side of Death—Scientifically Examined and Carefully Described* (Adyar, India: The Theosophical Publishing House, 1961), 653–654.
[42] William Crookes, *Researches in the Phenomena of Spiritualism* (Manchester, U.K.: The Two Worlds Publishing Co., Ltd., 1926), 54.

"That's the only way I can explain it to you, Aug. We don't have to use words on paper when communicating, you know that."

"And I also know that a goal for this book is to use words on paper, Tim. It's not possible to easily explain what just happened in a concrete way, but I can try to conceptualize it. I guess this is the time to discuss info-spheres."

Perhaps we can begin by reflecting Robert Monroe's concept of a Related Organized Thought Energy, or ROTE, a kind of "thought ball of energy." All the concepts encapsulated in this compacted energy form can be passed in one action from one entity to another or more. The information can be experienced and absorbed all in an instant, or stored for later access—a little at a time or all at once. It also possesses an organic, intelligent quality, absorbing new energy and changing from what it absorbs, producing more information. Tim gave me a compacted, very complex, multi-sensory laden and layered educational recording with which I interacted. In an instant I experienced what Tim had experienced, and I now have a personalized, working knowledge of what Tim meant when he said he had looked into my astral-etheric experience.

Bob Monroe, a pioneer, researcher, and writer about the out-of-body experience ("OOB") coined the acronym ROTE, to try to convey a sense of the phenomenon that he interpreted as a kind of recording or "mental book," which included sensory and emotional data or patterns.[43] While undergoing consciousness training at The Monroe Institute in Faber, Virginia, I recognized that the ROTE is yet another person's unique way to conceptualize something I'd already experienced with Tim and other Risen Ones. I sometimes see ROTEs clairvoyantly as balls of light, so I call them "light-information spheres" or info-spheres, if I have to call them anything. Because they exist far beyond the primitive system of the spoken and written word, of course it's a challenge to even discuss them.

"Still, Tim, even though you might not remember the experience of materializing in my bed, why couldn't you receive an info-sphere about it?"

"August, you're intuiting that I've received a very complex memory package that seems to release only those pieces of information that are relevant to the moment, such as those that come up while you and I are discussing your experience. The very act of communicating something seems to make it easier to remember, which releases more information from the info-sphere given to me. As you were just sharing your experience I was able to access your memories, aided by our bond of love and familiarity which activated the sphere, making it vibrate to resonate in a particular way, which in turn released more information. For me, it was like watching and being in a movie at the same time. In turn, I gave you an info-sphere about this experience."

---

[43] Robert A. Monroe, *Ultimate Journey* (New York: Doubleday, 1994).

"Tim, I'm now feeling an expansion of some sort, as if the information you shared with me has enlarged the original experience and my understanding of it at a much higher level of awareness. But who gave you *your* info-sphere?"

"*You* did, Aug. By just re-telling your original experience, you not only told me what you remembered, but you conveyed much, much more information—'between the lines' is one very simple way of putting it. But there is still a lot more than just lines of information. Your ability to share your personal multi-sensory and multi-emotional experience can manifest a light-filled sphere of information which I can then access. When emotional energy is directed into such a powerful memory, it continues to grow, to expand, and to live. It's like a living movie, and when I look at it and change it with my emotional energy, this makes a copy of it, a new info-sphere for me to play with and store information, but without erasing the original. I was able to enter into the movie and experience things that I had missed out on before. I'm even able to pose questions to it and try out ideas to see where something might go if a few words or actions had been done differently. I can co-creatively interact with what might be called 'a living archive.'"

"It boggles the mind. I'm impressed by how well you explain all this, and that we can make your explanation come out in rational-sounding sentences."

"It seems that one of the infinite capabilities of this information system is that it learns and finds ways to make our learning easier, so perhaps that's why you're finding it fairly easy to transcribe.

"But I know that you're interested in why I couldn't remember materializing in your bed. I could give you an info-sphere about it, but we want others to be able to understand it as they read now. An info-sphere can even include this printed text as one of its many elements. As you've pointed out, written words are symbols at least twice-removed from the actuality, so there is much within, beneath, and between the words and concepts that many will be able to discern and come to a personal understanding about on their own. As we will explore in greater detail later, even the words have resonance."

"Tim, you're right—a lot more information can be encoded in a single word when combined with other words, even on the written page. One word mysteriously changes another's meaning, even though it still looks and sounds the same. This reminds me of that metaphysical idea that when combined, the many create something that is greater than the whole."

"While a mysterious process to those on the material plane, it's less of one to those no longer in an earthly material body. It's not just the word itself that conveys information, but it's *how* the word is said, its tone and the music of its vibrations. A word spoken without intonation conveys much less meaning. Deeper meanings are encoded within sound vibrations, and when you want to make the meaning materialize, you create a particular sound to encapsulate the meaning of the symbol. This symbol is the spoken or written word. When I want to convey meaning to you I can do it with symbols, from which you then extract the meaning. Hopefully the symbol has meaning to you so that you understand it. Light and sound are difference expressions of the same energy and can do the same thing—I'm beginning to learn a lot about that here."

"I see what you mean—here on earth we use light to convey visual and aural information on a complex scale, such as the fiber optics used for telephones, and lasers to encode and read information on discs."

"We don't need earthly shadows of Risen technology like fiber-optics, Aug. I know *that* statement is sending your imagination aloft in all directions, but let's stick to the subject at hand and I'll try to come back to that later.

"Here is the simplified version of what happened in your bed that morning. When I had materialized, I wasn't fully conscious of it simply because I wasn't conscious that I was experiencing anything other than a very realistic dream. Remember when I said that my awakening into the Risen state was like a dream, coming and going in and out of different worlds while sleeping, and mostly non-conscious? I was not only traveling outside my earthly body during my illness but outside my astral body as well. I also said that your willful, loving desire to find me kept the way open between us, which otherwise might have closed. You were the door through which I could enter.

"Risen Healer-Scientists were able to draw on the light-filled qualities of the structure of your body, which was enlightened—meaning energized—by the light of your love for me. Our love for one another was the energy—the 'gravity' or the affinity that drew us closer. It may have seemed as if I was coming to you, but you were also coming to me in the altering of your consciousness. You had fallen into an altered state of consciousness, and I was put to sleep, so to speak, so that we would both be able to resonate and then awaken together, still resonating. I partially materialized because there was only so much atomic substance that could be used at the time, although in truth this substance goes far beyond so-called 'quantum' levels—but there is no way to convey these finer, higher vibrating realities in human mental concepts."

"Tim, I can safely say that my own quantum knowledge is quite limited. We've mentioned these Healer-Scientists several times before. I've had some encounters with them—notably Kauffmann—and I know that you're involved with them as well. My impression is that you're studying to be one, right?"[44]

---

[44] Erich Kaufmann, a medical doctor in early 19th century Germany, responded one night to a request to Spirit about back pain. While falling asleep, I was suddenly awakened by an abrupt, booming voice in the dark that barked out, "*Kaufmann here!*" Nothing else happened, and I drifted back to sleep. Again the voice suddenly shouted, "*Sensitive! Extremely sensitive here!*" I then felt someone poking and squeezing my back—in the morning I was completely pain free. A few months later, he showed up with Tim, who, to my surprise, was studying healing with him. – *AG*

"I've been steadily focusing on not only what I can tell you about my role as an Initiate Learner-Healer-Scientist, but on *how*—it will be very challenging. New concepts will have to be built, but with inadequate words.

"But wait, August—I'm being aided by what you might perceive as a *device*. Yet 'device' is not at all right. If you saw it, you'd agree that it could be more correctly defined as an 'organic personified pattern'—it's living and intelligent—yet it's not an info-sphere. It's a 'biological something,' so I think it would be more appropriate to call it a 'system.' And this one particularly seems to be a bit of a smart ass, which perhaps may be due to it appearing as a very large calico cat—as big as a tiger! I don't think this was intentional on my part, although Bigfoot, who's nearby, may very well have influenced this. He's quite partial to people with fur.

"It *could* be called a 'translator' but it also augments and teaches, and seems to affect how I want to say things. And get this—Kauffmann has sent it to me! It's very affable and already seems rather attached to me, and it's saying that it 'comes with its own instructions.' It suggests that a way to describe it would be with the word *biologic*, and as a noun. So we could call it a biologic, but it just corrected me by saying it would preferred to be called Prufrock. Now I know this is very strange, August, but cosmic life cannot exist without strangeness. In fact, that's rather a constant around here."

"Tim, I recognize the word 'Prufrock,' which means I must have encountered it somewhere, but really haven't the faintest idea what it means or where it's from. So I just looked it up on the Internet, and it could only be referring to T. S. Eliot's poem, *The Love Song of J. Alfred Prufrock*. Does this mean anything to you? I also just read it now, and it's so stunningly, weirdly, deeply reflective of our relationship, that it would take several chapters for me to explain it—I'm actually in tears. It appears that this strange, mystical poem is being used here as an info-sphere and Prufrock is incredibly brilliant! It somehow contains many implications regarding personal details that correspond to our lives—yours and mine, that is—and the poem feels like it has a living intelligence of its own. What strange mystery is this?"

"August, I'm also stunned. Prufrock is obviously pleased with himself and purring very loudly. He seems ready to begin now, and Kaufmann has stepped forward—he has brought others to assist as well. I'm definitely feeling something strange happening to me. [45]

"Prufrock is prompting me to tell you that now, in the beginning, we will influence you towards language that is structured by the deep loving

---

[45] T. S. Eliot, *Prufrock, and Other Observations* (London: The Egoist, Ltd, 1917). Because of the very personal nature of this communication, it would be next to impossible to convey to others the special intimate meanings interpenetrating this poem, which is fairly lengthy as well, and so our apologies for not reproducing here it for further discussion. – *AG*

connection we share, as well as by a 'lattice' of likely unfamiliar concepts. This structure will be frustratingly simplified and consist of a lot of space, and this space is for the manipulation of time. This seems to mean that the way I speak, or the way I come across to you, will not sound like the usual me and that Prufrock's influence will affect the level and quality of my communication. It would take so much time for this process to occur within the confines of your earthly space that the newly constructed lattice will allow for much less time to occur in your consciousness. Prufrock had already been stimulating you to seek out and read unfamiliar things. This has been going on for some time, apparently without your full conscious awareness. Know that this is Spirit stimulating you to learn new concepts, so that I will have more from which to draw upon as we move through our experience. Our love and commitment will be the guiding forces as resonance and learning proceed.

"You, August, are comparatively familiar with earthly terms and concepts about healing and about the human body—more so with non-allopathic approaches that are open to holistic awareness, and less so with formal, institutionalized medical agendas. Your linkages with other people who are even more familiar with the subjects are also useful here—with those still embodied who are far more educated than you in both polarities, and especially regarding the links with those who are most strongly affiliated with the practice of 'machineless healing.'

"You are also familiar with the human aspect of terrestrial being which is called 'psychology,' primarily from a westernized viewpoint, although your pursuit of knowledge has led you to many other cultural and therefore useful understandings, viewpoints, and channels towards growth in this area. Your relationship with Krishnamurti obviously adds many layers upon and connections with varied approaches and viewpoints, including those of shamanic, yogic, theosophical, and anthroposophical traditions.[46]

---

[46] *Theosophy* ("divine knowledge") – The system of beliefs and teachings of the Theosophical Society incorporates aspects of Buddhism, Brahmanism, and European occultism, with emphasis on beliefs in reincarnation and spiritual evolution and other aspects of ancient knowledge. Attributed to Madame H. P. Blavatsky, a pioneering esotericist of the 19th Century, the society was launched in New York City in 1875. Krishnamurti, who was the son of a theosophist and raised and educated by the Society, was considered to be their "Chosen One" until he publicly dissociated himself from it as a young man in 1929, and from all organized endeavors thereafter.

Anthroposophy ("human wisdom") – A worldwide spiritual movement developed by Rudolph Steiner in the early 20th Century as he moved away from Theosophy. Utilizing Christian and Rosicrucian influences, it is spiritual science based on knowledge from Steiner's alleged experience of the Spirit World through his conscious development of the higher faculties he believed existed in all human beings, although latently in most. It is said that Anthroposophy cannot be grasped except by the power of love, and the emphasis is on knowing, not faith. Both Blavatsky and Steiner were prolific, brilliant writers about their respective systems, which are intense and complex.

"A significant factor that will aid me is that you are also aware of what I shall call your 'mental-emotional intuition' and of your own respected work on multi-astral levels. I will conceptually label this work as a 'Healer-of-Drama-Through-Drama-Sciences'; as a 'Tangential-Tone-Through-Inner-and-Outer-Songs-Healer-Scientist'; and as a 'Healing-Scientist-Interpreter-for-Low-Lower-Lowest-Misconceived-Levels.' There are many others, some with an underlying designator of 'Artist-Artisan-Builder,' each exceedingly complex and difficult to symbolize at this present level of initial communication.

"Although I say that your awareness of your work can aid me, it is also a bit of a deterrent as much of your experience is very different from mine in terms of self-evolution. I've had to work like hell to catch up with you in some things! This you know—for how could you hope to conceal the fact that you've sometimes stopped the process of your own seeking and learning, thinking that it would allow for more time for me to catch up? I wish to assure you, Dear Heart, it is fine to release your fears about doing this. Everything that anyone does is timely and appropriate and supported by its own grace. It all fits into place, so relax into that which I share.

"I correctly reference our Risen Healings as 'Sciences' and also as 'Healings,' which is your word for what we might call 'whole-ing,' if we bothered with words in that way. Here, there are other manifestations of light, electromagnetism, heat, and matter not only unknown on the earth but cannot be known there. Here, we deal with image manifestation, which is a mild way of conveying what we are capable of achieving.

"The Healing-Sciences, at least in the environment where I exist, are utilized purely as a machineless approach and employ gentle interventions that seek understanding through merging—known as 'assessment' on your plane—and emerging—or 'diagnosis' on your plane. Unlike on earth, Healing-Scientists do not have 'prognoses' here. All healing is assured as soon as it's begun. Upon assembly, your earthly machines or devices are laden with expectations, and then perceived and experienced as separated individualizations or accessories from a dimensionally limited viewpoint.

"When the capabilities and productivities of terrestrial machines become predictabilities—or 'dependable'—they are delegated as slaves of the ego-mind, which seeks to assimilate your machines for its own use. Once assimilated on all these levels, the slaves become the masters, the masters become slaves, the interfacing becomes a relationship, and when given monetary value, co-dependency is established. The co-dependency is maintained and reinforced through tightly-held beliefs, which caused the original assemblage to begin with. It appears that 'progress' on earth is dependent almost entirely on factors of finance, of which the Risen have no need.

"Prufrock emphasizes that beliefs in the mechanization of the universe are especially adhered to by engineers, biologists, psychologists, chemists, and allopaths, yet less so by quantum physicists, who are abandoning neo-Darwinian beliefs, as their personal experiential realities reveal non-visible multi-universes, which are not machines to be deconstructed into smaller parts, but living, organic holograms of intelligence. Some of Earth's physicists now intuit that what was theorized to be the chaotic process of fragmentation of the larger into smaller, is also 'That-Which-Is-Ever-Increasingly-Greater,' achieving intelligently-driven expansion through the launching of holographic representatives seeding and nurturing consciousness, infinitely."

~ 17 ~

These words may not make conscious sense at this time,
but my spiritual senses comprehend and retain
this knowledge for Authentic Self.

"Those approaches that utilize machines on your level are considered antithetical and anti-ethical to Risen Scientists in the higher vibrating spheres. Some scientists from Earth bring their machine co-dependence with them, felt to be a necessary symbiotic component by their ego-self. Although the ego-self can no longer be sustained indefinitely in their new Risen reality, these recently-arrived scientists continue to act as if the ego-self still lives, and also proceed as if unconscious about its dominance in their new existence, as they did in their former lives on earth. Old habits are hard to release. They continue to build and 'improve' their machines here. They still believe in and invest energy into attempting to obtain measurements with their thought-objects, or machines. Their notions of measurement have no lasting validity in their present transitioned state, although they either cannot or will not accept this.

"Thus the energy needed to sustain their work is of a vibratory nature that repels them from the greater centers of healing here. Healing cannot be achieved here with the machines used on earth, which are opinionated, misinterpreted, stepped-down attempts to reproduce what many brilliant earth mentalities intuit as existing in the higher mentalities, meaning those multi-dimensional centers where true healing thought gathers at the call of Risen Healer-Scientists. Such Risen beings are healers first and scientists second, which is nearly opposite of the earth scientist-healers, who embody the reversed reflection of their astral memories to which their intuitive drives lead them, and which their ego minds mistake for their own creations, thus causing a reversal, as though looking in a mirror and thinking the reversed reflection is normal and real. Those here who are still machine-dependent scientist-healers continue seeking knowledge to refine their work. Those who so desire are able, to a certain extent, to communicate partial elements of their work to like-minded embodied ones on the earth, thus working as a kind of team, although in effect misguided as if the partially sighted are leading the blind.

"Prufrock also emphasizes that earth-like drugs which are machine-processed and machined into the body are entirely absent in the Risen realms. Risen plant life is endlessly more varied, most of it unknown on the earth, and the plants are never coerced or used against their will to aid in healing. The plants intelligently understand when it is appropriate to lend their light, that is, their energy, to aid in healing procedures. Prufrock is also showing me that on the astral levels closest to the earth, certain former earth scientists, now incorporeal but not yet fully Risen, are able to co-manifest corresponding plant life that meets their requirements of use that appears to supersede the will of the plants, and thus they believe they are continuing their work within the illusion that substantial results are achieved. Because of their close proximity to the earth plane, they are often able to influence their like-minded, similarly resonating embodied colleagues. Much of earth's medicine, including its ethics, is based on this misuse of energy that is illusory, unstable, and unpredictable, thereby labeled as 'accompanied by side-effects.'

"These same incorporeal scientists are attracted to the advanced planes beyond. Among their greatly varied communities closest to the earth plane there is much myth and misperception about the advanced Risen Scientist-Healers. Constant attempts are made to construct machines that will bring them into contact with the higher planes to observe and extract information about the evolved Scientist-Healers. In truth, all they have to do is ask but they insist on demanding, which closes doors rather than opening them. The demands are made through fear, a reaction that comes from their beliefs.

"As you and I have experienced, if asking opens a door—which is most often perceived by the mechanists as a literal door—the door opens so that one may step through. As predictable in their case, when a door is opened an arrogant demand is then made for information to be brought through to them. Sensing that nobody wishes to step through, the door closes upon such commands. A few grow to realize that *they* have to go through the door themselves in order to become part of the actualization process of their own growth and eventual self-authority—and so actually *do* go through the door. They then apparently vanish, taking the door with them, simply because the door really *is* them. Their successful efforts to self-evolve enabled them to make a channel through which they could move. The increased understanding they gained induces further compassion and enables them to seek ways to stay linked with their former colleagues. As always, love between individuals will remain as links. Much as our love, August, links us and has created a channel—and one day, a bridge—one of many bridges we will cross together into new, uncharted geographies.

"I sense you wondering about what I do here in my Risen geography. Prufrock's influence is somehow causing me to feel very stilted in trying to get my message through in a way that makes sense, and it's driving me crazy. Even 'do' is not the right verb. In fact, verbs aren't used here to begin with—they're only necessary and useful for the machinists and their devices. 'Things' are 'done' with 'devices.' 'Doing' here, where I am, in the way you 'do things' there, would be like using dynamite to create a delicate ice sculpture. It seems correct to say that I am a kind of intern or student, or better yet, a learner. Prufrock is telling me that Earthers will misinterpret 'learner.' The innermost meaning of 'disciple' would come closest, although it is also tainted by misconception and misuse. Not too helpful, is it? I will have to use verbs after all, since your material language, if you have not guessed it by now, is a machine as well, although new spiritual elements are ever-so-slowly trickling back down into it. Fully-spiritual language is non-mechanical, purely organic, and living.[47] You also must have noticed I've been using the building elements of your language differently than its original structured intentions at times. I don't find it at all very comfortable, and I can sense you don't either.

"During my transition, awakening within me was a yearning which was a response to an advanced pattern of love. I was invited to add my vibrational energy to the pattern. This pattern, in turn, was responding to a yet higher energy inviting it to join—and this invitation extended forever inward and outward. In short, I was being offered 'work' to do, whenever I felt ready. I was actually resonating with and gravitating toward a Greater Light.

"My suffering on earth had been seen by this Greater Light as a call for healing, and as potential energy to further enhance the Whole. During one exceptionally painful moment that overrode the medication, I cried out for help. This intensely emotional asking made a portal. I went through it and was taken into the arms of this Greater Light, which I perceived as a Being of Light or what you might call an angel, which is an earthly concept that could never sufficiently describe this Being. This Being had been drawn to the particular quality or tone of my suffering. I was comforted, soothed, rocked, and sung to, and knew peace on a new level. This Being of Light was a very great Original Healer-Scientist—'original' is also an inadequate descriptor—I am striving to convey the idea of deep antiquity outside of any time. This Light-Being healed me on a spiritual level, which was my new astral material level. It rewove broken threads into new patterns, strengthened weakened ones, revitalizing the light fabric of my own barely significant, visible pattern of individuality.

"The nature of peace is to bring peace. Foundations of peace are

---

[47] The earliest human language was based on spiritual sounds, which were best preserved in ancient Sanskrit. Language has since devolved into a mechanized system of sounds, but has recently begun to transmute extremely slightly by the re-introduction of a few of the original reverberations. – AG

continually built with peaceful energy. Serenity is yet another sharing of energy enacted through all individualized points of conscious light, forever gently expanding in intelligent awareness and growing consciousness. This expansion is also the invitation to share, to join, to add, and to invest joy. I was asked to en-joy with this Great Light. I surrendered, a response that you yourself, August, are very familiar with."

"I am, Tim. *Surrender* describes a self-empowered act of saying 'yes' to a loving offer from the Universe, because the offer also includes a sharing of information that makes me a conscious part of my own process, a direction toward greater self-awareness—it's a quiet, restful consent. Krishnamurti helped me comprehend a more evolved idea of surrender when he once said, 'To surrender is to dissolve into the perpetual motion of love.' Later, during a time of tremendous inner suffering, I heard a Risen voice clearly say, 'Surrender—put down your weapons—so that we may work peacefully together.' In that moment I gained further, comforting understanding of the concept of surrender as acquiescence."

"Yes, August, it's an invitation to manifest the garments of a co-creative co-healer. I don't have a signifier yet as a Healer-Scientist, and I wear the green robes of a seedling. I'm diving into unknown depths for words or concepts for the kind of spiritual healing-science I am involved with at this time."

"Getting this information from you, Tim, feels as if I've been holding my breath for too long. There's a lot of pressure, like being deep underwater. Then I have to come back up for air. If I want more information I have to hold my breath and dive down again—it's exhausting. I'm getting the feeling that Prufrock is also connecting with me in some way to help out. I can feel him enabling this communication by somehow accentuating and enriching our vibrations. How strange, I feel like it's getting trickier to use English myself."

"Just hang on, Aug—you're right about what you're picking up. You won't forget English, but it's not working as well for you right now. There's a term coming to me, connected with your work as a therapist—'population'—which suggests I might share about those whom I work with.

"When I am needed, I am asked. I always respond in the affirmative—otherwise, there'd be no need to ask me. Then I'm brought—never alone, but with others also asked—to a 'populated exceptionality' where those who are alike in their needs and pandemonium dwell—where they live, love, and dramatize in similar ways. 'Experience' in this space is the dramatization of states of consciousness. Is what I endeavor in and partake of *therapy*? It's therapeutic to me in that I am given the opportunity to serve others in healing ways, which is also therapeutic to them. Serving others serves me.

"It is spiritual therapy, of course, but that says little. Here, 'spiritual' is our 'physical.' It is *your* physical too, although people on earth generally believe the opposite. 'Metaphysical' or perhaps 'meta-spiritual' is a bit better, if poetical, guiding the abstract to return to a form that is health, and encouraging false fragmentation to coalesce through feeling. It is like calling out to the light, once sent into mirrors, to return to its source.

"I'm referring to certain Risen individuals who have brought with them unhealthy, clever parasites who appear as shadows to me, but as important advisors to the unhealthy persons themselves. These shadows are energized manifestations that are the semi-intelligent reflections of the earthly bio-device we've referred to as the simulate self—which are, in effect, 'tumor-mirrors.' My task is to reflect a particular quality of light into the tumor-mirror from a detached but intelligent, caring angle that is just enough to capture the mired one's attention. A clairvoyant person on the earth might discern my actions as a dramatized event where I am simply engaging in conversation with the person. The particular light I bring up and reflect would be seen as the word-pictures I use to communicate with this person.

"Simultaneously, another Healer-Scientist invisibly approaches the mired one's presence as a carrier of a link to another healthier mind, with whom there would be enough resonance to channel a slightly higher vibrating light. Under the Principle of Mutual Attraction, this action would then cause the mired one to become aware of the new and greater light. This greater light is enough to decrease attention to the artificial-mind mirror, making it less cohesive and thereby decreasing the tumor's grasp. 'Grasp' is implied here as in 'understanding,' for in order for the tumor to be successful it must generate a simulated self-reflection that is convincing enough to be accepted as real, necessary, and fulfilling. The echo or shadow of the former simulate self is then either blinded or immobilized by a greater light emerging from its own reflection. Unable to sense its host, it loses its grasp. Enlivened by the misappropriated energy of the mired one's true spirit-light, the tumor's mind shadows become entrapped in its own belief system that it originally used to lure and snare its prey. Two negatives become a positive—false duality vanishes to reveal the reality of true oneness—which results in dissolving or canceling out the original misunderstanding."

~ 18 ~

These words may not make conscious sense at this time,
but my spiritual senses comprehend and retain
this knowledge for Authentic Self.

"August, I apologize for this tedious idiom you appear to be getting. It feels like I've been speaking through a vacuum cleaner while it's turned on high. Perhaps we should stop and revisit this subject later, and see if we can re-do it in more comfortable language?"

"You're right, Tim, it's weird, uncomfortable, and giving me a headache. You sound like a Vulcan on acid, but there's powerful wisdom-energy within it all the same. Although we've been used to talking on inner intuitive levels for some years, this is really the first time you've tried to communicate something of this sort and on a higher level with the likes of Prufrock, while I try to capture it on paper. I would prefer to leave it as it is, and maybe other attempts later on will come through with more ease and less strain. Perhaps this process will build a template toward greater resonance within the morphic field."

"Prufrock is supposed to learn from all this and help us adapt, so maybe that means it will stop making this sound so mind-numbingly alien. I'd like to relax now and suggest you do, too—eat something and get rest, dear friend."

"I'm totally drained and I'm starving. It's late, so let's resume later after we've both rested, and ingested all that we just experienced."

"And after you've ingested those cookies I know you're heading for in a minute."

"No fair—let me indulge in my vices in peace."

"Goodnight, and see you in *Paradise*, Dear Heart."

The Risen will use any and every little thing to hint they're with us, regardless of its seeming insignificance. Tim's use of the word "Paradise" with an emphasis on the capital 'P' signaled to me that he was using some kind of double-entendre in his usual dry but witty manner. So I immediately looked further into T. S. Eliot's poem from which Prufrock took his name. I discovered that the poem is prefaced by an epigraph in Italian, taken from Dante Alighieri's *Inferno*. The first realization that struck me right away was that while on earth, Tim had been an *affezionato italiano*, and had taken Italian lessons for years. I often pretended to help him with his irregular verbs while we lay reading in bed at night. So of course Prufrock would reference himself to me via the only poem that could call attention to him in this way. The next significant thing that quickly presented itself to me was that *The Divine Comedy* was not just about Hell, or *Inferno*, but also about *Paradiso*, or Paradise!

Intent on relaxing with my cookies, I turned on the television a few minutes later, and the first thing that appeared was the movie "Enchanted April," from Elizabeth von Arnim's very charming 1922 novel of the same name. The story is about four English women who make an adventure by renting an Italian castle in Southern Italy, where the sun and flowers are like *paradise* to them, greatly contrasting the dreary, rain-sodden England they had left behind them. This "Italian coincidence," arriving almost immediately on the tail of the previous Italian coincidence, held particular and personal significance to me. It got my attention and held it. This was yet another communication being sounded on a Risen scale.[48]

To any skeptic, and understandably so, it might seem that I'm trying to see connections where there aren't any. Yet another way of conceptualizing this is that I'm seeing connections where they *are*. Obviously these subtle connections and the processes involved are highly personal, and only so to me in this particular instance. But don't ask me how it's done. I'm not responsible for television programming, but it's a wonderful "coincidence" if one wants to see it that way. Because of the nature of time in non-terrestrial planes of existence, it's not beyond Risen abilities to manipulate earthly things, especially electromagnetic ones like computers, radios, televisions and telephones, weather, and even bodily processes, as well as time, thoughts, and dreams as a means to a goal. In Tim's world there are highly skilled artists who manipulate and play with these things much like our modern multi-media artists on earth.

So it's not at all surprising to me that Tim had caught on fast and was utilizing a Prufrockian approach to continue to validate that it's really him, and that I really will someday leave this heavy, dreary place for an adventure with him in *Paradiso*. This ongoing validation process is typical of our beloved Risen Ones who maintain an interest in us, for they understand the obstacles we encounter in accepting the fact of their survival.

The actuality of contact and sustained communication is difficult enough to make it comparatively rare. Once someone incorporeal like Tim discovers or is taught how to achieve communication, as long as their corporeal counterparts continue to maintain a loving and active openness and awareness, the Risen will continue to pour out great energy and creativity to cause and validate communication, simply because they also want to be as close to us as possible. They have no intention of going anywhere that seems too far away, because the opportunity is as exciting to them as it is to us.

Those who are familiar with the multiplicity of such communications will eventually and instinctively recognize these *numina* for what they are, although everyone else around them may not. No matter how many times you share a particularly powerful astral-dream experience about a loved one who came and touched you in some way, the experience essentially remains yours and yours alone. Unless the person you're sharing it with is exceptionally empathic, they will never truly understand it at your level. It's all for you only.

---

[48] I'm reminded of our discussion in Chapter 5, which used the idea of an island *paradise* to present the paradoxical relationship between belief and experiential knowing. – *AG*

Consider, for example, when a Risen One leaves a message on an answering machine. This is a fiddly business, as often the messages are as indistinct as a badly transmitted fax. Most listeners would think it was just "noise on the line." But if the caller is someone that is an intimate of yours, there will be little or no doubt about their identity. All the subtle nuances in undertones and rhythms in their speech, which would go unnoticed by others, would never escape your inner ear. This is known as "emotional recognition"—meaning that you can hear your loved one's smile. There are also the higher vibrating, emotional connections you have with your Risen loved ones, which will resonate in your heart and mind as surely as if they had reached out and given you a hug. Those who never knew your loved ones as you do would not be able to have this experience. If they're the insensitive type they might even look at you as if you're in need of a psychiatrist. Be assured that you're not.

It often happens that *numinosum* that occurred days, weeks, or even months and years ago finally come together and make sense. This is due to the way time is utilized by Risen Ones as well as our inability to directly perceive and comprehend the complex realities involved. As we continue to strive to increase comprehension and become more open-minded, much will fall into place, like piecing together a large, complex jigsaw puzzle. The numinous becomes luminous, and we will begin to distinguish aspects of new worlds.

ASPECTS OF TRANSITION

"When we hear the music ringing in the bright celestial dome,
When sweet angel voices singing, gladly bid us welcome home,
To the land of ancient story where the spirit knows no care,
In that land of light and glory, shall we know each other there?"
~ Spiritualist Hymn

"Death is absolutely safe."
~ Emmanuel

Death is a normal human process like birth—and it is also a transition. Transition may begin quite some time before the material earthly body is cast off, especially with terminal illness or advanced age. Many people have reported temporarily leaving their bodies during near-death experiences—or NDEs—brought on by illness, an accident, or a coma from which they eventually recovered. Some shared about an awareness of *something* coming their way, a few days or weeks before their unexpected transition—just before a sudden stroke or a traffic accident, for example.

It's not uncommon for people to want to protect their dying loved ones by not telling them the truth about their impending death. But transitioning persons may be the first to ask for confirmation of what they already and intuitively know. They might even come right out and tell everyone else, because their experience is connecting them with deeper wisdom. Not surprisingly, the protectors may try to hush them up, insisting it's not true and not to worry. This effectively closes them off to each other and to any real good-byes. What keeps the process open is a response, not a reprimand— "Yes, you're right. Would you like to talk about it?"

Or the transitioning person, out of her own culturally programmed desire to protect others from the seeming negativity of death, may wait until the right moment and then send bedside watchers away on some unassuming errand. "Go take a nap. Get a cup of coffee. Make that phone call now—I'll be fine— I'll just close my eyes and nap." Then during the next few moments she quits her body in isolation, incapable of saying goodbye because of ignorance, fear, shame, or perhaps from a personal need for privacy.

Although the transitioning person's inability to deal with her experience and to let others share in the process might reflect the diminished level of her spiritual maturity, there will be many opportunities to work on these issues after she's transitioned. This can be achieved through continued communication between the parties after transition, resulting in a unique and exciting dynamic process between two worlds. Nothing is lost, while everything continues to be gained.

Yet such subterfuge by a transitioning person could also be spiritually inspired. She may have become more open to a greater awareness, intuiting that an essential factor in the lives of those about to be left behind is to *not* experience the actual moment of her passing. There is purpose in whatever happens.

For many of those who are finally and truly on their way Home, the normal and natural process of transition begins before they might be aware of it. An initial sign may be increased memories of dream life. At first they awaken from their dream experiences with little memory of them, other than that something now feels *different*. They may not tell anyone about these feelings, even when they finally realize the significance of them. On the other hand, the experiences will feel so real—because they are—that they may talk about them as if they happened during waking hours and not sleep. This indicates that their consciousness is transmuting and expanding, and able to accommodate an increased awareness of more levels of being.

They may awaken from vivid astral dreams with clear, emotionally-charged memories of flying, or seeing, talking, walking, and embracing loved ones who transitioned before them. These little treks outside the body are "preparatory flights" and each voyage will take them out a little further as they become increasingly familiar with their new way of living. These activities also facilitate the loosening of the astral body from the earthly material one, like a butterfly beginning to wriggle free from its chrysalis.

Sometimes there are songs, prayers, poetry, and stories they can recite or write down with great clarity after awakening. Such efforts can reap great rewards if encouraged by all involved in the departure. Those who are going to be temporarily left behind will have incredibly precious documents and artifacts in which to find great solace, comfort, and wisdom as they go through the inevitable grieving process to come. These works of art will also continue to keep both worlds connected, for their vibrations will set up a resonance that will act as transmitter and receiver, creating a catalyst that can facilitate communication with The Risen. They will be beacons of light in the darkest of moments for those feeling lost at sea in their grief.

While the transitioning person might see familiar faces during their astral experiences, sometimes the people they interact with are not at all recognizable. These are Risen Ones who are specifically there for this phase of the transition to help educate them about the new life ahead. Various Risen therapies are used to help deal with issues that may hinder the transition, such as shame, guilt, anger, and fear. Of course this assistance can only come with permission—it's never forced in any way.

Our Risen loved ones may stay in the background during this educational process until the transition is complete. It's not that they might not be highly skilled transition facilitators themselves, but there seems to be a tendency to "save the best for last." Just like the real people they are, the Risen love giving surprises and celebrations, and they get quite excited and giddy in their eager anticipation of the approaching reunion. Believe us, the Risen really know how to throw a "Welcome Home" party!

As the transition process continues, so do the astral-etheric experiences. The astral-etheric bodies become increasingly loosened from the material form, bringing experiences of clairvoyance, clairaudience, and clairsentience—and so the transitioning person begins to see, hear, and feel the Risen as they gather about in support and comfort. Most fully-embodied beings will see the dying loved one watching, gesturing, and talking to the empty air. Much of what they say may not make sense, because they have no adequate language for what they're experiencing.

Unfortunately most modern people, having lived in denial and disbelief about survival, are paralyzed by their ignorance and fear into further states of confusion or silence. The attempts of the transitioning person to tell others about what they're experiencing will be misinterpreted as some kind of delusional or hallucinatory symptom of their illness or medication. This pathologizing only serves as an unnecessary barrier between people who are soon going to be saying a very important "see you later!".

Dr. Elisabeth Kübler-Ross, one of the 20th century's foremost and courageous pioneers into the realms of death and dying—and who now continues her passionate exploration as a Risen One—shared that if we take the time to simply sit with transitioning persons, they will teach us many things about them and about ourselves.[49] Just being able to sit there shows an incredible caring that says we accept what's happening, and that we accept *them*. This creates a space that allows them to feel free to accept their experience as well. To just sit is much more difficult than it may sound, as our society tends to prefer the "don't sit there, do something" approach. Letting ourselves rest

---

[49] Elisabeth Kübler-Ross, *On Life After Death* (Berkeley, CA: CelestialArts, 1991). This interesting little book relates the author's personal experience about a transitioned former patient, who materialized in broad daylight to her in a public space, and then sat and talked with her.

quietly so that we can respond, rather than react, will greatly empower all involved. We may begin to realize that little or even no response is necessary, and then the silence may reveal answers to unasked questions. Our actual presence is a powerful energy that makes a difficult farewell easier.

Rather than marginalizing and isolating the transitioning person, there is a great deal of surprising beauty and intense intimacy that can be shared by being open and willing to be nonjudgmentally quiet. We really don't have to say anything to convey this willingness other than remaining present and listening, which is a gift to them. It must also be kept in mind that their life on earth is not yet finished, and so their purpose here is not yet over. They continue to have the ability to give back merely by the grace of their own presence.

Because of an inborn sensitivity or a heightened awareness brought about by increased stress, lack of sleep and food, worry, alcohol, medications and other substances, it's not at all rare for many at the bedside to be able to sense the increasing intensification of Risen activity around them. They may see brief twinkling blue and white lights, movements out of the corner of the eye, or subtle shadows and other forms appearing and disappearing, while hearing whispers, laughter, and soft music coming from *somewhere*. Increased and intense, even shared dreams may also become a part of their experiences.

Perhaps we can't be physically present with our loved ones as they transition. We can still set aside, as many times a day as we want, a few moments to sit quietly and reach out to them with our heart and mind, projecting our loving presence. This is not an exercise in fantasy. It is using our Source-given imaginal abilities, to experience the truth that none of us need be alone. There are only degrees of perceived separation, depending on how we choose to use our abilities. Up to this point these abilities may have been dormant, but the events themselves could easily activate and awaken them.

We can spend the last few moments before entering sleep to state our intentions that we wish to meet our loved one in the astral environment. While our physical bodies may present barriers while awake, they no longer matter once we are asleep and have a willfully intended place to go and someone to be with. It is most effective to state these intentions aloud—or at least, whisper them if you have a bed companion who might not understand. Make the request that your angel, or your guides, or someone else you know who has already made their transition, help you achieve this meeting, and remember it upon returning to your physical body. Upon awakening you will hopefully be able to speak about it to someone or write it down. Don't worry about what others may think, for in doing so you will be adding to your own spiritual growth while on earth, and planting seeds for growth in others.

Upon leaving their earthly body for good, many people will immediately be greeted by family and friends, whose presence will simultaneously shock and delight them in such a way that they will immediately become fully awake, healed, excited, and joyfully at ease. The transition will be as easy, if not easier, as stepping from one room to another or shrugging off a very heavy coat. I've heard it described as "leaving a humid room where I could barely breathe, to suddenly find myself in the purest, freshest air imaginable." Someone else shared, "I suddenly realized that life on earth was like wearing a strait-jacket most of the time." There is nothing painful involved here, since the neurological factors that informed the material brain to react with pain responses are left behind in the earthly material body—they are not a part of the new Risen body. Neither is there any lasting memory of the past physical discomforts, which were a cellular function of the old body. There simply is no need for any more of the old physical pain.

Tim reported that he experienced a falling in and out of a deep, dream-filled state, gradually awakening into a Risen consciousness. His experience appears to be fairly typical of those who endure a lingering or debilitating illness that exhausts and traumatizes the spirit. He was brought to a center of healing for recuperation, one of many such countless places. At these centers, Risen Ones who have gone through the same process themselves and now wish to offer their abilities and knowledge in service, care for the newly transitioned soul. Perhaps Tim would like to continue with more details?

"August, I'd be happy to share what I know from my own experience and that of others, especially because I'm now in service to new arrivals that need rest and healing. It's a specialized service, which seems to be typical of all services here, for everyone is uniquely qualified to assist directly due to their uniqueness. Something is made for everybody—or really, everybody is made for something.

"I am still fairly new to this work. I've had to return to the event of my own transition in order to observe and study it. Many if not most Risen individuals quickly forget their transition experience. It becomes absorbed into the greater awakened reality once the Risen person is up and about in her new world, a place that defies previously known ways of description and analysis, and requires a new way of manifesting thoughts and feelings. Like a newborn infant, she has to learn how to interpret her perceptions with a brand new sense of awareness.

"When someone has transitioned after ailing for a long, difficult period, very rarely can he jump up and instantly acclimate to a radical new way of living, thinking, moving, and feeling. Many on earth have the misguided notion that transitioning into a new body not only makes them young again, but that they're also instantly endowed with super-human or angelic powers that make them stronger, wiser, and more intelligent. But we'll be much the same as ever, and wisdom will come with accumulated, consciously aware experience, not as an automatic response. It's true that a Risen person may begin to regenerate a different looking body, and all disabilities will be replaced by whole and healthy parts—the blind will see, the deaf will hear, the paralyzed will dance. Everyone eventually manifests a body in which they feel comfortable and happy. The old may become young again while the young can grow to an appropriate maturity, should this be desired. Everybody has a unique vision of personal comfort. Regeneration depends upon the person's beliefs and feelings about themselves, their relationship to others, and their feelings of fit in the universe. Unresolved negative attitudes and feelings will need to be identified, acknowledged, disentangled, and released. There will be unlimited guidance and support offered to help with these tasks.

"You mentioned, August, that when a person sheds the earthly body, the new astral body is what remains upon transition. This needs some more clarification. This body is not necessarily completely formed and perfect, like something new just out of the wrapper. It *could* be, but often it's quite the reverse. The condition of our new body greatly depends on our achievements of personal growth and spiritual evolution on earth. This involves the conscious and underconscious qualities of self-awareness, which we've gathered and integrated into our constant beingness, as well as the extent of our awareness of and communication with Authentic Self. The more one has advanced within the level of one's consciousness, and able to maintain an awareness of that consciousness, the easier it is to translate the awareness into a higher vibration, which is a finer movement of the substance of being. We have become more light-filled because we have expanded our consciousness and thus can hold and maintain more light. I literally mean actual light, not something symbolic. Think about it—the more light there is in your presence, the more you can see. And seeing is achieved here with what we previously experienced on earth as inner sight, although now with greatly transmuted facility and completely replacing the former physical faculty of perception.

"Evidenced by the present depressed state of humankind, it's understandable that a great many people arriving here are not very light-filled and so literally don't have much to show for themselves. I'm a good example of someone who had to continue to work through some exceedingly important but neglected issues after I recovered sufficiently. August, you know now what I mean, don't you?"

"I do, Tim. But perhaps we'll share about that later on, if that's ok, since I'd like you to continue to explain about the healing centers for now."

"Then onward, ho! From my present position—or rather, my position of presence—I discern that my attempts to convey and to help you conceptualize these healing centers are inadequate. I fear this will be true for every aspect of my new reality. I'm not very good yet at finding concepts to transmit that the human brain can receive and interpret well. I know, we've both said that a hundred times. Still, I will try to give a description of what seems to me like the bare bones of some mystical creature.

~ 19 ~

These words may not make conscious sense at this time,
but my spiritual senses comprehend and retain
this knowledge for Authentic Self.

"I've already related what my awakening environment was like—inadequately, of course, because of its beauty beyond words—filled with lights and sounds and sensations your earthly senses can never know. As I became stronger and more awake, my awareness also expanded, and I was gradually able to see and hear more. At first there were others—healers—who were gathered around me as I rested. I was unaware of their presence but they entered my awareness as it expanded and clarified. They used 'healing devices' which I can only describe as living lights. The love that arose from the awareness of Bigfoot's presence strengthened and amplified my vibration even further. The bouquets of light-flowers you sent me, as well as those from others, brought more light and serenity into the environment. Those who attended upon me always smiled but remained silent and gave off a light of their own. Several times I thought I saw my father's form somewhere off in the distance, while I continued to rest my gaze on that blue, blue ocean.

"I was so much like a newborn infant that others patiently and repeatedly pointed out things so I could see or hear them. They helped me find and observe the events around my awakening and revitalization. I now have a clearer reference for these events, a kind of movie I can watch at anytime. This movie could be said to be an extremely complex system of info-spheres, where information is continually released, adapting and adjusting itself to my emergent understanding. From within it I can observe myself asleep in a huge bed, with Bigfoot always there beside me. Our beloved animal children are very often the first ones brought into our awakening awareness. There can never be any question of their pure and outright innocence. There might be fear and other negativity brought on by the appearance of a human person due to trauma we experienced through hardships they may have inflicted on us. But we will at once feel safe within the presence of our animal friends, who always and truly loved us without any reservations or judgment.

"Here is what I see as I now revisit that experience.

"I am in the bed, and both the bed and the place it's in seem to go through many continuous transformations in appearance and structure. Sometimes the environment is faint and misty, all lights and shadows, and at other times it's architecture, which shifts and shimmers as it interacts with my consciousness and emotions, and as the consciousness and emotions of others interact with me. The room, if that is the right word for this space, appears to let in light while simultaneously manifesting it, and continually adjusts to promote a healing atmosphere that supports physical, emotional, and mental health. I say 'physical' because I really *do* have a body here. Perhaps within your context, August, you would call my body 'astral' but here everything is as real to me as your environment and body are to you—although nothing here, including my body, seems to stay the same for long. Everything is alive, and in this life there is always movement, and this movement is transformation."

Tim gives me a mental image of this architecture, which transforms rapidly in appearance in my mind's clairvoyant sight. In one moment it looks like the original source of earth's classical Greek temples—immense, majestic, and perfect. In the next instant it dissolves and grows into transparent, rainbow-filled structures that might be highly structured plants, continually adjusting in apparent response to music coming from the pulsing of the rainbows. This architecture alters yet again, into forms resembling crystals, glowing from within with a living light of their own. This metamorphic process seems spontaneous and unpredictable, yet it's also orderly and harmonious.

"The process is also metaphoric, August, as it reflects who one is, as one is. At times the walls of this constantly shifting, pulsing structure open up to reveal other worlds, or vast constellations of stars, or sometimes just cloud-filled skies. You might call these openings 'windows,' but they're not just holes in a wall. Bigfoot often jumps through them—I've no idea where he goes—returning an instant later and appearing very self-pleased. Wherever they are, cats apparently continue to do whatever they want without an explanation.

"I'm now receiving some sort of visions or revelations. These are visuals that are real, and inform, educate, challenge, and strengthen my newly forming senses. As an awakening spirit, what I see also interacts with me as healing tools and as a healing process for mental functions. So as I grow stronger my senses continue to evolve, unfold, and multiply in this place. I feel like a flower bud opening further into the light."

(Tim shares some details about particular relatives and friends of ours who come from doors or down stairs that appear and then vanish. The content of these reunions is of a particularly personal nature to us both, so we have mutually agreed that the particular details should be kept confidential, while still sharing the nature of the experience.)

"Each appearance of these persons I once knew on earth, and who were essentially believed to be forever gone and non-existent, continues to surprise me. I can't say that I'm getting used to such things and frankly, I don't want to. Every single thing upon which I can focus my attention is like that here. Nothing is exempt from being able to evoke surprise, joy, laughter, delight, and mystery. I never knew that a reunion could be so intense. These loved ones take me on short jumps through these 'windows' to places nothing less than natural paradises—majestic forests, mountains, canyons, and idyllic summer meadows, where I explore how exquisitely soft the grass feels, and encounter the myriad ways in which flowers and butterflies are able to communicate to me with intelligence and humor. Together we experience the exquisite and peculiar qualities of water here, which sometimes looks and behaves like your water on earth, but also exhibits qualities of light and sound that would defy all the so-called laws and aspects of your reality.

"The complexity of life here, of all reality within my reach, is so vast and vivid that one way I might contrast mine with yours is that you're not even experiencing life as reality. You're merely lying on the bottom of a glass-bottomed boat, watching the dim movement of light and shadows but unable to interact with or feel what you see. My experience is without the boat, and I'm in the water where the light is clearer, more defining and tangible, and I'm able to interact with the experience. I'm quite aware that I'm just in the very top layer of a vast deep of interacting realities, which expand and proceed from all directions at once. I'm still capable of a kind of timid respect of this, something which you might call awe. When this happens I close my eyes and reach for Bigfoot, thankful that I can stay in the bed and in this place for as long as I need.

"There are unlimited places such as this, healing centers that adapt to the needs of those brought for regeneration, revitalization, and education. A newly transitioned person who finds comfort in a particular religious context might be received into an environment and by healers reflecting that context. If they find security and comfort in going to church, to church they might go, along with others, all brought together by their mutual affinity and resonance. Many have no particular religious preferences and so their reference will organically arise from other emotional, psychological, and spiritual sources. Some environments will be peaceful, some will not. Others will be hellish places, lonely prisons of darkness, dampened sound, or echoing silence. Each person is unique and continues to evolve and change, however slight. Even a snail's pace of advancement still occurs during the healing center experience, visibly and tangibly reflecting growth as transforming structures of energy."

"Tim, how can lonely prisons of darkness be places of healing?"

"All healing begins at some point of conscious awareness. This point is a location and first presents as a *quality* before manifesting as a structure of architecture, landscape, or a quantitative event. As it once did on earth, the Risen mind continues to construct one's reality, but the important distinction here is that the manifestation is *instantly* and responsively real and substantial, and continues to interact with one's mental processes and spiritual emotions. Whether the manifestation is calm or stormy, heavenly or hellish, depends totally on the quality of our consciousness, as well as the quality of any belief about who we are. Regardless of how or what we manifest, there will be absolutely no judgment awaiting anyone. None! Nada! Zip! *We* are our only judges—and we're capable of being the most unmerciful of judges where our own self is concerned. There are healers here who will step in to intervene with a kind word or gesture should we begin to judge ourselves, but often we won't be able to hear or see them until we arrive at the enlightened deduction that self-judgment is delusional self-damnation.

"If we do arrive with spiritual self-awareness, we may quickly evaluate our situation and see that dropping any remaining residue of ego-mind beliefs will free us and let our vibration rise to a higher state. Yet we could still continue to think we can judge others and judge ourselves. This judging is thinking in the extreme negative. Negativity, which is neither good nor bad, manifests particular conditions and worlds. Positive energy also results in its own manifestations. Each of us can decide for our self about the levels of comfort we find acceptable, whether in positive or in negative environments, or a distinctive mixture of both. There is no limit to the number of levels one can exist on, consciously or less than consciously. Loving our self may beget gardens of paradise, while unloving our self may beget lands of the lost. And yet who can judge where others should be, or what may be most comfortable? When we open our baggage, what will we have packed in it and what will we still want? The less baggage we bring with us, the more freedom we have to manifest anew and to settle peacefully."

Tim had an active role in his own healing at the healing center, facilitated by his response to the assistance that was offered to him, especially since his transition began during his illness. The beautiful, evolving nature of his healing center and his experience there also directly reflected his positive participation in his own process. Tim's transport to the healing center could not appropriately be called a "spirit rescue." But his reference to "lands of the lost" speaks directly to these issues, which I call liberation dramas—the subject of our next area of exploration.

LIBERATION DRAMAS

"I know of one religion; it is service."
~ Silver Birch

"I slept and dreamt that life was joy.
I awoke and saw that life was service.
I acted and behold, service was joy."
~ Rabindranath Tagore

Upon leaving the body for good, there are some who cannot or will not continue the journey that will lead them beyond the astral planes of earth and into the Risen lands. Because of confusion, fear, or outright denial, some transitioning persons will need assistance to find their way to the appropriate area. Once there, they will be cared for as needed until they regain their strength and an empowered sense of their new reality. Until this happens they will not be fully Risen, and they'll continue to live in a temporary state or place of existence. They might even refuse assistance, most often because they are afraid and misinterpret the well-meant intentions of attending healers. Strong negative emotions branching out from fear will form barriers, creating a force of repulsion that prevents healers and Risen loved ones from being felt, seen, heard, or sensed in any way. Acts of judgment are common reactions toward self and others, and will form obstacles with negative forces. Whereas judgment is a reaction—conscious or otherwise—non-judgment is an aware response of love, compassion, and curiosity.

An especially common but potent deterrent to becoming healthily Risen is a person's ignorance about life after death, which is worsened by an active disbelief in survival, and further exacerbated by hostility to any suggestions about changing or releasing such beliefs. This kind of mental positioning is a form of unrestrained unease that intensifies into dis-ease. This dis-ease is a reaction to anything that evokes fear and defensiveness, and will progress in its course as it continues to feed and grow from worry and other negative emotions. Mental disease on earth is a condition that reflects organic, chemical, and electromagnetic disturbances in and around the biological form, due to any number of multi-variable traumas, such as abuse inflicted by self and others, as well as pre-natal disorders resulting from the same kind of imbalances. Another disturbance is the pre- and/or post-natal loosening of the structured quantum-light grids that underlie the genetic codes. These light grids are associated with the phenomenon that scientists are now calling "dark energy-matter." The light grids are connected to this matter by the force that is Life, a force yet to be comprehended by modern scientists. These grids are also connected to the non-material worlds, which are built of the subtle energies of Life. These subtle worlds are infinite in number and in possibilities.

All unhealed and unresolved biopsychosocial disturbances, including addictions and ego-mind controlled mental conditions, will immediately transport a newly-disembodied person to less-than-positive geographies that reflect the existing state of mind. These mind-states may manifest as airless wastelands, cold-running sewers, dark jungles, scorching deserts, vast parking lots—to suggest just a few of the more hospitable planes of unhealed consciousness. Infinite in number, these planes may contain infinitely diverse communities, cities, and civilizations, populated by a continual influx of citizenry from many dimensions.

What conveys and unites these souls is the Principle of Affinity, which replaces the earthly expression of physical gravity. *Spiritual Affinity* is the force of the subtle matter that comprises astral-etheric existence. Sometimes in the Risen state there is complete isolation from all other life forms—if that is what is desired or if that is where one has spiritually evolved. It can become tortuously difficult to move away from such states and beyond to lighter planes of existence. Imagine this as if trying to break free of gravity on earth. The only way we could do that completely would be when our body dies. But in the lowest of astral geographies the body one has doesn't die as the earthly body did, so that method of release is no longer available. The way out of this potential astral nightmare is far more difficult to achieve than the death of an earthly body. In the astral, one no longer has time in which to free their immortal self—at least in the way time was available on earth.

"All you say has validity, August. What's so interesting here is how your material body colors your language. Your words are serious and heavy, lending their own gravity to the situation."

"You're telling me to lighten up, aren't you, Tim?"

"Well, yes, now that you mention it, there *is* a little too much solemnity to your words. You're too grave—pun intended, and I see I'm making you smile already. Let me add a little more light to this heavy subject, since this directly relates to what I was sharing earlier. I believe I can now better conceptualize it in ways that will make more sense to you and not sound so strange as it did before when Prufrock assisted me. It's easier to work with him now. I've learned from Prufrock as he has from me, and we've both grown together.

"There are Risen Ones who are Healing Interventionists and are with us at every moment of our transition process. They engage us in light-filled conversations and tasks of light, suggesting choices that will balance any of the negativities that would otherwise bring about the 'purgatories' and 'hells' you yourself have witnessed during liberation dramas. There are many kinds of healers involved in this kind of occupation, and I serve as such a Healer. We work in teams and on many levels. Not all Healing Interventionists are on the same level, and may actually exist on many different planes of reality, or geographies as you call them. While it might appear that we are working alone on a mission, we are in fact surrounded and supported by many others, who vibrate at such higher levels that they are out of the range of our current senses. This is reflected in the environment of all persons on the earthly level of vibration as well, meaning that those on the earth are never alone, even if their limited senses suggest otherwise. In the same way, my own Risen senses may be limited compared to others who are beyond me in vibration.

"As you've noted, there are those newly-transitioned who, for various reasons but mainly because of fear, simply refuse to move any further beyond their lifeless earth body and its former environment. They may become obsessed with their old body, accompanying it to the graveyard and remaining with it, unwilling to leave something that's no longer useful. Most healthy individuals have no interest in looking at their cast-off body, especially after getting a glimpse of it.

"Because of the Principle of Mutual Affinity, like-minded individuals will be drawn to each other—negative to negative, positive to positive, and all the infinite variations and combinations of these aspects. True opposites do not attract one another, although it can appear so if there are deeper, hidden aspects of likeness. Fears and fantasies of similar individuals will merge and instantly manifest environments, scenarios, and dramas that outwardly express what is experienced and shared inwardly. Childhood nightmares, real and imagined, are now no longer repressed and can emerge as fully realized environments. If a person had lived an earthly life feeling trapped by self and others, never feeling free or trying to feel free, then of course this is all that was ever known and accepted, and thus would provide the template for expression on the higher emotional planes of manifestation.

"The power of light-filled compassion and non-judgment must never be underestimated. Beneath every troubled human's ego-shell and within the human space known as the heart is the spark of Universal Source-Fire that responds instantly to any other spark that loves it—impersonally, yet wholly without judgment, without worry or fear. The response is automatic because like attracts like. As far as I have seen, which is still very little indeed, the purgatories and hells in which many awaken upon transition are short-lived. They may be nothing more than a brief memory, like a sharp intake of breath. Then, because the love response is instantly healing, they not only become consciously aware of their Rising but spontaneously accept it without regret.

"August, I'm quite aware of your missions that assist those in spirit who, for various reasons, have chosen not to respond to compassionate gestures. These are considered fascinating cases by the many Risen interested in helping them. The Risen have formed their own teams and communities, some of which are seldom seen, so far and deep do their research and rescue efforts take them. I know that you've been on several such teams and that you're aware of the particular kind of work involved, which you call liberation dramas."

"Thanks, Tim, for bringing some lighter energy into this conversation. The way in which you so good naturedly and lovingly did this makes me feel that we are growing ever onward in a loving relationship as well as our own working team, and part of a larger one, too. I hesitate whether I should share these so-called 'liberation dramas' from my journals although I find them quite fascinating, in spite of their dark under- and over-tones."

"Please, Aug, hesitation is fine, but only for a moment. I urge you to share whatever you feel you'd like to share, as it's all part of the same thing, and all is connected in this book.

"Alright, then, I will. The particular one that you're suggesting to me right now is a good one, and emotionally relevant to anyone alive on the planet. It will also provide a good comparison to other rescue missions, and a beginning look into the kinds of situations that can arise when transition is directed by negativity, especially fear."

LIBERATION DRAMA 1

This mission is still painful for me to revisit, because it involves the terrorist act upon the World Trade Center in New York City on September 11, 2001. Every emotional and spiritual human pattern on the planet of earth was changed on this day. There is nobody that this event has not touched in some way, and everybody has had or will have a part to play in this particular drama, which will be unfolding for decades to come.

 "September 12, 2001 . . . terribly long and horror-filled past 24 hours. Frustrated and afraid . . . no phone service, trying to track down friends who worked in or near the towers . . . exhausted, slept with difficulty. Each time as I began to fall asleep, I was assailed by mental noises of destruction, explosions, vast rumblings, and by the memory of the military planes that shrieked over the city all day long yesterday.

"I tried to nap . . . at some point I must have finally drifted off . . . and found myself in a smoke-filled area. I couldn't see the sky nor could I tell if I was inside or outside. The evidence of total chaos was everywhere— massive piles of stone and metal and chunks of concrete all around, as high as 30-story buildings. At first I saw what I thought was snow, but then realized were countless, minute pieces of paper, dust, and fabric falling and swirling all about. I felt that at any minute I would be overwhelmed by it all and could feel myself being pulled back into my body on the bed.

"I heard the cries of men somewhere beyond in the clouds of smoke and dust. Six or seven firefighters appeared out of the swirling cloud. In spite of the dirt and filth all about them they appeared perfectly clean, even their helmets and coats. They were holding onto each other as if afraid to take a step in any direction. Most of them were crying and groaning, calling out in despair, not in any intelligible words, just sobs of distress.

"Although I couldn't sense anyone else around me other than this frightened group of men, somehow I knew exactly what to do. One of them began screaming, "There are still people in there! For God's sake, we have to find them!" His screams frightened his companions all the more and they began to panic. I feared they might run back off into the nothingness and I would lose them. I stepped forward and grabbed the one that seemed to be strongest in character and pulled him into my arms to calm him with the serenity I knew always dwelled within me. I held him at arm's length and looked into his eyes, which were rolling wildly about, like an animal that knows death is all around. He never once questioned my presence. I shook him gently to get his attention, and firmly said that I would show them the way out. 'To the people?' he asked, meaning the people he believed to be trapped, and I answered, 'To the people who are waiting for you, yes, this way!' I turned, and taking his hand, told him to take the hand of the man next to him, and to tell that person to do the same to the man closest to him, and so on until we were all connected in a human chain.

"I had led them only a few steps forward when a large fire engine materialized out of nowhere. It looked absolutely brand new and shiny, totally unaffected by any of the disaster surrounding us. A beautiful golden light glowed on it from some unseen source. 'There!' I cried, 'There is your truck, get in it now!' The looks on their faces! They still didn't understand that they had died and so couldn't comprehend how a fire engine of such new and immaculate appearance could come out of nowhere. 'Don't be afraid,' I spoke loudly but gently and with total assurance. 'You don't have time to think about this, just get in and *go*!' I held one of the doors open for them, and then opened another. Somehow they managed to get in without any protests, although they were all sobbing like little children by that point. When the last one was in I shut all the doors behind them and shouted, 'Drive straight ahead!' I suddenly felt myself pulled away with great force, as if a rope were tied around my waist, and I was back in my bed, weeping from the intensity of the experience. After a short while I forced myself to get up and write down all I could remember.

"A little later that afternoon, still deeply disturbed by the events and not feeling rested in any way, I tried napping again and immediately left my body as soon as it relaxed. This time I found myself in what appeared to be some kind of shopping center, perhaps a clothing shop, which had the same war-torn appearance of the environment I had been in earlier with the firefighters. There was the feeling here of being buried alive, as if a great pressure was above and all around me. There was not the total darkness one would assume, but instead everything seemed lit by a dim, grayish phosphorescence. There was also a choking, god-awful smell.

"I found a woman lying on her side. When I touched her she jumped up with a start, eyes darting madly, mouth open as if wanting to scream but unable to take in any air. I held her hand tightly, for she seemed to want to run away. Another woman and two men ran up to us, crying and gesturing. Without warning they all stopped moving and became completely silent. Their eyes glazed over as if they could no longer see. I couldn't tell if they were even breathing, and could only assume they had gone into some kind of deep shock, overcome by utter fear and hopelessness.

"As I helplessly watched, each began to shrink in size and in an instant they were children. They were no longer catatonic but became animated with terror, caught in a nightmare from which they began to shriek for their mommies and daddies to come save them. Whereas a moment before I had hoped that I could somehow reach these poor souls in their adult forms, it was now impossible to contain the hysteria that had broken out amongst them like some contagious disease. I tried to get them to pay attention to me, because I somehow knew that there was an escalator nearby which would take them into the awaiting arms of Risen Ones who would help them. But they ran away screaming and crying into the pitch-blackness that had now descended upon us. I awoke in my bed, heart pounding and breaking from the agony I knew to be theirs, and from my frustration at not being able to help a group of terrified children."

Although the firefighters were mortally frightened, their years of intensive training, immense courage, and inestimable love and loyalty for one another had contributed to their ability to remain fairly stabilized and clear-headed, even under this unimaginably horrible circumstance. Death had never been far from their day-to-day lives. Surely, each and every one of them had privately thought about, and discussed late into many nights with one another, the probability of their deaths in such a dangerous profession. On that day duty called and they answered without hesitation. And when a Higher Duty called, they hesitated only briefly and then responded to the voice of authority they recognized—as voiced through me in order to guide them to their new destiny. The new fire engine was something they recognized with great familiarity and saw as a source of safety and a symbol of sanity amidst the total chaos. I am so very grateful to those unseen guides and guardians who materialized this symbol of security at the crucial moment.

I was never able to find my way back to the poor souls who had reverted to their child selves, overwhelmed by the most primitive of human fears of being completely abandoned. They had regressed like this as a kind of psychological defense against all monsters, in hopes that their parents would burst into the room and hold them soothingly, ending the nightmare.

I was only one of innumerable astral rescuers involved in this world-shattering event. Mediums and channelers, psychic healers, and sensitive persons all around the world answered the calls of spirit distress from the thousands who died in a few moments that day. Knowing this, I also know that all the victims of that event were eventually rescued. A few of the transitioning individuals understood exactly what was happening, but most did not, due almost entirely to the fact that our culture does not widely accept the truth of survival after death. Most were left unprepared for what could have been the most exciting day of their earthly lives. Instead, it became the most traumatic.

The prayers sent winging to them from all corners of the globe helped them all immensely. The spontaneous candle-lit ceremonies that sprang up on streets and in parks in every earthly community, and the emotionally intense rituals and ceremonies that were planned with great loving care, all contributed to bringing light and clarity into the fear-darkened minds of the fallen. They were enabled to find strength and eventually find their way to the comforting arms of their Risen families and loved ones awaiting them.

"I was also instantly drawn there, August, as if by a magnet. The emotional distress arising from that great city was a visual and audible explosion of fear, as much from those still embodied as from those who were instantly displaced from their physical forms. Billions upon billions of Risen Ones, countless light beings from other species and other dimensions, the highest of angelic creatures and elementals from water, earth, wind, and flame, entities that have never known what it is to be embodied, and even the vast, deep spirit of Mother Earth—all were instantly summoned to that one tiny spot of fixed location but inestimable value, to lend help to ensure that not one soul would be lost for very long. I assure you that all the souls were eventually brought to the surface of consciousness—some sooner than others, but not a single one went unfound. This was because of the intense wave upon wave of uplifting, positive light-filled emotion, the combined love of all their earthly siblings that washed over them with healing and living light, raising their vibrations until they could see and hear their new Reality as it knelt down to greet them and welcome them Home."

"Indeed, Tim, the world changed more in those few hours than it had in the past century, offering humanity the chance to make leaps in quantum qualities that could bring mass-consciousness to a new level of understanding. Each individual consciousness was challenged to either revert back to primitive reactions of fear, hatred, anger, and revenge, or to open and join hearts and hands to find the greater response of love within. It's obvious to many that a new foundation of love was begun that day. This speaks to a cosmic arrangement of the greatest yet subtle and mysterious complexity that is beyond the conceptual abilities of the human mind, but not beyond the human heart when it comes to joining and supporting. Humanity was catapulted into a greater reality, which reflects the even Greater Reality into which those newly Risen ones eventually found themselves."

The next intervention is one that's on a very personal scale. Yet many readers will resonate with it as they most likely did with the previous one. Every individual transition is unique, meaningful, and powerful. When brought to such an intimate level as the following one, I feel particularly blessed and honored to have been given this experience.

LIBERATION DRAMA 2

"Not having to work today, I slept late into the morning. I awoke very thirsty, and after drinking a glass of water got back into bed and had the following experience while sleeping.

"I found myself looking at a young man who was standing in a field. It seemed to be night, and he was at the other end of the field some distance away from me. Although it was dark I could see clearly, but couldn't discern any source of light. As I walked toward him through what seemed to be tall grass or hay, I felt that I knew him very well, that we had a history together that went very far back, and that I cared for him very much. Yet I had no idea who he was.

"As I got closer I noticed that he looked dazed and confused, as if he had just woken up. He appeared rather young, perhaps in his twenties, tanned and very healthy, with wavy, golden-brown hair and a bit of a goatee on his chin. I reached out and put my hand on his shoulder. When he felt this, he instantly became more alert and looked at me, saying, 'What are *you* doing here? I thought you didn't like me.' I felt very surprised to hear him say that, and replied, 'What do you mean, of course I like you. I *love* you, I always have—didn't you know?'

"'No, I didn't.'

"'Well, I *do* love you.' I put an arm around his waist and drew him next to me, and then he put his arm around mine. This contact felt very loving, and the feeling grew more intense as we began to slowly walk across the field together, arms around one another. It wasn't erotic in any way, and yet more intense than anything I can remember feeling here in my physical body. I continued to puzzle over his identity while we walked but then gave up and decided not to worry about it.

"It began to get foggy all around us, and there was some kind of spotlight that followed us as we moved on through the dark field. We walked for just a little bit in this spotlight, and then he seemed to grow weaker, as if he might faint. I supported him as we stumbled through the tall grass. We had crossed the field and had come to its edge, where a forest was faintly visible through the fog. And then, without any sound or warning, he was gone.

"I woke up back in my bed, bewildered—yet feeling intense love for this person. It stayed with me all day as I worked on a research project at a university library in the city. I was still puzzling over it the next day, trying to figure out who this person might be, but with no luck.

"I checked my email the next evening at home after another long session of working at the library. There was a message from my cousin, Thad, consisting of only a few, shocking words: 'Jerry had an accident last night, and he's dead. Call me.'

"I phoned Thad immediately. He told me that on the night before the day I had the astral experience, his brother Jerry had gone off into the fields on their farm to cut wood with a chainsaw. The sun had not yet set and Jerry must have thought there was still enough summer light left to work by, characteristically ignoring the cardinal rule to never use dangerous machinery alone. The saw had apparently slipped and cut an artery in his arm, and he bled to death almost instantly. Not knowing Jerry's plans, Thad had assumed that his brother had gone into town for a rowdy evening at the bar with friends, and so thought nothing of his not being home late at night. But Jerry hadn't returned by the next morning. His mind troubled, Thad went out into the fields and found his brother's lifeless body where it had fallen.

"With amazement and almost disbelief, I realized that it had been *Jerry*—dazed, confused, and in a younger body—whom I had helped across the field in the fog! For some reason, I had been summoned to assist in his transition.

"Since then, I've looked in on him in the Risen astral, and he's with his parents and other relatives who have passed. I learned that his parents had met him on the other side of the field after I had escorted him there. True to form, he's pretty pleased with himself and laughing about what happened. I have known these two brothers all my life. I grew up with them, sharing parents and families and summer vacations, and we were best friends as well as first cousins. Jerry was a real rough-and-tumble guy, very physical and getting cuts and bruises, burns and breaks as we grew up, playing and going camping and rock climbing together. He was always falling out of trees and tumbling down steep embankments, or wiping out on his motorcycle. I was continuously amazed at how he would just laugh off some pretty nasty injuries as if they were just scratches. He's still the same Jerry I've always known, but appears happier now than I've ever seen him."

A few weeks after Jerry's transition I had a vision during a meditation. I discovered that his initial, smooth sailing into the new world had not stayed that way for long. His father, who was my uncle and had transitioned several years earlier, came to me and showed me what seemed to be a "film" of Jerry suddenly collapsing and then waking up screaming. It then transpired that Jerry had initially thought that the event of his death was all a dream, including meeting me in the field and then being led into the arms of his Risen parents. But when he didn't wake up, fear overcame him—he not only didn't believe in an afterlife, but over the years had cultivated an intense fear of death. This was a fear even the sight of his Risen parents couldn't erase. When he couldn't wake up from this "nightmare" he came to the mistaken conclusion that he had somehow been given drugs which had trapped him on a very bad trip, or else that he had gone crazy and had lost his mind. Neither of these possibilities fit what he intuited as the truth, so when he regained memories of what had happened in the field, his only conclusion was that he really *was* dead. But because his mind couldn't get around this unbelievable conclusion, he lost control of his awareness and had a breakdown. He was sedated by Risen Healers into a deep sleep, and then taken to a healing center for rest.

Deeply disturbed, I asked Tim about this. I had thought that once somebody found themselves in an astral environment of great beauty and light and surrounded by loved ones, everything moved from there on a fairly uphill road. I had been so happy for Jerry, and relieved that his physical suffering from the accident had been practically non-existent, but now it seemed as if he were going to suffer terribly after all. Tim and I talked about the event.

"August, Jerry was completely unaware that he was no longer in his body, so you were summoned to the scene. He still considered himself as alive as ever, but was very dazed and confused, which is often the case with those who are so quickly disembodied. The great and rapid loss of blood caused him to swoon and faint, and it was from that faint that he immediately awoke, and in the dazed state that you found him. In no way was he aware of what had happened or what was taking place. His confusion was resolved by seeing you suddenly appear there in the darkness out of nowhere. And yet because he assumed with certainty that *you* were alive—that is, an embodied person—that meant most certainly *he* was also alive. This assumption, albeit wrong, helped him keep some sense of perspective and balance. *You* were the sole source of light in the field, which was otherwise completely dark due to his mental confusion as well as his ignorance about his situation. Any memory of the accident or of his death was completely absent, which evidenced the deepest terror that lurked in the darker reaches of his mind, the fear of death.

"He already knew without question that his parents had been dead for several years. If these dead people could be there with him, so plain and solid, then either they were 'ghosts'—another of his unresolved childhood fears—or he was as dead as they were. This last thought was inconceivable to him and would have been precarious if allowed to surface. So seeing you, a person he knew to be bodily alive and well, allowed him to bypass any thoughts about death and instead surmise that he had only fallen asleep and was just waking up. And he *never* would have allowed a ghost to escort him across a field at night! This process enabled him to gather the natural strength inherent in the astral body, which also gave it form and intent. He must have felt quite well, for he was manifesting as someone younger, and so much so that you didn't recognize him. And because Jerry was the last person on earth you could imagine being dead, such a thing never occurred to you either, until you were so informed in no uncertain terms by his brother."

"So, Tim, Jerry recognized me instantly since I still appeared as the middle-aged guy he'd known and grown up with. He was even surprised to see me there, saying he thought I had never cared for him much, which now brings great validation to me. Although his assumptions about my feelings for him were not true, there had always been a certain distance between us while growing up. He used to tease me pretty cruelly when we were kids, and it was often hard to tell when he was serious or not. I guess I distanced myself from him, never realizing that his spirit was much more sensitive than I gave his personality credit for. And now I remember that although he always acted macho and fearless, it was very easy to scare him, especially as kids, staying up late at night telling ghost stories or watching scary movies on TV. I could never tell if he was pretending or really *was* frightened, come to think of it. So what you say about why I was there to help him makes sense. What's more difficult to understand is why the plan to rescue him backfired."

"Silly goose, there was no backfire! You're allowing your ego-mind to hornswoggle you into a negative perspective for its own purposes. Try to bring a positive focus onto this. Each of us is ultimately responsible for our choices, such as an impulsive decision to go cut wood with a chainsaw alone in the woods at dusk. And also for all the thoughts, feelings, and beliefs that we choose to accept, embrace, nurture, or change—or distort, repress, or run from. Jerry's personal beliefs about death were his own, including how he chose to deal with them. Thoughts and feelings about something like death have much more far-reaching influences and effects, being completely relevant and necessary to one's transition. Jerry brought these kinds of thoughts and feelings with him, which were not very evolved. Because of your appearance, he could temporarily and conveniently forget his fearful notions of death, and he felt safe enough to be supported by you and led across the field he also knew so well. He didn't even think of questioning your appearance out of nowhere, since to do so would start the crack that would topple the foundations of his logic. It is especially significant that it was you and nobody else who was brought there. Also, you and Jerry were born only a few days apart, which produced a subtle but specific affinity and resonance between you. It all speaks to many things, including a testament to your spiritual sensitivity and your compassionate nature, and to the bond of the relationship itself.

"As Jerry's swoon wore off, he came back to more clarity of mind. It was then that he was in a better position—literally, in a better light—to see things for what they really were. His parents were there to help with that part of the transition, as he really was very much like a baby being born into an overwhelmingly new place full of bright lights and strange sounds. They laughed with joy as he recognized them, and he laughed with them. But he was also still very much a grown man with an earthly adult's rationale, and his mind was uneducated about this new process of the next step in his life. His reactions, or as you might say, his 'defense mechanisms,' were still very much imbedded in his memory of who he had been on the earth, for the ego-mind does not always fully make its own dissolution instantly upon the spirit's transition. Old habits die hard, as we've said before."

"Yes, now I can remember how Jerry acted when we were little kids, especially when something would scare him. When we would play 'monsters' at night out in the fields and woods he would run away, screaming at the top of his lungs for his mother! Later he would pretend it had never happened. And that is *so* very Jerry. We always used to think he was trying to be funny, but this doesn't sound comical in any way to me now."

"What's funny is that you should say that, Aug, because I'll bet that he'll look back upon this, should he choose to—and I'm sure he will—and he'll laugh harder than anyone else. The finer, evolved essence of humility is the gift of being able to laugh at the escapades of one's earthly self.

"Skilled Risen Healers utilized Jerry's inabilities and deficiencies of earthly origin in positive ways to dramatize both the power and the potential in terms of how the energy could be put to spiritual use. The sight of his parents acted as a cleansing jolt of energy but there was also a delayed reaction. As the truth began to emerge and then form in his mind—and hence as his environment— it frightened the very wits out of his residual ego-mind, thus rendering it incapable of keeping its hold on his Authentic Self's awareness any longer.

"This is akin to how certain healers on the earth will work in order to free a person possessed of 'unclean spirits'—which are, in effect, artificial semi-intelligences and dictatorial tyrants that live as parasites on the energy of their host. Once forced out into the open, they can no longer survive in the higher light of Authentic Self, which brings clarity to the afflicted while burning away the clouds of malignant, negative thoughts and beliefs. It was just such an artificial intelligence—albeit the very small, hypersensitive mechanism you call the ego-mind—which screamed and thrashed in terror when it came face to face with the true reality of Jerry's new life. No longer having a material body to control, it knew that its program had truly come to an end. Jerry was placed into a deep and healing sleep from which he gradually awoke, strengthened by the same prayers of 'light-flowers' that you had sent to my bedside when I was recovering.

"I can tell you that he is now having a truly authentic existence, hardly able to contain his excitement in exploring everything and anything, just like the little trouble-maker he was on earth. He eagerly awaits your own arrival. I only hope I'm invited along on some of the trips he has planned!"

"Tim, forgive me, but I can't help suspecting that you're a bit of a trouble maker just like Jerry was on earth."

"And you can never help smiling when you scold me for such things."

"I must be humble then, for I can't help laughing at myself for doing so."

"Yep, you're humble alright. Forgive me for changing the subject, but I believe you have some more liberation dramas you'd like to share?"

"I do, and thanks for reminding me, and also for sharing about my cousin. What a relief it is to know that his terror was temporary."

I've been waiting to hear from Jerry but that hasn't happened, and neither Tim nor anyone else will explain why. On this subject they are strangely silent, for reasons still unapparent to me. I did, however, briefly hear from Jerry through a friend who is a medium, but he was only able to quickly say, "thank you for helping me," and nothing more beyond that.

Before I move on to the next example of a liberation drama, I will share something of relevance that I came across in my researches after the incident with Jerry, which validates much of what happened. It's not uncommon for information to come to me in this way as a response to my mindfully seeking answers and insights about an experience.

Robert Crookall, (1890–1981) was a well-known and highly respected scientist in Britain and a member of the Geological Society. He resigned from his geological work in 1952 so that he could devote the rest of his life to psychological studies, with an emphasis on psychic phenomenon, out-of-body experiences, and the afterlife. A prolific scientific researcher and writer, perhaps his greatest work was *The Supreme Adventure—Analyses of Psychic Communications*, a painstakingly compiled volume examining the literature and evidence on the experiences of death and its survival.

Crookall's study is particularly important because it is the only one that has closely examined the differences between natural and enforced death and how they generally manifest. In meticulous detail he organized the transition process from beginning to end in a categorization of seven experiences. These are: 1-The Call; 2-The Life Review; 3-Shedding The Body; 4-The Sleep; 5-The Awakening; 6-The Judgment; and 7-The Assignment. So thorough is his examination that in Shedding the Body, he breaks the experience down further into three parts, which are Natural Death, Enforced Death Other Than By Explosion, and Enforced Death By Explosion. Crookall's explanations helped to confirm certain aspects of Jerry's experience. Much of Crookall's research information about enforced death came from mediumistic contact with disincarnated soldiers who had died in the World Wars.[50]

Experiences like Jerry's, where the shedding of the body had been enforced—but not through an explosion—are similar to natural deaths. Scant physical pain, if any, is felt. Detaching from the body through enforced causes usually results in little more than a brief coma. Commonly, the fact that they have permanently left the body is often unrealized for some time. Many see their own body right away but don't recognize it nor do they realize that they are no longer in it. Also, they can suffer from feeling the grief of still-embodied

---

[50] Robert Crookall, *The Supreme Adventure—Analyses of Psychic Communications* (Cambridge: James Clarke and Co. Limited, 1961), 21–22.

friends but usually cannot make embodied people see or hear them. Like Jerry, they often wonder if they might be dreaming.

While many of these factors are similar to non-enforced transitions, Crookall found marked differences regarding enforced death. In natural death experiences most people go into a kind of sleep for awhile, whereas in enforced death the transitioning person tends to be awake and alert at once or very soon thereafter. Instead of feeling normal peace and security, enforced death usually brings bewilderment and confusion, as it did to the people at the World Trade Center. Rather than finding themselves in an environment of light and beauty, those in situations like Jerry's will more likely manifest places reflecting their confusion, appearing as fog, mist, and other states ranging from blurred dimness to total darkness. Many of these criteria appear to directly relate to Jerry's experience, except I didn't notice any indication that he was able to perceive his deceased body.

The following liberation drama is especially fascinating as it further illustrates just how some souls might manifest their personal and environmental realities directly due to the state of their emotional, mental, and spiritual states upon transition. Although this seemingly unresolved rescue seems quite nightmarish—like Jerry's—it is temporary, meaning that the environment could last for a short or a long period of "time."

LIBERATION DRAMA 3

"Along with a team of others, I find myself exploring some sort of ship or vessel in space. I am aware that another team is exploring a similar one elsewhere, as we are in intermittent but faint contact. The interior of the ship consists primarily of long, low-lighted halls with raised platforms on either side, and the overall effect is of a museum or zoo without bars or other barriers. On the platforms, spaced evenly apart, are all kinds of animals, some familiar to me, others not. They all appear to be sleeping but closer inspection reveals that they are conscious but unable to move. Upon still closer examination, listening to their mental and verbal conversations with each other and with themselves suggests that these were once people, not animals—and that upon transition they manifested on this plane in their present condition now before us. Although none appear to be physically restrained, they are unable to move and lay flattened out against the floor, as if gravity is so great they can't lift even their heads or limbs. Their conversations range from calm, rational thinking to extremes of illogical, nonsensical thought processes, including confusion, fear, sadness, and anger, often punctuated by outbursts of growls, shrieks, tweets, and barks.

"I pause before what appears to be a bear-skin rug, but which actually *is* a bear, deflated in appearance and unable to move. Its female voice, which I hear mentally, is extremely preoccupied with her nails and which color to varnish them. Sometimes she mutters out loud or weeps softly to herself. A member of the team is attempting to communicate with one of the other beings but gives up after no apparent success. But as I'm kneeling before the bear I notice that the being my teammate had been with was apparently aware of his communication attempt. It begins talking about my colleague in an alarmed way with one of its neighbors, who in turn passes the message down the platform. With each new recipient the content of the message is escalated a bit more and an increasing panic starts to arise.

"I leave my position and inform my teammates that we had best not attempt any more direct communication with the ship's occupants, as it seems to only cause fear. We notice that the general atmosphere is starting to radiate a lot of negative emotional energy. The last thing that I can remember is that we are all standing in a room filled with some sort of machinery or controls, and strategizing about leaving."

LIBERATION DRAMA 4

This event involves people who had not completed their transition and were actually stuck in the midst of it. Certain factors, such as fear of death or ignorance about the process and reality of survival, as well as cultural influences, can affect the actual transition process. As this event shows, people who often cross over together—that is, those who die in some shared event— also often share the same mind-set and so may co-manifest their transition drama or scenario. It also demonstrates that once we have left our earthly bodies and the confines of the planet, space-time is no longer the same factor it once was. This particular drama suggests that the individuals involved are from an earlier century and had been trapped or inhibited for quite some "time."

"I find myself on an old sea-going ship, a large wooden one with many sails, from an era before the invention of steam engines. The overall feeling is early nineteenth century. I'm with a few others on the ship, who are rescuers like me, but most of the passengers are spirit women and children, all in poor shape and frightened, their clothes very dirty and tattered. It's a black night, stormy and freezing, and the ship rocks violently on the choppy water. The spirit men are being attended to on a separate ship—faintly visible in the distance. The reason for this segregation is not clear to me.

"It comes time to leave and the other ship in the distance is signaled. Rather than using technology that might be frightening, such as electric lights or lasers to signal them, one of the teams gets creative and hoists some large oil-soaked sheets and sets them aflame, by which the ship in the distance becomes suddenly and clearly visible. We see that the men's ship has also raised flaming sheets. We begin to sail in what we seem to naturally know to be the right direction, the men's ship following."

LIBERATION DRAMA 5

Finally, I share a very brief extract from an old dream journal that seems to indicate that I was somehow involved in a child's transition. It was written long before I was consciously aware of any such thing as rescue missions, and is in rather dreamy, mystical language.

"I meet others here and there along the way, many in different layers of time and space-reality than I, for they are not where I am yet, and still take instruction. But they know of The Journey. They will be there with me, for the The Journey is through time itself and beyond it and beyond space. Everything is so full of wonder and alien beauty. I touch down at spots where little ones receive education on their parents' roofs, on barn roofs, or on platforms constructed in the air of dream-space.

"I come upon a woman, a mother who is dreaming that she is by her little girl's bed; the child is dressed in blue clothes and blue beads. The child is asleep in this dream of mine. The mother cries, 'Why must you take her? Why? Why now?' I can only answer, 'It must be.' But I feel the mother's feelings, and tell her that this child is one of the youngest yet wisest we have ever seen. I smile, as again I remember teaching young ones how to swim in a pool of dream water, and to catch the art of flying in the wind."

I have been involved in many spirit interventions over the years. Some are simple events, such as helping my cousin Jerry cross a field, but most are extremely complex in approach and design, requiring creativity as well as experience and a certain mental and spiritual stability in one's life. Most of us still embodied on the earth will be involved during our terrestrial lives in some kind of service for others who have left their bodies—parents helping children, children helping parents, friends assisting friends, and strangers serving strangers.

TWENTY

DWELLING PLACES

"Each of us makes one's own weather, determines the color of
the skies, in the emotional universe which we inhabit."
~ Fulton J. Sheen

66 ugust, I know you sometimes sadly dwell on the very short time
we were together on the earth. Your thoughts go back to the cozy
apartment I once had in an older section of the city—I
understand completely. It was a special place, in one of those charming
buildings that fortunately became designated as a protected historical structure.
You were very sensitive to its unique spiritual ambience, and you loved all the
nuances that made it an impressive space in spite of its compactness—the
moldings, the floor-to-ceiling windows with their antique glass panes, the
fireplace you wanted to clean so it could be used once again, and the special
bookshelves with the magical fold-in typewriter constructed by a clever
craftsman. You yearn even for those wintry days when the wind whistled
through the poorly insulated windows, and you've not forgotten about the
spare set of pajamas I kept for you—too large, but you wore them anyway.

"You don't have to look back on that place and time as if it's all been lost,
never to be seen again. It's never left my mind—literally. I've manifested it
here where I am, including the building and even the neighborhood. I'm there
now, and it's more charming and special than ever. Remember how terribly
slow the plumbing was? No more, for my mind has repaired it and now the tub
fills in no time. *Of course* I can take a bath—why not? It's still a pleasure of mine
to soak forever, with nothing to do. I've even added some more kitchen space
and a window behind the sink that looks out onto a tropical sea, one that was
never there on the earth. There's also a new door looking out onto a garden of
willow trees around an elaborately carved and cascading fountain.

"You're wondering about the kitchen. I can cook if I want to—and I sometimes do because I enjoy it. I don't need food in the way you need earthly sustenance but I can still get pleasure from the same forms should I so desire. The newly Risen often continue to manifest and eat food from habit but eventually forget about it. I'm sure you and I will want to go on expeditions to other lands, and will bring along a big picnic basket just for the fun of it.

"Sustenance exists all around the Risen as light, and we ingest this light by being in it, or we can cause it to manifest as blackberry pie with vanilla ice-cream—I know that's your favorite. And to satisfy another question you have but won't ask—digestion occurs under higher, finer principles of chemical transformation in the Risen, so you won't see any outhouses around here.

"That apartment was also Bigfoot's while on earth. He's often there, anticipating my arrival. It represents a homey security to him—although I don't profess to understand the minds of cats anymore than before. Well, perhaps a little more, since we can now communicate mind to mind but he's often way ahead of me about many things. It seems he had much more mental clarity while on earth than I ever did. He remembered the summer vacations at the beach and so helped manifest the ocean environment in which I awoke.

"I don't live in the apartment all the time. The word 'live' is not quite correct in connection with the way dwelling spaces exist here—actually, 'dwell' works much better. And the word 'time' isn't exactly right either. I don't dwell there all the time—hardly ever, actually, for there is far too much beyond it. Infinooty! There are never-ending environments for me to explore or manifest and occupy for as long as I want. But that particular former earthly space still lives in your heart, for you often visit it in your mind, especially when you're feeling lonely and pining for the good old days.

"Whenever your mind is focused on that place, it draws me to it, too. I dwell in that space once more, and in feeling your loneliness I experience and share the same emotion of wistfulness with you. I lie on that same overly soft bed and wish you could be there with me, holding hands while reading or just being quiet together. I greatly miss you—did you not realize that? I'm not some omnipotent, omniscient being who can be with you whenever I want, as I want—if only I could. I'm not beyond feelings just because I am beyond my former earth life. I feel more intensely, more fiercely, now that the density of my terrestrial body is no longer dimming the light of my spirit. It's when your mind and heart create a welling-up of emotional outpouring that I can especially feel you. These feelings are like beacons in the mists separating our worlds. They guide me to my own inner space where I can find you once again. Much of our conversation takes place in this space—you in your mind and I in mine, as our minds and hearts strive to bring the two overlays of experience as close together as possible. Someday my experience will be yours and we'll build a fire in the fireplace together—the chimney is all clean and ready.

"In the greater expanse of mind that is now mine, I lie here at times in the bed, sharing your experience. I have the advantage of not having to dwell in earthly time, and freedom to go wherever my mind takes me, which is in spiritual time. I stay with you as best as I can, knowing that although I may be an invisible companion, I am one that you can feel and sometimes even see and hear with your inner spiritual senses. Those moments you feel something caressing your fingers, or tickling the side of your face? That's me, Dear Heart, reaching out to you with all the determination I can summon.

"For a short period after my transition I was closer to the earth plane and could find your dwelling place more easily, spending time with you practically within that same space, watching you as you went about your day. But my spirit body became increasingly rarified as the etheric components became finer in vibration. Any remaining residue of my terrestrial-astral body finally succumbed completely to earth's gravity and was drawn back into the cycle of materiality—as all material has for uncounted æons. It became progressively more difficult for me to be so close to you on the material plane. It seems to me that it was my mind's will that drew and kept me near as a response to your own evolution and self-awakening response to more spiritual light.

"As part of some mysterious process, it seems I had to search for you as my being responded to your love and the memories that swirled around me. Your memories had a gravity of their own and drew me to you, for my spirit body still trailed shadowy echoes of earth—etheric tendrils of barely a few atoms. They loosely vibrated in resonance to your own earthly environment and acted as a tuning device, eventually allowing me to find and reveal myself to you. Any more manifestations of the material kind may become less frequent and not more as we had hoped. Now I am more purified as spirit and it is the stronger, more infinite energy of love that draws us close. I'd like to see if we could find some way that you can continue to increasingly share my experience of dwelling here. Every day of your time is one day closer to when we will walk arm-in-arm down great tree-lined lanes, deep within ancient, majestic forests. Can you let yourself dwell within that knowing?

"I see you are wondering what lies beyond this tiny apartment where Bigfoot and I sometimes rest. Nothing and yet everything lies beyond it. When I go for walks through the old neighborhood, it's the same, yet so much more. Each and every thing is alive, suffused by glowing, pulsating, prismatic lights, filled with life and energy as the sun-filled trees in the parks, effervescent as the fountains which give forth music, their waters welling up and cascading down pieces of sculpture that are never the same. Birds, animals, butterflies, and flowers of exquisite and dramatic beauty populate this geography. It is all a manifestation of my mind, yet infinitely more. It is also a co-manifestation, for there are many other Risen here, drawn together by the resonance of our minds, united by curiosity and love and the never-ending desire to experience and share. Some of the people are familiar to me, many are not, but all are enjoying themselves and each other. Sometimes the landscape will gently change and appear as if several geographies exist in the same place, as many souls overlap here in similar ways of vibration of mind and emotion.

"Although many prefer to walk in this sort of environment, some float or fly. There are those who take pleasure in vehicles of every kind, from old Model T's to trains, planes, and even boats on gentle streams, scaled down for individual use or for small groups of people. I've never seen anything like your giant jets that carry hundreds of people at a time although there is nothing barring such things, so I'm sure they must exist somewhere. It all depends on what we allow our minds to manifest.

"Some travel through the purity of thoughtful desire, meaning that the mere thought of wanting to be somewhere results in instantly being there. Many prefer this method of movement to all others. We choose our method of passage according to taste and need, whatever pleases us.

"I can seemingly walk forever onward but never come to an end as if eternity is contained within a few short blocks. You and I have been shown and now understand, to a very limited degree, that one of the infinite truths about 'forever' is that *we* manifest it. Some might say we create it but to be nit-picky, everything has already been created and so everything already just is. We are the shapers and shifters of creation, causing it to manifest as it pleases us. There is no end to anything, no walls or boundaries. There are no finalities simply because wherever you go, there you are, something that people on earth already intuit. On the Risen level we say, 'As you go, you are.' This is the manifested realization of one's immortality.

"We are all one with That Which Created All—Original Creator Source. We are of the same Mind, and so wherever or whenever we are, Mind Is. There is no place or time Mind can't be. If we move 'outward,' that movement can continue without ceasing, manifesting environments within which to dwell. The very movement of Mind is manifestation. If we move in a way that we desire to be 'inward,' the result is the same. If I desire to dwell in light or darkness, or seasons and weather, there are no limitations imposed upon my desires except those I place upon them.[51]

"In your continual learning about Risen existence you're realizing more closeness to me and my existence and you're finding hints about some of the surprises I have waiting for you."

"I suspect you mean, Tim, the daydreams I've had lately, which sometimes feel as if they might burst into life but then fade quickly, often beyond the

---

[51] Tim's experiences sound very similar to the currently developing theory of *biocentrism*, which posits that consciousness manifests the Universe, and not the other way around. – *AG*

reach of memory. Although I can't picture these memories to myself, I seem to have the awareness that you're building some special places for me. Many times I've had a waking dream about being with you again in those especially beautiful parts of the city where the brownstones of yesteryears still stand, outside the wear and tear of time. I've always loved those quiet, tree-shaded places and have thought that when I've crossed over, I'll find or perhaps even make such a city dwelling for myself. Sharing such a place with you would make this fantasy perfect. You were listening in, weren't you?"

"What quiet joy it gives me to hear you say these things, August. We've begun to share our lives in the spirit worlds already. I would never wish to hide anything from you but I do indeed have surprises. I see that either you are becoming more skilled at reading my mind or our minds dwell in such similar states that we tend toward manifestations that are alike—I can hardly tell."

"Tim, there is some particular music I listen to that somehow brings me to exquisite states of mind—places, buildings, and landscapes filled with those things that bring me joy and comfort. While listening to it I often spend time mentally dwelling in one particular place, which I've come to know as my 'country cabin by the moon-lit lake.' Will you be there when I finally row my little boat to the dock across that lake and walk up the path?"

"I've already been there, awaiting you to join me on the porch swing. We meet there often while your body sleeps and your spirit flies free, visiting your manifestations of mind in person. I've also been to your wonderful estate, which looks like something no less out of 'Brideshead Revisited' and increases and beautifies in some way every time I visit there—as well as does the animal life. Did you know I just met the elephants there? Elephants! You have elephants roaming around there, along with countless cats, horses, dogs, and birds. Herb and flower gardens have been springing up recently, and since I've yet to see other people there, I can only assume it's all your doing."

"I *am* very fond of elephants, Tim, and I've made it a habit of inviting them to my lands for some time. I can only warn you to watch out for the thundering herds of dachshunds. What's your understanding of how these dwelling places of ours come to be? I can see how yours came about, as you're actually there as a Risen One, but what of mine?"

"You know of the mind's powers, August, as you've been creatively manifesting your own dwelling places all along. It's similar to how living spaces are manifested on earth. The place you live in now did not exist until you decided to find it, and then your mind began to conceive of possibilities—from there your inner vision proceeded to externalize them. Your entire world experience is one immense, complex manifestation on the material plane. Cities, towns, and houses on earth previously existed only in people's minds. Granted, the external manifestation process is much slower and tedious on your material plane than it is in the Risen states, but the principal is the same—

mind manifests reality. All the fantasies about places where you would love to dwell not only become possible once you transition into Risen life, but they can begin to manifest even before your transition. It depends on one's mental and emotional clarity, one's will, and especially one's self-evolution, which together bring enlightened understanding of Mind and its unlimited abundance.

"While you're dreaming of that cozy little cottage or even a castle tucked away in some hidden glen, the strength of your desires will cause the building elements to come together in the realm of the Higher Mind, which is your mind, my mind, our Mind—it is all One—and particular elements of light will coalesce into an actuality that reflects those desires. The more it becomes real to you in your mind, the more it becomes 'real–ized' on the higher planes where such things are meant to occur. The Risen are capable of manifesting realized wonders of landscape and architecture, which are their dwelling places and are far beyond the physical possibilities of the earth plane.

"Of course I'm speaking of the positive, spiritually inspired powers of the individual use of Mind. To the extent that one's thoughts, dreams and fantasies are able to manifest in ways that are beautiful and meaningful evidences the degree of spiritual evolution, of the self-love and self-esteem that enable and support the love and esteem of other individuals, and the level of understanding that Mind is a shared experience as well as an individual one. There are those on the earth, who, for whatever reasons unique to their experience, understanding, and individual evolution, are unable to manifest much more than a Risen tar-paper shack—if even that. While they might be able to fantasize about a sumptuous Hollywood mansion, more than likely the nature of that image is of the earth-bound, ego-mind's desires and so could not in any real way be imaginally expressed in the higher astral realms.

"For example, the nature of greed appears to manifest in the earthly realm as an energy that is able to acquire, accumulate, and manifest imagined wealth in all its forms of ego-mind desire. In the Risen Worlds, however, the nature of greed, having been individualized and nurtured through belief and habit on the earth, but now accepted into the infinite capacity of Authentic Self, is no longer a toy in the hands of the limited and now dissolved ego-mind. Instead, through the greater and unlimited power of the Higher Mind, the emptiness of greed is like dry air blowing over a parched landscape. And that is what most likely will manifest—landscapes of vast, empty expanses of dead and dying vegetation, unable to grow or revive from lack of the energy of a loving, serene spirit that is connected to Original Source, whence outpours all sustenance."

"A parched landscape—that sounds like hell."

"Hell is in the individual, self-enforced, separated mind. It *is* that manifestation of mind. Hell manifests when a small part of Mind tries to cordon off a section of Heaven for itself, which is as impossible as a piece of sunlight separating itself from the sun. I'm learning that Heaven is in the Mind, and Mind is the True Reality, existing beneath the illusory environments of the self-damned mind. Perfection is not something to be attained; it is something to be realized, to awaken to. Oh, the incredible ecstasy of awakening to the realization that there is no end to awakening! There is no end to Heaven, continually unfolding and revealing itself as we awaken to ever-increasing awareness of having our being in and as paradise."

"And yet, Tim, I've seen vast spirit geographies that reflect the neuroses and paranoias of the individual ego-mind, while still seeming to be grand and glorious in their own way. In other words, some might find these places hellish, but one person's Hell could be another person's idea of Heaven."

"I know these places you mention, August. Entire cities, civilizations, lands, worlds, and universes of expression can be realized by one mind resonating with another or by enjoining with countless other similarly resonating and resounding minds. Becoming a Risen One does not automatically change who we are. We can change ourselves because of the gift of free will from Original Source. We *are* our transition. Like attracts like here. And so beauty, for example, really is in the mind of the beholder, and the continual process of awakening to awareness is a continual realization of that beauty, ever refining and redefining, and never the same.[52]

"We've mentioned that not all ego-mentalities acquiesce to the greater Risen reality. Surrender cannot be forced in any way. Some ego-personalities crystallize and survive beyond the dissolution of the earthly body. Rather than relinquish the fear that immortality might not be a reality, these personalities believe that although they've survived an earthly death, true immortality is impossible, and 'real death' is still inevitable. Their intellectual arrogance traps them within this hard-shelled belief. Many of earth's greatest individual minds now exist in co-manifested ego-geographies of dazzling intellectual beauty, and because of their continued loyalty to and dependence on their earthly personalities, are located somewhere between terrestrial space-time and Risen time-space. They are still very aware of the Earth and continue to inspire other great but still-embodied intellects with their own delusions—often materializing in the form of theories, articles, books, and films on Earth. Because of the advanced scope of their individualized minds they inevitably comprehend much of Risen truth, and so while rarely wicked are often tricksters. Because they believe some sort of humorless cosmic joke has been played on them, they get their 'revenge' by passing it onto their earthly brethren. They are exceptionally resistant to any kind of rescue efforts, but may eventually discover the higher levels of Risen truth, usually through boredom.

---

[52] For a detailed, first-hand report on one such "sub-Risen" geography, see *The Diakka and Their Earthly Victims*, by Andrew Jackson Davis (Boston: Colby & Rich, 1886, reprinted by Health Research, Mokelumne Hill, CA, 1971).

"Words like 'hell' and 'damned' are not an indication of judgment, Aug. They are just words and it's as you suggest—we all find our pleasures in all ways. Where there is no judgment, all ways are permitted, always. Every individual is appropriate, and that is usually something learned after leaving the earth. We are extending our experience to others through this book to offer the opportunity to learn a few things before their transition. The great and loving nature of Original Creator Source works through change, which can be put on pause here forever if one wants. But we will all eventually grow weary and feel stagnated by the unchanged, and what was once beautiful loses its light because of the stagnation, which is the lessening or withdrawal of interest, which is a lessening of light. What was once considered wondrous loses its luster from the reduction of light and from a less focused attention.

"I see the greatest gift we have been given by Original Creator Source as the ability to change our mind. Many, many souls, upon coming to a stagnated state of mind, become trapped by their ignorance of their true nature, which is that the Mind of the Highest Self is also their own mind and is shared by all individualized minds. The illusion of ignorance further manifests as an illusion of fear, and thus seems to result in a trap or as 'hell.' Many of our spirit rescues here involve the answering of mental and emotional cries for help from souls imprisoned in the illusion of their fears. Others never seem to feel the need to ask for help, and some even knowingly resist it."

"Tim, thanks for finding ways to share your realizations with me, even though my human brain can barely conceive of your experience. My heart longs for more—more experience, more expansion, and more life with you."

"Longing implies a lengthening, a slowing of time—do not long, August. Instead, embrace your realizations as actual manifestations of the reality of which I am an undying part. Let these embraces bring us instantly together and leave the longing to fade away. Let your spirit awake into its own conscious reality, where the ego-sense of time will diminish. In doing so you will increasingly see and experience that the earth around you will begin to fade— and has been fading, signaling the truth that transition commenced at the timeless moment your spirit was sparked upon the earth. Turn your attention toward the direction of transition, and let your mind flow in the eternal present that is your true world, and is our true world and home together."

TWENTY-ONE

KRISHNAMURTI SPEAKS

"Sorrow is not in death but in loneliness,
and conflict comes when you seek consolation,
forgetfulness, explanations, and illusions."
~ J. Krishnamurti, *The Little Book on Living*

Tim has not been my only intimate contact within the worlds of the Risen. I've been prepared all my life for these experiences, and in many continuing ways that are often beyond my present understanding. It's clear that spiritual guides and guardians have used my love for books, healing, nature, art, music, research, and learning as inspired sources of motivation.

One particular individual turned out to be both guide and guardian. While he was still in his body on earth he had been my watchful astral mentor since I had been born. He continued to act in this service after he transitioned to a higher plane. An incredible aspect of this relationship is that I was unaware of him until after his transition. He didn't want me to be aware of him but it was a "cosmic occurrence of unexpected potentiality" that made it crucial that he reveal himself.

It shouldn't be any surprise by now that this cosmic occurrence is difficult to put into words. Yet for me there's a very clear, experiential understanding at the deepest of levels. This understanding was assisted by my guardian's explanations and I'll try to relay them as simply as possible. Much of it may sound very strange but keep an open mind as Tim and I have continually asked. Understanding will take place on other levels besides that of your present state of mind.

~ 20 ~

These words may not make conscious sense at this time,
but my spiritual senses comprehend and retain
this knowledge for Authentic Self.

Some metaphysical traditions have suggested that that which we experience as our single "-I-" actually appears to be many internalized "-I's-." There is the internalized -I- that is the child, the -I- that is the parent, the -I- that is the career person, the lover, the secret dark dæmon, the mischievous sprite. The number of these invisible -I's- is as unlimited as our constantly changing, moment-to-moment living experience. Each -I- has its own mental and emotional expressions and each one has its own world—worlds within worlds. These smaller "selves" are not the simulate selves. They're actually mental aspects that manifest as very complex, inner manifestations of our earthly life as it evolves towards increasing awareness of Authentic Self—a very high -I-, indeed.

Up to this point we've been referring to Authentic Self as a kind of separate self or entity. It's now time to begin conceptualizing It also as the conscious experience of *Higher* Authentic Self.

This seemingly highest -I- is not the final goal, for It is always adapting and evolving. As mental aspects, our smaller selves exist as potentialities, and not all will come into our sphere of awareness. Of those that do, some will remain longer than others—some will grow, while others diminish. Each is as valid as all the infinite colors of the light spectrum, visible and invisible, shimmering and changing as one's relationship to one's self changes. These multi-selves enrich us with infinite potential for all experiences.

Authentic Self may be portrayed as if it's the be–all and end–all to personal evolution, but Creator Source Mind, which encompasses all individuated Higher Authentic Selves, does not put such boundaries on Its manifestations. Higher Authentic Self is itself a conglomerate of many potential selves, of which the earthly experience is but a slower vibrating, reflective process. From this perspective the potential selves of Higher Authentic Self are experienced as real and valid within their respective realities.

It is indeed a momentous event when we reach the end of the need for our earthly body and leave it, once and forever. But it is not *the* final event, for an earthly transition is also a reflective, experiential process of the higher planes beyond the earth. We will not want to live eternally on the next astral plane or on the next after that, or on the one after that. As immortal beings we have infinity in which to live, work, and play. The metamorphosis of caterpillar into butterfly will express and re-express itself as we grow into new states of awareness and move on into new experiences of life. Even the caterpillar/butterfly metaphor will transmute into something completely novel.

Our Higher Self and its Potential Higher Selves, as well as our earthly self and its potential selves, all exist simultaneously within and without different kinds of time. Mystics have sometimes described this simultaneity as "the center that is also the circumference." The centered experience—Authentic Self—is defined by its experience, which is its circumference. The circumference encompasses its center, and the two cannot be divided. They also can't exist without each other. Paradoxically, we humans are able to perceptually separate them, an illusionary aspect of our dualistic outlook upon our material universe. In timelessness, every thing and every self is connected, whether or not any particular self is able to experience an awareness of connection.

Sometimes such connections can be experienced and observed. This happened to me, as far as my human mentality can comprehend. One of my Higher Selves, realizing its particular potentiality of greatest possible fullness within its particular dimension, began the transitional process that is akin to the same great event here on earth that we usually refer to as "death." The Authentic Self I know as my identity here on earth was connected in a particular way to this other Higher Self. Suddenly there were no barriers between that Self and the earthly self I experience as "August." I became aware of, and then resonant with, this other Higher Self to such an intimate extent that I found myself literally beginning the early stage of transition here on earth. I won't go into any of the details of what this was like, other than to simply say that it was very frightening and did not feel natural or appropriate, and that it wasn't a type of mental instability or breakdown. Since that experience I've wondered how many are diagnosed as mentally ill when they are in fact having a "spiritual emergency," something Christina and Stanislav Grof and others have explored and written about in great and caring detail.[53]

My guardian came forward to prevent my premature absorption into the experience of the transition of that Higher Self. He revealed himself to get my attention and ground me firmly back into my earthly awareness. I don't know if anyone can truly imagine my reactions to suddenly hearing, as loud and clear as an inner bell, a stern but kindly voice announcing himself as "Krishnamurti," that he had been with me since I was a child, and to not be afraid. I felt a certain amount of disbelief but then relief as his unwavering presence calmed and restored me to complete stability on all levels in less than a day.

---

[53] *Spiritual Emergency: When Personal Transformation Becomes a Crisis,* eds. S. Grof & C. Grof (New York: G.P. Putnam's Sons, 1989).

At first, and then for months afterward, he seemed to express what I can only call annoyance—as if this whole episode had been an inconvenience to him. He had no qualms about telling me that in *his* view nothing about the event should be retained in my conscious memory, as it could interfere with my experience while I still remained embodied on the earth.

This presence did indeed seem to be the gentle but sometimes impatient spiritual philosopher, "K."—as he referred to himself on earth. His appearance explained my lifelong attraction to and love for this person whom I had never met in the body. He made it clear that I had, up to that point, survived all my life without any conscious awareness of him, but now it was up to me if I wanted to continue this new conscious relationship, and on what level. As he insisted while on the earth, he would not be an authority in my life.[54]

I had no problem with returning to the way things were, but I didn't see how it was possible. So I suggested that our relationship, which I felt was now greatly changed by the event, should continue as one of exploration and sharing but tempered by our mutual need for solitude and personal authority in one's life. He agreed to this, pleased with my acknowledgement and use of my own authority. Although we rarely speak to one another I have had some very rewarding and enlightening dialogues with Krishnaji—a name that his brother, Nitya, who also once made his presence known to me in a small but precious way—suggested I was privileged to use. On earth he usually referred to himself as "K." and so that will do just as well here.

The K. with whom I occasionally communicate can no longer be called "K." in the sense of his former earth-defined personality. He no longer needs that name. In fact, he realized that the name "Krishnamurti" was no longer necessary while still on the earth, which is why he referred to himself as "K." or simply, as "one." When I spiritually reach out to connect with him it's toward his unique, core vibrational essence, his Higher Self aspect. I project some of the former K. aspects as a form of greeting process and he responds in kind as a resonance of those former aspects. As my own vibrations have ever-so-slightly increased over the years, it has become less necessary for him to maintain his "K-ness," and I've been able to experience him in new and intimate ways. This is also something I've been experiencing with Tim.

Following are some of the talks I've had with K.—while on solitary walks in the woods, or lying in bed trying to nap and unable to quiet my mind, or while sitting at my desk and working on some trivial writing matter. If near a computer when we began to communicate, I would just go to it, sit quietly and

---

[54] Jiddu Krishnamurti (1895–1986), a passionate advocate for psychological freedom, was known as a philosopher, teacher, and a gentle but obstinate and sometimes curmudgeonly saint. He left us to wonder at the inherent and clarified nobility in his refusal to neither lead nor follow—all the while remaining open, compassionate, insightful, and awake.

type what he said to me. Somehow I retained what he said even when I was walking somewhere, or while riding on a train—he would simply recall it for me while I sat at the keyboard later on. It's not unusual for him to ask me to refer to books of other writers or even the dictionary, as he's very picky about there being no misunderstanding about each word he chooses through me, and he still retains his characteristic fondness for symbols and their meanings.

This particular discourse continues from another begun several days earlier. Although such conversations would stop when I had to attend to something else, they would always begin where we left off, even days or weeks later. It's clear to me that much of my present understanding about my life and my experience in the universe is related to what K. has been sharing with me every since I was born. A good deal of his meaning still evades me and there are things that I personally don't agree with, but I continually find more to learn from and delight in whenever I re-read these valued talks.

 "Have you ever gone out at night when the sky is clear and cloudless, and gazed up at the countless stars, the myriads of galaxies that seem to be above you—and then realize they are also all around you? You are part of them because you are within them. What is this shift of realization that has taken place? Does one not feel at first overwhelmed, perhaps even frightened? Surely, one feels awe. One no longer wants to be here, but *there*. And so a feeling of longing arises, a complex feeling, one that we are not sure is pleasure or sadness, or both. Perhaps one suddenly sees that one is not so important, or so powerful, or so individual. Is this feeling informing us of an error in perception, or is it asking us to venture further? Depending upon our individual or group beliefs we may venture and become lost and found in any number of ways.

"We have come to see, you and I, how the word 'belief' is derived from the more basic definition of 'to like or to desire.' To desire something implies movement, an activity where we either move toward that which we desire, or when we focus our energy and attention on making that which we desire move toward us, which is usually quite often the case. That is, we reach out to attempt to take that which we desire. Even the act of reaching out implies movement away from one's experience of self.

"So there is this movement that appears to take us in a direction away from the Great Source, which is where we are and have been all along from the beginning. If this movement is taking us, then we are now in a position of powerlessness and seemingly having no choice in the matter. We do not want to simply be here where we are, but *there,* where we are not. And if in our own mind we manage to be where we are not, where is *that*? Is that not an illusion? What feelings arise when we are no longer present? We feel displaced, away from home, or homesick if you will. Where once we were aware, choosing neither here nor there, we are now caught in our act of choosing, which begins to take us further and further away from our home.

"To return home, to the place from where one's being and awareness of being arises, one must let go of belief, which is desire. Often this is discussed in terms of the word 'surrender' and immediately we have all kinds of reactions, none too favorable most of the time. Why is that? Let us look at that word, 'surrender.' Please be patient, and go now to the dictionary—let's explore this together. We see that the basic meaning of 'surrender' is to give up one's power over something else, so of course one can see mischief arising already, as we like power, don't we? And there is that word 'like' again, from which 'belief' is derived."

[I am again referred to the dictionary and note that 'surrender' means 'to render back in a direction which is literally above or beyond us.' 'Render,' which in Latin is *reddere*, means 'to restore back.' The Latin *re* means 'back' and *dere* is from *dare*, 'to give.']

"So, we see that 'to render' essentially means 'to give back.' Giving back does not mean that one will lose what one is giving in the process, or that someone will take the gift away, never to return it, lost from sight forever. We are giving something back because it was theirs to begin with. It means that in the act of surrender a movement is begun that is not out of desire, not out of grasping, not reaching out to take. Instead this movement joins with us and also enters us into the eternal flow of infinite, universal abundance.

"Surrender is the hand that reaches out to gently touch the awaiting pendulum of the clock, to begin its first movement that will allow it to continue on by giving back the service of marking chronological time. Surrender is the birth of a child into the awaiting world, to begin its first movements that will continue on in its newly found potential to give back to the world. Surrender is one's hand reaching out to another in an open gesture of human companionship, in giving some food to eat or clothes to wear; rendering an act that will live on and continue to allow the receiver to give back. To surrender is to dissolve into the perpetual motion of love. Reduced to its simplest terms, surrendering is giving, and so it is a gift.

"Surrendering is not giving up. It is giving. We give for many reasons. It has nothing to do with freedom, there is no such thing as a 'free' gift. We know in our heart that a true gift is one given without expectations, without beliefs, without desires, without likes or dislikes. Take away these things, which would otherwise be attached to the gift, thereby attaching us to it and which would take us away from our place of awareness, and then we are able to remain in the ever present rising of self-awareness.

"At first we give for the pleasure of giving alone and not expecting anything in return, although often we *are* expecting pleasure, you see? The attachment is still there. This still implies desire, a wanting to take, which implies movement and measurement, which is time. The so-called pleasure of giving is what one actually receives in return, regardless of one's desires. It is a simultaneous exchange and therefore infinite. That is to say, time is of no consequence during that exchange. As one surrenders one is no longer trapped in the violence of time and all that it implies. Instead, one is that surrender. Or more simply, one is that gift."

A few days later—

"You have become interested in the subject of awareness. What does it mean to be aware of one's own self? You might think that here is a very difficult and complicated concept, or else something of a totally different and simple nature. Most of us feel that we are certainly aware beings as we are right now. If we weren't we would be asleep, wouldn't we? We must maintain such a belief and are in fact already engaged in the difficult and complicated side, simply because we cannot see that we have already answered our own question.

"Those of us who are still circling in the slave's walk of hope and are desperate enough to long for something better, a simpler life with less demands and more rewards, are often more aware of ourselves through the medium of our suffering. Those who are, for whatever reasons, more intuitive than the average human being, might drift in and out of self-awareness through feelings and dreams. A very small child might be astutely self-aware, but that is quickly and tragically overshadowed and eventually extinguished by the hopes, dreams, and sufferings that are its parents' legacy, perhaps handed down over many generations, even many centuries, constantly being embellished with a peculiar type of refinement that is both alluring and addicting. If one could be totally and completely aware, totally free of unawareness, there would be nothing to be lost or gained, neither from the past nor from the future.

"Is self-awareness the same as self-knowledge? What does it mean to say, 'I know myself?' Let us examine this question closely without sentiment or criticism. Especially without criticism, for we are merely attempting to observe, and that is enough for now.

"Alright, I say, I know that I love to eat a certain food. But that is a thought where I think I know something about myself. So is the love of this food a fact, or something that I have simply acquired, perhaps because my family always ate it, or the companion I want to impress eats it now? It cannot be a fact, you see. One can exchange the word 'food' for any other word, such as 'belief,' 'country,' 'lover.' Let us remember that words are symbols and not the thing. But the thing itself, is not *that* a symbol? Our belief, our country, our lover represents or symbolizes something that is much deeper within our self, and for many reasons now appears as an apparent material object, circumstance, or entity. One's own perceived self is such a manifestation.

"Perhaps I love this particular food because my body needs it in some way, possibly due to some deficiency. It may be a fact that my body needs it, and this is knowledge that is apparent and easily verifiable. It does not matter if I love this food; I might even hate it. As continually manifesting materializations, our bodies already have a self-knowledge that sustains and regulates them to be able to survive. So it seems that it is possible to know about the body, which is what we mean here by our self, and to know about one's beliefs, one's country, and one's lover.

"One might say, then, that in order for there to be self-awareness one must have a body, for we need something of which to be aware, and it is only through the physical senses that we are able to be aware of this body. One, therefore, is self-aware. Look at your hand and you will find that you can apparently project some sort of attention into every part of it, provided it is healthy, right down to a fingertip. If you are now in your fingertip, what has happened to the rest of your body? It has not disappeared because you have withdrawn your attention from it. Or has it? Can one continue to send the attention further on, into the cells, into the cells' contents, into the blood, into the very molecules of the bone marrow?

"We may use this thought to rationalize a belief in an afterlife, for example. That is to say, a place where we will continue to live after we have finished our time on the earth, and where we will continue to have bodies. One needs a body to be self-conscious; if you take away the body one cannot be conscious. We need some sort of body of which to be aware. But we have just seen that what we have been calling the self is also the body, whether or not we realized this at first, and that the body does not need our attention to its blood and bone and cells in the way that we think our self needs attention. We learn how to take care of our body in the proper way because it tells us how, if we look and listen, if we use our senses. That is what our physical senses are for, to enable us to take care of our body, to keep it safe, warm, and nourished. We learn what is poisonous and harmful to the body and some of us avoid all or some of those things. The body has an established self-knowledge, and it can go on without our attention, even in the deepest sleep. So without knowing precisely how, we might feel that we can say we know our body is self-aware.

"There is, then, the arising feeling or sensation that we are *not* our body. That it is more like a vehicle in which we wake up in every day, to embark on yet another exciting or boring day's journey, until we can park it and leave it to rest. If we permit a close observation of this we might be able to see that at the deepest and most simple of levels, that which we call 'awareness of the body-vehicle' does not change—it only adds or subtracts, multiplies or divides all the various projections which we call 'the world.'

"The error that we make is the grandiose assumption that it is even possible to know anything. We may think we know, but we do not. I say, 'I know myself, for I do such-and-such a thing all the time.' Do you truly know why you do this thing all the time? In the same way that you can direct your attention to the tip of your finger, try to direct your attention to your behavior. You will travel endlessly back in mental time as you find one point of origin or cause for the behavior, but then this leads to the previous one, and then the one before that, and so on. You will discover that you will not be able to travel endlessly or even very far, for those people and places and things that transmitted the behavior, beliefs, and thoughts left the world long ago and cannot provide you with any more answers or clues. And so you will come to what will, at first, seem like a wall beyond which you cannot go.

"This is the point where one can say, 'Well, I see then that I do not know.' There is no physical wall, but rather only a projection that shows we are still being held and overpowered by thought. If there really is a wall, then surely you should be able to find the cause of it, and remove or remake it, but you would still be manipulating a projection. We can say now that here is the nearness of not knowing. Here is the edge of the world that we thought we knew, and which has now come to an end. Can we accept that? Perhaps not, and we will either turn back in fear and retreat to that which we think is safe, or else use our beliefs to continue projecting our personal worlds.

"However, can one sit for awhile at this cliff's edge of what was formerly thought of as the known and listen to the cries of fear, perhaps even rage, that sound all around and within the self? As these cries fade, like echoes at the edge of a great chasm, there is a silence that arises, unknown in the world of thoughts, beliefs, behavior, or time. Sitting in choiceless awareness, without thought or belief, without primal emotion, all sense of direction and time are now drawn into this awareness. One may seemingly and endlessly think about continuing on past the edge of the abyss into the unknown.

"But if this final thought is directed back in the direction from whence one came, it will be seen that what was formerly the present became the past as one traveled to this present point; and that the future, toward which one was just traveling, has also become the past into which one cannot go. Time has touched itself at all points, and pure awareness is now the center.

"This center of awareness rises, falls, and rests, again and again, as a wave within the universal expression of All-That-Is, which is also a constant center of awareness. The body's breathing is a resonance of this wave. That which could be called 'infinity' touches us over and over, becomes us as we become it, one flowing into the other, just as a fountain rises from the earth and is drawn back down into its source, to be expressed again back up through the fountain. The Self cannot be separated from its Source. If one is aware of Self, then one is aware of Source. This awareness is a beginning that never ends."

~ 21 ~

These words may not make conscious sense at this time,
but my spiritual senses comprehend and retain
this knowledge for Authentic Self.

TWENTY-TWO

BORROWED FROM ANGELS

"There is no drifting through life, then, but a built-in search for the fulfillment of values, whatever possible successes, conflicts, or failures may be involved, and no matter how modest or great or complex any of those qualities may be."
~ Robert F. Butts[55]

"If at first you don't succeed, try, try again."
~ William E. Hickson

When Tim physically materialized in my bed and embraced me, I was fully awake and knew without question that I wasn't experiencing any of the sleep paralysis that sometimes occurs while waking. I've had many such experiences, which can contain vivid imagery and sounds, even tangibly sensed elements, and so I know the differences between a biologically-induced mental state and a numinous state of mind.

It's not improbable that the experience could have been catalyzed by a mild effect of sleep paralysis as I was awakening. But then it transformed into something altogether different as the event unfolded. Unlike sleep paralysis, I was able to move, I could feel and hear, and I could speak. But Tim insisted I stay still and not talk, for personal reasons of his own as well as out of concern that too much movement might disturb and end the experience. When it was over and I had recovered from the shock of it, is it surprising to hear that I wanted to repeat it as soon as possible?

In spite of my intense efforts to somehow will Tim back, it didn't happen. I begged the air, made promises to not interfere with the process, meditated on my chakras, tried to induce the gong effect—and I would have drank cod liver oil if I thought it would have worked—but nothing happened. Finally I

---

[55] Jane Roberts, *The Magical Approach—Seth Speaks About the Art of Creative Living* (Novato, CA: Amber-Allen Publishing and New World Library, 1995) p. 50.

remembered to pray and ask for help, which appeared through the means most available to me, mainly channeled guidance as well as books brought to my attention by Risen guides. They often bring support through written material and other media, including the ones I'm about to share.

Many of my reference materials are books that were written and printed anywhere from recently to 150 years ago. Much of the technology we now take for granted was then in its infancy or not even conceptualized. Now, however, several of the methods that I've researched and personally used, with varying degrees of success, make use of modern technology.

Contact from the Risen is very often at *their* own choosing—from calling us on the telephone or leaving voice messages, to sending text and pictures through fax machines or leaving them on the hard drives of our computers. Within the general class of electronic voice phenomena are microphone recording and broadcast static recording, the latter including broadcasts via radio and television signals, and also white noise and video recording. Other non-electronic methods hark back to earlier times before these technologies were available but are still in use today. These include scrying and the séance methods, the latter utilizing automatic writing, Ouija boards and various channeling methods.

Electronic Voice Phenomena (EVP) has been around for several decades and seems to be rapidly becoming the method of choice for communication between the unseen worlds and our technologically dominated one. In 1959 Frederich Jurgenson, a Swedish documentary producer, used a tape recorder one day to capture birdsongs. Later, he heard on the tape a soft but distinct male voice whispering in Norwegian in the background, giving an on-the-spot lecture about the bird songs. As a true scientist, Jurgenson began to experiment for more. He eventually received all sorts of messages, even from his deceased mother. He published a booklet with an accompanying vinyl record disc in 1964, called "Voices From Space." Its European success led to more publications and attracted the attention of psychologist Konstantin Raudive. Jurgensen and Raudive began to collaborate and are attributed as the main source of the beginnings of serious EVP research. In the early 1970s psychologist Peter Bander wrote about these two scientists and the story of the voice phenomenon in *Voices From the Tapes—Recordings From the Other World*.

For those who feel inadequate about achieving contact, they needn't be too hasty to compare their futile attempts with my slightly successful ones. I, too, am a child of modern times, and natural abilities aside, often impatient because of my own encultured desires for instant gratification.

The very first method I tried was to attempt to capture voices of those in spirit on audio-magnetic tape. This involved allowing a new, blank cassette tape to run with the microphone switched on while playing some kind of static noise in the background. The working theory here is that those in spirit utilize the vibrations of the static and direct that energy to re-manifest as voices, music, and other sounds. To create the static I used a white noise machine, the kind sometimes used for sleep. I faithfully sat each night for an hour for two weeks, waiting for someone to speak to me. I detected some faint voice-like sounds after listening to them hundreds of times with high-priced headphones, but nothing was significant to me.

My research indicated that the voices would be hard to hear, sounding very soft or far off, sometimes mixed with other voices, talking or singing or even speaking backwards. To further acquaint myself with all of the possibilities I managed to track down a CD copy of *The Ghost Orchid*, an archival collection of EVP voices, some from over 40 years ago. The voices were captured in various ways, including from answering machines and radio broadcasts. Master-recorded in the United Kingdom through the efforts of The Parapsychic Acoustic Research Cooperative, some of the 79 track listings include "polyglot voices," "singing voices," "instant response voices," and "alien voices." The booklet with the CD contains a great deal of history and referrals to other important EVP resources worldwide. While I was able to develop a fairly good facility at comprehending some of the very strange things on this CD, my own tapes eluded me. True to my nature, my patience ran out quickly. I abandoned that method although I believe it had appreciable influence on my receptivity to future events awaiting me. It all adds up even when we don't think of it in that way, and perhaps the less we try to direct these kinds of phenomena, the more freely they'll be able to occur.

While reading some materials about studies on "Instrumental Trans-communication" I had my own first solid ITC experience. I had ordered several books on the subject, and the *The Ghost Orchid* had arrived with several books, all anonymous in their various wrappings. As I was opening up the third one—*The Ghost Orchid*—it slipped out of its brown paper wrapping and thumped to the floor. At that same instant the television came on by itself. I looked around for the remote-control unit, thinking I must have stepped on it, but saw that it was resting on top of the set. I had never had such a thing happen before—televisions just don't turn on by themselves! A bit bewildered, I switched it off and went back to the task of unwrapping books.

I settled into a favorite chair and began looking over the reading material that came with *The Ghost Orchid*. My telephone is close by in the next room, and although I normally keep the ringer turned off when occupied with work, the answering machine remains on and turned up so I can screen for any important calls. While deeply caught up in one particular passage, I heard, rather peripherally in the background, the answering machine switch on. The sounds I heard were not voices, however, but a mixture of static, beeps, and other strange noises. Curious, I dashed to the phone and picked up the receiver, but the caller had apparently hung up. I played the message back and could only hear static and odd mechanical noises but also what definitely sounded like a very faint voice in the background.

Blaming it on a phone company anomaly, I was about to hit "erase" when something stopped me, and I replayed it several times. The entire message was less than five seconds long but now that I was intensely focused on it I could clearly hear a voice, as if from far, far away, saying, *"Please answer it . . . something, something, something."* I then realized that this might have been someone in Spirit attempting to connect with me while I was actually reading about the subject, in the synchronistic way for which they're notorious. I turned the phone's ringer on and said aloud to the air, "Please call back!"

Frenzied from excitement, I paced the room. In less than a minute the phone rang again! Evocatively, it was a friend who was also involved in her own mediumistic explorations and she immediately asked why I sounded so strange. I told her what I thought might have just happened. After we marveled over the implications for a moment, we rang off. I then listened to the message again and this time I heard as clear as a bell, "PLEASE ANSWER IT – I LOVE YOU, AUGUST!" Stunned and in shock, I played it over and over, thinking I must have been hearing things. But it remained the same. "PLEASE ANSWER IT – I LOVE YOU, AUGUST!" This could only have been Tim!

At first the voice didn't sound quite human, and yet not quite like an artificial, computerized voice either. It sounded *very* far away, coming through over some light static and punctuated by tones and beeps. It reminded me of a tape recording that ran just a little bit faster than normal, and, oddly, the words were very evenly spaced apart, as if each syllable was being clearly annunciated or rehearsed. There was also a definite melodic quality to it, rather than just a straight speaking tone. I could detect great feeling within—a mix of deep emotional content, excitement, and even a hint of desperation. Somehow, it felt like Tim and nobody else.

After listening to it at least fifty times, I heard yet another voice. It was deeper and definitely more masculine sounding but still whispery, as if behind the main voice I heard as Tim's. I soon realized I was hearing this voice repeat the last four digits of my phone number. This realization seemed to bring me mentally into line with Tim on a psychic level, for it was suddenly clear to me that not only was this Tim but that he was working with others—technicians perhaps, who were orchestrating this call.

I managed to keep that message on my answering machine for several years so I could listen to it whenever I wanted. But I also made a separate copy of it, which I submitted to an audio technologist who cleaned it up. It still sounded exactly the same to me, but the technologist admitted to only hearing "something"—illustrating that while some people can hear certain EVP voices with ease, others can't. I've also learned that even those who are skilled at hearing EVP voices often cannot hear what another can because the message is meant for one person alone and no other. This is because the emotional content of the message is what reaches the listener's ears, above and beyond any of its electronic aspects.

I've received quite a few of these strange messages on my answering machine since that first one but none have been as clear. Most of them sound like there are many people laughing, talking, singing, and having a good time in the background, as if someone's calling me from a wild and wonderful party and hoping to be heard above all the noise. Machine-like noises, very technological and modern in sound, are also usually heard from beginning to end. I've never been able to extract much detail from them and it makes me wonder if these messages could be some kind of info-sphere.

Up to now, Tim and I never discussed this event, mainly because of others that eclipsed and thrust it into the background. And maybe because I never did get around to figuring out what his area code is. We had also not yet reached the point of development in our evolving relationship where we could mentally communicate for long periods of times, as we can now. What better opportunity than to finally ask him about it in this very moment?

"So *was* that your phone call, Tim?"

"You know it was, August. I've been following you here and everything you've said is pretty right on, mainly because you've done so much work on your own trying to find ways to learn how to consciously get in touch with me. If it seems that a lot of communications from the Risen are 'just coincidences' it's because there isn't a lot of support around the suspicion that maybe they're much more than serendipity. What you might call your suspicions about many of the things that happened are really your intuitions about what was actually going on.

"In fact, I had been trying for quite some time to get in touch with you. There were a number of times that I had tried to use the telephone before this particular instance, where I was finally successful in getting your attention. These things usually take a great deal of planning. It's much easier to utilize the answering machine, which is almost always on and ready to receive, whereas trying to align events to reach a live caller is much more problematic."

"When did you try to call me before that day? I can't say I was ever aware of it. And why didn't you keep talking, instead of only speaking a few words and then hanging up?"

"I'm not surprised you didn't recognize the calls for what they were. All of the successful attempts barely reached and registered in your sphere. Those that were recorded on your answering machine were interpreted by you as some sort of wrong number or cross-wired snafu from the telephone company. This kind of misunderstanding happens frequently in your world. But nearly everyone on the earth has a telephone, so you can be sure that people who have transitioned and are aware of the possibilities are certainly going to try to call. Many of the wrong numbers that people on earth think they get are really their Risen loved ones and friends managing to get through. In spite of our collective success, more often than not Earthers almost always dismiss it as a glitch of some sort in their system. True, it may actually be a glitch but that doesn't mean that we haven't been trying."

"How could there *not* be glitches to begin with? This kind of thing goes far beyond the concept of a long distance call!"

"This brings me to your question about why I didn't speak longer. Because of your musical background you have an exceptionally developed listening ear and you picked up on several things, notably that my voice sounded not quite human. You particularly noticed the peculiarity that while it sounded like a voice that had been recorded and slightly speeded up, it was only the tonal quality that sounded like that and not the actual speed. As Risen, we exist on higher wavelengths of vibration, which is why we usually can't be seen or heard by the senses of your lower vibrating bodies. My voice had actually been pre-recorded, in a manner of speaking, before it was analyzed, broken down, and reassembled by our technology here. Then it was broadcast at what you would call a 'wavelength' but what we experience as 'an echoic condition,' although that's really not quite the right phrase, which I sense you struggling to find. Don't worry about finding it—you're doing well enough at capturing the essence. But it wasn't quite this pre-recording that you really heard, although bits of it were interspersed in the background."

"Actually, Tim, you're confusing me again."

"Just stay with me, Aug. Much of Risen communication has to do with quantities as well as of qualities of light. Most of your scientists don't believe that light can be superluminal—that it can go faster than what they believe to be a fixed speed. But they're beginning to understand that there are *unlimited* expressions of light, and therefore some forms of it can be perceived and experienced as faster than others. But because light exists everywhere, measuring light in any ultimate terms becomes meaningless, especially where there is no terrestrial time. It took a lot of work to assemble the light of my speech, dissemble, and then reassemble it, very carefully and a little at a time, into a signal that could be read by your technology and sound coherent to your ears. Often this coherency doesn't happen.

"The message also had to resonate in such a way that your brain would be able to respond to it as well as interpret it. There were extra, added-in qualities that were tailored to get the attention of your emotional mind by evoking an emotional response. This was supposed to happen should you physically engage yourself in the process by actually picking up the phone. Those involved in this particular experiment wanted to see what would happen if you had actually answered the call, thereby linking yourself into our system. You *did* pick it up, but not soon enough. Yet it appears that something significant registered with you just in time to prevent you from erasing what you thought was a glitch. There have also been exciting reports of this happening with other teams elsewhere, and in varying degrees."

"Wait a minute, Tim. Who are these 'teams' you keep mentioning? In others' EVP events, they've actually recorded real-time conversations that took place over the phone, and even over radios. These conversations were with Risen technologists or scientists, and it sounds like you might be speaking about the same kind of individuals."

"And indeed, I am. There are many widely scattered collectives of Risen and non-Risen investigators and scientists who have devoted their energy to accomplish real-time conversations through the phone and radio. Still others are having some success with computers. But I feel your mind swimming in confusion, so let me slow down. As mentioned earlier, there are special Risen stations or centers for the communication sciences that seek to research and develop ways to bridge the gap between your world and many others."

"Have such places using advanced technology always existed, like the one with which you're involved?"

"Another *time* question again. I can tell you that since Earth's creation there have been Risen individuals who are passionately interested in not just communicating once or twice to loved ones left behind, but in developing ways to do so at any time and for extended periods. The Risen technology here is far in advance of anything ever known on earth. Much of Earth's present technology is the result of Risen influence. A lot of it simply doesn't translate between the different geographies, and most of the elements needed to construct the necessary technologies are simply not part of your physical world.

"I've been doing a lot of research into mediumship and Risen contact myself—you've been motivating me all along, Augie. I learned that when somebody had a séance during the time before electricity was discovered and used in modern ways, Risen technology was utilizing forms of energy that simply had no counterpart on Earth. Risen scientist-healers would often come together—literally in the hundreds—just to assist with a candle-lit, table-tipping event in some Victorian parlor. But in reality, incredible technology was underlying the event that wasn't visible from an earthly perspective. Through trial and error other phenomena began to appear, including what were called spirit lights, direct voices, materializations, and apports.[56] Although such 'side effects' often occurred, they were unintentional in the beginning.

---

[56] Apports are physical, material objects that the Risen, under certain conditions, can dematerialize from one place on the earth and rematerialize to another. Reported apports have included fresh flowers, jewelry, coins, and even freshly dug dirt with worms still wriggling in it.

"Risen Healer-Scientists constantly struggle to find ways in which their technology can interact with yours. History reflects that Risen efforts have often proved sporadic, iffy, nebulous, fleeting, questionable, and difficult to measure, record, or repeat. This isn't because nothing real is happening, as skeptics might insist, but because the scientific conditions are inadequate. Look at your own past few decades of computer technology and you'll see that a software program that was running perfectly well five years ago not only won't work on any of the existing hardware, but little of that earlier hardware even exists now. And those inadequate conditions continue to remain in place while everyone is still up and walking around and interacting on the same bodily plane. Technology improves but conditions don't always keep pace with it. Imagine trying to run our software on your hardware, or vice versa, between two different dimensions.

"As well, Risen Healer-Scientists often try to inspire your scientists and researchers who are mentally prepared and open to the possibilities in such ways that they can make earthly technology more sophisticated, and able to join with the higher forms of energy. As terrestrial understanding of quantum realities and even realities beyond the understood ones begins to become enlarged and enlightened, it seems that this might finally happen."

"Good lord, Tim, you seem awfully knowledgeable about all this, but I don't recall you being a techno-geek when you were on the earth."

"I'm still as helpless with any advanced stuff. I only know a little from my experience with the technicians who tried to contact you—twelve times."

"I still find it hard to believe that you actually left messages for me before, but I'll take your word for it. And twelve times! All the while I was trying so hard to contact you through automatic handwriting and then through tape recording, and blaming you for not trying just as hard. So I just gave up and probably way too soon."

"It's completely understandable, Aug, in spite of your impatience, as it's not easy. There are people on earth who have had to stick it out for *many* years before they were able to successfully establish a beginning link. Maintaining that link is yet another challenge."

"So establishing links are not only difficult and often chancy, but one has to keep at it once the channel is opened in order to keep it opened."

"Precisely. Unless there is sufficient energy to keep a space open, especially when dealing with the organic chemical forces of earth, the natural tendency is for it to close up to restore things back to their previous state in order to continue evolving. Opening up a link disrupts the evolving process— it's a shock to the system. Sometimes this shock can stimulate the system to a kind of quantum leap over the spiritual evolution process, otherwise known as transmutation."

"Well, that all makes sense to me, although it's frustrating that you just don't have an 800 number that I can use."

"Now there's an idea—who knows?"

"I'm kidding, but I'm sensing that you're not, Tim."

"Nothing's impossible, as you've been finding out, Augie."

"Then while I explain the next approach I tried, I draw your attention to the telephone next to me in case you want to try again."

While I'm waiting for his call, I'll move on to another method of contact with the Risen. I investigated the use of *scrying*, an ancient technique used to evoke a kind of clairvoyance using mirrors or natural bodies of calm water such as lakes or even crystal bowls of water. Sometimes black bowls are used, or ink placed in the water to darken it, making it easer to see any images that might appear. Several ancient cultures used highly reflective, polished black stone or metal. The crystal ball is a perfect example of a scrying instrument.

I opted for the inky-water-bowl method, scrying in a dark room with muted candlelight to activate the water's reflective surface. Several times I seemed to very briefly see what looked like real clouds forming and floating across the water's surface, almost as if I were looking down through a hole in the sky. But my impatient nature won out again and I gave up after a few days.

A week later I awoke in the wee hours, and saw what appeared to be a tiny television displaying some sort of "broadcast," glowing on the bedside stand. As I came up out of sleep and my eyesight cleared I saw movement in the scene on this "TV." There was a landscape with hills and fields, and a sky with gently moving clouds, while breezes could be seen rustling through the trees. I couldn't hear any sound and interestingly, everything was in black and white and shades of gray. At first I thought I must be dreaming while awake and was hesitant to reach out and touch whatever it was, afraid that any movement would make it disappear. So I carefully but firmly closed my eyes, held them shut for a moment, and then opened them. The scene was still there. I intentionally noticed that I could feel my body and my hands and feet, so I knew I was awake and not asleep and dreaming. I noticed the time—4 a.m. I watched the scene for a few moments and realized that the movement in the foreground was a person, totally blurred and out of focus, as objects become when a camera is focused on the background and away from the foreground. I couldn't discern who this figure was or what it was doing.

I was becoming very tired after watching this scene for about five minutes and having a hard time keeping my eyes open. I knew that I might fall back asleep at any moment. I made a decision and slowly reached out and turned on the bedside lamp. The "TV" vanished and in its place was the lead-crystal water carafe I kept there and had that very night refilled. It was gently lit from behind by the LED on my clock-radio. Puzzled but too tired to think about it, I fell back asleep.

Upon waking a few hours later I immediately recalled what had happened. As I lay there pondering, I remembered that just the night before I'd had a discussion with a friend about my earlier, unsuccessful attempts at scrying. So possibly there was a delayed reaction factor at play and the previous attempt, along with the conversation with my friend, had acted as a catalyst. It seems that the water-filled lead-crystal carafe served as a receiver in the way a crystal bowl of water was supposed to. The LED display of my clock must have provided just the right amount of light. Although I had blinked my eyes to clear my vision the scene did not change, and I had even forgotten about the fact that the carafe was supposed to be there. It appeared totally real, with no feeling or sensation of the unreal about it.

A few days later I was trying to take an afternoon nap. I was lying in bed with my eyes open for only a few moments when I became aware of a "scene" before my eyes. I was still mindful of the rest of my room—the window, the walls, and ceiling, but this scene seemed to be superimposed over the physical elements of the room like a projection, opaque enough to block out what was behind it. Again there was a landscape but this time it was in softly brilliant colors and as if lit from within. And of all people, my English grandmother was looking straight out at me! She appeared quite young—younger than I had known her. I wouldn't have been so sure of her identity if not for her glasses. I recalled seeing photographs of her wearing them—black-rimmed at the top and coming to points—"cat glasses," as they were called. The photographs were taken when she was much younger and before I was born. I noticed now that she appeared to be talking rather excitedly and gesturing behind her toward the hills and trees—the landscape was very summery and beautiful. But I couldn't hear a thing she was saying, as if the volume had been switched off. I tried mentally to tell her that I could see her quite plainly but couldn't hear her. But she kept on talking and gesturing without any indication that she could see or hear me. She seemed serious and a little urgent in her behavior, as if something was very important "back there" or "over that way." To my great disappointment the vision faded completely away after only a few moments.

Another method is usually referred to as "automatic handwriting." The medium's hand holds a writing implement over paper while being guided by a Risen One's hand or energy force, and thus communication takes place as the written word. Some mediums report hearing words in some way or sometimes feeling the transmitted message, which they then transcribe themselves. It's often a slow, laborious process, although there have been mediums who were able to write so fast when controlled by the communicator that someone had to sit next to them to remove and replace the paper as it quickly filled up. Entire books, including novels, have been written this way, but the phenomenon seems to have considerably lessened by the twenty-first century, perhaps due to everyone using keyboards to type instead of writing by hand. I've tried to use a pencil, sitting for over an hour in the dark. Other than a cramped wrist I got some extremely slowly-formed scribbles that might have been the word "Tim." Predictably, I didn't stick with that technique for very long, so I now utilize a computer keyboard for this kind of communication.

"That *was* my name, August. When I became aware of what you were trying to do, I found a teacher who specialized in the form of automatic writing you were attempting, in order to teach me how to do it. You intuited that it's not easy and takes time and so worried about it—which didn't help the process. Being the impatient perfectionist that you are, you stopped after only a few tries. I was only able to get you to write my name, which was difficult enough because you believed that it had to be in my handwriting in order to prove it was really me, and this belief was yet another form of control that got in the way. You have an aversion to writing by hand anyway, having used the computer for typing for so long. And while on earth I preferred my typewriter to writing. Although I transitioned before personal computers were available, we obviously resonate extremely well using a keyboard as the communication method.

"I admit that trying to control your hand's movements was difficult and uncomfortable for me. I couldn't find a way to stabilize myself within a vibration that was as close to your physical dimension as possible. It might have been easier if you were the kind of person who enjoyed the physicality of holding a pen and writing by hand. The fact is we both find typing faster and easier. My teacher quickly concluded that we should focus on the keyboard."[57]

"I'm wondering what you do while I sit at the keyboard, talking with you in this way, Tim. Is it a very different experience than when we're communing with each other when I'm away from the computer?"

"I'm actually sitting in my little apartment that we both loved so much, and I'm typing along with you. I'm still using my old Smith Corona—I wonder if you can hear it? When there are pauses, we are discerning each other's thoughts and feelings, as well as simply enjoying each other's presence, for it's a very intimate process. I've been experimenting with a more meditative approach, where I go into a park and sit in a tree, and join my mind with yours. It might be hard to conceive, but this still enables the process to be recorded. The more advanced Risen who have been communicating with you are very

[57] P. was an established writer when on the Earth, and always wrote his manuscripts by hand. While D., his companion, and I were discussing him shortly after his transition, her hand began making circling movements at the wrist, seemingly of its own volition. I recognized this as P. signaling for her to get a pen so he could communicate to her. Because she also primarily wrote by hand, they were able to engage for many weeks in direct, loving communication via pen and paper, until he moved on to a much higher state of vibration. – *AG*

often in some kind of nature setting or environment and not a specific structure as I'm in now."

"I think you meant sitting *beneath* a tree, not in one, didn't you, Tim?"

"I meant sitting *in* a tree. The reception seems to be a lot better if I'm up in the branches, and the view is better, too."

"If that's not validation that you're still the same eccentric Tim, I don't know what is."

"Compliment accepted. I've been using my typewriter as a kind of 'prop' by which we can make and strengthen a mutual connection. What I'm producing here is still much different than what's appearing on your computer screen there, as if we're writing two different books of a very similar nature. My version of our book is an astral one and can exist in many different forms. I've been told that our two different books are expressing themselves as a single one on a much higher level, which is kept in a particular Risen library, along with all the others that were ever written between the Risen and the embodied. They're considered to be distinctive artifacts, and some day you and I will have the pleasure of seeing our book together."

"It's extremely heart warming to think of that day. You know, I can actually hear in my mind's ear your typewriter tap-tapping away. It's going to get very annoying unless I can somehow push it to the background. If you can turn down the volume on that thing, I'd appreciate it."

"In case you can't tell, I'm rolling my eyes, August. All you have to do is forget about it and the tapping will vanish. It's the same thing that most people do when anything in the form of a Risen communication comes into their presence. Thinking that it shouldn't be there or even hoping it will go away, they dismiss it, and so away it goes."

"Tim, you just brought up something very important. In essence you're saying that closing my self off to Risen contact literally shuts the door on it, whereas opening up the door more, which means an effort on my part, will let in more information. Still, I think I'll close the window on the sound of your typewriter for now while fully supporting your method of tree-sitting. Can you share a little more about what the actual experience was like when you were attempting to reach me on my telephone?"

"I don't know if I can say too much in the way of description, simply because, yet again, there are few ways that I can find to conceptualize the experience with symbols in ways your human brain can receive and interpret. But I really am excited about trying, and while it will have to be simple it's going to take up quite a bit of space."

"Take up all the time and space you need, Tim."

"Thanks, then, I will. It appears that most disembodied people, upon reaching a consciously aware Risen state, naturally turn their earliest thoughts to their loved ones still on the Earth. More often than not they try to communicate mentally with them—usually the most accessible method available. But these newly Risen immediately run into walls of grief, barriers of disbelief or non-belief, and other forms of self-involved emotional aspects generated by the embodied loved ones. Such negative aspects of grief do little to help establish a positive connection but instead prevent any comfortable connection from happening at all. The Risen are people, too, and after a certain number of unsuccessful attempts at contact become discouraged. So instead they begin to respond more and more to the wondrous reality of their new Risen home, which constantly calls to them. Inevitably, they cease trying to communicate to those on Earth.

"Like many, August, you are extra-sensitively attuned to the thoughts and emotions of spiritual worlds. But you actually sent out *positive* communications to me, like beacons across the vastness of space, which could go nowhere else but to where they were intended. I've already shared about the impact your prayers and love had on my healing during my transition. Your abilities, combined with your willingness and energized by your love, actually made me a potential candidate for one of the communications programs which exist within certain areas of Risen society."

"What do you mean by a potential candidate?"

"Your focused attentions and intentions towards me made for a potentially successful communication. My wanting to contact you was not an uncommon thing but the fact that *you* wanted to contact me, and had actually succeeded through your own actions, was not so common. This factor made all the difference. A group of Risen Healer-Scientists, who were avidly involved in the various instrumental transcommunications of which you spoke earlier, discerned the energies of our relationship—our communications set up a resonance which they detected and investigated. They were also participants in the 'blissful occurrence veiled as a spontaneous event'—when I appeared to you on the subway train. How they detected our resonance, like so much around here, is still a mystery to me."

"I love mysteries, you love crosswords—seems like a perfect match."

"It *is* often just like trying to fill in the blanks of a crossword puzzle. I was asked if I would be willing to join them in one of their many ongoing communication experiments. I whole-heartedly agreed, for I longed to find a way to let you know I was alive and ok, which would be a great service for me to do."

"I can understand your enthusiasm to join them, but why did you want to do a service?"

"You understand the value and importance of being of service to others,

August. Freely giving of one's time and energy, however slight, adds to the greater whole so that all beings, who *are* the Greater Whole, have the experience of joyful, continual abundance."

"And since the one serving, the giver, is also part of the Greater Whole, he is also giving to himself."

"Exactly. I wasn't on the earth long enough to give of myself through service in many ways, but the truth is that I never even thought much about it until the end of my terrestrial life began to draw near. I intuited that something in the way of volunteer work was a spiritual thing to do. In spite of my not doing enough to really get what it was all about, what little I did still planted seeds that began to grow immediately upon my Rising.

"Let me try to convey what this particular service to the Greater Whole was like. I was brought to what I can only inadequately describe as a satellite-like station or a moon circling a larger planet-like body in a space-like environment. This moon is called something in a spiritual language that might be translated as 'Borrowed from Angels.' This is the meaning of the name as it seems to me, translated into your thinking language of Earth. But there is a multi-leveled meaning to it. The place itself has an incredibly sacred feel, so perhaps it really *is* borrowed from angels. The station is a world unto itself, with several million people living on, in, and above it. Although it's as beautiful in most places as some of the Earth's oldest rain forests, all of its nature evolved through the collective efforts of everyone living and working there. Every single entity is involved in some way with the scientific healing art they term as 'inter-astral communication.' And not just with your earth but with many other places—some like the earth, others not in the least like it, but all vibrating at the near-similar vibration of density. I say 'entity' because not all the people I've interacted with here have an earthly human history and so do not present themselves as human—or perhaps, more correctly, I can't perceive them as an earth-evolved human. Some are not even 'humanoid.' Oh, the wonder of it all, Dear Heart!

"This facility has been operating for a long 'time.' It has a particularly charmed history from its many successes in reaching those still embodied on earth, and is noted for its highly creative aspects and especially for its particular kind of humor. There's a widely-held theory there that all universes are built upon a foundation of humor.

"This particular facility also has a name, and again I struggle to find the right words to convey the multi-leveled meanings. As I can't seem to find a word or even two to do it justice, I will take the long route and offer just a few of the many phrases that convey some of its essence. Hence, 'Here We Go There and There We Go Here'; 'Mountainous Echoes of Reflected Love'; and 'Frustration Becomes You.' Personally, I think of it as 'The Sapphire Isle' because I work on an island in the middle of a deliciously blue sea of warm, shallow water, in which I get to swim whenever I want. There are dolphin-like people there who are Healer-Scientists and we often swim together. It seems to me that they're responsible for much of the interesting character of this place. They certainly know how to joke and laugh!

"The Sapphire Isle is involved with many forms of communication. Much of it is interrelated—meaning in the way a telephone can stand alone as a potential contact device, or augment another device, such as a computer or a fax machine."

"Tim, I tried to set up my computer for spirit contact according to the methods various ITC researchers have suggested. It seemed fairly simple—just open a blank document on the computer, leave it open all the time, and wait for someone to leave a message there. But nothing happened. Was I at fault somehow, perhaps by being too impatient again?"

"What little scientific understanding I have about these things comes to a halt here, August. I'm not clear about the complex selection process regarding the methods chosen to contact people. Since I wasn't involved with those particular approaches, I haven't a clue. I'm not even sure I would understand it if it was explained to me. But I must comment on your tendency to assume that when something doesn't work you're somehow at fault. If this belief of yours has been hidden or goes unacknowledged, you could have an unintended expectation to fail and therefore might produce failure."

"I have to agree with your astute observation. The fear of failing has always been an issue in my life that I've preferred to ignore—even thinking about it makes me fearful. You've given me some valuable insight into how my fear might sabotage certain things. It may explain the delayed effect with the technique of scrying I had tried. But please continue your fascinating story about The Sapphire Isle."

"This facility uses many techniques for inter-astral communication. One of the reasons the telephone was chosen for us is because it was discovered that I had spent a great deal of time on the telephone while on the Earth, and that you and I had talked on the phone several times a day, every day. Of course nobody had a home computer then, and neither the Internet nor cell phones were yet a reality, or else we probably would have been emailing and texting one another. Perhaps our lack of shared experience with computers explains why your computer experiment didn't work."

"You're just trying to make me feel better."

"I hope you heard me just sigh, August. The point I'm trying to make is that because we were connected to the concept of the telephone by our mutual understanding and use of it, the conditions were mutually favorable toward making an inter-astral connection through a phone.

"There were many components to the actual process of making contact through your telephone. It was done as a serious, scientific experiment. I received an orientation that included a fascinating history of the development of inter-astral communication. The presentations were such that I couldn't tell if I was watching something that had been recorded or if it was actually happening. I was told that it had happened and also *was* happening, or 'replayed.' Keep in mind that the concept of 'play' is an important one, and has more meanings and applications here than I can count.

"I was seated in a very comfy chair, and was instantly within the event being replayed for my orientation. This wasn't a movie projection on a screen. I was actually *in* the event itself, as a kind of non-participating observer—or so I thought. But then one of the persons in the event turned to me and asked me to step closer for a better view! This was an interactive, intelligent process, organically alive. Believe it or not, the person speaking to me introduced himself as Tom, and that he had been known on earth as Thomas Edison. The expression on my face made him laugh, but he went on to explain at great length—lectured, really—about what I was experiencing and how it could be used in many methods, including replaying and experiencing an event in an infinite variety of ways. I am sending an info-sphere for you to experience it, as it would take a very long time to explain it all. As it was, my mind was thoroughly rattled by having my hand shaken by someone claiming to be Thomas Edison."[58]

"If you say he said he was Thomas Edison, I believe you. I just got your info-sphere about this and my jaw is dropping. And I see you're right—it would take us many hundreds of pages at this point to try to go on any further about it, so we'd better move on for now. I think I have the gist of it, though."

"My orientation was an ongoing process and I was free to engage in it or not—but *of course* I wanted to. I began by stepping up onto a floating platform in the center of an immense space, so huge that it seemed ridiculously larger than necessary. I was informed that I was correct in sensing that I was within

---

[58] In the final years of his life, Thomas Alva Edison became interested in the possibility of communicating with "spirits." He considered himself an agnostic and claimed to have no particular belief about the afterlife. But he strongly believed that it might be possible to develop an apparatus of great sensitivity that would enable personalities in "another existence" to get in touch with us—if they existed and if they so desired. He began work on this device in 1920. He corresponded with British scientist Sir William Crooke, who had developed the vacuum tube that Edison and others adapted into the light bulb. Crooke was deeply involved in paranormal research, especially in spirit photography. Edison was so impressed by Crooke's collection of photographs that allegedly showed Risen Ones that he believed that if they could be shown on film, his device to capture their voices might also work. He worked on the prototype until his death in October 1931. As he was dying he sighed, "It is very beautiful over there." It's said that at the precise moment of his death, clocks all over his house and workshop stopped working. In spite of years of searching, neither the device nor its plans have supposedly been found.

an 'interiorized space,' which was comparable to fifteen earthly football fields in size. Strangely, the platform I was on in the center of it all was barely large enough for me to stand or sit. If there was a ceiling or walls I couldn't see them. There were other, larger platforms floating around and above me from where teams of individuals controlled and monitored whatever was going on, which didn't look like much to me. The dolphin people were also swimming around. When one dived straight through the ground beneath me I realized that I was floating over something more liquid than solid, which I couldn't see unless it moved when disturbed.

"I can't say that I saw what you might think of as computers although there were visual screens of some sort that floated and moved about. These panels appeared to be areas of light energy, solid but somewhat translucent. They distorted the space they occupied in some way so that the altered space was used to form their appearance. What looked like symbols and pictures of colored light and accompanied by sound—music, really—not only came out of these panels but left them and flew over to another one to join or pass through before moving on to somewhere else. It was all very fast, strange, and obviously intelligent. I was reminded of singing birds or buzzing insects flying with intended purpose. Sometimes the screen from one platform would glide across overhead and stop before another team member to share information. People wore devices of light over their clothes that encircled and covered their bodies, arms, legs, and heads. But as nothing seemed to be actually happening, I asked if they were taking measurements. Somebody laughingly replied, 'no, we're *making* measurements.' I still have no idea what that meant."

"Maybe you could ask Thomas Edison the next time you see him."

"Not a bad idea. Anyway, I couldn't identify the source of light, but then everything then went dark—I couldn't see or even feel my own body. I felt disembodied and floating, and the chair was gone. Then the light came back on and somebody said, 'Thank you, that will be all for now, unless you'd like to do some more.'

" 'More *what?*' I asked. I hadn't experienced anything, but I said I'd like to continue. Everybody seemed happy to proceed. When I say 'everybody' I'm talking about a lot of people, at least several hundred that I could see standing or sitting on the many platforms quietly hovering about me. The chair appeared next to me and I was asked to sit in it again. Five floating panels then assembled themselves around me, creating a pentagonal wall that began at the base of the platform and came up to just over my head, effectively closing me in. These panels were screens on which pictures and symbols appeared and floated across. The symbols were able to detach themselves and emerge out and away from the screens, joining together in the open space and forming very precise configurations into a grid of light around me. This was all done very quickly but not silently, for every symbol, every line or piece of light—I guess you could also say 'data'—emitted sound. The result was intensely musical yet very soothing.

"I watched and heard the data change colors and sounds while the grid became more defined, until it felt like it was taking on substance, which formed itself around my head and body. It was as if a wax impression was being made of me—although it wasn't wax, it was light and sound.

"I heard a voice from somewhere say 'Tim, you're doing very well, would you please repeat the following—and just humor us: '*This is Tim. I touched my nose, and then my toes, and then I took off all my clothes.*' Very confused, I did as I was asked but couldn't help bursting out laughing, for which I immediately apologized. 'Oh, but that's *perfect*, exactly the response we wanted,' someone replied in a deadpan voice. I then heard my voice played back, so it must have been recorded. It was played back maybe thousands of times in thousands of ways, almost all at once. The effects were dazzling as the grid reacted with its own lights and sounds, shifting and readjusting around my face and body.

"The panels around me glowed extremely brightly and I saw stars and planets in them. It seemed as if the chair I was sitting on was moving through space, and the stars and planets were zipping past me with incalculable speed. The earth appeared before me—at first very tiny, but then it quickly swelled up, and there was no mistaking which planet this was. At the sight of it I was moved to tears. I moved through some clouds and then briefly rested on the surface of an ocean. Then, unexpectedly, I was in a forest of redwoods, and then all at once over a city—*your* city!

"A voice said, 'Tim, your vision is going to go off for a bit, so you might want to close your eyes if that would be more comfortable.' I closed my eyes and then opened them right away, but I could only see blackness. The voice continued, 'You are presently back above the Earth and outside its atmosphere, situated in the middle of an area of electromagnetism that is going to be particularly noisy for a bit. We need you to listen to it but don't say anything.' My eyes were still open but I was unable to see anything. I heard a static-like noise coming from far away, which rose higher in pitch and volume and then fell, which it did several times. My eyesight cleared and I saw a dolphin person swimming off in the distance. Without warning I was back at The Sapphire Isle, the panels and grid were gone, and I could see and hear the others around me perfectly. They were all grinning at me.

"Before I could ask what the heck had happened I was suddenly back in the place of static. Again, I couldn't see but someone said, 'Close your eyes if you like, but you're doing great, Tim. Let's go ahead and try for a little more.' I heard another voice speaking in a mixture of words and numbers that made no sense to me. All at once I was overwhelmed by what must have been millions of voices simultaneously speaking, and I realized I was hearing all the telephone conversations being carried on at that moment on the earth. This lasted only for a few seconds, and then I heard nothing—just dead silence. Then came the distinct sound of a telephone being dialed, or rather, the buttons being pushed. It was so unexpected and strangely contrasting to all I'd experienced so far that I laughed out loud, but I stopped laughing when I heard *your* voice, August, and I immediately started shouting, 'It's me, it's Tim, here on your phone, please answer it, I love you, August!'—thinking that I was actually talking to you. But when you didn't respond I realized it was your recorded voice on your answering machine.

"Someone laughed and said 'nobody's home, Tim' and told me to just relax and wait, because we hadn't got to the good part yet. I heard the button-pushing noises again and your voice on your answering machine asking the caller to leave a message. This process happened at least a dozen times. I heard my voice echoing, "It's me, it's Tim, here on your phone, please answer it! I love you, August!' There was the very strange sensation that even though I wasn't actually speaking, it felt as if I was, as if the sound resonated from within me. Suddenly I felt very tired, and completely drained of energy.

"I came to at The Sapphire Isle. Oddly, I was lying down in a bed. It was gloriously comfortable and I fell back asleep immediately. When I awoke, Bigfoot and one of my teacher-guides were there with me. She sat on the bed and asked how I was doing. I felt perfectly fine but confused about what had happened. She explained that the emotional surge I had experienced had 'increased my density' a bit, making me slightly susceptible to what she called a 'particular aspect of gravitational force.' "

"Meaning?"

"Meaning that hearing your voice and feeling that I was so close to actually talking to you caused me to have a strong emotional experience that was both joyous and anxious. I guess I just passed out from the excitement."

"Good heavens! Were you ok?"

"Perfectly fine, and I was told that the experiment was a great success, and the facility would be greatly honored if I would continue with the project. I had no hesitation in agreeing to this and so I went through everything again. That first time, your answering machine actually *did* pick up my voice, but the researchers said that a follow-up analysis showed that the quality was so poor that only a few bits of the dolphin folk's vocalizations of data checking came through the background. What the team found so exciting was that while the longer, pre-recorded message registered as weak static, the emotional outburst I had at the beginning is what actually came through and what you heard, even when they thought they weren't transmitting at that point.

"By the way, I've since confirmed that the dolphin people are at the top of the hierarchy of scientists at The Sapphire Isle. They're light years ahead of non-cetacean people regarding communication. They established this particular facility among the many others on the satellite I described, and are the ones most intensely interested in the results between us."

"Tim, I'm wondering now if the vocalizations of the cetaceans might explain the clicks and beeps I've sometimes heard on other messages, which I thought were just the result of the equipment malfunctioning."

"This seems the right time to let you know that some, but not all, of the mysterious gong and bird sounds you've been hearing are your brain's attempts to render cetacean vibratory signals into human sound waves. Because you have a human brain and skull and not those of a cetacean, you experience a certain amount of discomfort and even some pain from intercepting those signals. Your human skeletal structure is actually a living system of crystals evolved from and toward resonance with every aspect of your physical environment, from changes in weather pressures to surges in emotional stress. The makeup of the non-corporeal signals is difficult to explain, although like all vibrations are a type of light, and effected by your space-time. To a certain extent these signals can be transmitted through the various earth technologies that use light pulses, like telephones. Unfortunately, non-corporeal transmissions cannot perfectly resonate with your technologies, and often cause equipment malfunction. And it's not beyond the capabilities of a cetacean to purposefully enhance or jam certain frequencies."

"Tim, I knew that we would be writing a book that wouldn't be easy to manifest. Now I'm starting to feel as if everything we've presented so far is a very insubstantial veneer on top of worlds within worlds within worlds. I'm feeling helplessly far out of my depth."

"Dear Heart, I'm delightfully surprised at how this is going, as I also had no great foreknowledge of how things would be. But you're tired and hungry and need to rest. I can sense you smiling in spite of being overwhelmed by the great and glorious adventure we're sharing here, and understandably so. Come back later and we'll pick up where we left off. And try not to worry about missing anything—you know I'm never far away."

"Thanks Tim, you're absolutely right. I'll do as you so lovingly suggest."

About a month after Tim shared this provocative information with me I found myself again confined to my bed with another severe headache. Instead of the usual large, booming gong sound that often accompanies this type of headache, I was experiencing smaller ones. They didn't last as long and were higher in pitch, but nonetheless were still very uncomfortable. Each time they resounded they produced a painful pressure behind my eyes and above the bridge of my nose, which occurred whenever I had relaxed into a particular state of mind, actually a light trance. As strange as it may sound, these pitches also responded to my inner dialogue, as if there was an intelligence speaking to me. Intuitively I asked if this was a particular spirit teacher of mine. The gonging seemed to "reply" several times, the cadence sounding just like somebody talking, although I couldn't understand anything. So somebody *was* trying to communicate with me in a very direct mind-to-mind way, but in a frequency I couldn't resonate with and which was physically uncomfortable to me. I continued to experiment to try to adjust my trance level to see if I could learn how to change my own vibratory rate, but after only a few minutes of this strange spirit Morse code it became too painfully dissonant to continue.

In spite of the discomfort, I was greatly intrigued. All of that ringing was sounding a bell for me in my memory somewhere. I finally found a journal entry that had been written almost a year before Tim's first momentous appearance in my bedroom. This demonstrates the necessity for writing things down in as great detail as possible, even the miraculous events we are convinced will never be forgotten. No matter how much we want to be able to remember all that numinously happens, psychospiritual amnesia invariably begins to arise once we're back in a normal state of consciousness.

"I fell asleep for a brief couple of hours this evening. The gong had been lightly sounding all day. Not quite asleep, not quite awake, I became aware that there was a new kind of noise near my left ear, drawing close, then away. It was unlike any earthly sound I knew. Through some sort of inspiration I realized that I was hearing a voice trying to communicate to me. The sound was too speeded up, or else affected in some way that might have sounded normal there, wherever *there* was, but didn't sound normal here. I inwardly voiced this idea to whoever was trying to speak to me (if indeed they were) and I immediately heard and felt someone speak against my ear. It was rather like a whisper in a somewhat toneless, breathy voice, but I clearly heard someone say, 'Hello, August!' Before I could respond, my body suddenly began to react by shaking, probably at a primal level of fear. I voiced inwardly that whoever it was, they needed to back off a bit because my body was reacting negatively. I felt someone move away from me, and then I internally saw a shadowy figure write something on a pad of paper, which was thrust before my inner eyes. On the paper was written 'Hello, August!'. There was the feeling of a great joke here, and a contagious sense of humor coming from the entity. Unfortunately, I then quickly came to complete wakefulness and lost all contact."

It seemed somebody was trying to communicate to me in a very direct way. But my physical senses reacted in fear, as if the higher vibration of the communicator was too much for them. I suspect this is often the case when people are confronted with disembodied spirit energy. Instead of turning off the fear and talking back, most of us can't find our anxiety's "off switch" and our body ends up wanting to run away.

In spite of the incredible nature of the material Tim had been sharing with me, my life on earth still had to go on. There was work to do, a cat to feed, bills to pay, laundry to ignore. A month passed before we could return to where we had left off regarding the telephone communication. During this time a close friend of mine transitioned after a long struggle with cancer.

Shortly thereafter, my grandfather, at the age of 93, made his transition one night while his body slept.

I had spent many hours with my dying friend in her final months while she courageously endured inestimable pain and discomfort. I was also with her for the last few weeks she spent in hospice. Powerful medication finally gave her some of the first true pain-free moments she'd had in years, while gently assisting her to cross over in her sleep in the early hours of a wintry dawn. It was some time afterwards before I could find her. When I did, I discovered she had been taken to a Risen healing facility, or as another medium I know puts it, "placed in the incubator." This reflected Tim's experience of being cared for in some kind of healing facility, which is often the case when someone has been very ill for some time in the material body. When in her body, my friend had the benefit of having a group of friends around her who all had—to various degrees—belief, knowledge, and faith systems that supported the reality of survival beyond the body.

Our coming together around her for several years during her illness was a process of individual and group self-discovery as well as spiritual evolution. Her own process of realizing that she was in the last days of her earthly sojourn was reflected in the group's experience of carefully finding ways to accept and eventually talk about this momentous realization. We came to a collective understanding that we were participating in a great and wondrous event. In the last few months we were able to let go of the old language of hope that chemotherapy and radiation had failed to instill in us. We found our own unique and personal language of love and compassion, which grew to anticipation and even celebration—one of us was going Home! Since her transition my friend has elected to stay close to the earth plane to assist her friends, lending support and grace to our own earthly struggles.

My grandfather and I were not especially close when he crossed over. He wasn't an emotionally sensitive person and never shared his feelings, but I was still grateful for many of the happy childhood memories he had given me. He was a loving and playful person in his own way where his grandchildren were concerned, especially during our childhood.

As he began to physically fail, there were family reports that he seemed to have mentally retreated from the world and was no longer "quite there" anymore. It was clear to me that he had almost completely left his physical form several months before it breathed its last. His very old body was finally wearing down to the point where it could no longer adequately hold his spirit as it increased in its vibration. In reality, he was spending most of his time as a spirit out of the body, although where he was exactly and what he was doing was something I was unable to discern. The fact that we never really knew each other well as adults or resonated on similar levels partially explained his absence from my higher senses after he transitioned.

Several months after his transition, while I was walking in the woods and reveling in the solitude as the first signs of spring were beginning to appear, my grandfather made himself known to me. The intensity of his presence was so intimate and loving that I was overwhelmed, as I had never experienced that side of him in my entire life. Often an arrogant and silently cold person on the earth—especially as he got older—there was now a new sweetness and humility, and a softening of the personality. I discerned that he had quickly transitioned to a very young and vibrant-looking man in his thirties. He spoke directly to me, expressing a great deal of regret for not taking advantage of the many opportunities given to him during life, especially where he could have continued to extend his caring efforts beyond the childhood years of his grandchildren as they became adults. The emotional truth I felt beneath what he said told me that this was indeed my grandfather.

I responded that the only regret I had was being unable to get closer to him as an adult. He shared that he was now being given the chance to "iron out some of the wrinkles and fill in some of the gaps" he had brought with him to his Risen life. He would watch, protect, and assist his adult grandchildren in ways that would allow him to progress away from his regretted earthly shortcomings. As his presence began to fade I thanked him, and welcomed his company at any time.

A few hours later I smelled something for the first time in years—the startling odor of a burning wooden match and then my grandfather's pipe, taking me back many decades in memory while bringing him directly into the present moment. Smell is the most powerful of our physical senses and it can give us access to memories we didn't even know we had. This particular scent took me back to some of my earliest ones, almost to the beginning of my life on earth. These kinds of numina make my present moments fuller and richer, almost spherical as the container that is my earthly life.

Shortly after my grandfather's visit, another coincidental surprise occurred.[59] Sometimes I have waking visions when meditating, where I clairvoyantly see things behind my closed eyelids—so vivid that it's like watching a movie, but with enhanced colors and greater details. Occasionally I'm immersed within the scene and am really there in some way. This time I found myself face-to-face with a young man—a boy, really, about twelve years old. He appeared directly in front and above me, as if in a window in space. He was sitting in a chair, and I immediately recognized that I knew him very well and intimately. Yet, paradoxically, I had no idea who he was. He showed a very direct and fearless, intense interest in me, and his serious looking face reminded me of someone I knew.

---

[59] Most use "coincidence" when meaning "by chance." Here it's being used to signify spiritual events *coinciding* in the same position or area in one's personal, experiential space. – *AG*

Then a little dog came up to him, which he put his arm around, pulling it closer. Another dog came to his side, jumping up with its front paws on his lap. At once I recognized two of the many dogs I'd grown up with. His identity was clear in an instant—this was my younger brother, who had died ten days after birth from serious physical defects more than forty years ago. I had seen him once before in a meditation, but he had appeared as a kind of energy field and not with a human body. At that time we had communicated in a distant, awkward kind of way. He didn't respond to the name he'd been given during his short stay on the earth, nor could he quite comprehend what "names" were, as well as other earthly concepts that seemed to have no significance to him in his Risen state of existence.

Yet it was clear that he knew who I was, and he impressed me with the understanding that he had been close by me all my life. But he wasn't bound to me in the way that we on the earth tend to experience family relationships, which are often conducted through emotional struggles via the ego-mind's manipulations. He didn't seem to feel obligated to me in any way, as if the "blood is thicker than water" supposition didn't include him. In short, he didn't seem to have an ego-mind. And yet he was very capable at projecting a deep sense of love and warm regard toward me while conveying a sophisticated sense of humor. He was interested in me and wanted me to be interested in him, and naturally I was. But I was at a loss at what to call him.

The vision then faded as we parted in brotherly conspiracy to meet again.

As for where Tim and I left off, I seem to have wandered away from our sheep again. Since it was Tim who had brought our last session to a close, I now turn it over to him.

"I wouldn't think of keeping you from wandering, August—I can see how much you like to ramble and saunter in the experience of your life. The story about your brother is wonderful and important as well. It shows how unlimited are the ways in which Risen and non-Risen can communicate. You and your brother interacted in such a genuine and spontaneous manner, complete with visuals. I can barely use the telephone even with the most seemingly sophisticated spirit technology. If not blood, then *something* must be thick enough between the two of you to enable such a real-time event to manifest, and a very lovely one at that. This 'something' is what we've both been referring to all along, in many different ways and concepts—vibrations, resonance, and harmony."

"I was wondering if we were ever going to actually talk about what we've been talking about. The two of us have a particular understanding and personal knowledge about vibration, but I was starting to worry that we were coming across in that New Agey way of sounding authoritative while remaining frustratingly ambiguous."

"So then what's the alternative? Middle Agey? Old Agey? Sorry, I couldn't resist. I agree that this would be a good point at which to introduce our experiential understanding of what we mean when we use words like 'vibration' and all the other ones related to it. This topic could be investigated in enough greater detail that it would demand another book or two on the subject, as you fretted about earlier. But as your Spirit Editor, it's clear to me that the subject, while intensely complicated, can still serve to lead us to an intriguing exploration about that most mysterious aspect of all life—vibrations."

VIBRATION, RESONANCE, & HARMONY

"As you experience it yourself you experience that the entire material world is nothing but vibration. We have to experience the ocean of infinite waves surging within, the river of inner sensations flowing within, the eternal dance of the countless vibrations within every atom of the body. We have to witness our continuously changing nature. All of this is happening at an extremely subtle level . . . As you experience the reality of matter to be vibration, you also start experiencing the reality of the mind: consciousness, perception, sensation and reaction. If you experience them properly with *Vipassana*, it will become clear how they work."[60]

~ *Excerpts from the discourses of Shri S N Goenka and Sayagyi U BA Khin on Vipassana*

We have been as simply direct as possible when presenting complex and challenging views about the paradoxes of transition. So while vibration is simply true, it's not truly simple.

Everything so far has led up to this topic, a little at a time, through our conversations and experiences—to carefully and gently enable sufficient understanding to unfold. If there is still a lot of mystery about vibration, be assured that your inner self—your spirit—has been keeping up with it all along.

~ 22 ~

These words may not make conscious sense at this time,
but my spiritual senses comprehend and retain
this knowledge for Authentic Self.

---

[60] *Vipassana* is an ancient Middle Indo-Aryan word for a process of observation—observing "what is" from moment-to-moment—observing "what is" as it is, thus gaining a "panoramic view" of one's life while immersed in all life. – *AG*

I've learned from Krishnamurti to never use words or concepts without an understanding of their meaning. The word "mystery" comes from the ancient Greek *myein*, meaning "to close or shut the eyes." From *myein* comes *mystes*, which is the origin of "mystic" and means "one who has been initiated." This suggests that something is closed to the eyes and ears unless one is an initiate. "Initiate" is from the Latin *inire*, "to go into, to begin." So the underlying message here about the mystery of vibration is that not all doors can be opened by everyone. This is fundamental to understanding Risen contact.

Human beings are a mystery to one another and to themselves as well. One might say—mysteriously—that this is what keeps us going. The intriguing allure of a mystery is that solving one often produces another. Opening one Risen door and going through it leads to another that may not yet be open. There is the distinct feeling of Greater Intelligence behind the doors of the Risen, waiting with childlike delight to help us find answers.

And let us consider another species of mystery—that which cannot be solved. For most of us, the great door of secrecy—death—won't fully open until we leave our earthly body for good.

Without going into all the scientific references that attempt to define vibration—and there are many—let it suffice to say that vibration is light that moves, and that which moves is alive. Every thing moves; every thing vibrates; every thing is alive. Life is filled with light.

Every thing is moving. With a little wrinkling of the brow we can see that this is true. This book is moving, whether or not you are holding it. The substance that it's made of, the finest of subatomic particles that our science is capable of detecting thus far, has been perceived to be in constant movement. Quantum mechanics scientists believe that matter "behaves," meaning that it moves in certain ways and that quanta—the units of energy without mass and substance that make up all things through the vibration of substance—are indivisible. Interestingly, biologists generally believe that life is nothing more or less than "chemical behaviors" that arise from certain structural arrangements of certain molecules in the presence of water.[61]

Scientists are technologically unable to carry their observations any further inward or outward to disprove these beliefs. They have observed that the charge of a material particle is what seems to give it boundaries and solidity; that its movement produces magnetic fields; and that the acceleration of its

---

[61] The subject of water and its divine, mysterious origins on Earth, including its dramatic differences in Risen geographies, would take several volumes to explore. For now, see *The Miracle of Water*, by Masaru Emoto, and his other books about his studies and findings that water transports the vibrations of our very thoughts and words, which cause a direct effect on the molecular structure of water, and therefore on our health, since our bodies are mostly water. This also supports science's observation that observation influences the behavior of matter.

movement appears to produce electromagnetic waves, or light. They have also noticed that the act of human observation, which is also behavior, directly and inexplicably affects the behavior of a particle. Even a scientist's act of noticing affects the observations. Can we ever see, then, what is *really* there?

This movement or behavior is what Tim and I are speaking of when we mention vibration. When a guitar string is plucked it vibrates, usually in visible waves. The faster it goes the less it can be seen. Our eyes are only capable of seeing within a certain range of vibration, just as our ears can only hear within a limited range of sound. The substance that makes up my material body is vibrating at a certain rate and this is also true for the substance of Tim's body.

We are not talking about *spirit* here, which is the light that moves us. We are speaking about that which spirit enlivens, meaning the particles of all matter and therefore of our bodies. The particles of Tim's body are finer, that is, smaller, and move faster than mine and so my physical senses cannot see or hear the electromagnetic waves—if that is what they indeed are at his level— that are produced by his body. For instance, a window fan that is not moving can be easily seen. But turn it on and quickly the blades begin to blur until barely visible. If they move fast enough they can't be seen at all. But our other senses of hearing and touch would inform us that something is definitely there.

Even "particles" are not ultimately real—rather, they are formations of energy, which moves the forms. But we will continue to speak of "particles" for the sake of being able to conceptualize this energy.

Where Western science is concerned nobody has yet determined how or why all things move or vibrate. We are speaking as Westerners, as neither Tim nor I can lay claim to being scholars of the Eastern traditions, although there are many resources for exploration that are inestimably older than those of the West. That this movement of matter has been assigned the quality of "behavior" by Western scientists is very intriguing, for behavior suggests nothing less than intelligence, of a kind far greater than anything we can begin to conceive—at work everywhere, all the time and in all ways. This intelligence is Spirit. Spirit—which is life—moves us.

Life moves in mysterious ways.

If we know what vibration is on a certain level, then what's the big mystery? It's that vibration is not life itself but rather *evidence* of life. What is the invisible energy that moves everything to begin with? How, and why?

It is Original Creator Source, simultaneously within and beyond us. It can be seen as the physical light we know on the Earth. It enables us to move things with our minds, like when we want to scratch our nose—we respond to the itch by using our mind to move our hand to relieve the itch. Clearly this demonstrates mind over matter. *We* do that. Gravity *can* be defied, as shown in that simple movement of our hand, or in the upward growth of a flower. When we leave our place of embodied occupancy—when we "die"—we can no longer raise the arm. Nor can a flower or a tree remain upright, as all material things eventually succumb to earth's gravity. And so *we* are also vibration.

Doors leading to other doors.

When Tim and I are communing, our spirits sense one another's particle vibrations, which are the evidence of the life, of spirit within us. We are sensing the spirit that enlivens the particles as well as the quality of mind we share during this sensing. This simultaneous co-sensing is part of the Principle of Rapport. Co-sensing needs no special "sixth sense" or psychic ability to do this, for the physical senses alone are capable of discerning much more than we are used to allowing.

Tim and I discern as much as we do on many sense levels because our vibrations are very similar to one another's—that is, we *resonate*. "Resonate" comes from the Latin *resonare*, to re-sound—to sound again, or to echo. When an acoustic guitar string is plucked near another similar guitar string, the second one will respond all by itself without being touched, reproducing and returning the vibrations of the first string. The energy that arises from this is called *frequency*.

❋ *This returning of vibration is the actual dynamic of communication of all manifested creation.* ❋

When two frequencies are close enough or identical in acoustics, as well as in electromagnetism, they become superimposed—or merge—and the result is a wave of amplification. So when Tim and I are resonating closely enough the result is an amplified experience. Recall that when a material particle is accelerated, visible light is produced. When amplification is accelerated, astounding things can happen, as will soon be seen.

Sometimes a new tone will arise from two resonant ones, called an *overtone*. Anyone who has sung in a large enough choir knows that at certain points, when everyone is in tune and resonating with one another as a group, a completely new and different note will majestically emerge above their heads, uniting all singularities into something larger. New ideas and new relationships that arise out of established ones are no less mysteriously majestic.

The similarity between two or more things is the resonance between them, or put in another way, the agreement between them. When we agree with someone we can also say that we resonate or are in resonance. When overtones arise from a particular resonance we have something new, which is *understanding*. When we resonate in different but still agreeable ways, which is another way of saying in similar ways, we are in harmony—from the Greek *harmonia*, or "means of joining."

Two waves that are different are said to interfere with each other—they don't change the nature of each other, they just manifest interference. When we resonate in different ways, we are in dissonance—from the Latin *dissonare* or "different in sound." What may resonate for one person might be dissonant to another, and vice versa. Therefore neither resonance nor dissonance can be equated with "good" or "not good" but are just qualitatively different.

The overtone produced by the understanding of difference is that of *non-judgment*. The vibrations that lead to this understanding are those of *sympathy* and *compassion*—from the Greek *sympathē*, "having like feelings together," and the Latin *compassus*, "together in suffering." Resonance and dissonance are sustained or suspended according to many factors.

Thoughts mingled with emotions manifest vibrations, which are feelings, which then manifest conditions. Keeping in line with the scientific observation that all is movement and that light and sound are vibrations, our thoughts are also vibrational in nature. A thought is the "seed of vibration" which, when planted or dispersed into the universe, sets up a vibration that will produce varying amounts and combinations of resonance and dissonance. From there, thoughts grow according to the condition of the ground onto which they fall. "Ground" means mind, and "condition" means mind's conscious awareness of itself. Thoughts are sustained, strengthened, weakened, suspended, or dissipated by the amount or lack of nourishment from attentive awareness upon them. Western scientists have not yet developed ways of detecting and measuring thought to their satisfaction—but the fact that they even try is interesting. Many of us have empowered these scientists to make decisions for us, because we haven't given much attentive awareness to our own individual thoughts about this. We haven't given much thought to the matter.

"Giving thought to matter? August, you speak in metaphors."

"To us, Tim, these metaphors reveal truths."

"I am in resonance with you about this."

"I love you too, you big lug. I sense that you wish to add more?"

"Yes—that light is also sound and therefore music is light. Each and every single unit of life is a light-filled tone and tone-filled light. Every thing vibrates and all movement produces light and sound. All universes are an ongoing symphony of infinite drama. Your life on earth and beyond it is a melody. This is less apparent on the earth due to its great density and lower vibration, which dulls and deadens the spirit, greatly lessening the connection every thing has with everything. It becomes more obvious on those planes beyond the Earth as we become more refined and of greater vibration."

"How have you experienced greater levels of vibration in your reality?"

"Where I am, all experience is vibrating at a greater level beyond a terrestrial experience, and descriptions are not easy to find."

"I share your frustration at being unable to find adequate descriptions, Tim. I also understand what you say about music, which seems to accomplish for us what literal transcription cannot. You and I have discovered that certain music and songs will cause one or both of us to vibrate in such a way as to make us strongly resonant, which sometimes become amplified, bringing us even closer together. This experience can be so intense for me that I hardly know where I am in that moment. It's as if I'm being transported to somewhere else not in this space or time where my body still seems to be. At other times negative thoughts or feelings of lesser vibrations will arise from the ego-mind, causing interference and lowering the resonance."

The Risen often share their experiences in ways that are beyond conception, such as formless energy patterns, or as the light information spheres mentioned before. Yet even the slightest description could still be useful to inspire others to locate what their own current inner and outer senses are capable of discerning.

"Let's together try to give an example, Tim, and in line with our mission, keeping it simple. When you were sharing the experience of your gradual awakening into your new Risen awareness, you spoke about flowers that were near and around you. In terms of vibration, light, and sound, can you share more about plants and nature where you are now?"

As Tim begins to share at this point, we each have to change the rate of our vibration in order to become more resonant. This is known as the Principle of Rapport. Rapport facilitates the exchange of energy, and this is established when the spiritual and/or physical vibrations of one entity vibrate in unison or near unison with those of another entity.

This means stilling the ego-mind's inner voices—the simulate selves—of past and future memory as much as possible. I raise my vibration by increasing my conscious self-awareness, for one's personal sense of awareness is that which enlivens materiality—or in other words, awareness accelerates vibration, which is amplification. There are unlimited ways to raise—or accelerate—one's awareness of self, as many as there are individuals. One cannot dictate to anyone other than to one's self what these ways might be. What unites us all is the primary realization of the sense of being that is known as I AM. One begins with feeling one's I AM-*ness*, one's Authentic Selfness, and from there the journey of growing self-awareness accelerates and expands—or amplifies—depending on one's ability to sustain that level of vibration as it transcends.

In this moment I now begin to imagine, and then see, with spiritual sight, a bright and clear, steady candle flame burning gently and silently in the air just before and above me. I don't question or comment on it but quietly accept and observe. I'm inspired to light a small blue glass votive candle. A material candle flame vibrates at a particularly gentle and even rate, and responds to subtle emotions by intensifying its own vibrations, which in turn help to slightly raise and clarify my own inner quiet. Blue is a tone on the area of the visible terrestrial light spectrum and also marks a particular vibration that resounds on the borderline of certain Risen states of consciousness.

"August, I've also manifested a candle flame in a darkened space before me. A single flower emerges out of the flame. This is a flower of my mind and my connection to Greater Mind. The flame, burning softly through the dark blue glass of your candle, causes you to think of blue flowers, and now I have a bouquet of blue flowers before me."

"The flowers I have in mind, Tim, are hyacinths, hydrangeas, and some exquisitely blue pansies I once saw in a window box many years ago. I can especially smell the intense perfume of the hyacinths."

"I have them here now before me. They have replaced the candle flame, and glow with many lights of their own, softly vibrating. There are beads of light pulsating up and down and through each petal of each flower, slowly, then more quickly. The faster the beads of light pulsate, the more solid the flowers appear, the more tangible to the touch. This pulsing is many sounds—stringed instruments, tinkling bells, running water—all which rise and fall as if there are voices singing in many tongues. This wavering of light is a perfume that reaches me in a wave of scent that takes me away, then brings me back, takes me away, then brings me back . . ."

"Takes you where, Tim?"

"To a garden of immense space and loveliness. I've emerged into a world where I can see enormous fields of flowers and sense intense but gentle movement, lights, and sounds. The bouquet I have been holding is responding to the other flowers around me and has left my arms, hovering through the air like dragonflies to join the verdant paradise around me. I see what might be other flowers, or butterflies and birds flying about, swooping low and sailing high and creating song as I move towards a tree in the center of this vast field.

"This tree is so gigantic as to be a world unto itself, and it would take you several days to walk around it. I cannot see how high it rises into the ice-blue sky, but there are a few wispy clouds in the lowest branches. I've changed my perspective now so that I can better see it. It is a Great Being, and also a world, which seems to me to have no dimensional end, for I cannot find a perspective from which to view this world all at once. As I move to place myself beneath this tree I experience many changes of vibration, as if distance and movement equal the same thing. The effect is as if I myself am like a buzzing of bees or a breeze upon my own cheeks.

"There is a civilization of beings living in this tree—so it's also a city. It is the source of life and a home to uncounted generations who have known nothing but a continuing coexistence of harmony. There are many seasons in this world, not just the few that you know, August. Each season is always a new one and never the same as any other, arising from the shared existence of all the beings that have lived in this tree for æons."

"What are these beings like, Tim?"

"They appear only as light and movement and far-off sounds. But I've just received an invitation to come closer and to visit for as long as I want. There is much curiosity about me, and I sense a lot of humor. There is an awareness of not just me but of you as well, August, and they are fascinated by us."

"Go visit them now, Tim. You've given me many strange and wonderful views, and I feel as if I could sit here and share in your experiences forever."

"Thanks, Aug. I'm asked by these beings to extend an invitation to you to come to this amazing place when you can, when your body rests and you can move freely through the higher planes."

While Tim is being received into the hospitality of his new-found friends, I sit quietly watching the candle flame wavering with its own voice, one I cannot hear but would be able to if I were Risen. Although Tim is elsewhere we are not separated, and I am quietly, distinctly aware of him as he continues to move through various astral geographies.

These are actual experiences with Tim, not insubstantial, intangible ideas of creative abstraction. So much of what we on earth may arrogantly assume are creations out of our own individual minds and dub "fictions" are, in absolute actuality, the memories of our own astral spirit experiences beyond this pale world. We spend enormous amounts of time and money trying to recreate these "fantasy lands" on earth and make them as perfect as possible. We take passionate delight in bringing these memories to life in books, plays, movies, and theme parks. We live for such surprises, wonder, and magic. Even the Scrooges and humbugs who deny such things have their evolving roles in the scheme of things, too. We all also intuitively know, to some degree, that the more we expand and open up, which means to have less fear, the more we are able to connect with greater opportunities for experiencing our unlimited heritage, which is nothing less than everything, including contact with the Risen. Within this limitlessness, we can continue to expand, to learn, and to trust our intuition with greater ease and acceptance.

It's greatly comforting and invigorating to know that Nature—that is, flowers, trees, gardens and forests, animals, birds, and people, are awaiting us when we leave this planet. Tim's experience with flowers touched something in my memory, and in going back through my journals, I found another astral experience with him that began with flowers.

Note that even though it was snowing in the land of my waking, physical plane, the weather was entirely different in the astral geography in which I found myself. Light and physics seemed to be poles apart as well.

"Heavy snows today—all was white and quiet as twilight arrived. I felt more distant and removed from my body than usual. While falling asleep I felt that I might be able to willfully go out of my body. Above all, I knew that I wanted to be with Tim. As my body fell asleep I concentrated and willed as hard as I could to leave and then felt something happening.

"In an instant and without any sensation of having traveled anywhere, I was standing in a field on a hillside, and knew I was no longer on Earth. Filling with joy, I began to sing, and saw that the tones caused plants to grow out of the ground and burst into bright purple flowers. I experimented with different sounds—the flowers responded, sometimes growing larger and brighter, sometimes receding. The flowers and I wove a pattern, a discourse upon levels I never knew possible. We were communicating, and we were all equally delighted with this surprise.

"I then walked up a very steep hill in the middle of a brook, stepping from rock to rock while the water tumbled around them. I came to a large tree and thought I saw somebody run behind it. My first thought was that it was Tim and so I called out his name. As I walked around the tree, all became dark, and it felt as if my eyelids were closed. I couldn't open them but could still sense light and shapes. Then Tim was suddenly there holding me; I was speechless. Knowing that I couldn't see him, he kissed me to prove who it was. It's been a long time since he's kissed me, and yet there was no mistake whose mouth it was upon mine. I began to cry as I held him tightly around the neck.

"My eyesight then cleared somewhat, but it was like seeing through watery glass. We were sitting in a room with another man I seemed to know and like quite well. But now I have no idea who this man was, as I sit here back in the material world writing it all down. There, however, we talked and laughed and spoke about other people we knew. I can't recall what we specifically said. I was simply, incredibly happy in a deeply peaceful way to just be with Tim.

"All too soon I felt myself being pulled back, a familiar feeling that told me we were about to part, so we quickly said good-bye. There was no sadness in this parting. Being there seemed so much more real than where I was being pulled back to, that it didn't matter in the overall scheme of things. Going back was temporary—being with Tim forever was ultimately inevitable."

Mentioned earlier, the topic of amplification reminded me of an exceptional event that took place between us, which contained elements of the ways in which vibrations, light, and sound interplayed and affected us both. It speaks of wonders that can hardly be believed, while cautioning that care must always be taken in terms of health where mediumistic experiences are concerned. I've already shared about the time Tim actually materialized in my bed. But this was not the only time that this incredible miracle happened. The following journal account is somewhat lengthy but invaluable in its details.

"While meditating in bed early this evening, I thought of Tim and felt an intense desire to much more consciously be with him. I remembered the revelation that amplifying such a desire is the key, so decided to direct my meditation in that way and concentrated on my desire to be with him. It was difficult and took lot of energy that I didn't seem to have that day. I soon found myself growing bored with it and decided to take a nap instead.

"While lying on my side and wondering if I should ever drift off to sleep, I felt a hand on my shoulder. I didn't feel it fall there—it was just there. I knew immediately that it was Tim. I've had this experience once before, but it was when awakening one morning with his hand on my shoulder. This time I was already awake, and not dreaming. I then began to move into an astral-etheric level, vacillating just slightly out of sync with the material world, yet fully conscious and intensely aware of his fingers pressing into my shoulder. I reached back and grasped his hand. It was definitely a hand, but seemed very small for an adult. Tim tried to pull away from me but I only held on more firmly. As we each pulled in opposite directions his fingers stretched as if made of raw bread dough. Without letting go, I stopped pulling and so did he, and I felt his hand fill out until it felt like a normal, adult-sized hand.

"As before, when I had tried to turn around to look at him, he whispered for me not to. The last time I obeyed. This time I ignored his request, and keeping a firm hold on his hand, turned over onto my back to face him. My room is always kept quite dim, even during the day, so it's much darker at night with very little light entering in. But my eyes were used to the darkness and I could clearly see that this was Tim, leaning over me and looking into my face with a somewhat surprised and slightly worried expression. Letting go of his hand, I reached up to feel his hair—it was full, luxurious, and wavy, just as it had been when he was on earth. When I released his hand he grasped me around the wrist, hanging onto it as I touched his hair, his brow, and then his face, which my fingertips could feel smiling.

"I felt intensely sleepy and lay back on the pillow. I started to fade in and out of consciousness—or I assume so, since my memory of what happened is sketchy. We had a long and intimate conversation about things I can't recall. It was as if time no longer existed. The conversation seemed infinite and my human brain is unable to retain the memory of the enormity of it all.

"Because I was experiencing it on a slightly higher astral level, my bedroom appeared altered. The differences were insignificant, such as the desk being placed elsewhere and certain pictures moved to other walls.

"I noticed that Tim wasn't looking well, and actually rather ill and undernourished. The closer I looked the more I saw that he appeared as he might have when he had been so sick on earth, wasted by his illness. I had the impression that it was becoming difficult for him to maintain his form and that he was uncomfortable and uneasy. I didn't know if this was actually the case or if he was just having a hard time maintaining the form of his astral body. The room then got totally dark, making it difficult to see. We emerged onto another level of consciousness, manifesting into a different geography of reality. He was standing now and trying to talk to somebody about what was happening into something that looked like a cell phone. I heard him identify himself and then call out for a person whose name I didn't recognize and can't recall. He sounded panicky. I heard him mention the group he was affiliated with, a rather long esoteric-sounding name which connoted some sort of scientific spiritual group.

"Something white was scattered around Tim's feet. It appeared to be a kind of white powder, which at first I thought was sugar. I saw what looked like broken glass and wondered if Tim had dropped a container of this substance. It was sparkly and glittered like fireflies, and there was quite a lot of it lying in little piles on the floor. I could see little flecks of light twinkling within this substance. Touching it caused it to crackle and pop, its reaction when coming in contact with my body—physical, etheric, or astral body, I can't say at this point. I intuited that this substance was largely involved with Tim being able to materialize to the point where we could see and feel each other—not entirely on the low physical plane where I inhabit my earth body but as close to it as possible, on just the other near side of light sleep.

"At this point I returned to an awakened conscious state, but still in higher vibration and not fully back on the physical plane. Tim was nowhere to be seen or felt. I rested for a bit while my mind boggled in wonder over the events that had just occurred.

"I lay in bed for at least an hour going over the events. My body felt uncomfortably charged with energy. Wave after wave of currents of energy seemed to be passing through it, as if cold breezes were coming from the inside out, and as if a great deal of static electricity was playing all over me. It was strong enough to be frightening but I told myself to not be afraid, that there was no reason for fear and that I was safe—but I still prayed for help and support. The electric effect lasted for almost an hour, and I noticed that the right side of the bed where Tim had materialized was inexplicably cold. The cold quickly reached my body and I pulled the comforter over me to get warm. I felt hungry, so got up and went to the kitchen to find something to eat—a few swallows of juice seemed to suffice. The static effect seemed to follow me as I walked from and back to the bed. Eventually I was able to fall into a deep, dreamless sleep."

When Tim had materialized in the first experience I had shared earlier, it also began with a hand on my shoulder. In that instance I was coming *from* an astral experience, which then culminated in a physical one. In the most recent one detailed above it was the opposite—a physical experience that moved *into* an astral one. In either case, this overlapping of the astral with the physical resulted in a temporary condition of surrealistic-like qualities, which some might call supernatural and others might label as hallucinogenic or delusional. What's actually apparent here is an event of worlds intermingling and achieving *entrainment*, as various states of amplified, conscious awareness revealed their interpenetration—an aspect of the unlimited nature of the universe.

An out-of-body experience is when the spiritual astral-etheric bodies temporarily leave the physical body. The range of such an experience is complex and infinite, for it varies according to our individual nature, which is always evolving and expanding. The nature of time on the various astral planes has fewer boundaries and restrictions than on the earthly plane, and also interpenetrates—it fluctuates and overlaps, extends, and expands according to principles very different from terrestrial ones.

For instance, my imaginal perception was able to manifest and experience my bedroom simultaneously on at least two planes or versions of reality. One was a physical level and the other was astral. In the astral version, my bedroom was the same but differed in small ways as it reflected the constantly changeable nature of my mind and its emotional states. It's not uncommon to find normally fixed aspects like doors and windows to be reversed or even missing in their astral counterparts. Such aspects serve different purposes in the astral as it adjusts accordingly to these purposes. Walls may be a different color as they reflect emotional states, or non-earthly paintings may appear on the walls, reflecting our thoughts and ideas. The terrestrial principles that govern perception, awareness, time, and other psychobiological experiences of an earthy existence are still flexible enough to enable us to utilize and practice our manifestation abilities on the astral planes closest to our own.

There are greater, expanded principles that underlie astral projection and all earthly manifestations, which not only allow our experiences to occur but guide and protect us within the ultimate compassion of the universe. Some might refer to these principles as laws—the "Law of Karma" or the "Laws of Nature," for example. However, human laws—which are reactionary efforts of a group mind seeking to control the actions of others—are not equitable to these cosmic principles. Nor are these principles like scientific laws, which are also reactionary expressions of group-mind perceptions, aimed towards gaining control over what's perceived as "chaos needing measurement and domination." In essence, there are no laws outside those that humanity makes, adjusts, or discards. As mentioned before, "law" is not the best descriptor when speaking of higher vibrating realities, as it implies humanly observed boundaries, restrictions, judgments, rewards, and punishments. Perhaps "guidelines" might better relay the concept of the higher reality, although for present purposes the Risen concept of *principle* will serve well enough.

In our human physical state we can't even begin to comprehend the structure of the nearest, higher principled reality. Dr. Robert Crookall, the well-known scientific researcher mentioned earlier, has written the most comprehensive book on the subject—*The Study and Practice of Astral Projection*. A large part of the book deals with the Risen and the various processes around their transitions as well. His systematic study and presentation of many cases corroborates many of my own experiences, including his finding that many people, upon awakening from a semi-conscious dream, find themselves instantly projected back into the astral while in a conscious state—as well as the other way around. As one of Crookall's studied subjects stated—

" . . . I have, on many occasions, wakened from a dream of 'dead' loved ones INTO the projected state. They seem to inhabit a 'sphere' that is further away than that I appear to be in, whilst projected. I have come to regard projection as a stage on my journey back from the places I believe I visit in sleep. Though probably it is not a case of moving through actual distance so much as becoming attuned to different vibrations, and hence to different states of being."[62]

In this experience with Tim, many powerful forces were at work and play, on many levels of existence—mental, emotional, and physical. Vibration, rapport, resonance, resonance amplification, and interference can all be identified. *Entrainment* is also apparent when my being vacillates, a phenomenon of resonance first observed in the 17th century, and which has an effect on all of us. It is defined as the tendency for two oscillating bodies to synchronize and lock into phase so that they vibrate in harmony. Entrainment is universal, appearing in chemistry, biology, psychology, astronomy, architecture and many more realms. Examples are playground swings that are swinging out of sync but then adjust, or one may be in a clock store and notice the pendulum clocks of the same size swinging back and forth in unison. Scientists believe that small amounts of energy are transferred between the two systems when they are out of phase in such a way as to produce negative feedback, thereby manifesting a more stable phase relationship.

It is clear that the meeting of two beings from two different realms had an impact upon a multitude of aspects of our lives, intensifying and changing them in unexpected ways. I have no doubt that I had guides and guardians close by, watching everything and taking care of me. Tim has since shared that he came with others as part of a support plan, and was instructed by his own guides to stay in close touch and let them know when he needed help, utilizing some kind of Risen technology. I later recalled that we had met previously before this event in the astral state and had discussed it and what it entailed, but I had forgotten this discussion, something that Tim and his colleagues were aware might happen. As it was, I did remember bits and pieces, such as vaguely comprehending the sparkling substance that had been sprinkled around.

Tim informed me that there were many individuals who were involved in this experiment, including Risen Researchers and Healer-Scientists from more than one astral level. Obviously Tim and I had each manifested in more than one particular physical way. There was liberal use of the sparkly stuff—a form of ectoplasmic matter that was specially fabricated by the Risen technologists involved in this experiment. Ectoplasm, as noted before, is a highly sensitive and sometimes volatile substance, which occurs naturally in varying amounts in

---

62 Robert Crookall, *The Study and Practice of Astral Projection* (Secaucus, NJ: The Citadel Press, 1960), 163.

all of us, but to a greater extent in mediums. The Risen have been utilizing their technology in many ways to express and impress their presences upon our physical plane. Sources suggest that Risen technologists have been experimenting with ectoplasm for at least two earth centuries and perhaps much longer. Advanced Risen techniques of chemistry, physics, and other sciences are involved, which are unknown and inaccessible on earth.

Clairvoyance and Materialisation: A Record of Experiments, written in 1927 by Dr. Gustave Geley, is documented with photographs of ectoplasmic manifestations and records his extensive scientific analyses of the many surprising forms of this enigmatic stuff. Most manifestations take place best in completely darkened spaces, as it did in my bedroom, because of ectoplasm's great sensitivity to the coarse form of our plane's light. For this same reason ectoplasm is extremely difficult to photograph. Dr. Geley and other researchers worked directly with Risen technologists in experimenting with various ways to overcome this difficulty. They used different colored lamps to see which would interfere least with the ectoplasm, while still giving off enough light to allow successful photography. A particular color of red light was found to facilitate the process. Occasionally the Risen technologists could somehow enable the ectoplasm to be photographed with a regular flash, but only for a brief instant.

Geley's work took place over eight decades ago when photography was still in its early stages. For reasons not yet clear, such direct materialization phenomena seem to have comparatively tapered off to almost nothing in the twenty-first century. For those that do occur, modern photographic techniques would surely be able to overcome some of the previous difficulties encountered. There are now advanced techniques such as high-speed photography and microphotography, which enable us to see and capture images impossible for the naked eye to detect, right down to the atomic levels of matter. The science for detecting and recording many forms of light within and beyond our known galaxy has also made incredible advances. Who knows what could be revealed if our terrestrial scientists seriously turned their eyes and hearts toward the Risen worlds?[63]

---

[63] As earthly technology increasingly aligns with that of the Risen—primarily due to advanced forays into quantum realities—the manifestation of ectoplasm is giving way to far more fantastic forms and limitless possibilities, as most notably seen in The Scole Experiment, where the Risen were able to fully materialize utilizing new forms of energy and light that accessed other dimensions. See *Witnessing the Impossible* by Robin Foy, and www.thescoleexperiment.com. – *AG*

TWENTY-FOUR

WATER TO THE OCEAN

"You've no idea how hard I've looked for a gift to bring You.
Nothing seemed right. What's the point of bringing gold to the gold
mine, or water to the Ocean? Everything I came up with was like
taking spices to the Orient. It's no good giving my heart and my soul
because you already have these.
So—I've brought you a mirror. Look at yourself and remember me."
~ Rumi

Tim's state of mind and being had evolved to a point where it was difficult for him to materialize. Such astounding experiences with him were occurring with less frequency. A dry spell seemed to have arrived, for he was beginning to move on to a higher vibration that inhibited his abilities to contact me on my physical level. I worried this might affect the intuitive and mental intimacy we'd enjoyed over the years. It seemed as if I couldn't sense him as strongly anymore, as if my usual awareness was no longer tuned in to his presence. I hadn't mentally heard his voice lately, and while this was not unusual, it had gone on long enough to cause me stress and sadness.

Tim once guided me into doing heart work when I had somehow gotten emotionally closed off to the world around me. I wondered if this was happening again, and so began doing exercises to expand my emotional awareness and feelings. This affirmative action brought my awareness closer to Tim in subtly different ways, but not as clear as in earlier days. I began to realize that as I changed, so did our relationship. And as our relationship continued to change, so would we, as part of the unending spiral of life.

He helped me understand that my awareness of him was initially based on the "Tim" I'd known before his transition—which meant the Tim of the past, the Tim of my memories. To a large degree, the relationship in my mind was built on those memories. If I were to continue to approach him and our relationship in terms of those memories, the sensation of the relationship would eventually fade—as memories do—and so would what I thought of as my awareness of him. Instead, I was to actively seek to experience him in the present—to let the memories fade and disengage from them, freeing myself and my mind for movement and growth with him, as he is *now*.

Tim has also pointed out that we each experience the evolution of our personal self and our relationship in different ways from one another. One of us might appear to be moving on because of the other's seemingly slow advances on his plane. I once expressed that it felt as if for every two steps forward I took, the next step was often one backward, and he shared that it was often the same for him. He added that when both of our sporadic growth movements are taken into a wholistic consideration, it must look like we're dancing a very strange dance. It's only when we're able to coordinate our movements that we can actually progress without falling over one another or stepping on toes. To be able to slow dance together is probably the most challenging, yet rewarding, thing to do.

After a few weeks of exercises for opening my heart, I awoke from sleep one night with the quickly fading memory that Tim and I had made love in a way I'd never experienced before—simply because it's not possible on this earthly plane. It was the ultimate, intimate act of *merging*—not just our astral bodies but our spirits and minds as well. It was ecstatic, intense, overwhelming, and utterly new to me. I have since been told by the Risen that such experiences are what the embodied on earth are trying to compulsively recreate through their physical sexual union on the material plane, which utterly pales in comparison. This means we *are* experiencing such thrilling consummations on the astral levels but can rarely remember them, having nothing to compare them with in our material life, although we intuitively try in our own physical ways. Opening the heart to greater and higher vibrating realities may enable us to remember such events. Yet much of the psychospiritual amnesia around such experiences is for the best. We would have so much longing for more that we wouldn't be able to fully live our lives on the earth, and may even become ill from the conscious awareness of such unfulfilled needs.

Many experienced OBE travelers might classify my materialization experiences with Tim as "astral traveling." I would agree on certain levels, although their complexity seems to take them into areas beyond the astral. While reading some old spiritualist books late into one night, I realized that in spite of these intense experiences since Tim's transition, I still had very few, clear recollections of being with him upon waking from a night's sleep. Although I knew that I spent a great deal of time with Tim while sleeping, I could barely remember much beyond jumbled feelings and fading recollections.

As I readied for sleep one night, I made a request out loud to Tim for us to meet during my sleep, and also affirmed that I would be enabled to remember as much as possible upon returning. Upon awakening in the morning, I recalled the following—

"I was riding the subway with two friends, both still living on the earth. We were standing while we chatted. Then a man got suddenly on, jumping through the doorway. I recognized him but couldn't quite remember from where or when. He acted as if he knew me quite well, and he had a rather self-possessed attitude, a-cat-with-the-canary smile on his face. I got off at my stop after saying good-bye to my friends, and he came with me to a place that greatly resembled my grandmother's house. I've always loved it, as it represented peace and safety to me. This fellow sat with me on the couch in the living room. We both had been carrying books and he asked me what I was studying. I looked at mine and they seemed to be in some sort of Asian language, and so I answered, 'Chinese poetry, I think, but I didn't know that I knew any.' I asked him what he was studying and he said something about a project that his father and brother were doing. While I was sitting there I was acutely aware of the great attraction I had for this man and how wonderful it felt to be with him, as if he were someone I had known well for a long time. I even felt lust for him. But I had to confess to him, "I must apologize, because although I seem to know you, I don't know your name."

" 'That's ok,' he laughed.

" 'And,' I added, 'I can't seem to remember my own name, either.'

" 'That's ok, too,' he answered with a grin.

"I made another apology for keeping him from his original destination, but right away he answered, 'Oh no, I wanted to be with you, and spend this time with you. That's why I'm here—I'm *very* happy to be with you right now!'

"I put my hand on his as we sat next to each other and I felt an incredible thrill at touching him, and found myself, rather embarrassingly, impulsively reaching out to touch his hair and stroke his face—I even leaned over to kiss him. But then he inexplicably pulled away so that I had to be content with just sitting next to him. Although he wouldn't look in my eyes, he never stopped smiling.

"To my great chagrin, upon waking I immediately recognized that this person was Tim. Even now I have a very good picture of him in my mind. He had appeared much more as I remembered him from his earthly days, and not as the unrecognizable youth I had seen on the train when he had materialized to me and Bridget over a year ago. As always, he was so handsome and had completely enchanted me.

"As I write this I am being impressed that *this* is the Tim of the present and not the one of the past. The fact that I was able to be with him in the astral, maybe consciously for the first time, attests to the success that I'm having in terms of opening up my heart and letting go of the past. I can more easily focus my attention and presence into the now, where we both are in reality. I recall having an immediate reaction of dismay and even fear when he had been gently rebuffing my advances. But almost as immediately I was also impressed that there was no need for my negative reactions, as his actions were a reflection of our two separate states of being. We were not perfectly resonant in vibration and so certain interactions were not feasible, and possibly might not have been comfortable. This inspired explanation relaxed me and removed my worries, and I was able to continue to just be happy with the memory of his presence."

Although my consciously intended attempt to be with Tim was a success, it's obvious where I had made the mistake, which accounted for my frustrating inability to recognize him as I sat face to face with him, even while touching him. I had forgotten to state in my intentions that while being able to remember as much as possible upon awakening, I would also be able to recognize him while in the astral state. I felt abashed by this oversight. I knew that the astral planes were capable of causing great distortion of familiar places and faces, as well as mental confusion in the physical brain, which can only interpret the experiences in limited ways.

In spite of this achievement, my worries of growing apart from Tim continued to color my day-to-day thinking. But I was learning, and that was a key point of many of these experiences. Tim and I knew that by intentionally reaching out and making and maintaining contact, the very vibrational energies raised and focused would result in something—often a surprise. Even when we seem to have given up, like when I lost patience with automatic writing and scrying, one cannot predict in an earthly scientific way what will happen. One sure thing I've learned is that the element of astonishment is directly affiliated with the Risen. When their lives begin to intersect and interact with ours, we can *never* be totally prepared for what may happen.

I learned my lesson. A few nights later after the astral train incident, I engaged myself in a period of deep meditation, an important component in inducing amplification and then conscious astral experiences. I poured all my energy into the intention to not only find Tim and then awaken with the memory of it intact, but I prayed with great willful desire to recognize him when I was with him. Relatedly, I had just finished reading a certain section in Stewart Edward White's *The Betty Book*, where Betty was in contact with "The Invisibles," her spirit contacts. They wanted her to learn how to enter *their* conditions, because they became dulled and confused when having to "come down" to her earth plane. These conditional aspects also seemed to be similar with the experience that was about to happen with Tim.

I brought my mind to a place of focused emotional intention, praying with great intensity to be with Tim, to recognize him, and to remember him upon awakening. I recalled that during the last time he had materialized I had been sleeping on my left side, so I purposely arranged myself the same way again. Such ritualizing can be helpful in focusing the intent. It was a little after midnight and there had been a full moon the day before. I couldn't be sure if the moon has anything to do with these things—I suspect that in some way it might—but I always note in my journal the astronomical conditions and the weather and time of day as well. I quickly fell into a deep sleep.

At some point I awoke, still on my side, and felt someone touching my shoulder and breathing on my neck. An arm was under my waist while a hand was resting on my shoulder. I immediately whispered, "Tim!"

"Yessss," he murmured very faintly, as if with a voice coming not from human vocal cords but sounding like a soft funnel of wind. I reached up and gently grasped his hand, and this time he didn't pull away, nor did I try to turn around. As before, his hand felt just like bread dough and I could feel it moving and swelling as the hand and arm gained shape and strength. Although it didn't feel like a human hand, I knew it was Tim's all the same, and I caressed the fingers softly and carefully as they caressed mine back. I continued to whisper with growing excitement, "Oh my god, it's really *you*, you're *here!*" I was ecstatic!

He replied, "Yessss . . . it's meee . . ." in the same breathy sound. His arm moved beneath me. I could feel his upper body against my back, but not his lower body or legs. His soft breathing against my neck was neither warm nor cool, neither dry nor moist—it can't be really described.

Like the previous experiences, maintaining such a physical-world juxtaposition became too difficult for us. Without warning we were displaced into the back of a kind of wooden wagon in an astral landscape. His body was now fully formed and clothed. We carried on a brief conversation while sitting across from each other, holding hands. In mid-sentence he fell over as if struck, barely able to move or speak. At first I was startled and thought he was seriously ill but I intuited that he was merely very weak. I found a blanket in the wagon and covered him with it—then he seemed to fall unconscious, at which point I grew alarmed. It was dark all around as if night had fallen, and there was a full moon shining on the landscape. The wagon was in some kind of field with hedges and trees scattered about.

A young man came running across the field, followed closely by about a dozen other people. Frightened, I flattened myself down but the young man popped his head over the side of the wagon and said not to be afraid because he had come to help Tim. The other people ran on past us. I didn't know this man and couldn't tell if Tim did, who was sleeping heavily. We somehow instantly traveled to a building that looked like a barn. I understood there was a kind of apparatus there that could transport Tim to where he would be cared for. A young woman was operating this apparatus, and asked me for "something of yours." When I didn't respond she reached around my neck and tore the tag off the back of my shirt. Tim seemed to have "deflated" and she folded him up as if he were a shirt, put him in a drawer in the apparatus and then put my shirt tag in another, smaller compartment. He obviously and literally was in no shape to go anywhere on his own. I deduced that she took the tag from my shirt to take back with her as part of an experiment.

With no sense of movement or transition I next found myself back in my bed and completely awake—the clock read 2:25 a.m. There were no sensations of having fallen asleep and then awakening. I was just suddenly not there and instantly back here. Strong chills began to rapidly run up and down my body, as if cold breezes were blowing across and even through me. The sensation was very light and not as dramatic and uncomfortable as it had been before. I felt tears welling up from joy over the experience, and immediately wanted to go back or else somehow enable Tim to come back to me. I very clearly heard Tim mentally tell me to get out of bed and go eat something immediately. I didn't feel hungry and wanted only to stay where I was but he kept insisting I go eat something. So I got up and went to the kitchen and ate some cold soup, shivering all the time although the room was quite warm, and found that I was very hungry. I got back into bed a few minutes later and instantly fell into a deep sleep. I awoke a few hours after sunrise, a bit groggy but not wiped out and ill like I had at other times. I felt elated, and prayed this meant that we were making progress.

Later, I began to experience feelings of guilt, as if somehow *I* had caused Tim to get ill. All the ego-mind's voices started in, accusing me of dabbling and interfering in things that were not my domain, going against the "Universe's Laws" that were meant to keep the two worlds apart, and so on. This shows how the ego-mind will continue to advocate for itself at our own expense, even when such experiences as mine unmistakably illustrate the profound and intelligent love that accompanies and rises from them. I acknowledged the ego-mind's interest in controlling my life by facing it directly and letting it know that I would not be dictated to by it, and that it was not being useful—enveloping it with light quickly silenced it.

I had referred earlier to Leadbeater's observations that spirit activities on such physical levels as this put great stress on those involved. These materialization experiments did indeed have consequences where Tim's and my health were concerned, which could explain their relative rarity in my life—or in anyone's life, for that matter.

We continued to meet and spend time with one another in the astral while my body slept, and it seemed as if the heretofore uncontrollable and crazy aspects of these encounters were beginning to balance out. The day before my birthday brought one such astral experience, and I noted this very special gift in my journal.

"I was with others whom I knew, and we had gathered in a huge hall with many hundreds, maybe even a few thousand people. Our chairs each had a program on it. We were graduate students of some sort and this was our commencement ceremony. It seemed quite casual, as everyone was dressed in any way they wanted, although I don't recall what I was wearing. It was as if we were graduating not from a specific school or program but from a former existence of some sort, or a way of being, and now we were ready to move on. Everyone was smiling, talking, and laughing. I met up with about a dozen people I knew, men and women, and we all had seats close together. I knew them all well, as good friends, and can still see their faces, but none of them are anyone that I remember now from my waking earth life.

"Except for Tim. I knew that he was to be there, graduating with me. His seat was next to mine and he was late, not an unusual thing for him but I was still a little nervous. The ceremony started but I wasn't listening, being too preoccupied anxiously watching for him.

"Someone said, 'Here he is!' as he strode in and sat down next to me. He said he had stopped in a movie theatre on his way there. He thought he was going to be too early and the last thing he remembered was thinking he wanted some popcorn. He fell asleep in the theatre and then woke up, late for the ceremony. He didn't act pleased to see me or even kiss me, but then, I didn't seem to be overjoyed either, just relieved that he had made it—it was all so forthright and natural. Although I felt calmer now that he was there, some distant part of me (the one in my earth bed?) was quietly growing more astonished at being there and being with him. I felt so very much in love with him and so grateful that we were together.

"I reached over and put my hand on his knee. He was wearing tan-colored twills and there was some kind of lint on them. I noticed it was a patch of black cat hair (so he had been with Bigfoot, his big black cat!) and I picked it off. He felt me do that and put his hand over mine and squeezed it, and we continued to hold hands. While he was reading from his program we communicated in silence with our hands, softly and slowly caressing each other's fingers and fingernails. His fingers were marvelously long and strong, and I could feel the warmth and humorous intelligence in them as our hands played and talked together.

"I heard him whisper that he was still hungry, because he'd never gotten the popcorn. He was thinking of leaving to look for something, maybe some fried chicken—we hushed him and told him not to be silly.

"Each program was designed specifically for each graduate, but I was too caught up being with Tim to care. I realized that he was reading mine aloud, and I heard something odd and said 'What? Let me see!' He said, 'It's talking about olive trees, imagine that.' There seemed to be some kind of 'astrological prediction' for each person. Mine said that 'after the ceremony, you will go back to your cabin and find nautical maps and books, and begin studying them right away as you begin your new voyage.' It continued, 'you might find yourself later becoming interested in gardens, especially olive trees and in the cultivation of great groves of them on sunny hillsides.'

"I was taken aback and not so amused, but I now see that it probably wasn't being all that literal. I made the slightly sarcastic remark, 'Well, Zohar isn't necessarily right all the time,' and Tim asked, 'Who's Zohar?' I replied, 'An astrologer I remember from some Earth newspaper, I think.' Some of our friends overheard me and laughed.

"Through all this exchange there were people up front going on with the ceremony and giving speeches, but I hadn't listened to a word being said. I could only think of how happy I was being with Tim and how beautiful he was. At one point I leaned over and kissed him on the cheek. Although he kept reading his program (and presumably his own prediction) his hand never stopped caressing mine.

"I began to slowly awaken in my bed on earth. Even as I grew more earth-conscious, I could still feel our hands clasped together as they continued to speak in their language of love. The touch of our hands was the last thing I felt as I became fully conscious. I can feel his hand even now as I write this."

There was great personal validation for me from this experience. All the ways in which Tim behaved were so perfectly typical of him. Many were very subtle behaviors that I couldn't do justice to in words, and which nobody else would ever notice, but which I know as well as my own body. They were so very "Tim." His warmth, his intelligence, his sense of humor and love of film, his lateness, his wanting to just leave to go eat something, and his typical air of goofy distraction were just some of the more obvious characteristics that made the experience so completely real and matter-of-fact.

This was the first experience since his transition in which everything seemed very balanced, and where we both consciously recognized each other. There was a sense of rightness, calmness, and normalcy about it. "Graduation" is about reaching a certain place of self-knowledge that feels realized and assimilated. We seemed to be finally growing up into our experience, which was changing as we changed.

Much about these astral-etheric experiences has been explained to me by Tim and other Risen Ones, but mysterious aspects still remain. I've referred to many individuals that have been part of these experiences, and they all seem to have one thing in common—I don't know who they are. Or, perhaps due to psychospiritual amnesia, I don't *remember* who they are. I recognize them when we're together in the other dimension, but upon returning to my embodied existence all traces of their identity seem to vanish from my mind. What remains is the strong and certain feeling that I know many of these people on very intimate terms—perhaps as friends, teachers, even lovers. It's clear that Tim knows more about their identities yet refers to them only in terms of their roles—teachers, healers, guides, friends—but never using specific names.

This still gives rise to many questions. Who are the mysterious figures that seem to have important roles in my astral experiences? How and why do I know them? What are we doing together in the same astral geographies? Did I know any of them on earth, and what are our relationships now? For many these questions might make them wonder if they had a history with such individuals in a past life. Reincarnation has been a topic of intense interest for countless cultures and religions for innumerable millennia. As guided by the Risen, we've saved this subject for last—the most challenging one to address. Not just because it's interesting and exciting—but because for the vast majority of us on Earth it's quite probable that it doesn't happen, and never will—at least in the way we're used to thinking.

TWENTY-FIVE

THE PASTIME OF REINCARNATION

"Wherever you go, there you are."
~ *Zen Buddhist Saying*

"Do not adjust your screens. This is not a test."
~ *Zen Risen Saying*

Thanks to Tim for one of the above quotes. If this chapter could consist only of these two ideas, a lot of earthly time might be saved.

"De nada, Aug. I agree—they more or less say it all—if *all* could be more or less to begin with, especially regarding the ideas of reincarnation and pre-existence. A lot of 'time' *would* be wasted if such ideas actualized in the way most tend to believe. There are always certain individuals who dare to journey over the edge where the world is believed to end. They discover that there are more worlds to explore beyond this edge and beyond every perceived edge. 'Edge' is yet another way to say 'belief.' We're going to explore from a Risen viewpoint what many will consider an outrageous and even heretical suggestion—that beliefs about reincarnation are *mythical*. And that it's all just a game, a pastime—literally, a 'past time.'

"Many may be disturbed by the idea that returning to the Earth isn't necessary. To suggest that it may not be a fact, well, that may get more than a few folks riled up and defensive about a much-perpetuated and intensely-embraced belief. Perhaps we could say 're-embodied, yes—reincarnated, not exactly.'"

"Well said, Tim—the simpler the better. I'm all for this being the shortest chapter, if possible—the subject somewhat intimidates me. But I know you want to tackle this pretty much on your own, right? That's fine with me."

"Indeed I do, but I make no apologies about length or if I seem to diverge at certain points, which are really all connected.

"I'm speaking about the subject from my comparatively limited Risen experience, and certainly not as any final authority. With every piece of knowledge I acquire, more implications arise, suggesting that a particular fragment of knowledge is just that—a fragment—and is not a definitive description. Although I'll be speaking in what appears to be definitive ways, I ask those reading and listening to keep their attention open and the ego-mind quiet, while not accepting what I say as the be-all and end-all. I'll draw some conclusions but others may decide differently, while perhaps investigating further on their own. I propose that we consider the following information as suggestions and perhaps as implications, but not necessarily facts. Think 'unconfined' instead of 'restricted.' The universe is eternal and it cannot be said that anything is written forever in stone or in anything else, since everything, including stone, eventually changes into something else."

~ 23 ~

These words may not make conscious sense at this time,
but my spiritual senses comprehend and retain
this knowledge for Authentic Self.

"The ideas of reincarnation and pre-existence were part of a belief system I brought into my Risen existence. I kept expecting the subjects to crop up but they never did. When I asked about them I was met with varied responses. But some Risen folks, including a few I knew from my earth life, seemed to believe as I did and we spent a lot of energy discussing and debating, wondering and worrying. 'What should we be doing to get ready for our next life on the earth? Who are the teachers to help me with this? Where and when should we start?'

"Someone suggested that maybe there was a special learning center with a library that dealt solely with the subject, but nobody knew how to get there. Usually if we desire something strongly enough here it will manifest within our reach. But perhaps we didn't know enough about what to desire in the way of a learning center or library on this particular subject, because nothing of the kind appeared. And nobody seemed to know how to direct us.

"But I continued to ask. The responses continued to range from gentle giggling and shrugging of the shoulders to polite but firm answers of 'Don't worry about it, have a nice day.' This attitude annoyed me because I believed it was important to start planning for an eventual return to life on earth so I could start over and do a better job. I also believed that we choose our parents each time we return to the earth, and this time I wanted to make a few changes!

"Being the pest that I am, I sought out not only my guides but others I perceived as having more experience and knowledge than myself, thinking they would confirm my assumptions of rightness. Being enlightened beings, they immediately sent me to a special school for pests, where even know-it-alls can be educated.

"Those lectures and class trips were extremely enlightening, and I'm honored to share what I now understand at this point. I can't say I understand with completeness or even have all the information—in fact, I know I don't. Keeping that in mind, here's the first suggestion I offer—

~ I ~
One's reality is defined by three I's ~
Individuality, Intensity, and Infinity.

"This will become more comprehensible as we begin to perceive certain essentials as they emerge from certain myths.

"Although a myth is usually regarded in your modern world as completely fictional, it's based upon certain realities that were misplaced from the present consciousness of the embodied collective. Myths arise from the collective perspectives of all individuals as perceived through their physical senses, and become stories about a particular earthly hearth experience—'hearth' meaning 'home,' and on many levels. Notice that 'hearth' contains the word 'heart.'

"Individual and collective experiences co-exist within simultaneous inner and outer spheres of consciousness. The inner and outer are really one whole experience, but limited human sense perception continuously manifests boundaries. In spite of every intentional belief to maintain these boundaries, mainly through stories, they are in constant flux and flow. These stories continue to be supported by everyone's collective bodily memories of the hearth, which then become legends. These legends are collected, retold, deconstructed, reconstructed, often embellished, and even dismissed, forgotten, reviled, or destroyed according to present beliefs.

"Regardless of the form of their transformation, the legends continue to move further away from their source of origination. The use of writing and other arts allows many more people to share the stories outside the more restrictive oral collective, and hence the stories become changed, diluted, embellished, and so on, according to personal and societal preferences.

"No story is ever really lost, even as it sinks into the ever-deepening lower layers of the collective underconscious—to borrow your term, August—from where they can be accessed and retrieved at any time and by anyone. Many of these resurrected stories are alike and inspire new versions to fit a modern world. Because these stories may no longer make sense to a modern mind, they are often distorted by the retriever in order to make them fit.

"The rituals that were evolved to store and access the stories often deteriorate or are lost, and the surviving ones might not translate to fit into the present cultural paradigm. These stories are evidence of past lives, but each life, while enjoining the collective, belongs individually to the one who lives it. Here, then, is another suggestion—

~ II ~
Only one individual
can claim that individual's life experience.

"A myth is based upon facts that have not been lost but instead misinterpreted, mislabeled, or misinformed. The truths imbedded within the stories are still there right before people's eyes, but they can't or won't see or listen to what the stories are actually saying. The older and smaller, simpler societies who experienced their collective as imbedded Truths-Within-Nature-As-Nature observed that when a tree dies and falls down, baby trees often emerged from its roots. They knew that this was not the original, individual tree being reborn itself, but that new individual trees were arising from their shared source, the same source from which the former parent tree itself had emerged. For them, this was direct evidence of a Universal Creator Source and of that Source's universal love.

"They comprehended that the essence, or the spirit, of the parent tree, now invisible on their particular reality plane, was free of earth's embracing forces—including gravity—and re-embraced by new forces, manifesting elsewhere beyond the usual physical senses. That this former tree of earth still left behind a discernable imprint within the energy grid did not escape their attention. By focusing their awareness on this imprint they not only honored the sacred mystery of the tree's individual spirit, but also were able through this awareness to achieve heightened awareness of those astral geographies closest to the earthly plane. Eventually, through the particular path of survival-by-dominance that the evolving ego-mind was taking, most people relinquished these heightened senses, replacing them with ego-mind assertions that such experiences were not valid and could not keep them safe from death.

"The above outline of a tree's transition is directly reflective of the astral processes that echo earthly biologic processes. It also reflects the development of the human psychological component whereby the *healthy* ego-mind, through trial and error, branches out by assembling simulate selves as tools for Authentic Self. Those that are deemed to be inadequate or inappropriate are "pruned from the vine" by the awake Authentic Self. Those that are positive are tended to blossom and bear fruit. These are bare-bones examples of how life appears to emerge in those Risen astral planes that resonate with and still interpenetrate humankind's environments.

"Because of the withering of such finer ancient senses, the reigning earthly cultural view disables any abilities to perceive the underlying realities, thus rendering them invisible to the mind. Now, in your time, Nature itself is being disabled and destroyed by humankind, which means that humankind is destroying itself. When you attempt to destroy Nature you are literally destroying your hearth. Destructive thinking leads to manifested violence. Humankind is an inextricable part of Nature because, like the baby trees, their spirits arise out of the same spirit of Greater Nature. Humankind is now increasingly dismantling its own hearth, which contains the collective memories of countless individual homes. Decreased access to the collective under-conscious leaves a feeling of emptiness and longing, and so people are filled with increasing urges escalated by their ego-minds to fill that emptiness—even with stories that aren't completely true or which have yet to be realized. These urges demand instant satisfaction regardless of the damages incurred, while neglecting the health of the overall collective and causing severe imbalances within the greater system.

"There are countless debates within the various Risen geographies closest to the earth about the meaning of the present ongoing and unchecked destruction of your planet. The Risen inhabitants of these areas generally still have a lot of interest and emotional mentality invested in their former earthly home, not having yet arrived at the evolved point where the associated resonance has ceased. Although this isn't the place to go into it, I've become involved with another Risen book project. It will explore the evolution of the earthly ego-mind, its role, purpose, and how it mutates in order to survive the very recent upsurge of increasing numbers of embodied people who seek to erase, sublimate, or put it back in its proper role. The study is in aid of Risen Healers who assist new arrivals, whose ego-minds are still dominant and only able to navigate their surroundings through the fear the ego-minds used to achieve and maintain that dominance. Normally the ego-mind dissipates or sometimes transitions to a different, appropriate form that enhances rather than compromises the surviving individuality. Some Risen Healers feel that the ego-mind is retrainable before arriving, hence the upsurge in new books about it on your world."

"A new book? Ye gods, Tim—can't we finish this one first? And besides, I know next to nothing about what you're studying."

"Fear not, for not only Risen pests can be taught. And don't worry, Dear Heart, this other book will be primarily the Risen's duty to orchestrate, while your role will be to deliver the discernment."

"Oh, *that's* all? What a relief."

"Just remember that sarcasm is a poor man's laughter and you are far too rich to pretend to it anymore."

"Thanks, I needed that. But pray, continue."

"I give you an image here of your blue planet swimming in the Cosmic Ocean of Ceaseless Voyaging. Its never-ending development continually advances it as a new species in every unit of space-time. Although Earth appears finite, it is, in countless and generally unknown ways, infinite and non-predictable in its own evolution. This is because it is a living, organic being itself. Although it has long been studied by earth-born Risen, our terrestrial home is still a great creature of greater mysteries. Citing the repetitive tendencies of human histories, some see Earthkind's present destructive actions as signs of evolution and an element of the process of earth's unfolding nature, where growth appears as an occurrence from a four-dimensional perspective, like the movement of a pendulum swinging to and fro, further and wider. They wonder what the limits of this pendulum are and if it is reaching the state of its final limitations—many believe that it has. From multi-dimensional perspectives that are beyond the usual four—within most of humankind's ken—there are yet other models. The spiral is one that well-describes the Risen perspective, a model that is greatly downsized and a relatively static example of higher dimensions.

"One related theory ponders that Earthkind's actions may be part of a manufactured, collective human plan with the goal to eventually tear down their planet until it can no longer sustain them. Earthkind is always tearing down and rebuilding and this seems to be in its nature, possibly reflecting all of earthly substance's process of growth and decay. These processes are maintained by uncounted numbers of species of terrestrial intelligences indiscernible to most humans. The term 'manufactured' is used here because of the apparent direct interrelatedness between these imperceptible species and that of humanity, suggesting extremely higher co-creative forces that enable, guide, and watch all life on earth, down to the last microbe's little sneeze.[64]

"It has also been suggested that humankind has somehow been programmed to dismantle the present, near-consensual dominant civilization on earth. This would result in the dissolution of the basis of Earthkind's collective of life stories. Physical life on earth would no longer be sustainable,

---

[64] Tim is referring here to the sub-angelic nature beings, or *devas*—also known as the earth, water, fire, and air elementals and nature spirits of the astral-ethereal worlds. – *AG*

and so Earthers' spirits would be stimulated, as if by a catalyst, to seek out new homes elsewhere. It's theorized that 'Higher Powers' have initiated and are guiding this process. Earthkind has reached a kind of self-actualized barrier over which it cannot cross, primarily because it has resisted becoming appropriately individualized and has instead intensified its collective state as a defensive reaction of the dominant and collective ego-mindset. These collective efforts of destruction will automatically vest all individuals with the responsibility of having done so, therefore collectively binding them, to be swept up into a cosmic event that will take them to a new geography of being. From there they can recover from their earthly experience and begin to experience new levels of awareness, which were formerly inaccessible on earth.

"This theory suggests that Earthkind is being shown how to give itself a foot up. This would be no simple undertaking. Those who have succeeded in breaking free of the less- or non-conscious collective while on earth will have effectively reached an advanced individual awareness that will become their own evolving, conscious experience. They will no longer be subject to the binding powers of the collective, each having achieved a greater degree of personal freedom to leave and explore beyond the collective. Only the denser ego-mind, individually and collectively, would be able to survive on an earth of its shaping. And if it *did* survive such a cosmic event, it would have to return to the dense earth to pick up the pieces and start life anew—to reincarnate. However, neither the collective nor the individual ego-mind would survive such an event, therefore freeing all individuals of the dominance of their ego-mind and of the necessity for reincarnating upon the same earth left behind. This theory is one of evolution, and seems to suggest that some kind of earthly reincarnation has perhaps been occurring but is now being phased out in an evolutionary way—which is the subject of other related studies.

"The theories mentioned so far center upon individuality, particularly upon the individual's unique ability to perceive, acknowledge, and live a distinctive life. Such individuals differ from those who try to focus those same abilities to maintain beliefs of reincarnation, where the goals are different.

"Even Risen views about the knowledge gained about who we are and where we came from are still seen as 'ideas,' no matter how close to the truth they might seem. People on earth require evidence as proof, and so do the Risen who seek answers about these ideas. Many Risen desire confirmation, not just about earthly subjects but on every facet of Risen life as well.

"There appears to be some indication that the vast majority of Risen— perhaps all—did not exist as individuals prior to their human existence on the earth. This would mean that those of us who were born on the earth first came into existence there as individuals, from out of the timeless movement that became the first movement of all the finite time to be used for our individual life experience on earth. We have to start somewhere, and that is what the earth is for. We arose for the very first time on Mother Earth, sparked into life to grow and become increasingly light-filled. It's like planting flowers—each year new seeds are planted and new flowers arise. The new flowers do not get replanted themselves nor do they revert back to their primal seed state. Instead they appear to be designed to extend life through a particular process known as 'reproduction' which is tailored—or 'designed,' as some Risen theorists assert—specifically for life on a planet such as the earth. The new seeds produced are then planted while the parent flower moves on elsewhere as a different state of energy. It has been observed on worlds in other dimensions that the life-extension process does not always follow this plan, which varies without limit beyond earthly comprehension.

"Evidence also suggests that we do not come from somewhere else before that moment of primal birth because there is no moment for us until we become individuated. There is no 'where' or 'when' until self-awareness awakes as the spark of light bestowed by Original Creator Source. From thereon, however, each of us is entirely and infinitely unique and always will be. This individuality, like the baby tree mentioned before, is seen to be Original Source's way of experiencing Itself over and over again, unto infinity. Here is an indescribably glorious and forever variable event of Life-Creating-Itself, becoming Self-Aware and ever evolving until Self-Awareness merges into All-Awareness with Itself, Original Source. Individuality is never lost, never assimilated, never watered down. It will never cease to grow and expand while becoming more individualized, all the while exploring its environment in relation to itself. So in terms of our individuality, there's always going to be plenty more where we came from and from where we're going. Within this context Earth is seen as the cradle of our nativity and highly honored by many Risen. As touched on earlier, there are others who would rather just forget that they ever came from Earth. And so they *do* forget.

"The purpose of Earth, then, would be as the starting place for our birth as an individual. It provides us with an initial environment in which to begin to get a sense of the individuality that is ours forever, and nothing more than that. If this is truly the primary purpose of an earthly life, and if that life is eternal, then people could stop trying to make it anything more. They could ease up and enjoy the wonder of ever-growing consciousness, of ever-rising awareness of self. What freedom there is in that! Even if they *could* be reborn back onto the planet, they would never be able to learn all there is to know, no matter how many times they return—which some seem to believe is the absolute requirement for eventual de-planeting. As their time on the earth is, by default, limited in an earthly fashion, so then are the experiences within that time.

"There are Risen schools of thought that support the idea that we, as original, individuated sparks of life, do indeed newly rise from the womb of Earth, to live on and eventually leave, never to return. There are some in these groups who are also investigating another related theory—that each life itself is but a spark from an unimaginably vast and older individuation that re-seeds itself, singly as well as inestimably, on countless worlds, in countless dimensions. These vast and ancient individuals are innumerable as well, and each was seeded from yet other even larger and older individuations. This process has been occurring on levels of complexity impossible to comprehend, as the potential collaborations, combinations, and groupings between all such individuals are infinite and unlimited. Within this context, each individuating person on the earth will also eventually expand to immense dimensions where they, too, will seed yet further sparks, all from an Original Source. This seems very like the 'baby tree' idea that earth's earliest cultures had intuited.

"There are other theories spun off from this notion of mega-individuals. One of the simpler ones involves the notion of a group soul, where many individuals are sparked from a mega-being. Perhaps they will eventually all reunite into yet another mega-being, and/or merge, while expanding, with Original Source Being. These sparks would be seeded possibly on just one world, such as earth, or on several, depending on choices made by the Source Being. Perhaps even other dimensions would be utilized. Not all would necessarily be seeded at the same time in the same era, but most likely would be scattered across many time periods in order to gain a multi-experience as wide and rich as possible for the sake of the group mind and that of Source Mind. Thus they would all have varying awareness of Source, which might account for awareness of one another as well as individual feelings of pre-existence. This might explain the feelings of having lived other lives in other times. Individuals would also be connected to each other through their own evolving group underconscious. Their rate of return to Original Source Mind would be greatly different amongst them, spanning perhaps what an earth-mind might experience as trillions of millennia, or longer. There would still be an intuitive connection between those who have transitioned into the astral dimensions. The configurations would be creatively endless in order to achieve the maximal amount of experience, information gathering, and communication. Those who have strong intuitive connections with the sparked individuals in other dimensions might struggle with confusion about where their real natal home is.

"We might question why the advanced, more evolved beings simply don't make themselves available to verify or disprove such Risen theories. It's rumored that this sometimes happens, but on vastly advanced levels beyond Risen perception. For much the same reason that Earthkind seldom receives such definitive answers from the Risen, neither do the Risen receive answers from the higher levels of vibration. It is as much a matter of creation and manifestation as it is of learning, and while guidance might come from higher sources, giving the answers would not only be interfering but premature. In essence, there are no answers to be given, only to be uncovered—or manifested, and, eventually, created. Earthkind and the Risen all have unlimited universes as their think tanks, laboratories, and playgrounds to explore, discover, debate, and wonder.

"Some Risen who exist in higher vibrational states intuit that there are astonishingly vast intelligences that watch, guide, and support our efforts, and take great joy and delight in doing so, as if caring for their children while not interfering in their unique processes. Some of these Higher Intuitives feel that if we came from anywhere before rising from the earth, we came from the All, which is all there is, and so therefore we are simultaneously each *and* collectively All-There-Is. It can then be said that we have always existed, and more succinctly, that our essence has always been an element of the Greater—and still is, as a *now-individualized* element of the Greater. Here and now, we are *individuated* All—all of us, and each of us.

"The dominant cultures of Earth's 21st century are based on a sustained belief in limitation, as evidenced by the collective custom to unconscionably allow only a scant few to accumulate, limit, and control material wealth, paralleled by exponential increases in consumption and waste. After I was Risen I still carried my beliefs of limitation for a while, which kept me waiting and looking to be graded and tested on how well I did while on earth. Of course I expected to not do so well, and to fail at most things. The fear this generated made for a certain amount of confusion and chaos. When I saw that no tests were forthcoming, I asked about it. I was told point blank that tests could be arranged if that's what I wanted, but there weren't any prepared for me and never would be. At the same time I heard this, I saw and understood in a flash that so much of my life as lived on the earth was about using great amounts of energy to attract and create situations that would challenge and test me, rationalizing that it would be an indication of how good and worthy I was and was becoming, and also how 'evolved' I was. What I misinterpreted as tests were actually natural occurrences manifested by the Principle of Novelty—accidents, mishaps, mistakes, trials, whatever one might call them—which are the natural movements of manifestation. These occurrences were actually novel opportunities offered through the abundant gifts of Creator Source to enable me to move and grow in my immortal life.

"A lot of beliefs were instilled in me at an early age on earth, and I never thought to question them. Not questioning succeeded in strengthening all the illusions around the central belief of not being good enough, which then kept the belief of limitations going. The belief was strong enough to even convince me that something greater than me was arranging life situations to test me. This took me even further away from realizing the truth that it was little ol' me who was doing it to myself, by completely denying that I was in any way responsible for manifesting the situations that I believed had to happen in the first place. Here, then, is my third suggestion —

~ III ~

When Original Creator Source gifts us with individuality,
It always gets it entirely right the first time.

"And so, I submit that the evidence strongly indicates that we cannot be re-individuated again. We are our own birthday present. I like to say that with increased awareness we become our own presence. My observation is that there is never any need to go back to do it again, for the universe is infinite and never-ending and will provide me with unceasing opportunities, always new, fresh, and alive, to explore, learn, and expand my self-awareness on a continual basis. I don't need to claim more than one life because my one life is enough. Because this one life is eternal it will always be more than enough, which is the core meaning of 'abundance.' Other individuals will perhaps come to different, even radical observations of their own.

"Clearly, we *are* reborn upon our transition, but this rebirth is always into a new world and a unique state of existence, not back into the old one. The old one no longer exists—life is experienced in the continual *now*. We develop and carry forward the template for our new life. *We* are the template, and a new world will simultaneously arise from us as we arise from it, as a direct result of how we lived our lives on earth or from wherever we are continuously transitioning. The more brilliantly we live—that is, the more light-filled—the more spectacular will our lives manifest as we transmute ever onward. There are no limits to brilliance except as self-imposed. But even that is an illusion, for there is no real limit to anything.

"The beauty of the earthly material body is very temporary, for it serves to house the spirit body, which grows along with and as part of the material body. The body is like the shell of a seed and the spirit is the life-kernel of potentiality within. Both are a product of the original force of light that ignited the seeds planted within the darkness of the mother's womb to grow, flower, and fruit. Another analogy is that our material body is the cocoon and the spirit body the future butterfly. In the process of the butterfly, the cocoon is quickly formed and then needs no more attention as it ages, becoming dry and brown. So, too, does the body quickly form and age, so that the spirit within can have a home to grow in, and from which it inevitably leaves. The more attention we give to nourishing the growing spirit body within us, the easier and more spectacular will our emergence be into our newly Risen state. The earthly human cocoon needs to fully and healthily form, and it's disheartening to see how much attention is focused on preventing it from properly aging, while very little consideration is given to tending the growing beauty of the spirit within. If not cared for while on earth, this neglect will have to be addressed afterwards—I speak from experience.

"It's sometimes inferred that our spirits will take on new bodies again. Actually, our spirit will be our actual body, and then at some point it becomes the cocoon for the next transition. A higher vibrating form of spiritual being will then evolve from that event, eventually moving on to yet another new geography. So transition occurs due to the advanced state of spirit, meaning the higher evolution of the spiritual body's vibration.

"As transition is inevitable to all on the earth, so is increased vibration, even if it's just a little bit. Even the most seemingly undeveloped or malevolent persons eventually reach a point of higher vibration while on earth, and it's always just enough to catalyze the process of transition and jettison them out of the material plane. Those who leave via forced or violent circumstances have enabled that means by their very vibration.

"At some point in your earthly life, Nature will induce 'labor contractions' that will culminate in your being reborn into a new life. Once the spirit vibrates at a high-enough rate, it will no longer be able to tolerate the gradual lowering of vibrations of a disintegrating earthly body, which eventually ceases to vibrate. The higher vibrations of the spirit body will literally begin to shake the earthly casing free and the two will start to separate. In spite of earthly medical attempts to interfere with this inevitable process, the material body can only continue to slow its vibrations until all its activity ceases. No matter how healthy you keep your body, it will eventually cease to function. It will then be reabsorbed back into the earth as well as into the many cosmic rays that continually wash over and through the material world.

"The spirit then becomes a newer form of body that is appropriate to the higher vibration. It cannot return to earth to be reborn once again because its new and higher state of vibration would no longer be appropriate there. Upon transition one is no longer spiritually human because of the higher vibration, and so cannot return to being earthly human in the equivalent way. The higher vibrating spirit cannot be made to vibrate lower for very long, as I've learned when having to temporarily lower my vibrations for the experiments with materializing to August on his earthly plane. And even then I had to use materials that came from his body, plus substances supplied by Risen Technician-Chemists, so that a suitable mix resulting in appropriate vibrations could be fabricated to contain my spirit. In spite of the great care taken I was often in discomfort, paralleling August's experience where his lower-vibrating spirit was not comfortable in the higher vibrating material for very long.

"Upon Rising, it seems quite obvious that we will continue to evolve ever onward through higher—and sometimes, lower—vibrations, which means the birth experience also continues and evolves. It's beyond my ken how long this cycle repeats, until it perhaps transmutes to a different process. The transition experience is at its most primitive regarding our primal earthly birth. In the higher astral geographies, rebirth is a much different experience, where it's no longer a material matter of blood, sweat, and tears. It becomes a vibrant, living prophecy and gives great, ecstatic cause for joyful celebration. Although it's not the modern norm, there is just as much cause for celebration when someone transitions on Earth.

"Being fully Risen means being consciously aware of the present. There are those whose crystallized ego-minds and beliefs will temporarily bind them to the earth plane, so that they're disabled from immediately moving forward to become fully Risen on the higher planes away from earth. Intense fear, anger, resentment, and hatred are especially powerful elements that will cause such entrapments—longing and nostalgia will intensify these elements. If such negative emotions are outside of one's awareness or actively denied, this makes it tricky to find and get a handle on them to address and correct the malfunctions they cause. If such negative emotions are conscious and willful, embraced and energized, then a strong barrier is fashioned around the soul, making it opaque to the light of consciousness and sealing it off from light. This love-filled light, this light-which-is-love and true consciousness, is the only energy that can dissolve such barriers, and ultimately it does. It doesn't so much dissolve darkness as to simply illuminate that, in reality, there is no darkness there. Still, it may be æons before such self-imprisoned individuals can let in enough light to even adequately perceive their environment.

"These disabled spirits are by no means inactive, for they can influence still-embodied people, by attempting to continue to experience an earthly existence through somebody else's body, or more commonly by trying to share or displace an embodied ego-mind with their own will. They cannot do this in a permanent way, but due to their willful self-suppression and lowering of their vibrations they may achieve a form of rapport and thus influence an embodied ego-mind, and possibly gain near or total control of that mind's perceptions and then control of its behavior. The earthly embodied person then has the experience of losing their mind, and may be labeled by other embodied ego-minds as being off their head, deranged, unhinged, or mentally ill.

"I have heard one Risen theorist comment that 'those who try to reincarnate are attempting to swim back upstream in the wrong direction.' These disincarnates are unaware that they are leading less-than-healthy existences while swimming in the astral waters being 'polluted' by those attempting the same thing further upstream. This pollution arises on the earthly plane as contaminated emotional energy that is misinterpreted as evidence of past life histories. Those who elect to focus their minds on such energies in this way are unmindful of the miraculous gift of their own individuality, which is theirs forever to do with as they please. This freedom of individual will allows people to focus on anything and in any way that brings pleasure. As always and forever, there will be no interference or judgment from Creator Source. 'One's pain is another's pleasure,' as it has been said.

"The inappropriate actions of interfering disembodied persons are just some of the factors that may shape the beliefs of pre-existence and of reincarnation. Their influences are mistaken by the embodied for their own thoughts. With these outside thoughts can come all the personality characteristics of the disincarnate, as well as the influences *they* inherited from others who influenced them while on the earth and then while disembodied as earth-bound spirits. This includes characteristics inherited from generations of earthly ancestors. Likes, dislikes, and even long-lost languages may be learned and assimilated between resonating disincarnate and incarnate spirits.

"The experience of remembering past lives may also be from the projection of character elements of an earthbound spirit onto the ego-mind of a receptive embodied person. Those who are convinced they have lived a previous life are actually recalling memories of those who have gone before them. Each disembodied spirit had its own individual life on earth, which the embodied person would 'remember,' seemingly quite clearly, and believing it to be a past life memory. The more closely resonating spirits there are who are involved in the influence, the more past lives may appear to be present. Risen Healers who work on the lower levels have said that word gets around fast when there are willing Earthers who desire to have 'reincarnation experiences.' Earthbound spirits will seek them out to try to relive their own previous earth life in order to relieve certain discomforts, all the while ignoring their own actual spiritual existence. There is a noticeable parallel here between those on earth who mentally and emotionally cannot or will not move on through difficult life challenges, and those on the lower astral planes who cannot or will not accept the change and move on with their transition.

"Hypnotists and their clients may give disincarnated individuals chances to reexperience the memory of what it feels like to have a material body with physical senses. The embodied who seek hypnotic past-life regressions are entering into an agreement to have their bodily energy fields altered. This enables the ideal conditions that attract, invite, and nourish the invasive projections of those disincarnates who are often influencing a susceptible incarnate. These same spirits influence the hypnotist to make suggestions to the client to maximize the conditions necessary to enable their agenda. A hypnotist can be hypnotized by spirits who are better at it and without the hypnotist's awareness of it happening. The hypnotist may also have a personal agenda to appear competent as well as a need to prove the existence of past lives, and so is a perfect subject for spirit influence. 'Buried past lives' that become 'uncovered' are really the dramas of other previously embodied individuals. Their stories may appear in the conscious awareness of the embodied client at that time, but do not evidence that client's previous lives. In reality, the information is of someone else's life history.

"Like hypnotic states, daydreams and wandering thoughts are vulnerable mental conditions that are exceptionally open and impressionable and can be quite vivid in their reality. It's easy to lose a sense of self in these states. It's also simple for a disembodied spirit to induce trance states, and then insinuate impressions of itself while the daydreamer is unaware of it happening. Because the embodied person will be able to share in the discarnate person's memories, it will seem to be proof that they're beginning to recall a past life. But all that's being recalled is the past and even the present life of the influencing spirit. Unless someone has studied their own mental processes thoroughly enough to be able to recognize the difference between their own thoughts and the thoughts of others, all memories in the same thinking space will seem to be the same and therefore seem to be their own.

"Children, who have a minimum of life experience, are especially open and vulnerable to invasive earth-bound spirits, and easily confused and led to believe they have led a previous life. The misconception becomes more solidified when adults actively promote and push the child to continue the belief while pressuring them to produce more 'evidence' to promote their own adult agenda of fear-based beliefs in reincarnation.[65]

"The Principle of Affinity enables the mutual attraction between similarly vibrating embodied spirits and earth-bound spirits. If Earthers are actively engaged in beliefs that encourage seeking what they believe to be 'reincarnational information,' they will attract that information, possibly in the form of an earthbound spirit, who then might join and even merge with their thought processes. Information may also come to them in the form of books or from other embodied people who carry intensified, energetic beliefs mirroring their own. The disembodied person's previous earth history, along with all experiential memories, thoughts, and emotions will not only become accessible to the embodied seeker but will rush in to fill the gaps that ought to be filled by the embodied person's own awareness of presence. Lack of self-awareness and intentionally opening oneself up to non-self influences, as well as the use of alcohol and certain drugs, will further ensure the receptivity of invasive forces. Continued and extensive substance abuse will cause the body-spirit-mind components to malfunction and thus will leave an embodied earth mind exposed to outside influences, and with lessened recourse and protection. Self-healing and scientific prayer can restore the correct energies needed to re-strengthen protection and immunity. Such prayerful techniques may also come

---

65 In her book, *The Field*, Lynne McTaggart suggests that children who profess past lives have actually picked up another person's life memories stored in the Zero Point Field, which is intimately related to Rupert Sheldrake's conceptual theories of morphogenic fields and current emerging findings in quantum physics that everything and everyone is connected. – *AG*

from another to assist in regaining strength.

"Mental depression and low self-esteem caused and maintained by the ego-mind's controlling hold on the embodied person can create receptive conditions for invasive influences. One of the great psychological afflictions of most of modern earthly societies is the pervasive lack of self-love, reinforced by society's insistence that no one is ever smart, rich, attractive, or good enough. This seemingly inescapable lack, while totally delusional, is embraced as a personal belief by the majority and therefore reinforced by mass reactive behavior. That which is reinforced by the masses can be very difficult to breach. Certain drugs, which can often override the body's organic natural and even artificial structures, are inappropriately encouraged to correct what are misperceived as pathologies. Often these drugs are suggested to the embodied by incorporeal persons. By rejecting their true, unique individual selves and wanting to be someone else, the embodied become ideal receptacles for those disincarnate who wish to have earthly corporeal experiences again. Although possession of a body is comparatively rare, possession of a mind via spirit influence is not. This cannot be debated for long after looking objectively at the obvious successful influence of the Global Madison Avenue. Those in spirit have even more direct access to minds easily hypnotized by such suggestive influences.

"Note that qualities of good or evil haven't been attributed to invading spirit persons. While their lower vibrational conditions may provide harbor for negative emotions—often intense ones—not all of the disincarnate seeking to reexperience an earthly life have ill intentions. Some are malevolent and some are not, although all are misguided in some way because some form of fear motivates them. Any attempt to invade and use another's life for one's own is a misinterpretation of one of the most essential of spiritual reminders, 'Do unto others as you would have them do unto you.' Another way of phrasing this suggestion is 'Each in all ways to one's own.' A simpler yet powerful Risen version is 'Do not.' I remember on earth when the saying 'Do your own thing' became popular and was later rebuked by society-at-large for promoting selfishness within the younger generation. Yet when 'Do your own thing' is instilled with tones of love, joy, and discovery it becomes a responsible, powerful, and positive affirmation for the evolution of one's individuality.

"Those Risen who are particularly evolved may make themselves available for help and inspiration when called upon, but inspiration does not mean infestation. Some disembodied are so ego-self-absorbed that they become parasitical to survive. They become engorged on the embodied person's energy to feed the crystallized ego-mind's unyielding need for a sense of existence. They then gain more energy and the ability to continue to influence the embodied person. The embodied person's ego-mind becomes a co-conspirator with the spirit's crystallized ego-mind and the enlarged sensation becomes puffed up with self-assigned importance—it's more gratifying to have once been a wealthy prince instead of some menial ditch digger.

"The widespread beliefs in pre-lives, past lives, between-lives, and so on, show just how easily the embodied can be influenced. Mediums and channelers who do not properly prepare themselves, or are ignorant of or arrogant towards certain parameters, are even more prone to receiving and passing on misinformation, while reinforcing the mistaken perception-beliefs of others. If mediums are devoted supporters of reincarnation they may readily accept information from spirit persons who claim to be the past life of a client. They may rationalize any discrepancies by their own ego-mind-driven belief that they are 'reading the client's past life'—unaware that this spirit person is actually a separate entity from the client. This type of denial may feed the medium's personal agenda of wanting to appear competent, powerful, important, special, and valuable. Of course a client who is needy for such validations will be led and drawn to the medium that will help fulfill that need, as directed through the Principle of Affinity. All involved become invested in one another's fantasy. You wouldn't believe the astral knots that arise from these kinds of relationship ties! And all the while, the one truly great marvel, the great gift of one's own inimitable and unending individuality goes unacknowledged and ignored—and thus the spirit languishes.

"Down through the æons, innumerable influences have surfaced from the multi-dimensional depths of the human collective underconscious. These influences have sometimes been labeled as 'archetypes.' Individuals can and do share the energy of various archetypes, which are a natural result of the collective mind-experience of everyone who has even been born on the earth. A struggling young mother can find a source of strength by resonating with the archetype of THE MOTHER, which is the collective experience of all mothers. Or somebody who has been leading a repressed, stuffy life will somehow find access to THE FOOL archetype and finally be able to laugh at himself, and possibly be transformed by cosmic humor into a higher vibrating spirit. This particular type of laughter always raises the spirits—*double entendre* intended.

"The archetypes are your goddesses and gods, which have evolved in their own way to become various kinds of templates for human behavior. When accessed by individuals experiencing heightened awareness, these templates can trigger memories down to and beyond the cellular level—indwelling memories that belong not to the individual, but to the Collective of Individuals. Day-dreams, songs, walking into a room and smelling perfume, or a particular piece of architecture can activate these collective memories. Many individuals have attempted to explain their strong emotional reactions from these triggered experiences as evidence of having lived before as a certain person in a particular place and time. Because of the vast and complex connectedness of the Collective of Individuals, synchronicity and serendipity arise naturally, seemingly lending support to the notion of reincarnation.

"Practicing conscious awareness of one's individual self will enlarge the individual awareness. This means that one participates as one's self with one's self. The act of accessing collective memories adds to them while coloring, shaping, and enriching the overall Collective. This act of conscious observation does not increase the quantity of the individual's self-awareness, but rather enriches its *quality*. Every individual human mind is a bud on a branch of the earthly Collective Tree. Those who are openly sensitive will be able to reach into other branches or collectives of other world-dimensions, which together continually co-manifest as a particular Universal Collective. Those who are less aware of their individuality will be more prone to believe that their experience of others is but a memory of another life of their own. But those who are *more* aware and take a conscious, active role in their budding individuality will be enabled to realize and honor all the other individualities with which they share existence upon the Tree of Life, while maintaining a separate—but not separated—expanding experience of individual awareness of one's self.

"It has been observed that those of like mind and emotions are more likely able to find and access memories of each other, achieving an empathic connection that allows them to share past, present, and future timelines—this is the Principle of Rapport. Lives that are similar, regardless of where and when, resonate at all times—the Principle of Resonance. Spirit influence can also occur before the final transition from earth. When the body is asleep and the spirit is traveling in the astral, anyone can gravitate toward others of similar resonance. Time is extremely more variable away from the material body.

"For example—because of strong resonance, a 21st century person astrally travels to someone in the 14th century, who shares some of the same feelings and beliefs, and they may develop a relationship of a certain intensity. The 14th century person will experience influences from the mind and emotions of the 21st century person, who in turn will be affected and influenced by the 14th century person's reactions and responses. Depending on the amount of self-awareness, either or both might treat any sketchy dream memories as real or not. Depending on her cultural and personal belief systems, the person of the 21st century might think she is remembering her own 'past life experience' rather than recognizing the fact that she is recalling somebody else's life story in the past. The 14th century person might interpret his dream memories of 21st century technology as demonic and believe he's being assailed or possessed by an evil spirit in his present. If one is negatively inclined and fearful, it might be perceived as an ill-intentioned being, or its actions interpreted as trying to 'possess its victim.' Although it's now fashionable to believe that a past life is being recalled, if enough rapport is achieved between the two lives it may also feel like one is actually being personally contacted by another life form.

"*Consciously* sensing the lives of others who lived before us is now a mostly hibernating ability. The ego-mind, in its quest for maintaining an infinite earthly existence, influences its embodied host to steal others' past identities to enlarge and extend its own sense of self. This extending of the ego-mind is in aggressive opposition to the divine truth that each of us, as a co-inheritor of all that our Source enjoys, is able to access a greater sense of self by realizing and feeling the actuality of one's individualized self.

"The incarnate on the Earth spend most of their sleeping time in the astral, where they continue to live their lives. They form relationships with others, engage in manifesting and studying new things, go to lots of events and parties, manifest art, and explore other dimensional states of being. In short, your life does not come to a standstill when you hit the hay, to remain in stasis until you awaken and continue from where you think you left off. Your night lives are immensely more full, rich, varied, and utterly fantastic than your day lives. These astral life experiences are so unlike the waking life that it's not difficult, for those who are so inclined, to rationalize any unusual memories as evidence of past lives. What's more, most are completely incapable of consciously remembering even a thimble-full of their astral lives. Everything that happens in the astral becomes a memory stored in the collective mind, and these hidden memories will surface in infinitely subtle ways when invoked by resonating events as well as emotional and sensual triggers. Because they are not recognized for what they really are they become diminished and may be misinterpreted and reassigned as past-life memories by the ego-mind.

"For instance, a person is attracted by affinity to a particular Risen ancestor. They meet and converse on an astral plane, drawn together by their similarities, and generate resonance and amplification of thought and emotions. Upon leaving the astral the embodied kin will feel different—enlarged, enriched, and energized by the relationship—but because he hasn't learned how to access the memory of their meeting may instead rationalize his feelings as having experienced a past life. To induce and support this rationalization, his ego-mind will search his memory's store for suitable images and scenarios.

"During astral experiences, there is no 'thinking' as a person does while in the body because the bodily brain has been temporarily vacated. Instead there is a process whereby the astral-etheric mind-body experiences, observes, and records events while in the astral geography. Upon return to the earthly body, brain thinking resumes and the astral-etheric memory quickly disintegrates, broken up by the invasive, decision-making mechanics—or judgment—of the ego-mind. The ego-mind does this by using the brain to pick apart—or analyze—whatever it can access of the astral-etheric body-mind's experiences.

"The ego-mind cannot communicate with the astral-etheric mind. Instead it reacts to the vibrations of the astral-etheric mind by producing emotions, which then produce images culled from a personal and limited memory store of past events. These memories have suffered the inevitable disintegrative and warping effects of the ego-mind in its parasitical drive to govern everything from within its perceived, delusional domain. A desperate ego-mind will even feed upon itself, causing a unique form of exquisite pain that is the core feeling of all addictions, and to which the ego-mind compulsively returns again and again, unwilling and unable to cease its self-destructive thinking.

"Belief in survival in another body as a different life may be directly due to Authentic Self's deeper knowledge that one *does* survive and arise in a new body—as Risen. This awareness is generally not explored sufficiently to allow for a following through to the correct conclusion. The conclusion would be that one does not start over in a new life in a different body but rather continues on with one's single immortal life in limitless, infinite forms and relationships. This 'one' is just that—one—meaning it is *all* there is. And all is more than enough, isn't it? So it appears we don't get reborn backwards, which is yet another way of saying that we don't return to do it again.

~ 24 ~

These words may not make conscious sense at this time,
but my spiritual senses comprehend and retain
this knowledge for Authentic Self.

"Is this so hard to conceive? Those on earth are quite aware that the body they start out with is not the same body at the age of seven, twenty-one, or ninety-one. It's not difficult to see that it is in continual fluctuation and never the same in any given moment. And yet it is also apparent that one is somehow still the same individual while this individuality expands and contracts, waxes and wanes, ever changing, ever responding to the Principle of Novelty.

"The underlying factor consistently supporting the generally unchallenged belief in reincarnation is that old nemesis, the fear of death. Authentic Self, which unfortunately is usually *not* a conscious part of most people's lives, still inherently possesses the fact of survival after the material body's ending. As we have tried to show in this book, the success of the ego-mind's campaign to control the beliefs of the human-encapsulated mind is due primarily to its constant use of the fear of mortality—and even fear of immortality. The thought that one is immortal and will have to move beyond the earth, never to return, can be extremely threatening, especially if one has not taken the time to become informed of the facts about the process. Ignorance does not equal bliss but engenders fear. It's not difficult for an ignorant and insecure mind to pretend it will be safe when sustained by the belief in a return to the well-known environment for more earth-based living. Westerners particularly have the misconceived notion that they are 'pioneers' of some sort and so have built an entire culture around 'blazing new trails' and 'conquering new vistas.' This notion about dominating the earth is so embedded in their psyche that many may feel a compulsive need to return to continue to divide and conquer as a means to identify and to acquire power.

"And if one has to come back, why not do it differently—better, bigger, richer, more beautiful, less boring, more successful, less painful? Who wants to come back as the same person living the same life all over again? From there it is only a few steps to the construction of an entire belief-system, perhaps a philosophy or a religion based on such fear-inspired motivations. Somebody will then have to play the role of judge to decide how and when a person can come back, who deserves a better life, and who deserves less. But since there is no judge outside the individual there is complete freedom to act as one thinks appropriate, including the belief that one must submit to the judgment of others in order to be rewarded or punished, as the belief system dictates.

"The Great Wheel of Rebirth is an idealized, self-perpetuating system—not one of gentle self-transition. This cosmic merry-go-round quickly gets very old. Yet 'stop, I want to get off!' is a cry seldom seriously heard. Only a very few individuals on the Earth who courageously take the idea of reincarnation to its final conclusion—and each in one's own way—become self-aware enough to literally see it as an illusion projected onto a background of fear.

"Before what I've shared begins to sound too serious, the good news is that upon Rising most people will never feel any longing to jump back into an earth experience. Once they see what awaits them for having successfully left, the urge to return quickly fades. And everyone *is* successful. Even I, with my own beliefs about returning, soon came to see that deep down I really didn't want to go back—I just thought I was supposed to want it. Be assured that everyone will eventually come to the self-realization that their one individual self is enough and always will be abundantly enough.

"It appears that there are a very few and rare individuals who return for specific roles as teachers and 'spiritual politicians'—sometimes referred to as *bodhisattvas*.[66] But even they would not start all over in completely brand new lives. They might assume different personas for the part they are required to play, but they would have complete conscious awareness of their roles. Even for them returning is not a simple thing to accomplish and requires a greatly advanced evolution, intensive training, and much compassion. But it's clear that like everyone else they will continue to remain the individual they have been since their own beginning. A bodhisattva might not even have originations on the earth. In just this way all who transition from their earth

---

[66] From the Sanskrit, "one whose essence is enlightenment."

lives to Risen existence may have the opportunity to have an experience as a bodhisattva on any of the innumerable worlds in the infinite dimensions of Being. Infinity is there to explore, share, teach, learn, and love.

"OK, now I rest my case. In fact, I just rest."

"What a grand presentation, Tim! In spite of the strangeness and complexity I find it all reassuring to hear. Although I've intuitively known since I was a child that I've never had a past life on the earth, there were times when I felt I was being excluded in some way. So many people I've known strongly believed that they've had loads of past lives, with stories that sounded so real and fascinating. I always wondered why I couldn't recall my own."

"Because, August, you listened to those Risen who served by inspiring rather than influencing you to develop particular ego-beliefs, and who led you to search for and study the facts until you were aware of your personal truth."

"I realize that this inspiration has been going on all my life, Tim. But here's a question. If there is no real judgment, other than that which we inflict upon ourselves and on others, and we are free to form and pursue our beliefs as we see fit, isn't it a violation of the Principles of Universal Compassion and Non-Interference for someone to *not* be able to reincarnate if they want to?"

"What an awkward sentence and what a pill you are, Augie. There was always one in class—I should know, since I was usually the one, and which is why I have an answer all ready for you. Welcome to 'Higher Meta-Astralphysics For Dummies.'

"It's as you suggest—Creator Source will not interfere with what one desires, for Its greatest pleasure is to give us whatever we want, not to withhold it. The so-called 'Principles of the Universe' are really more like suggestions or guidelines. No, that's not quite right, they're more than that—they're gifts. And then it's all up to us if we want to accept them, and in what spirit, or rather in what spirit form. We also have the option to refuse them with no questions asked. The wonderful, mysterious thing about these gifts is that because they are infinite and unlimited in nature, we can use them in any way we want. There might be a Returns Department somewhere, but I would never dream of giving back an unopened present!

"Protests will arise from those who believe that Original Creator Source, or The Universe, or God, or however they prefer to label It, overrides our requests and makes decisions for our own good. But Creator Source does this only if we ask It to. All decisions are ours alone to make. In my experience it seems clear that our Source makes no judgments or decisions. As individuals, *we* make the judgments and decisions thanks to the gift of free will, which cannot be revoked. For the Source to revoke Itself would be like It holding Its breath until It turned blue. Your physical body can't hold its breath forever either, because it is a direct manifested reflection of the Original Source Body.

"If one wants to reincarnate, it's not possible in the ultimate way of creating another original life for oneself. One is infinitely enough as one. However, if you want to have the *experience* of a pre-existence to the primal birth on the home planet, or the *experience* of reincarnation, you can have it, including that of being a co-creative manifestor. As we make our own self-experiences we also make our own 'rules' or 'laws' about our experiences. As for choosing our parents, it is *after* our primal birth on earth that we enter into any kind of 'contracts' with them, not before. This we do while awake and while in the astral realms during sleep. Of course, if later you want to have the *experience* of choosing your own parents before birth, well then, why not?

"There is one thing that we cannot do—we cannot create our individuated Self. We can manifest the experiences that *appear* to recreate the individuated Self—including personalities, characters, actors, and roles. We really *do* have a Creator Source, which is the only Source Reality and which shares Its reality with our reality. We also exist as that Reality where all is possible, including all experiences and all illusions. The exception is that as we cannot create ourselves, we cannot uncreate ourselves. If we wanted, we could create the *experience* of being uncreated as easily as we can create the experience of having another life and being somebody else. But such an experience wouldn't be real, only a realistic illusion. You on earth do it all the time, trying to be somebody you aren't. Like reincarnation, it's a pastime, and called 'let's pretend.' It works spectacularly well and you have a wonderful time playing in this way, enough to fool yourself and most of the people most of the time, but sooner or later you always come back to where you started from—your Self.

"Here's the awesome part. Many now reading or hearing these words are actually experiencing the novelty of a manifested recreation in this very moment. Remember that 'novel' means *new*, 'creative' means *fun*, and 'recreation'—or re-creation—means *play*. Anyone might very well have done this hundreds, thousands, millions of times already. When one gazes into one's life deeply enough, it will be seen that this is so—or perhaps recognize that one just might truly be a 'first-timer.' It will be up to only the individual to choose what to do with the self-knowledge gained. This includes doing it again, like a child going up and down the slide over and over, or deciding to try something new on the playground—to let go, mature, transition, and transmute."

"Ok, Tim, this all makes sense to me. But what about the people who are total strangers to me, who come into my life for a brief moment and then depart, never to be seen again? Yet I feel that I have known them before and perhaps even for a very long time. Sometimes they stay in my life in some way—as a friend, colleague, or even lover. Sometimes there are people I just see on the street in passing, but when our eyes meet it's as if we recognize each other instantly and on a very deep level. Then they're gone like a ship in the night, but I find myself thinking of them for the rest of the day or more—

maybe longer. These aren't people I've known from past lives?"

"By now, August, you're probably realizing as you ask the question that the answer is obvious, so you must be playing ego-mind's advocate. These are individuals with whom you have some kind of relationship on the astral-etheric levels, and who will carry a familiar resonance that resounds like a tuning fork when you are near each other on the material plane. These relationships interpenetrate one another, not only during sleep but also during your waking day and for your entire life while on the earth. During particularly less active moments—daydreaming in light trance, for instance—you may even begin to remember these astral relationships through certain feelings. Your conscious mind can't reconcile this in most instances, but depending upon your level of self awareness it may actually be able to do so as your spirits recognize one another. If you and the other person carry specific beliefs about past lives and reincarnation, you might resolve the mystery in your waking lives within this context. Perhaps you'll even interact with one another as if it were true, and any kind of life drama can then be manifested to support your shared beliefs, which you might passionately refer to as 'fate' or 'karma.'

"There are those on Earth with belief systems that entail the planning of life events before entering the terrestrial geography. This system is used to explain why some people are friends or enemies, or parents and children to one another, and why others come into one's life at specific moments to perform certain 'tasks,' often deemed as 'karmic retributions' as connected to another past life relationship. However, when viewed from a vaster Risen perspective, 'karma' is seen as a solely embodied human invention. Such systems appear as the immensely complicated clockworks they would have to be—machined lives running according to cogs and springs, levers and pendulums. It is proposed from within certain Risen circles that such systems would contradict the known truths of free will, spontaneity, and cosmic humor—unless one counts the irony that emerges from such systems as humor. It is quite clear from the greater range of a Risen viewpoint that terrestrial relationships are formed as they are forming and any pre-planning of them is done not only on conscious levels but on underconscious levels as well. The dramas of such individual and group relationships are also pre-shaped in the various astral geographies while the body sleeps, but this happens as life is happening all around, and not before the life and the living of it begins.

"The machine-system of reincarnation may be a reflected and projected extension of a kind of Newtonian system. This could only manifest as an effective social structure when quarantined from Original Source in order to maintain that social structure. The use of projection and reflection is nothing more than smoke and mirrors to produce a very large and entertaining play. But to be effectively quarantined from Original Source would also result in deep feelings of loss, abandonment, and isolation."

"Tim, it really does sound as if it's all an immense and dramatic soap opera, or some kind of game."

"So why can't it be? If you want to step into the part and play it to the hilt, who says you can't? If you want to make up a game about reincarnation and make it seem so real that it appears real, why not? No reason whatsoever. And isn't it interesting that the word 'game' is synonymous with *pastime*?"

"As I've often said before, Tim, the mind boggles. The Risen theories you shared seem to suggest that we don't experience this game of reincarnation—this pastime—on Original Planet Earth. Dare I ask how it's done?"

"Well. It's really a strange pair of ducks. You're familiar with the concepts of the infinity of universes and unlimited dimensions, of possibilities never-ending and probabilities ever-awaiting. It appears that any manifestation of reincarnation is not played upon one's particular *original version* of earth. But there's no reason why a person can't manifest yet another experience on *another version* of earth that is completely like the one they left. Mind *is* that powerful. Everyone can manifest their very own earth to return to—exactly like the one they left. Of course there would have to be a built-in restriction of self-imposed amnesia to make it suit one's beliefs and needs, and this amnesia can be tailored in any way. And if they want, souls can co-creatively manifest the experience of being together or finding one another as their own desires for drama dictate. Sometimes there are 'leaks' that get past the amnesia—hence, feelings of *déjà vu*, past lives, and all kinds of 'evidence' that would manifest to help sustain the illusion. Since the illusion is built directly upon a foundation of Reality it has an apparent feeling of reality all its own and will respond to its manifestor's mind as directed. In this way we are given dominion over our worlds, as promised to the symbolic human, *Adama-Æve*. 'In my house are many mansions,' as the saying goes. 'My house' is Creator Source, and 'many mansions' are the infinitely emerging, individualized spirit-sparks—us. These mansions are also the unlimited possibilities in Mind.

"Our minds share our Source's Mind. If you want to adhere to the 'rules' your beliefs dictate, such as being reborn as an animal because you think you were a rotten sort and deserved nothing better, nobody and nothing will interfere with you from having the experience of that illusion. Of course there will always be someone nearby ready to help when help is asked for. Like the liberation drama where you found people who were presenting as animals—someone there must have had enough of that experience and had sent out a call for assistance, to which your team responded.

"*The Tibetan Book of the Dead*—and all such books—are excellent examples of beliefs-made-manifest—or 'manuals'—with the potential to manifest, support, encourage, and sustain other-worldly patterns of group-perceived existence, pre-existence, and re-existence. These other worlds may be thought of as no less real than Reality. Nevertheless, they are not Reality, but *thoughts about Reality.* Yet while thinking is powerful, it's not the only pastime in town. There is neither limitation to the universe or to potential universes, nor to individual experience within all potentiality. Why should there be? Any answer to that question would only be a belief, and beliefs can always be changed or discarded. That's what makes them fun—until it's decided to take them seriously. Then again, what is serious to one might be fun to another."

"Following your lead, Tim, I could answer that by saying there should be something only if one wants it, right?"

"Go to the head of the class."

"So then it follows that because Original Creator Source is unlimited, so are we, and there must be unlimited room for all potential worlds, universes, and experiences to interpenetrate, and for all time—or not-time, as the case may be."

"By Jove, you've got it. So while you might not be interested in experiencing an earth-type life again, others might. Choices are up to the individual, and the choices are unlimited. The quality of the choice is proportional to the individual's choice as well. We can appear to self-judge and to judge others, for better or worse, cycle upon cycle, countless æons upon æons. Yet judgment is still an illusory misperception. Eventually the desire for change overrides the fear of change and true transition can then take place."

"And so, Tim, it comes right back to Original Creator Source being non-judgmental and non-interfering in anyone's experience. The more like my Source I realize I am—Self Realization—the less judgmental I am about my own and about others' life experiences. It simply doesn't matter whether or not those reading this believe in reincarnation, and it never will matter."

"Yes, ultimately it doesn't matter because there *is* no ultimate matter—the eternal paradox. Our real service here is to demonstrate, as one very tiny example, that it's possible for two loving, resonating individual souls to engage in exploration across dimensions, and especially how much fun it is."

"Thank God, I'm glad it doesn't matter. I thought we were going to end up looking like we're taking ourselves way too seriously."

"But isn't it fun pretending to scare ourselves like that sometimes?"

"If *that's* your idea of fun. I love scary movies, but I'm ready now for something much more serene."

"Hmm. Well. Wait until *after* you see what we've planned for your Homecoming."

TWENTY-SIX

MOON SHADOWS

"I see the moon and the moon sees me,
I love you and you love me."
~ *Nursery Rhyme*

L ast night was the full lunar eclipse. The weather was cold and crisp, and the drama was played out on an immense stage, the evening sky swept bare of clouds by late autumn winds. In childish awe I watched as the Moon, the Night Mother, masked herself with the face of the Sun, the Father of Day. For a few transitory moments she assumed a persona whose origins were of a very different world, transmuted into something shockingly new and seemingly real. The mystery was revealed upon her unmasking, and order was quickly restored to the heavens. Many people never looked up. They were too weighed down by the gravity of materiality and by their own thoughts, unconscious of the majestic interplay of celestial bodies over their heads.

For those who watched with worry, the ending brought relief. For the surprised and delighted, the return to normality would feel enriched and blessed, perhaps tinged with a little disappointment, wishing it could have lasted longer. Some might even come back the next evening with hopes of seeing it again. And a few, especially sensitive individuals would have felt transformed by a brief peek into worlds within worlds, where hints of great vastness and deep secrets are whispered by distant beings of light.

My experiences with the Risen are reflected in the eclipse of the moon. There are few words to describe the immeasurable depth of what is still mostly unfathomable to me, and I feel my own twinges of disappointment in these two-dimensional pages I'm leaving behind as mere hints of evidence. Like the intermingling of the sun and moon, there are transitory moments of an overwhelming inner experience, of nameless feelings-within-feelings, of Tim being so very near to me and yet so impossibly remote. From within these mystical moments I'm sad and miss him because we seem to be separated. Simultaneously, I've entered a new state of mind and heart where I'm experiencing his presence in a profound and original way, as if I've stumbled upon an unfamiliar species of flower in a hidden garden.

Whatever this particular emotional experience is, whatever it is trying to tell me, I cannot put a worldly definition to it. Nor does Tim answer my appeal for help in understanding this experience—yet it's clear that he's still with me in supportive love. He's within the garden of my soul, but for some reason, right now he's beyond the range of true clear sight and hearing, concealed somewhere in the undergrowth. I find myself wondering if he's asleep and dreaming under a blossoming tree, and if I'm in that dream.

Perhaps I'm not in a dream but in a new kind of waking consciousness. What I do feel is Tim waiting for me somewhere in the distant landscape that both expands and contracts around us, like some vast sea creature breathing with the tides of conscious awareness, rising and falling with the cycles of sun and moon and stars.

After spinning for a while in these peculiar non-time states, I begin to feel Tim willing me to relax and enjoy the sweet mysteries of life and to let myself rest in this inner garden of strange tranquility, beneath the celestial dome of spiritual mind.

And in this moment I also feel an ending. Tim and I have come to a place in the road where it is time to sit and rest, to ponder over all that we have experienced since I first saw the little snake's body that marked the beginning of this spiraling journey. We sit in silence as only true friends can.

A few days ago, just before the eclipse of the moon, I came across another small, lifeless snake's body on the forest path. It was less than three feet away from where I had seen the first one, which had marked the beginning of this book and the many adventures that were to materialize. It was six years later, almost to the day. Like the first, this one also had its tail in its mouth but with some differences. It was slightly bigger, and where the other had displayed one coil, frozen in the moments of its body's final movements, this one had three coils—an unmistakable spiral.

It seemed to be a sign, the empty shell still embodying the truth of transition—an ending that is the foreknowledge of a beginning. The serpent with three coils is also an ancient symbol of the kundalini energy, coiled in sleep at the base of the spine. Was the Universe alluding to my own kundalini experience, which had catalyzed from contact with the Risen?

Ouroboros, the serpent with its tail in its mouth, is a pan-mythical symbol of time and the continuity of life. An alchemical sign of completeness, it depicts the Alpha and the Omega—eternal life. Ouroboros contains the idea of cycles, of returning to one's self through one's self. It suggests birth within death's jaws—doors opening. It also intimates death within birth's jaws—doors closing. It is life emerging out of death, then emerging out of life, year after year, over and over, seemingly without end.

But *does* it ever end?

Yes, say the Risen, for cycles aren't forever. Each and every cycle is a beginning and yet also part of a greater cycle, the vast spiral of movement of an individualized immortal soul through space and through time—and then beyond time and space.

This movement never ceases.

Quietly, quickly, like the masking of the moon and a snake's brief, precious life, this book's journey seems to have ended. Something else has begun, yet with no clear sign about what it might be.

"I'm here, August. It's strange for me, too. I've been feeling you as if far away somewhere, in a dream I cannot enter. Like the stars, we seem separated by great distances, while inextricably joined by the sharing of the lights and shadows cast amongst them. What functions as my intuition here, my connection with that which is greater and deeper, tells me that this feeling of separation is an illusion—and so then must the dream be an illusion.

"Your dream-time on earth is temporary. I feel your dream ending as you sense another phase of your life beginning. Although the phases of the moon and seasons seem to repeat themselves forever, never altering, never redefined, you are unable to see from a greater perspective that each phase is a door leading to another door—slowly, surely, and with great dignity. It may feel as if all the doors are connected in a great circle, causing you to repeat the same life with different masks and dramas over and over. Dreams on earth are moments of Higher Reality slowed down, where life is measured in steps and pauses. The life within the dream seems to be brief and mortal, yet the traveling unending. Higher Reality, wherein the dream is contained, continues all around the dreamer, expanding and evolving, using the dream matter as material for building yet more dreams. The dreams continue to become absorbed by Higher Reality, which is blessed and enriched by them."

"Thank you, Tim, for your brilliant, compassionate insights. You really see so much more than I. Your knowledge strengthens my own, which will someday be assimilated into my Risen experience. Then we'll share mind and spirit, unobstructed by the barriers of earthly materiality."

"I'm never far from you, August. Anticipation, trust, faith—each is temporary. You are preparing for something beyond the temporal lands of the earth. Let your feelings continue to guide you as best you can, loving and honoring them as you love and honor the body that is carrying you toward the last terrestrial door. When you step through it, you will have come Home, where I and so many, many, *many* others await you."

"Keep the home fires burning, Tim."

"Your wish is mine, Dear Heart."

"And Tim, about the snakes—now, really—*what* do they mean?"

"We shall never know how or why, Aug."

"That's what I thought."

We begin as spirits in worldly human bodies, not yet fully descended into our dreams about these forms. Each day humankind draws closer to some unimaginable accomplishment of its evolution. Even when we, as spirits, leave these bodies to rejoin the others waiting for us in the Risen Lands, the Divine Dream of One Mind's Reality will continue on.

What will it be like when that moment arrives—sometimes called "the Omega Point" or "the Event Horizon"—the achievement of body, mind, and spirit fully emerging and then merging amidst the ending of psychological time? There is much worldly speculation on this and it all falls short, as we are unable to conceptualize such an event. The Risen strive to help us with our understanding. Some modern terrestrial explorers of consciousness anticipate that we will discover that the physical expression of light will be revealed to be the outer fabric of the substance of real world consciousness—the window of time. Deepest intuition suggests that at the very least, the veils that have existed between the Risen and the yet-to-Rise will be dissolved completely. Time will be transmuted into an experience of *nowness* as it is experienced by the Risen in their state of existence. Communication and even travel between the innumerable states of being will be unhindered. When one feels ready to leave the body, rather than waiting for it to grow ill and painful and then die, every person, with guidance, care, support, and celebration, will consciously choose their own day of birth into the greater dimensions of continuing immortal existence. The final liberation from the custody of materiality will have arrived.

We'll be Home.

OOLONG RISES

"Cats come and go without ever leaving."
~ Martha Curtis

A few weeks after the Risen pronounced this "little project" finished, I was making coffee, a mug awaiting on the counter behind me. Whoever the Invisible was that pushed it off has not yet owned up. It had split perfectly in half, something I'd never seen happen before. I knew that this was A Significance. The next morning, Oolong, my feline companion of eighteen years and two months, made a peaceful transition in my arms.

It was obvious that for the past few weeks she had been on more frequent astral expeditions while leaving her body to rest on the brown velvet pillow that had been her throne for so many seasons. She intently watched and listened to things that were beyond my physical senses. Although her body remained quite strong up until the last few days, I knew . . . I knew.

Around the same time that she began to fail, I dreamt about a tiny kitten. Guilty thoughts assailed me, accusing me of heartlessly thinking about someone new before the Queen was in her grave. It was Tim who quickly brought me back to reality—"Silly one, the kitten is your own daughter, beginning to enjoy a bit of heaven on earth."

After she was gone, thundershowers of intense grief swept through my being, fading into distant echoes until the next one stormed through. Gradually the sun emerged unscathed, to reveal Oolong in her new spirit body, healthy and unharmed, watching me from her pillow with a calm, bemused expression.

"What's the fuss? I'm right here."

I awakened, and remembered that life truly goes on, and will never end.

THE EDGE & WAITING

> "How do you know but ev'ry Bird that cuts the airy way,
> Is an immense world of delight, clos'd by your senses five?"
> ~ William Blake, *The Marriage of Heaven and Hell*

The visionary Blake wrote a great deal about Authentic Self's experience in a material mind-body, constrained by the reduction of five senses and by societal and institutional conventions—"the mind-forg'd manacles," as he called them. He realized that having only two or three senses would not give us the ability to predict any more beyond them—and so it would be with but five. He lived in the knowledge that imagination flies free above the senses, and that it is the actual image of God in which we are made. God is imagination, which is the act of imaging. Imagination is not present to the five senses, which are mind-body components that filter incoming evidence of Greater Reality.

The ego-mind makes all decisions for the embodied, sleeping Authentic Self about what is acceptable as real. From these decisions simulate selves emerge. Because a simulate self is manifested from the ego-mind, its experiences and its choices about the universe are not authentic—they are not real but simulated. Authentic choices come only from a fully-conscious, self-aware Authentic Self. Authentic Self is the true author of one's life—the script-writer of its dramas, the set designer, the decider of staging and dialogue.

~ 25 ~

These words may not make conscious sense at this time,
but my spiritual senses comprehend and retain
this knowledge for Authentic Self.

THE EDGE

The edge is the perimeter of the reduced life experience within an unlimited personal universe. Lacking imagination, the ego-mind limits experience, utilizing the restrictive five senses as motivated through anxiety and fear. The imposed limitation is a "sphere of experience" that surrounds an individualized mind-body, which in turn seems disconnected from the conscious awareness of Authentic Self. Because of its spherical affect, which surrounds us on all sides, it appears to be all there is. But it is no more than a human goldfish bowl, its curvature reflecting back only that which the ego-mind projects. This sphere of forced experience is the kingdom of the simulate selves as ruled by the ego-mind. The ego-mind enforces the belief that its kingdom is unlimited and supreme. The result of this base inconsistency is a constant feeling of emotional strife to Authentic Self—*angst*—or worry and anguish.

The ego-mind may allow for a permeability of the edge if this fits its agenda. Individualized mind-bodies can then join and develop a group sphere of experience, attracted by like vibration and held together by like beliefs as dictated by the ego-mind. A group can be small like a couple or a family, or a larger sphere of several groups such as tribes, organizations, corporations, and nations. The separate ego-minds are never fully in agreement and so strife and dissention are inherent in these systems. The spheres of many ego-minds often interpenetrate one another. Intergenerational transmission of beliefs is also highly likely, as parents, usually in total unawareness, pass on belief systems to their children, sometimes down through many centuries. Formalized institutions of the ego-mind such as governments and churches also transmit and strengthen barriers to authentic and unlimited experience.

The edge of the sphere of experience is seldom visited by its inhabitant—there is usually no awareness of its existence. This edge can be seen in the belief of the flat earth, which successfully kept people from exploring their physical environment for fear of falling off into an abyss of unknown territory. Even though it has since been realized that the earth is not flat, the same fear-generated scheme, which was developed by the ego-mind, still actively exists in the ego-mind collective. Although we can now venture around the material globe, most of us are still encased in our invisible, protective sphere of ego-mentality, the flatland of the simulate self.

The ego-mind maintains the structure of its kingdom through beliefs that are engendered by deception. The edge or border of its kingdom is held in place by a force field of anxiety, like an electric fence. Should one move too close to this edge, alarms go off and trigger the feeling of anxiety. One of the ego-mind's lies is that the anxiety is unlimited beyond the perimeter, and that once the edge is transgressed the anxiety will go on forever. What makes this lie believable is that the sleeping Authentic Self is still aware of the actual limitlessness beyond the edge. The ego-mind lies that this limitlessness is identical to unrelieved anxiety and so we the avoid the edge. Unlimited, authentic living is effectively pinched off into a limited, simulated experience. This experiential avoidance results in a feeling of having "split," manifesting a "less-than" experience for Authentic Self, which remains unconscious of the reality, while sensing the loss as inexplicable sadness, grief, and depression. Although the feeling of being split is ultimately an illusion, we feel compelled to correct it and bring the two "halves" back together—typically by looking for other people, or careers—anything—to join with and complete us.

Change is the nature of the manifested material universe, enabling individualized manifestations of Authentic Self to move about from one geography of experience to another. Transformation of vibration cannot take place without this movement. Inherent in the design of humankind is ever-arising stimuli, causing individual forms to shift and change form in some way—that is, to transform. This stimulus, which is Original Creator Source's aspiration for novelty—or newness—is equally inherent in, and activated and detected, by our senses. That is, if we didn't have senses, we wouldn't be stimulated to transform. All physical and non-physical senses are affected in this way.

What lies beyond this edge? Nothing until we get there. As a natural course, one is brought up against one's edge as a result of Authentic Self's directive to transform. One feels suffocated in a relationship, or stifled by a career, or bored by the current lifestyle. A barrier to movement, the edge is a result of the ego-mind's need to control. It uses anxiety to keep an individuated Authentic Self from moving beyond the edge and hence from transforming. The ego-mind drives our mind-body vehicle around and around the perimeter of our experiential sphere. This habitual circumnavigation, which often becomes obsessive and compulsive behavior, causes unrelenting emotional, mental, and physical stress. As a result, Authentic Self is unable to inherit its Divine Realm as infinitely bestowed by Original Creator Source, and instead endures a frozen hell of restrictive movement, masterminded and ruled by the ego-mind. This restricted movement, as directed by the ego-mind, is also a limited attempt to simulate Original Creative Source.

WAITING

Being future-oriented, the ego-mind cannot wait. Instant gratification is its motivation. Addiction of some kind—mild to wild—is the eventual consequence. The ego-mind can simulate waiting in the form of a simulate self, which uses patience as a form of control to endure hardship, difficulty, or inconvenience against one's true, authentic desire. The ego-mind neutralizes our ability for self-control and the ability to tolerate delay.

Waiting, which is inherent in the nature of Authentic Self, is not meant here as patience. Because it is oriented in the present, Authentic Self has no need for patience and instead resides in resting in the feeling experience of Selfness. For Authentic Self, waiting is rest—and it is always at rest. For the ego-mind, which uses thoughts to generate a simulation of experience, waiting is unthinkable and unimaginable. Imagination and rest belongs to Authentic Self; worry and unrest belong to the ego-mind. Authentic Self has neither knowledge nor fear of death; the ego-mind lives to destroy this serenity.

Authentic Self can imagine experiences that appear to call for endurance if It so desires. But its nature is to enjoy rather than endure an experience. "Enjoy" is not meant here as the ego-mind's concept of getting joy out of something. Rather, putting joy *into* something is what Authentic Self brings to the table of experience, at which It serves as the Good Steward. For the Good Steward, to enjoy is to give. To reside and rest in the feeling of authentic enjoyment is Authentic Self's motivation. Joy is another word for *that which gives life*, or Original Creator Source, which is never-ending and unceasingly pours into one's universe through the channel of Authentic Self. When joy is withheld from outflowing, the feeling of life shuts down. Depression, illness, and the eventual cessation of material existence are the resulting effects.

Authentic Self becomes consciously aware of anxiety when it finds the edge of a simulate self's sphere of existence. If Authentic Self is in the driver's seat it can choose to pull over and stop and make observations and choices about what it sees as opportunities for change, rather than as barriers against danger. We all know what it's like to come up against our life's edges. For those who have been endeavoring to raise and sustain spiritual consciousness there may be the additional experience of not being able to turn around and go back, once up against the edge. This has been described as being on the edge of a cliff, over a dark abyss, or within a cloud of unknowing.

This is where waiting, or resting in the feeling of Authentic Self, comes in. When unknowing arises, one has simultaneously reached the feeling of Authentic Source. A simulate self will avoid the cliff's edge. Authentic Self, having awakened to the truth of its immortal existence and to the lie of death, will be able to contain anxiety while resting in mental stillness at the edge, and even bring joy to the experience. It may choose to rest as long as it wants, or to examine the belief system generating the barrier. It makes this examination by focusing its full, attentive awareness upon the belief system. Under Its quiet gaze—"quiet" meaning without the ego-mind's critical chatter—the belief system will be revealed as a misunderstanding, and then fade back into the nothingness from whence it came. The barrier dissolves and Authentic Self, as an individuated mind-body, can then move in the direction it chooses.

Authentic Self may also decide not to move, or perhaps to jump off the cliff. Having reached an awareness of its wings of immortality, fear no longer prevents or accompanies its choices. Whatever happens, there will be unlimited opportunity to bring joy along as a companion.

A Course In Miracles. Tiburon, CA: Foundation For Inner Peace, 1985.

Almaas, A.H., *The Pearl Beyond Price–Integration of Personality into Being: An Object Relations Approach.* Berkely, CA: Diamond Books, 1998.

Arcangel, D. and Schwartz, G. E. (2005). *Afterlife Encounters: Ordinary People, Extraordinary Experiences.* Charlottesville, VA: Hampton Roads.

Bander, Peter, *Voices From the Tapes—Recordings From the Other World.* New York: Drake Publishers Inc., 1973.

Beischel, J. (2007/2008). "Contemporary methods used in laboratory-based mediumship research." *Journal of Parapsychology,* 71, 37-68.

Beischel, J., & Rock, A. J. (2009). "Addressing the survival vs. psi debate through process-focused mediumship research". *Journal of Parapsychology,* 73, 71–90.

Beischel, J. (2010). "The Reincarnation of Mediumship Research". *Edgescience* 3 April-June.

Bolendas, Joa, *Alive in God's World: Human Life on Earth and in Heaven.* Great Barrington, MA: Lindisfarn Books, 2001.

Braude, Stephen E., *Immortal Remains—The Evidence for Life After Death.* New York: Rowman & Littlefield Publishers, Inc., 2003.

Chödrön, Pema, *When Things Fall Apart.* Boston: Shambhala Publications, Inc., 1997.

Corbin, Henry, *Swedenborg and Esoteric Islam.* Translated by Leonard Fox. West Chester, Pennsylvania: Swedenborg Foundation, 1995.

Crookall, Robert, *The Study and Practice of Astral Projection.* Secaucus, NJ: The Citadel Press, 1960.

Crookall, Robert, *The Supreme Adventure—Analyses of Psychic Communications.* Cambridge: James Clarke & Co. Limited, 1961.

Crookes, William, *Researches in the Phenomena of Spiritualism.* Manchester, U.K.: The Two Worlds Publishing Co., Ltd., 1926.

Davis, Andrew Jackson, *The Diakka and Their Earthly Victims,* Boston: Colby & Rich, 1886; reprinted by Health Research, Mokelumne Hill, CA, 1971.

Dembski, William A., and Michael Ruse, eds. *Debating Design: From Darwin to DNA.* Cambridge University Press, 2004.

Eliot, Thomas Stearns, *Prufrock, and Other Observations.* London: The Egoist, Ltd, 1917.

Emmanuel's Book: A Manual for Living Comfortably in the Cosmos. Compiled by Pat Rodegast and Judith Stanton. New York: Bantam Books, 1987.

Emoto, Masaru, *The Miracle of Water.* New York: Simon & Schuster/Atria, 2007.

Fawcett, Douglas, *The Oberland Dialogues.* London: Macmillan & Co., 1939.

Fawcett, Douglas, *The Zermatt Dialogues.* London: Macmillan & Co., 1931.

Feynman, Richard, *The Pleasure of Finding Things Out: The Best Short Works of Richard P. Feynman.* New York: Penguin Books Ltd., 2001.

Findlay, Arthur, *Where Two Worlds Meet.* London: Psychic Press Limited, 1951.

Foy, Robin P., *Witnessing the Impossible: The Only Complete and Accurate Eyewitness Account of the Amazing Physical Psychic Phenomena Experienced at Scole, Norfolk, UK and Overseas During the Scole Experiment.* Diss, Norfolk, UK: Torcal Publications, 2008.

Geley, Gustave, *Clairvoyance and Materialization: A Record of Experiments*. (out of print) New York: George H. Doran Company, 1927.

Goenka, Shri S N, & U BA Khin, Sayagyi. *Vipassana–The Essence of The Teachings*, 1995. http://www.buddhanet.net/bvk_study/bvk21d.htm.

Greeley, A.M., *The sociology of the paranormal: A reconnaissance*. Beverly Hills and London: Sage Publications, 1975.

Guggenheim, B. and J. (1997). *Hello from Heaven: A New Field of Research-After-Death Communication Confirms That Life and Love Are Eternal*. New York: Bantam.

Gurdjieff, G. I., *Beelzebub's Tales to His Grandson*, New York: E.P. Dutton & Co., Inc., 1973.

Hart, H., *The Enigma of Survival: The Case For and Against an After Life*. London: Rider, 1959

Harvey, Bill, *Freeing Creative Effectiveness: Doorways Into the Upper Mind*. Gardiner: New York: The Human Effectiveness Institute, 2002.

Hogan, C. (2016) In Grimes, R. *Seek Reality* podcast episode "Dr. R. Craig Hogan talks about The North American Station May 9th 2006. http://webtalkradio.net/internet-talk-radio/2016/05/09/seek-reality-dr-r-craig-hogan-talks-about-the-north-american-station/

Holmes, Ernest, *The Science of Mind*. New York: Penguin Putnam Inc., 1938.

Holzer, H., *Ghosts I've Met*. New York: Bobbs Merril Co., 1965.

Institute of Noetic Sciences. http://www.noetic.org.

Johnson, Raynor C., *Nurslings of Immortality*. London: Hodder and Stoughton, Ltd., 1957.

Jung, C.G., *Memories, Dreams, Reflections*. New York: Random House, 1965.

Kazanis, Deno, *The Reintegration of Science and Spirituality: Subtle Bodies, "Dark Matter," and the Science of Correspondence*. Tampa, FL: Styra Publications, 2000.

Krishnamurti, Jiddu, *The Little Book on Living*. Penguin Books, 1999.

Kübler-Ross, Elisabeth, *On Life After Death*. Berkeley, CA: CelestialArts, 1991.

Leadbeater, C. W., *The Other Side of Death—Scientifically Examined and Carefully Described*. Adyar, India: The Theosophical Publishing House, 1961.

Lees, Robert James, *The Life Elysian*. Leicester, U.K.: Eva Lees, 1905.

LeShan, Lawrence, *The Medium, the Mystic, and the Physicist*. New York: Helios Press, 2003.

Lodge, Oliver J., *Raymond, or Life and Death*. New York: George H. Doran Company, 1916.

Marris P., Widows and their Families. London: Routledge and Kegan Paul, 1958.

Maslow, A.H., *The Farther Reaches of Human Nature*. New York: Viking, 1971.

McTaggart, Lynne, *The Field: The Quest for the Secret Force of the Universe*. New York: Harper, 2008.

Monroe, Robert A., *Ultimate Journey*. New York: Doubleday, 1994.

Morse, M. and Perry, P., *Parting Visions: An Exploration of pre-Death Psychic and Spiritual Experiences*. New York: Piatkus, 1994.

Neville, *The Power of Awareness*. Marina del Rey, CA: DeVorss and Company, 1992.

Nicoll, Maurice, *Psychological Commentaries on the Teachings of Gurdjieff and Ouspensky, Volumes 1–6*. York Beach: Maine; Red Wheel/Weiser, LLC, 1980.

Rees, W. D. (1971). "The Hallucinations of Widowhood". *British Medical Journal* Vol. 4, 37-41.

Roberts, Jane, *The Magical Approach—Seth Speaks About the Art of Creative Living*. Novato, CA: Amber-Allen Publishing and New World Library, 1995.

Roberts, Jane, *The Nature of Personal Reality*. San Rafael, CA: New World Library, 1994.

Roy, A. E. & Robertson, T. J. (2004). "Results of the application of the Robertson-Roy protocol to a series of experiments with mediums and participants". *Journal of the Society for Psychical Research*, 68, 18–34.

Sannella, Lee, *The Kundalini Experience: Psychosis or Transcendence*. Lower Lake, CA: Integral Publishing, 1987.

Satprem, *Mother or The Mutation of Death*. New York: Institute for Evolutionary Resarch, 1976.

Satprem, *Sri Aurobindo*. Pondicherry, India: Sri Aurobindo Ashram Press, 1968.

Schrenck Notzing, Baron von, *Phenomena of Materialisation: A Contribution to the Investigation of Mediumistic Teleplastics*. New York: E. P. Dutton & Co., 1920.

Schwartz, G. (2001). "Accuracy and Replicability of Anomolous After-Death Communication Across Highly Skilled Mediums". *Journal of the Society of Psychical Research*, London, January.

Schwartz, G. (2016). In Grimes, R. *Seek Reality* podcast episode "Gary and Rhonda Schwartz Talk About Their Soul Phone Research." May 2nd 2006. http://webtalkradio.net/internet-talk-radio/2016/05/02/seek-reality-gary-and-rhonda-schwartz-talk-about-their-soul-phone-research/

Sheldrake, Rupert, *A New Science of Life: The Hypothesis of Morphic Resonance*. Los Angeles: J. P. Tarcher, 1995.

Sidgwick, H., Johnson, A., Myers, A.T., Podmore, F. and Sidgwick, E. (1894). Report on the Census of Hallucinations. *Proceedings of the Society for Psychical Research*. 26 (10) 25-422.

Solomon, Grant and Solomon, Jane, *The Scole Experiment: The: Scientific Evidence for Life After Death*. London: Piatkus, 1999.

Spiritual Emergency: When Personal Transformation Becomes a Crisis, edited by S. Grof and C. Grof. New York: G.P. Putnam's Sons, 1989.

Sri Nisargadatta Maharaj, *I Am That*, trans. Maurice Frydman, published by K. Dubhash Marg, India, 1973.

Swedenborg, Emanuel, *The Universal Human and Soul-body Interaction*, edited and translated by G. F. Dole. New York: Paulist Press, 1984.

The American Heritage Dictionary of the English Language, 4th Ed., Boston: Houghton Mifflin, 2000.

The Basic Bible, edited by S. H. Hooke., Cambridge: The University Press, 1949.

The Complete Tao Te Ching, by Lao Tzu, trans. Gia-fu Feng & Jane English, Vintage Books, 1989.

The Holy Bible, King James Version. New York: American Bible Society: 1999.

The Parapsychic Acoustic Research Cooperative, *The Ghost Orchid—An Introduction to EVP*, ed. Chatburn & MSH Harding. http://www.ashinternational.com.html.

Tolle, Eckhart, *The Power of Now: A Guide to Spiritual Enlightenment*. Novato, CA: New World Library, 1999.

Tyrrell G., *Apparitions*. Collier Books: New York, 1963.

White, Rhea A., "Exceptional Human Experience and the Experiential Paradigm," *ReVision*, 1995; #182, 18-25.

White, Stewart Edward, *The Betty Book*. New York: E .P. Dutton & Company, 1937.

White, Stewart Edward, *The Gaelic Manuscripts*. http://www.isleofavalon.co.uk/GlastonburyArchive/gaelic/.

Zammit, Victor and Wendy, *A Lawyer Presents the Evidence for the Afterlife*. Hove, U.K.: White Crow Books, 2013.

"WHEREOF ONE CANNOT SPEAK, THEREOF ONE MUST BE SILENT."
LUDWIG WITTGENSTEIN

THE AUTHORSHIP

August Goforth, a psychotherapist in private practice in New York City, is also an intuitive-mental, contemplative and psychophysical spirit medium. He was given this name as a child by Risen guides and mentors, and uses it here for the sake of his personal privacy and that of his therapy patients. He does not utilize his mediumistic abilities for therapy sessions, nor does he work as a professional medium to give readings for others. This is a professional bias as well as a personal choice, and may serve as an example for other therapists who might be misguided to inappropriately use mediumistic abilities in their work. However, he believes there will be an eventual spiritual evolution of humanity, as enriched by Risen contact, whereby the various human therapies will all successfully and appropriately be able to utilize mediumistic abilities for healing purposes. August is a member of several groups of non-embodied entities who are working to develop approaches of therapeutic support for psychospiritual challenges arising from imbalances between Authentic Self and the ego-mind and its simulate selves. This book, *The Risen*, has been a work-in-progress for seven years.

Timothy Gray was a writer, editor, and photographer in New York City until he made his transition to his present Risen existence in the early 1990s. He became keenly interested and active in meditation and the development of psychic abilities in the final two years of his existence on the Earth. His final terrestrial project was the co-authorship of *Dreams, Symbols & Psychic Power* with Dr. Alex Tanous, the noted psychic and parapsychologist (Bantam Books, 1990.) He has been intimately involved with the transmission of much of the Risen Project's material since its inception, and continues to interact with his Risen team members who have been specifically involved with this book's physical manifestation on Earth. Tim is a fledgling Risen Learner-Healer with a vast array of interests, including the study of the evolution of terrestrial ego-mind, its impact on the transition process to the Risen state, and its eventual dissolution to other energy forms. He is a member of an expanding interdisciplinary team of Risen Healer-Scientists who work together in the spiritual geography known as "Borrowed From Angels" and also partakes in expeditions to other vastly distant and previously unexplored dimensions. Tim has been August's partner in life and love since they met in the late 1980s.

The Risen Collective, which has been the primary force behind the orchestration of this book, is composed of over 1,500 non-terrestrial beings, plus inestimable *devas* of various ranges of intelligence, status, self-awareness, and time-spans. All are colleagues in a cooperative of higher-vibrating multidisciplinary groups, which reside in spiritual geographies outside the normal range of terrestrial psychic access. This collective includes educators, scientists, healers, philosophers, and artists from multicultural and multi-temporal backgrounds of Earth and of other dimensional systems, and who have an intensely committed interest in the advancement of communicative relationships with those still embodied on Earth and in other dimensional systems. In turn, they are contributing this service under the direction and auspices of an even higher-vibrating gathering, **The Risen Assembly**.

The Risen Assembly has indicated that there are more books to come, and would like to extend an invitation to those so interested to submit any questions or areas of interest they would like to see addressed to AugustGoforth@therisenbooks.com.